DANCING
A L O N E

DANCING
ALONE

The Quest for Orthodox Faith in the Age of False Religion

by

FRANK SCHAEFFER

HOLY CROSS ORTHODOX PRESS
Brookline, Massachusetts 02146

© Copyright 1994 by Frank Schaeffer

Published by Holy Cross Orthodox Press
50 Goddard Avenue
Brookline, Massachusetts 02146

ISBN 0-917651-36-7

Library of Congress Cataloging-in-Publication Data

Schaeffer, Frank. Dancing alone:
the quest for Orthodox faith in the age of false religion /
by Frank Schaeffer; foreword by Bishop Methodios
p.   cm.
ISBN 0-917651-36-7
1. Schaeffer, Frank. 2. Orthodox Eastern converts –
United States – Biography. 3. Greek Orthodox Archdiocese
of North and South America – Biography.
4. Orthodox Eastern Church – Apologetic works.
5. Protestantism – Controversial Literature.
6. United States – Church history.
7. United States – Moral conditions. I. Title.

248.2'4 – dc20   94-16213
(B)   CIP

About the Cover Illustration.

The cover illustration, by artist Diane Morrow, is not meant to be
confused with a real icon. However the painting of the broken image
illustrates a point made repeatedly by the author of *Dancing Alone*
concerning the fragmentation of the Christian community since the
advent of the Protestant Reformation. As modern Christians attempt to
piece together the flotsam and jetsam of Christian life, worship and
theology, they often do so unguided and with no reference to Christian
tradition. As a result their attempts resemble a badly repaired icon
symbolizing a type of "Christianity" that does not achieve the fullness of
spiritual life found only within the one, undivided church of the ages, the
Orthodox Church.

To those who introduced me to the Orthodox Church

Jim Buchfuehrer
Father Weldon Hardenbrook
Father Jon Braun
Father Peter Gilquist
Father Richard Ballew
Father Jack Sparks

To those who welcomed me into the Church

Bishop Methodios of Boston
Father Christopher and Claire Foustoukos
Father Alexander and Xanthi Karloutsos
and . . .
all the parishioners
of the Annunciation Greek Orthodox Church
of Newburyport, Massachusetts

God bless you all.

TABLE OF CONTENTS

FOREWORD

DANCING ALONE chronicles the spiritual journey of Frank Schaeffer to Orthodox Christianity, a pilgrimage which began in 1976. He set out on this quest, as he himself writes, "because of my deep desire to find answers to my own pressing questions and because of my longing to grow toward Christ rather than away from Him."

Converting to Orthodoxy is undoubtedly an act of inner spiritual strength and courage for any proselyte. It was an especially courageous decision for Frank Schaeffer, who is the son of a world-renowned and respected Protestant author and preacher. What especially impressed me about the text which follows is that it is imbued by a genuine Orthodox ethos and reflects the fact that the author is thoroughly knowledgeable of patristic thought and tradition. I was particularly appreciative of the author's careful examination and evaluation of religious life in America as he masterfully traced its history to our nation's founding fathers and prominent religious thinkers. His assessment of present reality is right on target.

In addition to being a very informative book for Orthodox and non-Orthodox alike, I firmly believe that it will be a missionary tool which could be used by the Orthodox Church to reach out to brethren who thirst for the eternal truths of the Orthodox Christian Faith.

M E T H O D I O S
Bishop of Boston
Greek Orthodox Diocese of Boston
January 21, 1993

AUTHOR'S NOTE OF ACKNOWLEDGEMENT

I began to write this book in mid-1988, two years before I converted to Orthodoxy, and completed it in 1994. I am a novelist and film director, not a historian or theologian. I have no research staff. I am not a scholar. I offer this book merely as the record of a personal journey, from Protestantism to the Orthodox Church, not as a work of history, theology, or scholarship.

Several people read this book at various stages in manuscript form and offered criticism that was invaluable. I am particularly grateful to His Grace, Bishop Methodios of Boston, for the time he took to read my book and for his generous foreword. The comments of Father Hanse Jacobse, Professor Kimberley Patton, Father David Tillman, Father David Anderson, my old friend and colleague Jim Buchfuehrer and Sophronia Tomaras were all very helpful.

My wife, Regina, as always, patient, kind and intelligent, gave me much good advice as she typed many early drafts of the manuscript. Beth Walker and Ivy Valory cheerfully typed several later drafts. (I write long-hand and to wade through my scribbling in good humor is quite a feat!)

I also wish to thank Fr. Nomikos Vaporis, editor at Holy Cross Orthodox Press, for his patience and kindness during the final stages of preparing this book for publication, and Professor Bruce MacBain for preparing the index.

My spiritual Father, Christopher Foustoukos, not only read the manuscript twice but, more importantly, has, by example and instruction, given me an ideal by which to live.

I also owe a special debt to the writings of Father George S. Florovsky, Bishop Timothy (Kallistos) Ware, Father Alexander Schmemann and Jaroslav Pelikan. In particular, Jaroslav Pelikan's *The Christian Tradition*, Volumes One through Four (University of Chicago Press); and Father George S. Florovsky's collected works in fourteen volumes (Notable and Academic Books), especially Volume 1, *Bible, Church Tradition: An Eastern Orthodox View*, were very helpful.

Since I am no historian, in writing this book I had to decide which comprehensive American history to use as a reference. Several suggested themselves; for instance, *The Oxford History of the American People*, Volumes One to Three. But in the end I chose to use the more accessible, and longer, *A People's History of America*, Volumes One to Five, by Page Smith (Viking Penguin). The reader will find a number of references to this fine historian's work but should not assume that my point of view in reference to American history was informed exclusively by Smith. Indeed, I believe it to be largely borne out by almost any standard text on the subject in reference to both the secularizing influence of Protestantism and the Enlightenment philosophy that influenced so many of our founding Fathers.

In any case I am indebted to all those mentioned above who know so much more about Orthodoxy, history, theology and spirituality than I do. Many thanks to you all for your help and inspiration. The failings of this work are my own.

INTRODUCTION

America is a nation in which we say we believe in God, while at the same time we behave like atheists. When judged by even a remotely traditional Christian standard of behavior, Americans can hardly be described as a "Christian people."

Measured against other cultures, we Americans are perhaps the most materialistic and desacralized people on earth. But, according to what we say about ourselves, we Americans are a "religious," even a "good" people. One's view of American society will therefore depend on whether one judges Americans by what we say or by what we do. We say we love our families. But fifty percent of our marriages are shattered by divorce. We Americans say we love our children. But almost one third of all American children conceived are aborted (1.6 million per year), and millions more who are born are abandoned to a failed educational system and to the tender mercies of our divorce courts, social workers and "day care" orphanages.

From a vantage point which accepts the inherent truth of historical Christianity, the moral problems which surround us are not the result of a lack of religion in our society, but the consequences of too much faith in the wrong religions. We live in a nation that believes itself to be intensely religious. However, religious fervor notwithstanding, faith in the historical teaching of the Church — in other words, Orthodox Christianity — is out of fashion in America. It is out of fashion in the secularized circles of our Knowledge Class (as some have called the academics, media personalities, educators, judges and business leaders who together shape the intellectual, political and social fashions of our society), and it is equally out of fashion in the Protestant community of rampant denominationalism. In the former, historical Christianity has been abandoned, along with traditional metaphysical and transcendent ideas, and replaced with a secular ideal, blind chance and nature not God, makes man and his morals. In the latter, there is faith of a kind, but it is the highly subjective personalized faith of the "born again" variety. It seems to me that such "faith" is actually more a form of psychotherapy than a commitment to historical Christianity, with the latter's demand that one must conform one's life to a certain sacramental and ascetic moral code.

Today very few serious people who study the moral or cultural-historical problems our society faces are willing to propose historical Christian solutions to those problems. And yet some of these same people maintain a fiction that they are Christians or religious, even though what they *do* contradicts what they *say* they believe. This dualism is possible because we have come to believe that reality is divided into compartments. In one compartment cultural and political life is carried on as if it is a purely secular-scientific pursuit. In another, we keep our religion. We act as if religion is only a private psychological and subjective experiential matter. Rarely is spiritual truth presented as part of everyday life, or as the solution to what are regarded as secular, political, or even moral problems. Even less is historical Christian teaching presented as the sacramental truth that transcends all other truth claims and causes us to regard all of life as sacramental, beautiful and full of meaning.

Modern life is fractured into spiritual and secular spheres. The great Orthodox theologian, Father Alexander Schmemann, has referred to this fracturing as a sin. "The sin was not that man neglected his religious duties. The sin was that he thought of God in terms of religion, i.e., opposing Him to life."

Sometimes we go so far as to formalize this rather curious and arbitrary division of reality. For instance, it has become an article of modern academic "faith" that historical Christian religious truth has little or nothing to offer pluralistic democratic secular people with worldly problems. Indeed in our pluralistic society, we hold that morality is largely a personal matter and that freedom, including freedom from moral or religious tradition, is desirable and beneficial. As a result, traditional religion often takes second place to secularized "religions," like politics, as the source of "morality" in our culture today. Spirituality has largely been privatized and removed from the public forum to the extent that it is now seen as normal for people to claim to be spiritual and, at the same time, to act as if nothing but materialistic hedonism rules their lives.

But the teaching of the historical Christian Church, the Orthodox Church on these matters, is very different from our contemporary secularized beliefs. The historical Church embraces a world view which posits that individual choices, for good or evil, are the root cause of human problems and triumphs — the foundation of human history. According to the Church, humanity's secular, social and political problems cannot be understood except in the context of the moral choices people make as they exercise their free will. Thus, spiritual belief is as relevant to cultural, political and historical trends as scientific theory, politics or education. This is because, according to the Holy Tradition of the historical Church, God — not nature — is the ultimate source of truth. Moreover, according to the historical Church, salvation involves a spiritual journey toward God, not only the pursuit of internal feelings.

According to Holy Tradition, it should be possible to write a book that attempts to critique social and political problems of the day and to simultaneously suggest a religious solution to those problems. If Christianity is truth in the sense that the teaching of the historical Church actually describes reality as it is, and offers sure guidance to people as to how to live in harmony with God, even how to become God-like, then Christian ideas will relate to *all* dimensions of human existence. If this is so, there will be no off-limits sign posted between the religious and secular. Both will be understood to have the same source. Thus, law will be understood to be related to religious morality, and politics will fall into a legitimate sphere of influence by religious people with religious ideas. Moreover, the beliefs of individuals will come to have a correlation with their external behavior.

A PERSONAL JOURNEY

This book is a map of a journey of intellectual and spiritual curiosity and discovery. It is not a work of scholarship but rather charts an odyssey that took me from the Evangelical Protestant community, to which I once belonged by default, to the Orthodox Church, which I chose on the basis of the conclusions described herein. I was chrismated into my local Orthodox parish in December, 1990. My reasons for becoming Orthodox are described in this book.

My journey to Orthodoxy began unwittingly around 1976 when I started to ask questions about what seemed to me to be the evident spiritual bankruptcy of Protestantism and the intensely secularized pluralistic culture it had produced. Seeking something more permanent than subjective, make-it-up-as-you-go-along Protestant religion, I began to read the Church Fathers and study Church history. I read, not in the abstract, as a scholar might, but rather to learn for myself if the historical Church, and its forms of worship and Holy Tradition, could still be located in the modern world. I did not do this to prove a point but rather because of my own deep desire to find answers to my own pressing questions and because of my longing to grow toward Christ rather than away from Him.

I bought some 200 books and practically annotated them into oblivion. The more I read, the more I realized that I had not been introduced to the historical Christian Church at all even though I had grown up in an informed, even "intellectual" Evangelical Protestant home. Nor had I ever experienced the forms of sacramental worship that had been taken for granted by countless generations of Christians before the relatively recent Protestant revolution against history and tradition. A day came when it became clear to me that if I was to believe the history books I was reading, and the writings of the Fathers of the Church, then I had to choose between the Protestant world view and the Holy Tradition. What was obvious was that they were not one and the same.

G. K. Chesterton once said that: "It ought to be the oldest things that are taught to the youngest people." As I studied the historical Church, I found that I had spent half a lifetime in the Evangelical Protestant world without learning one iota about the oldest things. It almost seemed to me that I had been kept from them. It was as if a lobotomy had been performed on the Protestant community and that the history, faith and practices of the ancient church had been obliterated in the operation. It seemed to me that we Protestants had deliberately avoided the study of the historical Church and concentrated on endless theological debates. Perhaps theological theories are easier to manipulate than history.

DANCING ALONE is a book that reflects my own discovery of historical Christian truths that I should not have had to "discover" at all. By rights they are, I believe, the basic historical and spiritual legacy that form the essential fabric, and common heritage, that should belong to *all* Christians of *all* ages, in *all* ages.

I have written this book in the hope that those already in the Orthodox Church will be informed as to the bankruptcy of their surrounding culture and defend themselves accordingly, and that those presently on the outside of the Orthodox Church may find it a useful tool in their pilgrimage. Perhaps this far from perfect work will at least provide a short cut to some of the truth I discovered by reading far too many books!

Frank Schaeffer
March 1994

Part One:

The Age of
False Religion

CHAPTER ONE

THE PROBLEM

Those of us who grew up as Evangelical Protestants were told that, unlike Orthodox or Roman Catholic Christians, we Protestants worshipped God in spirit and in truth. That is why, we were told, we needed no liturgy or "empty rituals" to help us to worship God. We did not need to study church history because our personal salvation histories were all that mattered. We did not need the Holy Tradition because we had a direct personalized relationship with Jesus. If we felt spiritual, then we were. What we did or how we worshipped had nothing to do with our salvation, which we understood to be a one-time, almost magical, predestined occurrence, not a journey. We believed in the Bible, but not in the Church. We did not need to confess to a priest, to celebrate the Eucharist, let alone light a candle, venerate an icon or say a written prayer.[1] We were taught that we were free of all such "neo-pagan superstitions." How other Christians had done things for millennia, or what they had believed, or how they had come to believe was no concern of ours. We needed no interpretation but our own in deciphering the meaning of the Scriptures.

No bishop, apostolic or otherwise, had any special authority over us regarding the true meaning of Scripture. No Father of the Church or Council had any special wisdom to which we should hearken. In fact we were told that our Christianity was like the rest of life in our pluralistic, free society-up to the in-dividual, a personal choice, a question of individual "leading."

---

[1] "The word liturgy . . . unfortunately dropped out of use long ago in Protestantism. . . ." Thomas Howard, *Evangelical Is Not Enough* (Nashville, 1984), pp. 91-104.

1

Our Christianity was, in fact, anything we wanted it to be, though perhaps we never admitted as much. We said that what we believed was biblical. But it often turned out that the Bible said anything we wanted it to. We tended to reject the ancient Christian idea that the Holy Spirit had led the Church. Yet we readily enough claimed the Spirit's "leading," on a personal sub-jective level, as proof that we were correct about matters theological and "doing the Lord's Will" in matters personal. If we disagreed with the teaching of one denomination or minister, we would shop for a new "church" until we found one we liked.

Ironically, claims of freedom from tradition and the Church's authority notwithstanding, we doggedly stuck to our "free" habits of worship. Our order of self-styled church services rarely varied within any given denomination. We always prayed the same repetitive way whether we read our prayers or not, ("Dear heavenly Father, we just this, we just that . . ."). If we were Reformed Presbyterians, we stuck to our Calvinist tradition — church consisted of four white walls and a lengthy sermon — and "worship" was the feeling you got if the sermon was good. If we were Southern Baptists, then baptize we did — adults only. If we happened to be in a so-called charismatic denomination, then our chaos of worship, tongues, prophesy, signs and wonders and the like was an organized chaos that, in its own extroverted way, was as repetitive and predictable as filing a tax return. It was not really a question of Protestant freedom versus ancient Holy Tradition, but rather of choosing which tradition, ritual and liturgy to follow.[2]

Each Protestant "tradition" took itself very seriously. Yet in our pluralistic society it was rare that anyone, or group, claimed that their relatively new "traditions" were better or truer than others in some absolute sense. Thus, perhaps unwitting-ly, our belief in pluralism came to be held by many as more absolute than any single religious tradition.[3] To claim that

---

[2] This inconsistency is not a new problem to Protestantism. As Jaroslav Pelikan writes, "Protestants, while rehearsing the Reformer's attacks on the scholastic doctrine of penance, were forced in turn to admit that by now an unthinking repetition of the formulas of con-fession substituted by the Reformers, had itself led to a new externalism." Jaroslav Pelikan, *The Christian Tradition*, vol. 5: Christian Doctrine and Modern Culture (Chicago, 1989), p. 52.

[3] ". . . the fragmentation produced by Protestantism was central in that a monolithic . . . religious culture would have provided greater resistance to secularization." Steve Bruce, *A House Divided: Protestantism, Schism and Secularization* (London, 1990), p. 27.

one's church was better, or worshipped more truly than another, branded one as a crank, even as un-American. In such an atmosphere of dogmatic tolerance, ideas of absolute transcendent or eternal, non-negotiable truth became almost impossible to defend. This was especially true regarding questions related to morals and worship. Surrounded by a consensus of multidenominational Protestantism it became harder and harder for Americans to define any idea, or denomination's teaching, as being true to the exclusion of other ideas. With the exception of expressions in regard to a few politically correct ideas about racism and the like, "I'm right and you're wrong," was a sentence that became almost unspeakable in mainstream modern American moral discourse, not to mention discourse about religion. After the authoritarian fervor of early Puritanism dissipated, the idea "This is my way of doing things but yours is fine too," typically represented the sentiment of most Protestants. After all, weren't all Americans created equal? Weren't all ideas equally valuable? Wasn't individualistic free expression the greatest of all gifts? How then could one sect, group, or denomination claim to be right about worship, doctrine or morals at the expense of what another had to say? Surely the genius of America was that all special interest groups could thrive as equal within our democratic culture? Apparently American individualism could only work as long as all ideas about truth were regarded as fundamentally relativistic.[4]

It was one small step from the idea that all denominations, even whole religions, must be equally respected, to the belief that all religions are equally true. In the end, the inexorable logic of denominational pluralism led to only one possible conclusion: since all religious ideas are equally true, even when they contradict each other, then they must be equally irrelevant to public life and serve no purpose beyond private individual therapeutic needs.

By the dawn of the twentieth century, the only absolute that effectively survived in the public arena was secularized politics. Only in a political system which included a powerful judiciary that protected the right to materialistic happiness did most

---

[4] ". . . the essence of reformed Protestantism may be described sociologically as individualistic . . ." Ibid. p. 229.

Americans share a common vision.[5] What was understood to be constitutional was held as far more relevant to public life than what had once been believed to be morally right or wrong. Religion was relegated to mere subjective opinion; a "personal faith."

In the 1970s, when Evangelical Protestants woke up to the threat to their well-being posed by the rising tide of moral chaos, even anarchy, in our desacralized American culture, there was little sense left of absolute non-negotiable moral right and wrong to which they could appeal. At best, all the Protestants could do was to use isolated Bible verses or secular arguments, the results of scientific studies, to support their calls for a "return to Christian values." They had lost the ability to argue for changeless truth beyond personal appeals to "what the Bible says to me," or the type of generic political arguments that began with the words, "Studies have shown . . ."

By promoting the abandonment of Holy Tradition, the concept of Natural Law, embodied in the authority and moral wisdom passed down from the Fathers of the Christian Church, and by accepting the idea that it was normal for the "Church" to be divided into 23,000 competing and often contradictory denominations,[6] what appeal could now be made by Protestant Christians to the historical understanding of morality, let alone non-negotiable truth? How could one shore up some foundational principle when historical precedent had been abandoned in favor of self-made "progress?"

By the late twentieth century the Protestant community had lost its ability to challenge in any credible fashion the secular culture that threatened it. Protestants could wring their hands, or organize politically, as did every other special interest group, however, they had clearly lost the moral high ground. By accepting as normal a plurality of various competing denominations, as equally valid expressions of multi-denominational Christianity, Protestantism had contributed so much to the creation of our culture's pluralism that it had lost the ability to call for a return to the high ground of moral absolutes.[7] As

[5] "The inevitable but unintended consequence of the rise of religious pluralism was the expansion of the secular state." Ibid.

[6] United Nations statistics on Protestant denominations in the world. *World Census of Religious Activities* (U.N. Information Center, N.Y. 1989).

[7] "However much conservatives may try to construe 'secular humanism' as a

a religious group Protestants could not even agree on the meaning of their sacraments and religious history. The foundational principal of Protestantism had been that it must make a break with its own sacramental history. How then could Protestants presume to dictate terms, or even make suggestions, to the secular culture around them in the name of eternal, changeless sacramental truth?

Perhaps the early Protestant Reformers had no idea of the mortal danger they had unleashed, danger to their own culture's underpinnings. Yet within the lifetime of Luther and Calvin, the rapidly proliferating Protestant denominations found themselves in need of a historically legitimating tradition. This need arose because Protestants began contradicting (and killing) one another over their various interpretations of Scripture. Having no one Holy Tradition to which all Protestants subscribed, the only recourse for the divided Protestant denominations was to individual and subjective appeals to Scripture. One problem became glaringly evident: one person's interpretation of Scripture often disagreed with that of others.[8] Protestants soon found themselves ensnared in their endless warring, where they remain adrift today. There is, though, one important difference: no one in the larger secularized culture listens anymore.[9]

Pluralism has pulled the teeth and claws of most religious people. To the so-called Knowledge Class, only politics is sacrosanct.[10] Religion is now often perceived as merely an annoying footnote to politics. The culture has passed Protestantism by. Alone with their Bibles, and their own subjective in-

---

coherent ideology which threatens their religion, it is the democratic attitude to religion expressed in that wonderful section on American forms which invites one to fill in 'the religion of your preference' which will do the damage . . . Protestants will never again achieve cultural dominance because their success is self-limiting." Steve Bruce, *A House Divided*, pp. 230-31.

[8] "It would soon become evident (during the Reformation) that various biblical interpretations clashed with one another. . . . To Roman Catholic and Eastern Orthodox teachers, meanwhile, all of this (Protestant confusion) proved again the need for an infallible church." Jaroslav Pelikan, *Christian Doctrine and Modern Culture*, pp. 73-74.

[9] "In the cycles of religious (revivals) growth and decline which have characterized the last two centuries, each wave of growth has involved either fewer people, or made less impact, or both." Steve Bruce, *A House Divided*, p. 223.

[10] "In this manner, a perverse notion of the disestablishment of religion leads to the establishment of the state as church." Richard John Neuhaus, *The Naked Public Square* (Grand Rapids, 1984), p. 86.

terpretations of the Scriptures, with no fixed changeless historic moral foundation, with which to legitimate their ideas or claims, Protestants have crafted their own demise and have unwittingly undermined the idea of transcendent, sacramental absolutes in the bargain.[11] Protestant denominations lost their relevance to the wider culture, in essence, by becoming that culture.

WORSHIP

Even in the area of personal spirituality all is far from well within the Protestant community. Protestantism has been plagued by extremes in the sphere of worship, ranging from dry and unsatisfying sermons-as-worship, to what can only be described as hysterical "charismatic" lunacy. This is due, I believe, to Protestantism's self-inflicted divorce from the authority and stabilizing influence of Holy Tradition, the apostolic succession, and the rich, balanced, tried and true ancient liturgies of the historical Church.[12]

Protestants are now so far removed from the living sacramental worship of the Church of the ages, administered by bishops and priests, with an historical, apostolic legitimacy and inheritance, that they have clearly placed themselves outside of the continuity of the historical Church and its Holy Tradition, the tradition of what has been believed by all Christians everywhere and at all times.[13] Protestantism and secularism are interchangeable in that both are equally desacralized — Protestantism in its anti-sacramentality, and secularism in its pure and hostile materialism.

Judging by the failure of modern Protestantism to lead its people along the sacramental paths of the ancient Church, it appears that no amount of being popular, relevant, evangelistic or trendy — or even Bible believing — can replace the basic need of Christians to fulfill their destiny as worshippers of God in the

---

[11] This is what Professor Steve Bruce describes as the phenomena of reformed Protestantism as its own "grave digger." This is a theme he repeats in *A House Divided*.

[12] In describing his own journey to the historic Church, Thomas Howard writes, "Evangelicalism . . . had in effect left me with nothing but the Bible and the modern world." Thomas Howard, *Evangelical Is Not Enough*, p. 58.

[13] For a definition of the development of the Holy Tradition see Chapter I of Jaroslav Pelikan's, *The Spirit of Eastern Christendom* (Chicago, 1974).

context of One Holy Catholic (i.e., complete, universal) and Apostolic Church.[14]

Many Protestants obey some of the rules of the ancient Christian faith. As a result many have produced good spiritual fruit. For instance the Salvation Army, or the more than one thousand crisis pregnancy centers that offer compassionate alternatives to abortion and care for women and children in the name of Christ, are largely run by Evangelical Protestants. Yet I believe that as a result of the loss of historical continuity by the Protestant denominations, regardless of what they say they may feel Protestants, and many protestantized, modernized Roman Catholics, are not living in the fullness of true and historical Christianity. From personal experience and observation, I believe they know very little about the light of historical Christianity, even though they talk about the light, read and write about the light, and claim to be in the light. The light many Protestants perceive is necessarily dim because they have no tools to use to help them come into the fullness of it, especially in the area of worship. The Protestant, and to a great extent the modernized American Roman Catholic, who is often thoroughly protestantized, is the child who presses his face against the candy store window. He, or she, can dimly perceive the Apostolic sacramental faith of the ages but cannot taste it! Like scavengers picking through wreckage on a beach Protestants, and many of today's Roman Catholics, have bits and pieces of the ancient faith, but little more.[15]

As compared to the well-documented worship practices of the Orthodox Church, most Protestants have no authentic sacraments or historical liturgical prayers. They may have fragments—echoes of the historical Christian past—but these are mere disconnected remembrances. They are the flotsam and jetsam of the historical faith, washed up on the modern shore. Many Protestants may well be deeply spiritual, but nevertheless they have been denied the tools of faith that the historical Church has at its disposal.

A study of Church history shows that Protestant worship, as it is usually practiced today, bears almost no resemblance

---

[14]"It is hard to overestimate the damage done through this traumatic loss of bearings in the Evangelical tradition." Richard F. Lovelace, *Dynamics of the Spiritual Life* (Downers Grove, IL, 1979), p. 235.

[15]Convert from Protestantism to Orthodoxy Jon E. Braun writes, "Yet in spite of my

to the sacramental liturgical worship of the entire Church for the better part of two thousand years in both the East and West. This is not a theological opinion, much less a moral judgment, but simply a statement of historical fact. The Church's practices are well documented.[16]

So entertainment-oriented, even trivial, has the majority of Protestant worship become that even the fear of God, according to the teaching of the Church, the most basic prerequisite for individual repentance, seems to have been largely lost. The mystery of faith has been replaced with rationalistic theology on the one hand, and frivolous, internalized, "touchy-feely," entertainments on the other.

The Fathers of the Church warned of the consequences of desacralization long ago. Today those warnings seem to fall largely on unhearing ears. Saint Evagrios the Solitary, one of the desert Fathers of the fourth century, writes,

> For prayer is truly vain and useless when not performed with fear and trembling, with inner watchfulness and vigilance. When someone approaches an earthly King, he treats him with fear, and trembling and attention; so much the more, then, should he stand and pray in this manner before God the Father, the Master of all, and before Christ the King of Kings.[17]

In comparison to the ancient liturgical worship of the historical Church, even the so-called liturgical Protestant denominations, like the Lutherans and Episcopalians (and

---

efforts to the contrary, I continued plunging down from my spiritual high until I bottomed out at a consistently low spiritual plateau. My failure was to be the source of fervent searching for years to come." *Divine Energy: The Orthodox Path to Christian Victory* (Ben Lomond, CA, 1991), p. 7.

[16]See Jaroslav Pelikan's masterful summery of the devolution of Protestant theology and practices of worship, which went so far from the unquestioned dogmas of the faith, that Pelikan writes: "Yet if it was good and proper (for the Reformers) to oppose all the structures of continuity by which the church for more than a millennium had been identifying itself as 'apostolic,' namely, the 'apostolic succession' of the episcopate . . . what was to prevent such opposition from attacking . . . the very dogmas of the Councils of Nicea and Chalcedon, the 'apostolic doctrine' by which the church for more than a millennium had been identifying itself as orthodox?" *The Christian Tradition*, vol. IV: Reformation of Church and Dogma (Chicago, 1984), p. 321. See also Chapter 6 entire, "Challenges to Apostolic Continuity," pp. 304-331.

[17]Saint Evagrios the Solitary, "On Asceticism and Stillness," *The Philokalia*, vol. 1, translated by G. E. H. Palmer, Philip Sherrard and Kallistos Ware (Boston and London, 1979), p. 37.

tragically, many americanized Roman Catholic parishes), have left behind their respect for Apostolic authority. Outside of the more liturgically inclined Protestant denominations, in the place of the ancient liturgies of the Church, we have seen a host of self-invented, irreverent, subjective spectacles ranging from comedy, to one-man shows, mass hysteria, political correctness, ego-centric preaching, flippancy, to cultic intensity, and warmed-over popular culture.[18]These religious spectacles are led by a myriad of self-appointed personalities, whose authority to teach, baptize or serve the sacraments, seems to rest not on the Apostolic succession, the Holy Tradition, or even doctrine, but on their personal popularity or celebrity status.

In spite of the fact that many Protestants love and follow Jesus, they are vulnerable to every passing spiritual or political fad. They live, as I did, before my conversion to Orthodoxy, from one day to the next, spiritually rooted in nothing beyond their own emotions and feelings and their own subjective denominational, or personal, interpretations of the Scriptures. Whatever fad is then sweeping their denomination as the latest cure-all for their spiritual listlessness, doubt and sense of deracinated drifting (the common lot of all people who do not care to know their own history) carries them along until yet another fad develops.[19] In their heart of hearts many Protestants are far from satisfied. Many Protestants are instinctively aware that a great deal of the "biblical" teaching they follow is man-made, recent, and little more than a cult of personality. But awareness that all is far from well is not enough. To most Protestants the fact that there is a real alternative is not a consideration. They are condemned by habit, ignorance and misinformation to create one man-made "church" after another; an attempt to invent the Apostolic wheel out of thin air.

---

[18]"It was as though the Church had never really existed. It was as though the Bible had been written yesterday and I was the first man to open it." Thomas Howard, *Evangelical Is Not Enough*, p. 67.

[19]"Establishment religion in the United States is fragmented in a way that is more fundamental than the familiar denominational mosaic. It displays a bewildering kaleidoscope of conflicting and shifting beliefs. To a large extent it reflects the diversity of American society, the nation's division into competing civil religions. . . ." Herbert Schlossberg, *Idols For Destruction: Christian Faith and Its Confrontation with American Society* (Nashville, 1983), p. 253.

THE NEW DOGMA

It is my belief that the root moral problem of modern America is the fact that we now look for political, psychological, social or scientific solutions to what are in fact moral-religious problems. The reasons for this state of affairs may be found in the dreadful mixture of dehistoricalized Evangelical Protestantism, Enlightenment Secularism and secularized, American-style Roman Catholicism that has become our nation's civil religion. It is a religion that has its historical roots in an amalgam of utopian sentimentality, corrupted Christianity and Western rationalism. Its philosophical foundation is the humanism of the Enlightenment, the sentimentality of the Romantic movement, the truncated rationalistic theology of the Reformation, and the materialism of the so-called American Dream.

Members of each cultural faction—Enlightenment-humanists, Evangelical Protestants and secularized protestant-ized Roman Catholics—only imagine each other to be ideological opponents. In fact, I believe that each represents a different side of the same coin: a hybrid composed of the fragments of the ancient Christian faith and thoroughly modern, anti-traditional, materialistic, and often utopian ideas.

The Protestant-Enlightenment civil religion of America has at its core a belief in a dogma of instantaneous, effortless, magical conversion and change. To the fundamentalist Protestant this manifests itself as being "born again." But the modern descendent of the Enlightenment humanists, and our secularized American Roman Catholics, also believe in being born again, in a form of secular "conversion."

The secular, scientific world also has its own versions of the "born again" experience. Secular conversion is a commitment to civic virtue, the politically correct route to secular "grace." For the fervent secularists conversion is not to a belief in Jesus, as it is for the Protestant fundamentalist, but to any one of the myriad of idealistic, political, and civil cults that are so much a part of American public consciousness today, and that are so typical of the sort of pronouncements that the politicized secular bishops of the American Roman Catholic Church like to make, as they desperately try to shore up their diminishing influence.[20] Environmentalism, third worldism, anti-nuclearism, feminism, homosexual rights, self-determinism, democratism, multi-culturalism, new world orderism, pacifism, African-Americanism, consumerism, abortion rights, sensitivitism, all of these "faiths," and many more besides, have their zealously "religious" adherents.

Some of our modern revivalists go out to witness for Jesus, others to witness for the cause of the whales, multiculturalism, homeless people, expanded government social programs, African-Americans, lesbians, redwoods, the constitutional right to bear arms, to be Native Americans, to protect migratory birds, or restore prayer to public schools.

We live in an intensely "religious," fractured and tribalized culture. In this milieu, even so-called secularists are religiously intense in their pursuit of a host of private and public moralistic causes, while the so-called religiously believing seem to be more zealous in the pursuit of political relevance than in the pursuit of holiness.

RELIGIOUS SECULARISM

The fact that our religious culture is intensely secularized is not necessarily a contradiction in terms. We have secularized our religion and given our secular pursuits the fervor of a tent meeting revival.[21] We are religious, but we are not Christian in any traditional sense. We are, it seems to me, utopian sentimentalists who believe in our ability to solve our problems with instant technical and political solutions, psychology, good feelings, and various brands of politically correct ideology and a myriad of state-funded social programs.

Americans seem to believe in their Puritan-utopian- millennial enlightened, self-proclaimed goodness, in being converted to see the light, in having some sort of special call or covenant that sets them apart from the normal rules of history. The sentimental feeling of having a special call, of being, as Lincoln

---

[20]See Rael J. Isaac and Erich Isaac, *The Coercive Utopians* (Chicago, 1983), especially Chapter 2, "Sanctifying Revolution: Churches in Pursuit of Perfection," pp. 15-44.

[21]See Chapter 1 in *The Coercive Utopians*, pp. 1-14.

said, "an almost chosen nation," has bred a uniquely American style of populist religion cut off from Christianity's historical roots. It is the religion of the born-again experience variety. It is the religion of the circuit-riding preacher and the televangelist. It is also the secularized religion of secular politics and social causes mistaken for faith.

Americans still cling to the theocratic, coercive, utopian and millennial vision of the early Puritans. They are still trying to legislate morality. The only difference is that we have changed our focus to suit individual tastes and secularized self-invented "covenants".

But, it seems to me, all—the secularists, the religious, the political leftists and rightists—are united in their faith in the American civil religion and its sentimental utopian vision of its own self-enlightened goodness. They may disagree on the means to achieve the "American Dream" but, at heart, all sides are largely materialistic and utopian. They all believe that humanity's, or at least America's, purpose on earth is to be converted to right-thinking ways, improve itself, become wealthy, comfortable, politically correct, environmentally aware and fix the world's problems through political change, medical-social engineering and technical solutions, which, if all else fails, should be imposed on the public through coercive taxation, education and law. Today almost all Americans seem to share this common world view—what is wrong in the world can be fixed by scientific, political, legal, educational or psychological means. Our problems are not related to sinful behavior, let alone individual moral accountability to God or His law, but to social, political and psychological causes.[22]

Echoing the born-again Protestant, the secularist also looks for instant, "born again" solutions to his problems. Rather than viewing life as a long struggle—let alone a sacramental journey toward a spiritual goal—the secularist and the Protestant fundamentalist share the same world view, the same commitment to the great American quick fix. The one looks to the government, the other to Jesus. Neither seems willing to travel a difficult, life-long road of spiritual struggle toward salvation. All

---

[22]"One has to search hard among evangelical and fundamentalist sources to find much about the core practices and values of the modern world which they reject, which is perhaps not surprising given the important role that conservative Protestantism played in bringing such a world into being." Steve Bruce, *A House Divided*, p. 174.

want instant results. To this end, American left-wing Roman Catholic bishops, right-wing Protestant Fundamentalists, atheistic Jews or militant homosexuals, all seem to be united in their devotion to good feelings and social and material "progress." They all agree that advancement is to be achieved through political or legal means or simply a quick born-again change of heart, a conversion to the American religion of self-esteem, self-realization and "rights."

ANOTHER VISION

The teaching of the historical Church holds out a very different vision of the meaning of life from that of our contemporaries. The Church teaches that the purpose of existence is communion with God, not economic growth, the redistribution of wealth, or even good feelings. The historical Church teaches that the sacraments are not mere object lessons, or empty memorials to truth, but truth itself in action. The purpose of life, the Church teaches, is not well being, much less the pursuit of happiness; but sanctity.[23] It is, we are taught, not self-realization but re-creation into the Image of God. The fact that we are sinful, but nevertheless may choose to become like God, is at the heart of Christian teaching.[24]

The Church Father, Lactantius, (A.D. 250-317), writes,

> It is on this condition that we are made to exist: that we pay the debt of service justly owed to the God who makes us to exist, and that we recognize and follow only Him. We are fastened and bound to God by this bond of piety . . .
>
> The world was made for this reason, that we might be born. We, in turn, are born, that we might know God, the maker of the world and of us. We know, in turn, that we may worship. And again, we worship so that we may receive immortality as the reward of our labors—for the worship

[23]Matthew the Poor, *The Communion of Love* (Crestwood, NY, 1984), particularly Chapter 5, pp. 79-84.

[24]"The world is a fallen world because it has fallen away from the awareness that God is in all." Alexander Schmemann, *For the Life of the World* (Crestwood, NY, 1963), p. 16.

of God entails great labors indeed. And, in turn, we are recompensed with the reward of immortality, so that, having been made like the angels, we may serve the most high Father and Lord forever, and may be an ever-lasting kingdom unto God. This is the sum of things; this is the secret of God; this, the mystery of the world.[25]

Starting from the changeless faith of the Fathers, we come to see that selfless worship of God, expressed sacramentally in all areas of life, is the point of life. Life's goal is not conversion to civic goodness in order to create man-made "perfection." We come to realize that life is primarily sacramental, not political, in its essence. And we come to see that authentically Christian political ideas about freedom, or justice, lose their meaning if they become an end in themselves, isolated from their true historical, religious, and moral foundation which gives moral principles meaning beyond mere self-interest.[26]

Life, as understood by the Fathers of the historical Church, is a mysterious living sacrament. If we believe this, our ideas about our lives, society, and politics will be drastically different than those of people who believe that conversion, secular or religious, to right-thinking ways and self-realization is the point of life.

---

[25]Lactantius, "On the Divine Institutions, A.D. 304," in *The Faith of the Early Fathers*, vol. 2, trans. W. A. Jurgens (Collegeville, MN, 1970), pp. 266-268.

[26]"If there is no appeal (to transcendent religious truth) beyond king or court, the law is finally capricious." Richard John Neuhaus, *The Naked Public Square*, p. 256.

CHAPTER TWO

THE CULTURAL "WAR"

There is an ideological war raging within our borders. This "war" is being fought between those who disavow the history, religion and society of Christian civilization, and those who continue to cherish our cultural and religious inheritance. It is being fought between those who have taken the Protestant pluralistic impulse to its logical conclusion and those Jews, Roman Catholic, Eastern Orthodox, and Protestant Christians who are struggling to establish some sense of moral order, beauty and mystery in our desacralized, materialistic, and morally anarchic society.[1]

From the pages of the popular press to the law courts, from the arts to the humanities, people holding to secularist, rationalistic social and political beliefs are often on a collision course with traditional Christians and Jews as well as others who cherish religious faith.[2]

Those seeking to destroy the traditions of our Judeo-Christian inheritance, have politicized the world around us in

---

[1] Richard John Neuhaus explains the cultural war — or at least its roots: "When the bearers have lost confidence in the tradition they bear, then that tradition must be ridiculed, lest it be suspected that it has in fact been betrayed . . . there is (a) new elite of people. It is a 'knowledge elite' . . . It is made up of people who are self-conscious about being well educated and 'enlightened' . . . (T)he new class is 'statist' in orientation, it favors increased government intervention in all aspects of society." Ibid. pp. 237-240.

[2] Describing the often unequal contest between those who hold traditional religious beliefs and secular ones in the world of academia, Page Smith, Provost of the University of California at Santa Cruz, writes, "Excluded (are) such ancient and classic human concerns as love, faith, hope, courage, passion and compassion, spirituality, religion, fidelity — indeed, one is tempted to say, anything that might be somewhat encouraging to young people." *Killing the Spirit: Higher Education in America* (New York, 1990), p. 20.

an effort to achieve their ends. Through a myriad of social engineering projects, they have radically altered, perhaps for the foreseeable future, the way our society thinks about the meaning and purpose of life, truth, morality and religion. Politics has, at all levels in our society, replaced religious truth as the principle source of morality.[3] Government officials, bureaucrats and judges now address concerns that were once the preserve of religion and individual conscience. This new materialistic political "morality" is thoroughly secularized; as such it is relativistic.[4]

A few specific examples serve to illustrate the far reaching, not to say cataclysmic, consequences of the banishment of traditional religious belief in favor of relativistic secular politics and social engineering as the source of "mortality" in our public life today.[5]

THE LAW

In the legal arena we have witnessed a host of legal scholars, law professors and judges actively abandoning the idea of the rule of law as disciplined by the original intent of the Constitution.[6] They have even gone so far as to manipulate the law to

[3] The roots of the erosion of the transcendent in favor of the "scientific"-political have been described as follows: "Darwinism promised that evolution to higher human and societal forms through natural selection and survival of the fittest was 'scientifically' inevitable. For the more politically advanced, Marxism promised a similar outcome to human history . . . ." Page Smith, *Killing the Spirit*, p. 35.

[4] It has been described as: "The right of the individual to believe whatever he wishes as long as he accepts the doctrine that it is this very right itself which is the supreme (political) dogma of the 'common faith.' " Thomas Hopko, *All the Fullness of God* (Crestwood, NY, 1982), p. 153.

[5] The subject of the secularizing and politicizing of American life and culture has been investigated in a wide ranging literature including: Neuhaus, *The Naked Public Square* (Eerdmans); Smith, *Killing the Spirit* (Viking-Penguin); Isaac, *The Coercive Utopians* (Regnary Gateway); Schaeffer, *How Shall We Then Live?* (Crossway Books); and many more. Several scholarly journals have also paid a great deal of attention to the secularizing of American life, among them, *Commentary, The Human Life Review* and *First Things.* A range of writers of various persuasions has noted the secularizing of America and the politicizing of American life. These would include Jewish scholars such as Norman Podhoretz, Irving Kristol and Jon Levenson, Roman Catholics such as Michael Novak and Peter Kreeft, Protestants such as Dr. Francis Schaeffer and Martin Marty and agnostics like Alan Bloom. The phenomena has been explored by writers on the political Left, like Germaine Greer (*Sex and Destiny,* Harper) to writers on the Right like Robert Nisbet (*History of the Idea of Progress,* Basic Books).

[6] See Robert H. Bork, *The Tempting of America: The Political Seduction of the Law,*

achieve their political ends by non-democratic, even non-constitutional means.[7] Typical of these abuses was the 1973 Supreme Court decision of Roe vs. Wade in which the laws prohibiting or restricting abortion were struck down in every state in the union. Not only state laws prohibiting abortion on demand, but two thousand years of Christian tradition regarding the sanctity of born and unborn human life was overturned by the "discovery," in the Constitution, of the so-called right to privacy — a "right" that is nowhere stated in the Constitution and that American jurists were unable to "discover" for 200 years.[8]

In the general public's mind, the legality of abortion was soon equated with its moral acceptability. This is well demonstrated by the staggering number of abortions performed each year in the United States — over a million and a half. Abortion was, at first, in the initial debate, described as an "agonizing choice" but soon came to be so routine that a high percentage of abortions are done at the demand of women who have already had several abortions. In the end, abortion became such an accepted "procedure" that it even became part of a subsidiary medical industry when experimentation with the tissue of aborted babies was given government funding on January 22, 1993 by President Clinton.

Roe v. Wade was only one manifestation of a revolutionary ideological impulse that has been driving America further and further along the path toward total secularization. From the radical leftist Critical Legal Studies program at Harvard University, to the politicized confirmation hearings of Judge Robert H. Bork in 1988, to the social engineering policies of the Clin-

---

especially Chapters 1 and 2 (New York, 1990).

[7] "When a court strikes down a statute, it always denies the freedom of the people who voted for the representatives who enacted the law . . . that act substitutes the will of a majority of nine lawyers for the will of the people." Ibid. p. 264.

[8] "From the beginning of the Republic until that day, January 22, 1973, the moral question of what abortions should be lawful had been left entirely to the state legislatures. . . . Unfortunately, in the entire opinion there is not one line of explanation, not one sentence that qualifies as a legal argument. Nor has the Court in the sixteen years since ever provided the explanation lacking in 1973. It is unlikely that it ever will, because the right to abort, whatever one thinks of it, is not to be found in the Constitution. . . .

In the years since 1973, no one, however pro-abortion, has ever thought of an argument that even remotely begins to justify Roe vs. Wade as a Constitutional decision." Ibid. pp. 112-15.

ton administration (fetal experimentation, government-funded abortion programs, etc.), we have seen the politicizing of the law — or rather the abandonment of the rule of law — in favor of the prosecuting various political agendas — by our judges, our politicians and their secularist political fellow travelers who teach in the law schools.

As Judge Robert Bork writes,

> Law school moral philosophy . . . turns out upon examination to be only a convoluted way of reaching the standard liberal or ultra-liberal prescriptions of the moment . . .What the students learn, to put it bluntly, is that legal reasoning of the sort that served us for centuries is now utterly outmoded and a verbal formulation can always be devised to reach the correct political result. . . . Law is a critical battle ground because, like the arts and humanities, like sociology, history, political science, and other areas that have become politicized, law has the capacity to affect ways of thinking and our culture through its educative and symbolic influence.[9]

THE HUMANITIES

A steady assault on the literature of the Greco-Roman, Jewish and Christian West and on its art has also been gaining momentum. This is true particularly in our universities which, since the ideological leftist political upheavals of the 1960's, have been dominated by people who hold highly secularized and philosophically relativistic views.[10] As Charles E. Donovan, S.J., wrote in 1963,

> The history of American higher education is a sad story of loss of faith by religious institutions. The presence in so many parts of the country of secularized, non-religious, at times even anti-religious institutions whose foundations

---

[9] Ibid. pp. 135-38.

[10]"Cultural relativism succeeds in destroying the West's universal . . . claims." Alan Bloom, *The Closing of the American Mind: How Higher Education Has Failed* (New York, 1987), p. 39.

were inspired by religious zeal and apostolic motives seems almost like empirical proof of the contention of positivists that faith and intelligence are incompatible.[11]

Those who believe that Christian faith and intelligence are incompatible are now in control of the educational endeavor in America. They have become dogmatically hostile to people who hold traditional, not to mention religious, historical, or even politically conservative views.[12]

A radical process of debunking has taken place. We find that the academic guardians of the humanities have themselves become those most avid to irreparably change; even undermine, their own fields of study in pursuit of their secular, ideological, usually left-wing, politicized agendas. This has been true in the field of theology as well as in the humanities. Many of the loudest voices raised in a chorus debunking the historical Christian faith have been those of Protestant and Roman Catholic, so-called, liberal theologians.[13] The phenomenon of the destruction of the liberal arts from within has manifested itself in a general disparaging of Western culture and history in the name of a new multiculturalism — what George F. Will calls a "curriculum (that) aims at delegitimizing Western civilization by discrediting the books and ideas that gave birth to it."[14]

In the forefront of this delegitimizing attack are the deconstructionist literary critics, who claim that the traditional meaning of literature must be "deconstructed" in order to liberate it from conventional interpretation. Gertrude Himmelfarb, Professor Emeritus of History at City University of New York, writes about how deconstructionist theory has invaded the other disciplines:

---

[11]Cited by James Turnstead Burtchaell in *First Things* (April, 1991).

[12]"The spiritual illness of 'post-modernism,' afflicting not just America but the Western world, obviously extends far beyond university walls, but it is in the university that I believe its destructive effects are most keenly felt." Page Smith, *Killing the Spirit*, p. 5.

[13]"In its public interventions today, mainline Protestant religion is typically advancing a view of politics and society in which (traditional) religion has no right to intervene." Richard J. Neuhaus, *The Naked Public Square*, p. 138. Also see Paul V. Markowski, "Academic Religion: Playground of the Vandals," *First Things* (May, 1992).

[14]George F. Will, "Literary Politics," *Newsweek*, April 22, 1991.

It is deconstruction . . . that taught a generation of literary critics that there is no text (fixed meaning) apart from interpretation, that the author has no more "authority" than the critic, that there is no objective reality. Historians, eager to be on the cutting edge of their discipline, soon discovered that history too could be deconstructed, that the events of the past have no objective reality, that they are no more than texts to be interpreted, invented, or imagined by the historian. And with literature and history, so with law; if events and texts have no reality or authority, then statutes, precedents and constitutional principles are equally indeterminate. In one discipline after another, the deconstructionists promise to do what the Marxists before them had tried to do: to demystify received truth and to liberate us from the tyranny of facticity.[15]

Page Smith, historian and founding provost of the University of California at Santa Cruz, has examined the deterioration of the academic community that has followed in the wake of its dogmatic secularization. He writes in particular of how we, in the West, have passed from an academic world view, that had at its heart a sense of transcendent spiritual truth, to a new "faith" in pure secularism hostile to Christianity. This is what Smith calls "academic fundamentalism." Smith writes,

The spiritual illness of post-modernism, afflicting not just America but the Western world, obviously extends far beyond university walls, but it is in the university that I believe its destructive effects are most keenly felt. . . . There is a mad reductionism at work. God is not a proper topic for discussion, but 'lesbian politics' is. . . . Academic fundamentalism is the issue, the stubborn refusal of the academy to acknowledge any truth that does not conform to professional (secular) dogmas. In the famous market place of ideas, where all ideas are equal and where there must be no value judgments and therefore no values, certain ideas are simply excluded, (i.e., historical Christian religious ideas) and woe to those who espouse them. Such individuals are terminated, lest their corruption spread to others. . . .[16]

[15]Gertrude Himmelfarb, *Commentary* (April, 1991).
[16]Page Smith, *Killing the Spirit*, p. 5.

The secularizing, or more accurately the pluralistic relativizing, of American education has a long history. Harvard University president Charles W. Eliot was typical of the dogmatic secularizers, products of the nineteenth century generation of Protestant unbelief and inheritors of the Unitarian rejection of historical Christianity. These scholars created the modern climate of academic fundamentalism, which is now so hostile to all but its own secular ideas. In Eliot's 1869 inaugural address at Harvard University he said,

> The very word education is a standing protest against dogmatic (Christian religious) teaching. The notion that education consists in the authoritative inculcating of what the teacher deems true may be logical and appropriate in a convent, or a seminary for priests, but it is intolerable in universities and public schools, from primary to professional.[17]

In other words, the idea that academic inquiry could be informed by religious truth was, according to the President of Harvard in 1869, an outmoded idea whose time had passed into oblivion. So it was that the idea of education informed by Judeo-Christian principles, an idea that found expression in an unbroken continuity from Byzantium in the East through the high Middle Ages and Renaissance in the West and up to the dawn of our own era, was abandoned. The word education now came to be understood to mean secular education, and a gulf between religious-philosophical ideas and secular-scientific academic learning was arbitrarily imposed.[18]

Prior to our modern age, all learning, scientific or otherwise, was perceived to have moral, ethical, religious content or meaning. Questions of morality and existence were understood to be inextricably religious by nature. Indeed, until late in the final stages of the secularization of the American universities, it was usually the president of a university who alone was entrusted with the responsibility of teaching all entering freshmen a course in moral, i.e., religious philosophy.[19]

---

[17] Cited by James Turnstead Burtchaell, *First Things*, April 1991.

[18] Page Smith, *Killing the Spirit*, particularly Chapters 1 and 2.

[19] The relationship between faith and learning was soon challenged in the new American Republic: "From 1800 to the outbreak of the Civil War, higher education in the new republic was distinguished by major trends. Religious orthodoxy was constantly challenged . . . the debate over classical versus practical education went on as contentiously as ever. . . ." Ibid. p. 37.

FEMINISTS

It seems that no single political interest group has more devoutly proclaimed the new secularized gospel of academic fundamentalism than have the feminists.[20] No single group has pushed harder to have traditional Christian religion relegated to the inconsequential nether world of personal experience or fought harder to perpetuate the idea that traditional Jewish and Christian religious truth is "regressive" and, therefore, does not belong in the public arena; and should not even be given a hearing.

Feminist literary criticism has followed deconstructionist ideological lines by reading into all literature, past and present, a radically revisionist interpretation that superimposes an image of patriarchal tyranny and gender oppression onto all literature at the expense of most traditional interpretations or spiritual and transcendent themes once held to be common to all people, races and sexes down through the ages. The feminists are in the forefront of a movement that has supplanted esthetic, religious and moral responses to literature and the arts, and replaced the traditional esthetic vision of the arts and humanities with a mere index of political one upman-or womanship.

Feminist literary theory has largely abandoned esthetics and become a study, not of literature, but of who has power over whom. The feminist agenda is one of reducing the human race to a collection of victims of patriarchal tyranny and of reducing the study of literature and history to political warfare carried on by other means. The politicizing of the study of history and literature results in a sort of cultural amnesia — a deculturation in which our secularized cultural elite seem to be bent on forcing the members of our society into forgetting who they are and where they came from as the first necessary step in engineering our society into a new secular "utopia."

Since the 1970's, the feminists have become so extreme in their war on academic tradition, that many women have

---

[20]Peter Shaw, *The War Against the Intellect: Episodes in the Decline of Discourse* (Iowa City, IA, 1989), particularly pp. 67-91.

begun to speak out against what they perceive to be an attack on humanity itself, and the West in general, by their intolerant academic fundamentalist sisters. For instance, Christina Hoff Sommers, Associate Professor of Philosophy at Clark University, wrote this stinging indictment of her feminist colleagues:

> Feminist complaints against the traditional curriculum are based on the notion that Western culture — all the received knowledge of thousands of years — is a flawed concept from the start. For everything that has been recorded and passed on to succeeding generations has been dominated by a male bias. This means that not only the humanities are under attack. One of the busiest areas of feminist research today is the gender critique of the sciences. . . . . The new feminism . . . is not concerned with more opportunities for women, or for that matter, with including women's achievements in the curriculum. Its aim is to transform our understanding of our past, our present and our future. How? By convincing people to accept the central insight of contemporary feminist philosophy: that the sex/gender system is the most important aspect of human relations.[21]

THE DEMOTION OF HUMANITY

Our schools and universities have become so anti-Christian that even Christendom's traditional high view of human beings has been abandoned and a concerted effort to demote and to delegitimize mankind in general, and Western Christian society in particular, has been made.

Today's ideological demotion of humanity has manifested itself through the propaganda of the more extreme members of some environmentalist groups who act as if people are an immoral intrusion into otherwise pristine nature.[22]

---

[21]Christina Hoff Sommers, *Imprimis* 19, vol. 6 (June, 1990).

[22]Ironically, they do this while claiming that people have no special meaning, are merely creatures evolved by chance, mere animals themselves, which logically would place humanity in nature as "just another species" with no special moral accountability to be responsible for his or her actions vis-à-vis the rest of nature.

When people are not demoted wholesale by some of today's anti-Christian thinkers, then the Western culture that we inherited from ancient Israel, Greece, Rome and Byzantium is demoted to a lower status than all other cultures. Exhortations to humbly learn from non-Western, non-Christian pagan societies are thrust upon us not only through university courses but by the popular media. At the same time the actual historical heritage of Christendom, its past, culture and civilization is increasingly ignored while the glaring problems of non-Christian societies are covered up.

If one reads the average history text book used in our schools today, one would think that the one thousand years of Byzantine civilization with its art, theology, humane philanthropic institutions, commerce and literature had never existed and had nothing to do with us. Our students are urged to study Australian aborigine culture or rain forest ecology or the literary proclamations of lesbian African-Americans or homosexual "life-styles," while not learning about St. Constantine the Great, St. John Chrysostom, Shakespeare, Dostoevsky, Chaucer, Charlotte Bronte, or Mark Twain.

Western civilization's remarkable achievements have been disparaged in comparison to other cultures. Confidence in Jewish and Christian civilization has been replaced by the remarkable belief that there is moral, artistic and religious equivalency between all cultures no matter how they behave, what they produce, or how they treat people. Furthermore, in many quarters the Christian East and West are now held to be inferior cultures to all others. This belief has reduced sociology and anthropology, like literature and history, to mere political ideological assertion in the secular campaign to de-Christianize our culture on the way to replacing it with a socially engineered, dogmatically secular super-state.

If the nineteenth century could be characterized as the age of Protestant missionary zeal, the twentieth century can be characterized as the age of the internal secularization of the West. Neo-pagan thought is promulgated in the name of ecological, sexual, racial or cultural "sensitivity," "diversity" and "multiculturalism," in the hope that these new mantras will replace the teachings of Judaism and Christianity with a new age of enlightenment, fraternity and happiness based, not on transcendent faith, but rather, on politically correct ideology and government programs.

SPECIEISM

The latest trend away from Christian tradition is "specieism," in which it is claimed people are equal to or lower than the rest of the biological kingdom. Literary scholar and author Peter Shaw writes concerning the specieist, radical-chic demotion of mankind,

> The unfavorable comparison of man with cockroach has become a familiar staple of biological discussion — although Stephen Jay Gould (media personality and Harvard University biologist) is ready to take a stunning step even further down the scale:
>
> "Evolution is a copiously branching network, not a ladder, and I do not see how we, the titular spokesmen for a few thousand mammalian species, can claim superiority over three-quarters of a million species of insects who will surely outlive us, not to mention the bacteria, who have shown remarkable staying power for more than three billion years."
>
> Here we have very nearly the ultimate demotion of man, the inferior not only of primitive peoples, other mammals and the cockroach, but even of bacteria.[23]

This demotion of humanity has gone so far that it hardly seems possible that only a few short years ago, the West was a rather self-confident society and that comparisons with other cultures usually left inhabitants of Christendom feeling grateful for their Jewish, Greco-Roman, Byzantine-Latin, Christian heritage.

It seems that most of the battles of the cultural war have so far been won by those who wish to eradicate the last traces of our venerable Christian civilization from the face of the earth.

---

[23]Peter Shaw, *The War Against the Intellect*, pp. 140 and 151-152. Harvard University paleontologist George Gaylord Simpson writes, "Man is the result of a purposeless and natural process that did not have him in mind." As cited by Phillip E. Johnson in *First Things* (January, 1993).

The question is, of course, what principals will replace the old, in order that our fractured society can remain a nation and a community, now that the philosophical presuppositions of Christian thought have been abandoned by our cultural elite?

The coercive, intolerant mentality of our Knowledge Class, wherein they ignore or denigrate opinions they find politically incorrect — as "homophobic," "sexist," "regressive," "oppressive" or "fascist" — and wherein law, education, politics and religion are perceived only to have the utilitarian value of being a means by which to indoctrinate the population with "progressive" (in other words, aggressively secular) ideology, does not bode well for the cause of traditional religion, not to mention the sanctity of life, civil liberty and freedom of speech.

CHAPTER THREE

THE FAILURE
OF AMERICAN
SECULARISM

One of the first Christian writers of the twentieth century to articulate his suspicion that the modern state had failed to provide a humane community for its citizens was C. S. Lewis. Lewis's ultimate expression of the horror of this process was in his novel *That Hideous Strength,* where an elite of scientifically trained technocrats is intent on exterminating most of the human race in order to insure the dominance of their own 'inner circle.' C. S. Lewis wrote, "I do think the State is increasingly tyrannical . . . (it) exists not to protect our rights but to do us good or make us good — anyway, to do something to us or make us something. Hence the new name 'leaders' for those who were once 'rulers.' We are less their subjects than their wards, pupils or domestic animals. There is nothing left of which we can say to them, 'Mind your own business.' Our whole lives are their business."[1]

BLIND GUIDES

Our sense of transcendent meaning, purpose and beauty has been lost. However, the failure of secularism, in America, to provide a humane alternative to Christian morality, is beginning to show. From crime to illiteracy, from family breakdown to

[1] 1954 correspondence to a civil servant by C. S. Lewis, as cited by Joseph Sobran in *Single Issues* (New York, 1983), p. 177.

the degradation of our cities, cracks in the secular utopia are turning into gaping canyons.

Yet, in spite of one failure after another, in spite of our secularized state's inability to provide authentic solutions for poverty, educational reform, public welfare, public safety, economic stability, or to undergird families, our secular elite — the Knowledge Class that dominates education, the media, the entertainment business, the courts, government, the educational unions and bureaucracies — continues to masquerade as those to whom we should look for yet more answers to our problems.[2] The Knowledge Class even audaciously proposes to solve the very social pathologies they themselves often contributed to creating. They continue to demand that we give them more money, more time, and even allow them to raise our taxes again and again to underwrite yet more utopian experiments in social engineering and state-sponsored "virtue,"[3] in spite of the fact that the least productive people in our society are often those with whom our social engineers and their government programs, have had the most to do.[4]

Have sex education and values clarification techniques of moral instruction led to a tripling of illegitimate births in the last thirty years? Not to worry! Government-funded legal abortion will provide the casual consumer of sex with a cure! Has militantly secularized, amoral public education failed to discipline, educate or produce responsible, self-governing, literate citizens? Not to worry! More money, teachers and facilities will solve the problem; experts in "conflict resolution" will help stem the tide of violence that is sweeping through our schools; psychiatry and social welfare agencies will replace the need for religious faith! If all else fails, we will lower our standard of academic excellence in the name of politically correct ethnic diversity! After all, isn't feeling good about yourself the most important goal in life?[5]

[2]See Thomas Sowell, *The Economics and Politics of Race* (New York, 1983) and *Civil Rights: Rhetoric or Reality* by the same author (New York, 1984).

[3]Jessica Gress-Wright, "Liberals, Conservatives and the Family," *Commentary*, April, 1992.

[4]Jared Taylor, *Paved With Good Intentions: The Failure of Race Relations in Contemporary America* (New York, 1992).

[5]"'Sensitivity' has proven to be a powerful political weapon. By redefining ideology in non-ideological terms, it has provided a pretext for sweeping changes in American universities, but also in the larger society, by radically changing the standards of equity

Yet, to all but the most reflexively conditioned, the constant refrain of America's educational and governmental Knowledge Class — more programs, more money, less traditional Christian religion — seems to be the battle cry of a failed philosophy.

It is no mystery that our Knowledge Class is at least partially to blame for the social chaos that surrounds us. The secularist and statist missionary crusade, that has overwhelmed American institutions in the twentieth century, has generated a vast, self-important, documentary literature. We know, as Hilton Kramer writes, "what secularized leftist elements in our political life organized the destruction of the public school system."[6] We also know what part of our culture created the legitimization of drugs, even who celebrated drug-taking as a legitimate "life style." We know who launched the black power movement that destroyed the civil rights movement and replaced it with the enslavement of statist entitlement programs that have condemned a whole generation of African-Americans to the welfare plantation. It is no secret as to who it was, in the feminist-lesbian movement, who preached the "gospel" of single-parent, female-headed households as equal to, if not superior to, traditional marriage. Our libraries contain whole rooms full of demands for "new family structures."[7]

However, the jury is no longer out regarding the results produced by the American secularist experiment. Enough time has passed so that our brave new secular theorists have had their ideas tested. We now know that contrary to feminist claims, female-headed families have been a financial and moral disaster, largely incapable of disciplining boys or of escaping poverty — welfare, day care and affirmative action programs

---

and evidence. . .Once status was determined by the degree of one's victimhood, every nuance of oppression became crucial — one's rights now depended on the constantly shifting scorecard of aggrievement." "The Ideology of Sensitivity," *Imprimis*, July, 1992. Also see William K. Kilpatrick, *Why Johnny Can't Tell Right From Wrong* (New York, 1992).

[6] *Commentary* (December, 1990).

[7] Any issue of almost any women's magazine printed from the mid-1970s to the mid-1980s is replete with pro-job, anti-family articles, "research" and "studies." Beyond the original feminists (Germaine Greer, Betty Friedan, Gloria Steinem, etc.) popularizers such as Helen Gurley Brown took the image of the "new" woman to a vast general public.

notwithstanding.[8] We have seen that abortion was not legalized, as feminists once loudly proclaimed, to help twelve-year-old rape victims and other "hard cases," but rather so that one million, six hundred thousand "sexual partners" per year can use abortion as a casual means of birth control, or to search for and destroy "imperfect" babies, or to facilitate their career ambitions and to make possible their consumption of sex as a consumer product unrelated to responsibility, commitment and child-bearing. We know who it was that created the climate in which sexual license was encouraged, in the name of liberation from our much-maligned, so-called traditional values. And we have seen the results: the highest incidence of illegitimacy in the world (with the exception of Sweden, whose secularized socialist welfare policies have encouraged an even higher rate of illegitimate births than our own in an all-white, all-middle class, well-educated population). We also know that the proponents of sexual liberation have been nowhere to be found, in order to explain, let alone apologize for, or remedy, their failed sexual utopia that has degenerated into a blizzard of illegitimate births, the AIDS epidemic and a political climate in which the statistics of rape and abortion (now even "date rape"), are the only numbers multiplying as fast as the national debt.

THE SECULARIST AGENDA

Chaos and human misery have followed in the wake of the state's social and educational programs, and in the wake of our secularized Knowledge Class' social engineering projects as they have successfully prosecuted their war on tradition. Evidence of the social pathology of America's failed "progressive" experiment is conclusive, nowhere more so than in the field of education. Professor of Psychology at Boston College, William K. Kilpatrick has documented the recent moral breakdown in American schools.

An estimated 325,000 attacks, shakedowns and robberies

---

[8] See James Q. Wilson, "The Family Values Debate," *Commentary* (April, 1993) for a comprehensive review of available material on the failure of the feminist agenda regarding single-parent households and working mothers.

occur in public high schools each month. Each year nearly three million crimes are committed on or near school property. . . . About 135,000 students carry guns. . . . Suicides among young people has risen by 300 percent over the last thirty years, (1962-92). . . . Teenage sexual activity seems to be at an all time high. Despite a much smaller teen population and despite more frequent contraceptive use, about 1.1 million teenagers became pregnant in 1991 . . . . Many youngsters have a difficult time seeing any moral dimension to their actions.

One natural response to these grim statistics might be to ask: "Why aren't they teaching values in the schools?" . . . It might come as a surprise to learn that . . . more attention and research have been devoted to moral education in recent years than at any time in our history. Unfortunately these attempts at moral education have been a resounding failure.

Why?

(Because) the same educators and experts (who espouse the Liberal 'value-neutral' philosophy that introduced 'progressive' educational ideas in the first place) . . . want desperately to hold on to their failed philosophy of moral education.[9]

It seems to me that a political gun has been put to the head of American society: the threat of social chaos. According to most "progressive" political theories, things must be made worse before revolution, or social engineering, can make them better. The more threatened and bewildered people are made to feel, whether by exaggerated environmental doom-saying, the threat of a "population explosion," neighborhood crime or educational chaos, the sooner they will abdicate their self-government to the political, academic or media "experts" who stand in the wings ready to help restore order with their utopian statist social engineering programs. As historian Paul Johnson writes,

To archetypes of the new class, such as Lenin, Hitler and Mao Tse-tung, politics — by which they meant the engineer-

---

[9] William K. Kilpatrick, *Why Johnny Can't Tell Right From Wrong*, pp. 14-15.

ing of society for lofty purpose — was the one legitimate form of moral activity, the only sure means of improving humanity. This view which would have struck an earlier age as fantastic, became to some extent the orthodoxy everywhere.[10]

In the absence of religiously motivated self-restraint and the mitigating communitarian influence of traditional social structures such as churches and families, all that remains as a bulwark against the nightmare of complete social breakdown is the expanding, apparently limitlessly intrusive power of the secular state. The social engineer, the doctor, the tax man, the coercive "progressive" condom-dispensing school-teacher-sex-educator, the regulatory bureaucrat, ever-expanding government programs, absent family integrity, religious faith and individual responsibility, are constantly presented, by our governmental and media Knowledge Class, as the last best hope for maintaining social order.[11]

In a sense, those secularists who often shout the loudest for new programs and initiatives to combat our growing social anarchy are like stone-throwing window-smashers who also happen to own the only window repair shop in town. The failure of their own coercive and intrusive programs seems only to provide them with further "evidence" for the need of even more intrusion into people's lives in order to create a "new society," a "new man," a "new woman," a "new world order," a "new multi-cultural, gender-neutral utopia" in which everything will be tolerated except politically incorrect, "old-fashioned," "regressive" religious ideas.

We have seen not only evidence of the failed secularistic utopian program but also, it seems to me, a cynical double game being played with people's lives — usually the lives of individuals who can least afford to become pawns in an experimental charade of political maneuvering. This is a game that takes unborn babies, old people, black children in inner cities, white children in suburbia, and teenage welfare mothers

---

[10]Paul Johnson, *Modern Times*, p. 729.

[11]See Angelo M. Codevilla, "The Euromess," *Commentary* (February, 1993), for a detailed examination of the role of the expanding state in Europe in the twentieth century and its continuing failure to justify expanding intrusiveness into the private sphere of life.

and treats them not as persons with aspirations, with God-given and transcendent sacramental meaning, but rather as pawns. They are the pawns of ideologically committed, secularized academic and political social planners, who now measure human worth in dollars and who no longer believe that the ultimate meaning of life is best expressed in worship, love, sacrifice, personal moral accountability and compassion. Rather, they believe that life's purpose is to become a productive member of the secular super state and "global community," or a dependent victim — a mere statistic in a bureaucratically controlled enterprise of economic production — a "human resource" rather than a child of God.

EDUCRATS

A good example of the anti-human attitude of our secularized Knowledge Class can be found in the field of education. Our educational elite have failed to truly educate, but nevertheless have tried to redefine the purpose of education as that of preparing the campus proletariat to "compete" in a "competitive world" of "interdependent, international trade." Listening to modern educators and educational bureaucrats, one would have to conclude that if a surgical procedure, genetic engineering technique or eugenic program could make American workers "competitive," and that if such innovations could eliminate the need for learning altogether, they would be welcomed!

Once it was believed that education had intrinsic worth because morality, virtue, art, beauty and life were worthwhile enterprises — because life had eternal, sacramental, transcendent, spiritual meaning. Such old-fashioned ideas have been replaced by the gray sterility, the Orwellian sameness, of an "educational program" to train a compliant, cooperative work force to "compete" in "world markets" and to provide a reliable tax base. Many modern secularists, in the field of education, have abandoned even the pretense of love for real learning for its own sake, learning undertaken because a human soul is worth nurturing, loving, enlightening.

According to our secularized "educrats," the ultimate purpose of life is apparently the ability to compete successfully with the Japanese. Where God was once seen to have been the guarantor of meaning, now the growth of the Gross National Product seems to be our ultimate human end. Where St. Basil the Great, Shakespeare and DaVinci were once found edifying and uplifting, the purpose of learning has been reduced to mastering "computer science," not in order to enjoy the fullness of life, but rather to build a more economical car or to lower "health care" costs. According to the educrat's creed, the chief end of the human being is apparently the continuity of the state.

However, the sullen subjects of the utilitarian secular educational experiment seem to be in a rebellious mood. The Knowledge Class may have decided that there is no ultimate transcendent purpose to life, and that becoming a productive drone ought to be enough of a "goal" for the young people with whom our educrats love to experiment, but the young people themselves seem strangely uninspired. Instead of being good little taxpayers-in-training, they have rebelled. They have lost interest in learning. They stab each other. They rape each other. They abuse drugs. They spray graffiti on public monuments and fail tests. They fail to learn to read or to think. They molest their dates in college dorms. They watch mind-numbing quantities of moronic television. They abort their babies. They steal from their employers, cheat on their examinations and, when they graduate, they cheat on their taxes. And yet their secularized mentors, or rather their social engineering, educrat masters, do not see the need to change their philosophical presuppositions.[12]

Simple arrogance does not seem to adequately explain the unrepentent behavior of our social elite, our Knowledge Class, our educrats, in the face of the bankruptcy of their programs. It seems to me that greed for power, and an irrational, almost pathological, hatred of tradition, especially Jewish and Christian traditions of morality, must motivate our failed secularists.

Far from taking responsibility for their failures, members of America's secularized Knowledge Class simply sweep them under the carpet and press on to what end no one can say.

---

[12]"Was not human planning to produce a 'classless society' not only intrinsically unattainable but positively harmful . . . . The experience of modern times, when human activism led so often, and on so grandiose a scale, to inhuman destruction, suggested as much." Paul Johnson, *Modern Times*, p. 734.

These so-called liberals seem to have trouble describing the sort of society in which they would be conservatives. Change and rebellion against convention have become the status quo.

THE EMPEROR'S NEW FAMILIES

Let us briefly examine just one specific failure, one small item in the secular catechism, the so-called new family structures that were to replace old-fashioned two parent households.[13] Research has shown that young men whose parents divorce during their teen years are far more likely to commit a crime than peers who did not experience parental divorce during adolescence: fifty-three percent compared to twenty-eight percent.[14] Dr. Robert W. Sweet, Jr. has found that "disproportionately, teenagers are running from families with step-parents and live-in boyfriends or girlfriends . . . runaways reflect the disintegration of the American family."[15] Another study found that children of parents who divorce are much more likely to cohabit before marriage than children of parents whose marriages endure. "A parental marital disruption is associated with at least a doubling of the cohabitation rate. Among young adults reared by continuously married parents, half had not cohabited before entering marriage compared to only twenty percent among the three groups of young adults who had experienced marital disruption."[16] Beverly Raphael, in a study on *The Impact of Parental Loss on Adolescent Psychological Characteristics*, finds that teens living in single parent or step-parent households, suffer from a number of serious problems less commonly seen among peers in intact families. "Adolescents from disrupted families report higher

---

[13]James Q. Wilson, Charles Murray, Thomas Sowell, Angelo M. Codevilla, Paul Johnson, Irving Kristol, et al. have written on the subject of the failure of the social engineering programs of the "New Left" at length. The whole literature of the Neo-Conservative movement has worked together to effectively debunk and discredit the human engineering programs of the Left in our time without, however, having produced much of a change of heart.

[14]"Patterns of Family Instability In Crime," *Journal of Youth and Adolescents*, 19 (1990) 201-18.

[15]U.S. Department of Justice, "Missing Children Found Facts," *NIJ Reports*, No. 222 (November-December, 1990), pp. 15-18.

[16]Richard Lauv, *Childhood Teacher* (Boston, 1990), pp. 5 and 108.

levels of general health problems, were more neurotic, less extroverted, had poor perceptions of their bodies, were more im-
pulsive, and had more negative views of their school performance. They were also more likely to report more alcohol and
psychological problems in their families."[17]

In a recent study at York University, Sociologist Mary Ann
D. Parsons analyzed the life course of 45,000 Canadians between the ages of 14-34. In this national survey she found that
adults raised in father-only households reported the lowest
educational achievement, lower than that of mother-only
households and adult men raised in mother-only families
reported "the lowest level of occupational attainment of all off-
spring from the different family types." She also found that
children raised in lone parent families in Canada are socio-
economically disadvantaged in adulthood. "The lone parent
population has risen dramatically since the early 1970s and
all indicators point to a worsening situation for the children
raised in this family structure."[18]

Fred Siegal, Professor of History at Cooper Union University,
writes,

> What, then, caused the growing gap between rich and poor?
> . . . The fraying of the American family. "The empirical evi-
> dence is in," says the *Washington Post's* Paul Taylor. "When
> marriage atrophies, so does fatherhood and so does society."
> Gordon Green of the Census Bureau has found that changes
> in household structure — the increasing number of people
> who are single or divorced — explains half the growth in in-
> come inequality over the past twenty years: families without
> fathers are six times more likely to be poor . . . . .[19]

Thomas Sowell, the noted African-American economist, who
is a Senior Fellow at the Hoover Institute, sums up the failure,
indeed the perniciousness, of the "liberal," statist programs of
the last decades.

---

[17] *Adolescents*, 25 (1990) 698-700.

[18] "Lone Parent Canadian Families and the Socio-Economic Achievement of Children as
Adults," *Journal of Comparative Family Studies*, 21 (1990) 353-65.

[19] "The End of Equality," *The American Spectator* (September, 1992).

The role of the family is crucial, and the systematic under-
mining of its effectiveness and legitimacy in recent decades
has produced social disasters. . . .

Social-service agencies, public schools, and judicial activists
have all amputated functions of the family and transferred
them elsewhere. The choice of the age at which children
are to be introduced to sexual matters, for example, and
the manner of introducing them and with what moral
values, was long ago taken out of the hands of parents. As
with so many other assumptions of superior wisdom in our
avant-garde elite, the actual results have been disastrous,
whether measured in soaring teenage pregnancy rates —
after years of *decline* before 'sex education' was widely introduced into American schools — or in the growing incidence of venereal diseases, including, AIDS. . . .

Today, and for the foreseeable future, families are besieged.
They face the intrusions of social workers, the brainwashing
of their children in the public schools, and now the threat
of lawyers grabbing a piece of the action by representing
children in lawsuits against parents, if the so-called Children
Defense Fund has its way . . . .

Family values are the antithesis of the values of the welfare
state . . . (the) partisans of the welfare state measure their
'commitment' to the family the way they measure so many
other commitments, by how many billions of tax dollars they
are willing to pour down the bottomless pit of government
programs.[20]

Yet in spite of the ruin left in the wake of sexual liberation,
no-fault divorce, the abandonment of the understanding of
marriage as a holy sacrament, the "progressive" leaders of the
movement to "liberate" America from religious or traditional
ideas and morality, are not only unrepentant but in fact, are
shrilly demanding more of the same.

As David Horowitz, (author with Peter Collier of *Deconstruc-
ting the Left*), writes,

For the left, it is not socialism, but only the language of
socialism, that is finally dead. In the universe of postmodern

---

[20]"Have the Democrats Really Changed?" *Commentary* (September, 1992).

relativists, there is no truth, no lesson that can be derived from this terrible experience . . . . To be reborn the left has only to rename itself in terms that do not carry the memory of insurmountable defeat, to appropriate a 'narrative' in which the leftist utopia can still propose itself as a moral 'solution.'[21]

Like the last of the old guard, Eastern European and Soviet Communists, our "progressive" Knowledge Class seems immune to any sense of personal responsibility for the failure of their theories. They seem to evince no desire at all to reconsider their cherished anti-traditional, anti-Christian beliefs in the light of the empirical evidence — the broken lives, smashed homes, and destroyed communities their "progressive" ideas have produced. The last of the Communist dictators, when confronted with the mountain of evidence concerning the manifest failure of Communist policy to produce the New Man and New Order, were no more obdurate than our own Knowledge Class when confronted with the reality of their own failures.[22]

THE VICTIMS

Greek Orthodox Archbishop Iakovos writes, "Perhaps the greatest losers in the fragmentation and decline of our culture and morality have been our children. Through near-criminal neglect, we've robbed them of their spiritual birthright."[23]

Government tax and welfare policies favoring divorce and illegitimacy over marriage, the deconstruction of education, the feminist juggernaut of the 1970s which glorified single-parent, female-headed households and advocated easy divorce and hard-nosed careerism as a panacea to women in order that they might escape "oppressive" traditional home life, the manipulation of the court system to force society to adopt the eugenic pro-abortion programs of Planned Parenthood,[24] the use of aborted babies in

[21]"Utopian Passions," *First Things* (April, 1992).

[22]Owen Harris and Martin Malia, "Communism, the Cold War and the Intellectuals," *Commentary* (October, 1991).

[23]Archbishop Iakovos, *Faith for a Lifetime* (New York, 1988), p. 123.

[24]See Robert Marshall and Charles Donovan, *Planned Barrenhood: The Social Policy and History of Planned Parenthood* (Harris, NY, 1990).

medical experimentation, the abandonment of parental responsibility by thousands of American men in favor of careerism and perpetual adolescence, the so-called sexual liberation of men from their traditional roles as protectors of women and children, the so-called liberation of women from motherhood and nurturing, our punitive anti-family tax codes, the failure of public education (a failure that forces families who care about their children to pay twice for schooling, once in taxes and a second time for private tuition), all these things — in other words, the whole program of the American secularized Knowledge Class evolved over fifty years — have played a crucial part in creating the social pathology of our time.[25]

Our secularist elite have not produced utopia by waging their war on tradition. Instead they have presided over the disintegration of what little sense of individual responsibility and community our individualistic American society once had. The rise of government interference in Americans' lives has been mirrored by the dramatic escalation of the very social pathologies — crime, abortion, illegitimacy, illiteracy, the loss of meaning — which the secularists say social engineering programs were designed to cure.[26]

[25]Jessica Gress-Wright, "Liberals, Conservatives and the Family," *Commentary* (April, 1992).

[26]William K. Kilpatrick, *Why Johnny Can't Tell Right From Wrong*, especially Chapters 1-6.

CHAPTER FOUR

THE FAILURE OF THE SECULAR RIGHT

In the 1960's, 1970's and 1980's, some members of the Knowledge Class switched sides in the cultural war. Given the failures of the secularists to achieve their social engineering goals, this is not surprising. Some secularists did repent, after a fashion, and admitted the error of their utopian coercive ways. They became tired of being moral anarchists. They no longer relished the role of self-flagellation, of always hating their own history and culture, of seeing themselves as the representatives of "oppressor, imperialist" Western culture in an otherwise pristine, primitive and good world. Above all they clearly saw the inhuman bankruptcy of the Communist world view and broke ranks with the Western Left and became anti-Communists long before the failure of Communism was acknowledged by the predominantly left-wing Knowledge Class.

These people came to be known as the Neo-Conservatives. They were thinkers, writers and academics who began to say that perhaps historical evidence and a more traditional interpretation of history, as well as rational discourse, should not have been so hastily abandoned by the Knowledge Class. The Neo-Conservatives began to contradict the ideas of their leftist, academic fundamentalist peers. They went so far as to challenge the Left's political received wisdom, that all things Judeo-Christian in origin, were inherently evil, and that all things secular in origin especially Socialist and Communist ideas, were good. Finally, the Neo-Conservatives went mildly on the intellectual offensive and began to criticize their colleagues in the universities, the media and corporate and government bureaucracies. These thinkers compared anti-Western revisionist claims of the Left unfavorably to the objective historical data. They also compared the results of the anti-Christian elite's negligible cultural and social achievements to their often spurious and inflated idealistic claims.[1]

What the Neo-conservatives exposed for all to see was that by and large the secularist anti-Christian (and sometimes pro-Communist) Left had failed to produce a viable moral alternative with which to replace the traditional Judeo-Christian values they were blithely liquidating. Far from creating a new human being, the secular Left had only succeeded in producing inhuman chaos and dependency on big government. Far from following the will of the people, the American Left increasingly had turned to non-democratic and coercive means — using the courts, media propaganda, even school curriculum censorship, to realize their utopian socialist agenda by coercion where legitimate persuasion failed.

It is largely due to the Neo-Conservative movement that emerged in reaction to the extremes of the New Left of the 1960's, that the cultural war has not been entirely lost, in America, to the anti-Judeo-Christian rationalistic Knowledge Class. Unfortunately few of the Neo-Conservatives, or indeed of today's Conservatives, have challenged the basic anti-Christian assumptions of the intellectual inheritance of the Enlightenment philosophers, let alone the rebellious iconoclastic spirit of Protestantism, which has permeated our egocentric, consumeristic, individualistic culture and rendered it so excessive, inhumane, subjective and anti-communitarian. Few of the Neo-Conservatives have exposed the limitations of the secular god of representative democracy, nor have they discussed its inability to provide anything more than big government. For this seems to be the result when the state is secularized, and transcendent, non-negotiable religious moral absolutes are abandoned as the ultimate check in the system of democratic checks and balances.

---

[1]The Neo-Conservatives included, amongst many others, such luminary intellectual figures as Norman Podhoretz (editor of *Commentary* magazine), Michael Novak, Hilton Kramer, Irving Kristol, Midge Decter, Richard John Neuhaus (editor of *First Things*), Gertrude Himmelfarb, Robert Nisbet, Thomas Sowell, Peter Berger, Paul Johnson, P. T. Bauer and Julian Simon.

THE FUNDAMENTAL PROBLEM

Even less have the Conservatives, "neo-" or otherwise, forthrightly critiqued the pluralistic secularism inherent in the Protestant-Enlightenment American experiment.[2] For all their laudable contributions in defense of the good, the sensible and the workable in our cultural war, it seems to me that the Neo-Conservatives, and many Conservatives as well, have largely failed to address the fundamental problem underlying our social decay. This problem, it seems to me, is not one of economics, race-relations or welfarism gone wild, but rather the resulting chaos following in the wake of the rejection of the humane communitarian tradition of historical Christianity in favor of Protestant-Enlightenment individualism and secularism.

Conservatives have tried to defend what little remains of Western civilization, yet have been largely unable or unwilling to critique the foundational principles of American cultural-religious history that, I believe, have led to the selfish chaos of rights they now deplore.

Conservatives dispute the *conclusions* of the secularistic Left but seem to often share the Left's secularism. Conservatives, too, have tended to disregard religious ideas in favor of materialistic economic and social models. They, like other Americans, tend to see things in terms of technical, legal, economic or political reality, not religion. They are more comfortable discussing economic trends than Holy Tradition, issues of pragmatic workability rather than those of non-negotiable sacramentality.

Many Conservatives have long since begun to worship at the altar of American democracy which they seem to adore instead of the God of Abraham, let alone Holy Christian or Jewish Tradition. They do this in such a way as to seem to imply that American democracy is a magical or even "spiritual" idea that can exist independent of moral and religious belief. It is as if democracy were some sort of natural phenomenon

---

[2] In fact, many Conservatives are distinguished by their seemingly mindless adulation of the American experiment. One only has to be familiar with the editorial page of the *Wall Street Journal* to know that there is a breed of Conservatism that takes refuge in projected statistics related to productivity as if American "success" was unrelated to divorce, abortion, abandoned children and the spiritual illiteracy that is creeping over the tribalized and barbaric society America has become.

unrelated to foundational religious principles. They seem to imagine that democracy will work for anyone, no matter what his or her philosophical or religious presuppositions. And they assume that it will continue to work for America no matter how depraved individual Americans become.[3]

WHOSE GOD?

The important question which the Neo-Conservatives, as well as most political Conservatives, seem to refuse to ask is: If the West is to be restored to cultural unity and moral integrity, what is to be its philosophical and religious basis? In other words, what, besides the mutual pursuit of free market materialism, can Conservatives promote that will be a large enough truth to provide us with a sense of community and individual accountability? Or even more to the point: is it even possible to be a Conservative and yet be loyal to a Protestant-Enlightenment society founded on revolution and the debunking of tradition?

The quest for an answer to these questions should be even more urgent to those who believe — even if only in some vague theoretical way, as do most Neo-Conservatives and Conservatives — that our culture needs some sort of "moral foundation" if it is to be free, humane and communitarian.[4]

But for all his or her good intentions, these are the vital questions that the non-religious Neo-Conservative and non-religious political Conservative do not seem eager to ask. Yet as long as questions of ultimate meanings are not tackled, I believe that the West, Western ideals and ideas cannot be restored.

---

[3]Typical of the sort of "conservatism" that refuses to ask the real questions concerning American society was George Bush's statement in his 1992 State of the Union address that "Americans are a good people." This misty-eyed sentiment seems to ignore a larger reality, one in which one-third of pregnancies end in abortion, 50% of marriages in divorce, and in which a whole generation of American adults have not bothered to educate their youngsters in the rudiments of good character.

Most conservatives have, along with most liberals, forgotten that "(R)eal self-esteem is a by-product of real learning and achievement. We feel good about ourselves because we've done something good or worthy." Kilpatrick, *Why Johnny Can't Tell Right From Wrong*, p. 41.

[4]"Religion as an institution. . . is very highly esteemed by conservative thinkers — though not all are devoutly religious. They believe that society requires the sense of morality and the sharply defined notions of right and wrong central to religions anchored in Judeo-Christian teaching." Burton Yale Pines, *Back to Basics* (New York, 1982), p. 248.

Moral chaos will continue to reign supreme in our cultural, legal, familial and political spheres of life. In the end, even the practice of democracy, once it is thoroughly secularized, will begin to fade away under the hammer blows of individualism run amok and statist coercion.

The loss of democracy seems to be already occurring. We have seen ample evidence in our politicized courts of non-elected judges imposing social change in a manner which is patently non-democratic. We have seen that those who hold to secularist political ideologies even seek to overturn the Constitution.[5] We have seen family and other social structures break down in the wake of the receding religious certainties and expanding state power.[6] We have seen the curtailment of free speech in the name of politically correct sensitivity. It is not surprising that the secularist ideologues who dominate our Knowledge Class have not admitted the correlation between the decline of traditional religion and morality and social chaos and loss of liberty. What *is* surprising is that so many Conservatives also seem to see the world through almost exclusively secular spectacles.[7]

WHO WON?

It seems to me that the loss of Christian moral values continues to take place even though the West has triumphed over Communism. The inability of non-Western, or ex-Communist, secularized systems to produce humane workable communitarian cultures does not automatically imply the continuance of the secularized West's livability, prosperity or freedom. Since human rights are inextricably bound up with religious conceptions of transcendent truth, the loss of faith profoundly affects all of life, including politics.[8]

[5]Robert Bork, *The Tempting of America*.

[6]Kilpatrick, *Why Johnny Can't Tell Right From Wrong*, Chapters 1-3. Weldon Hardenbrook, *Missing From Action*. Burton Yale Pines, *Back To Basics*.

[7]A point that Richard John Neuhaus has addressed on numerous occasions in *First Things*. See "The Public Square: A Continuing Survey of Religion and Public Life" in almost any issue.

[8]See footnote 4 of this chapter.

The squalid debacle of non-Western ideology does not imply that moral enlightenment will rise from the ashes of the squandered Christian culture. The fact that Communism's godless, materialistic, secularist society decayed even faster than our own is no reason to think that democracy's godless, materialistic, secularist society will not also slide into the oblivion of moral anarchy or authoritarian repression. For this may indeed be the self-wrought apocalypse awaiting us once our society has altogether forgotten and, more importantly, ceased to practice, traditional Jewish and Christian religious moral truth.

At the very moment that the Berlin Wall fell in 1989, and we were told triumphantly by many Conservatives that the West had won the "Cold War" against tyranny and barbarism, the United States was aborting 1.6 million unborn children a year. Our public school system was grossly failing to educate; illiteracy rates were proportionately higher than those of 1887. We had a drug epidemic in our inner cities. A seemingly permanent underclass of professional "victims" had emerged to drain the national coffers. Single mothers, who had reaped the feminist whirl-wind of "no-fault" divorce and misguided welfare policies (and who bore the brunt of the loss of men's sense of responsibility for their children), were heading impoverished households and had become a permanent core of the newly "liberated" Poverty Class. Violent crimes of all kinds continued to rise more or less steadily as did the incidence of cheating in schools and businesses. Malfeasance of all sorts seemed to become normative in the political process. The litigation explosion continued to expand in a culture of greed and failed trust. Affluent middle class citizens continued to mortgage the future of their children through greedily clinging to their own welfare entitlements like Medicare. This was their "right," in spite of the fact that they were thereby impoverishing the future of their children with an insurmountable, crushing, national debt so large that by the end of 1992, the third highest budget item of the federal government was the interest paid to service the national debt. And the search-and-destroy mission against "imperfect" babies, implicit in pre-natal testing, began to gain momentum in the same country that less than half a century before had tried Nazis in Nuremberg for "crimes against humanity" resulting from the Nazi eugenics program!

In 1991, during the one hundred hours that US-led ground

forces defeated Iraq's army, with less than two hundred American casualties, there were more than eighteen thousand abortions performed in the country which claimed to be "winning the war against tyranny." Many more young men were murdered on the crime-infested streets of our cities than were killed by the "uncivilized" Iraqis in the battle to liberate Kuwait City. In the time it took to complete Operation Desert Storm, thousands of divorce cases came to court, leaving many more children orphans to self-indulgence than were ever orphaned by our Iraqi enemies.

As Soviet Communism stumbled and fell on its rotting face in the summer of 1991, news footage of Boris Yeltsin defying tanks was interspersed with television coverage of a forty-day stand-off between anti-abortion demonstrators and "abortion rights" advocates in Wisconsin in the ongoing second American civil war over the re-legalized trade in human flesh. As newly freed Eastern European nations turned toward America and Europe for inspiration, we, in the West, continued to slide inexorably toward bigger and bigger government, the bureaucratization of all of life, more government regulation and a stagnating top-heavy economy. One might expect that these realities would remind those Conservatives with eyes to see that the so-called triumph of technology in the West and/or the economic and human failures of Communism, Socialism and Third World despotism are not necessarily the same thing as the *moral* triumph of modern, secular, Western society.

Some idealistic Conservatives have written and spoken as if the boundless wonder of computer technology and biotechnology and the so-called information revolution hold the key to a better future for the West. But this optimism seems to beg the question that is symbolically posed by the mute thugs huddled over video games in the dimly lit arcades that blight the American landscape, a question of a poverty of the spirit, immoral behavior and an attitude of perpetual vandalism against meaning, a mindless viciousness punctuated only by sex and drug-stupefied sleep. What price new, improved computers when their users cannot read the instruction booklet? What price the "information revolution" when no one has anything worthwhile to say?

I would suggest that the loss of moral will power in the West *is directly related* to the loss of belief in transcendent sacramental religion and therefore that our spiritual and social decline cannot be reversed by economic or scientific tricks, however spectacular their wizardry. Technical know-how cannot replace character. All the talk of the promise of new genetic discoveries rings hollow when the end product is merely the creation of new "compelling reasons" for abortion. The triumphalism of many American Conservatives of the "we're still number one" variety is given the lie by the fact that, morally speaking, the "American Dream" is beginning to look like a nightmare of selfishly motivated, inter-tribal warfare, punctuated by greed, prurience and thuggery.[9]

In the lexicon of conservative causes, politics, economics, education and science take precedence over religion, morals and ethics. For instance, the social engineering proposals made by such Conservatives as Charles Murray, (Losing Ground), are no less secular and manipulative than those of the Left. Conservatives all too often act as if our problems were solvable by merely fine-tuning secular governmental programs, diplomatic or military initiatives, inventing new computer chips, or investing in "bio-tech." While Conservatives may bewail the moral decadence of our age (for instance in speaking of "family break-down"), they seem largely incapable of offering a solution beyond calling for supply side economic measures, right to work laws, improved teaching methods, defense spending, longer prison terms for criminals, "family values" (a term that conjures up images of Disneyland as the New Jerusalem), more research and development spending, more savings, more (or less) consumption, lower taxes, reduced welfare spending — scarcely the medicine required to heal millions of ailing souls made sick by large doses of secularist American hedonism.

SNATCHING DEFEAT FROM THE JAWS OF VICTORY

As the moral anarchy of our present age demonstrates, a

[9] One could, for instance, read *Commentary* for a year and find a few articles that correlate economic problems or educational dysfunction with the decline in religious faith — beyond vague talk of declining "family values." The same could be said of *The American Spectator*.

culture cannot simply proceed on spiritual inertia. People need to believe in something transcendent in order to form a workable, let alone, humane society. Moreover, belief is not enough. People not only need to believe, but to act. There has to be a foundation that is greater than mere individualism, or American triumphalism, or even the desire to prosper, in order to produce the cooperation needed to forge individual people into a nation. Faith in faith, or in America, is not enough. It must be the faith of the profound, life-changing sort that leads to changed behavior even to selflessness. It must begin with repentance. Adam Smith, Hobbes and Locke have been proved wrong by history. When it comes to building a society, self-interest is not a satisfactory alternative to moral, religious virtue. As a foundation that will forge individuals into a community, selfishness is a resounding failure. There must be more than selfishness; "Man does not live by bread alone."

Whatever people believe in is always religious in nature, because ultimately it is by faith of one sort or another that we guide our lives. It can be the drum-beating pseudo-religion of nationalism, of the kind the American political Right delights in, or it can be the religiously zealous fervored commitment to politics, social programs and the worship of state power favored by the political Left. It could also be historical Orthodox Christianity. But in the absence of a faith in true religion, the very democratic enterprise — so beloved by the Conservatives — seems to me to be in jeopardy. Perhaps Fisher Ames foresaw modern secularized America when he wrote to Thomas Dwight in the eighteenth century: "Our country is too big for union, too sordid for patriotism, too democratic for liberty." Looking at the legion of abandoned old people, the love-starved infant population of our day care centers and the mangled bodies of our unborn children filling hospital and abortion clinic dumpsters, the amoral pursuit of health, wealth and happiness seems to provide a sorrowful and listless human agenda even when that agenda is dressed up as the "American Dream."

CHOICES

I believe that only two fundamental ways exist to affect

human behavior. Only two incentives exist by which to limit our human inclination toward selfishness, evil and anarchy. Each is illustrated by the respective phrases, *"There ought to be a law,"* and *"What you are doing is wrong."* The first expresses the power of politics and state coercion to regulate human affairs; the second pre-supposes a common shared commitment to sacramental religious truth to inspire individual moral restraint, charity and self-effacement. These phrases also represent the two philosophies that are squared off against each other in our bitter cultural war that pits secularized legal, political, media and social elites against traditionally religious people.

Pro-Western hubris is not a big enough base upon which a society can be built or rebuilt. Something more is needed than a jingoistic love affair with hi-tech electronics, the "right to bear arms," a sentimental attachment to the Bill of Rights, the free market or faith in the inherent goodness of the American people. And something more is needed than a return to the beliefs of the American Founding Fathers, since it was their short-sighted, Protestant, utopian, humanistic ideas that began the whole process of the radical secularization of American society to begin with.

NOSTALGIA

Some secularized Conservatives look back nostalgically to a time when there was a more or less commonly accepted Judeo-Christian cultural and philosophical foundation in European and, to some extent, American society. They recall a time when parents bothered to pass on their religious faith to their children, and a time when the words education and moral instruction were synonymous.[10] Yet lip service and nostalgia notwithstanding, today's Conservatives all too often fight the cultural war on purely rationalistic, secular ground.[11]

---

[10] See Robert Nisbet, *The History of the Idea of Progress;* Page Smith, *Killing the Spirit;* and Burton Yale Pines, *Back to Basics,* for three studies typical of the nostalgic Neo-Conservative hankering for a past that is unspecifically "religious."

[11] Many of Robert L. Bartly's editorials in the *Wall Street Journal* could be summed up as, "in spite of everything, America is still the greatest, most productive nation on earth and all the studies of the computer chip industry show . . ."

Conservatives may extol the virtues of human rights but rarely address the fact that the concept of human rights is ultimately
meaningless unless grounded in religious faith.[12]

Our secularized conservatives praise the idea of stable families
and faithful marriages.[13] But, it seems to me, unless such
praise is rooted in more than what is perceived to be "for the
good of society," it rings hollow and is just an expression of what
amounts to secularized pietism, one more social preference for
a Conservative form of social engineering, not a moral non-
negotiable truth.[14]

DEAD END

I believe that there are good reasons why Conservatives have
ignored religion and not looked to the modern Protestant
denominations for moral guidance. As Neil Postman correctly
points out, American religion has become trivialized:

> Not long ago, I saw Billy Graham join with Shecky Green,
> Red Buttons, Dionne Warwick, Milton Berle and other
> 'theologians' in a tribute to George Burns. . . . The Reverend
> Graham exchanged one-liners with Burns about making
> preparations for eternity. . . . Rev. Graham assured the au-
> dience that God loves those who make people laugh. It was
> an honest mistake. He merely mistook N.B.C. for God. . . .

> On television, religion, like everything else, is presented
> . . . as entertainment. Everything that makes religion an
> historical, profound and sacred human activity is stripped
> away; there is no ritual, no dogma, no tradition, no theology
> and above all no sense of spiritual transcendence. On these
> shows, the preacher is tops. God comes out as second
> banana.[15]

---

[12]Typical of such a-religious arguments are the many "religion-neutral" pieces that appear in *Commentary*, for instance, Giuseppe Sacco, "Saving Europe from Itself," *Commentary* (September, 1991), which discusses the danger of abandoning the "original Euro-
peanist vision . . ." without mentioning the Christian ethics, and fervent Christian faith,
that motivated the calls for a united Europe by the architect of European unity, Jean
Monett.

[13]See, for instance, Rita Kramer's *In Defense of the Family* (New York, 1984).

[14]Typical of such a technical approach to the family is the work of such social critics
as that of Roman Catholic William F. Buckley Jr.

[15]Neil Postman, *Amusing Ourselves to Death* (New York, 1985), pp. 5 and 117.

Given the trivialization of religion in America by many of its own Protestant leaders, the reluctance by thoughtful Conservatives to become embroiled in religion is not unreasonable. No serious person could possibly believe that the Protestant denominations, with their offerings of trivial entertainments as "worship," could produce any workable alternative to the secular chaos around us. It seems to me that this is yet another reason why, even by Conservatives, most serious social debate is carried on in purely secular, political and economic terms. The Protestant denominations ranging from the bizarre to the paranoid, from the libertine to the apostate, are largely ignored, left squabbling on the sidelines of their culture. Tragically, the American Roman Catholic Church has also become almost as trivialized as its Protestant counterpart. Just as the culture around it most needs the transcendent religious hope that non-politicized, pure, ancient religion alone can offer, many Roman Catholic bishops are acting like politicians and Roman Catholic liturgies have become mere popular entertainments, and not very tasteful ones at that.[16]

SECULAR BOUNDARIES

The self-imposed secular boundaries of today's cultural debate — what Fr. Richard John Neuhaus has called the phenomenon of the "naked public square" wherein religious ideas are excluded from public discourse[17] — means that the cultural war is being fought on secular ground. Thus its venue is an alien territory that gives the anti-Christian Knowledge Class a distinct advantage over religious traditionalist and secular conservatives.

To fight for ideals of freedom and justice without mentioning the Ten Commandments, Judaism, Jesus Christ, Orthodox Holy Tradition, The Fathers, the Sacraments, and Byzantine and Latin Christendom, is like trying to defend the

[15]Neil Postman, *Amusing Ourselves to Death* (New York, 1985), pp. 5 and 117.

[16]"In the liturgy of the (historical) Church we approach that perfect harmony between the outward and the inward. We celebrate Redemption, which has begun to knit things back together." Thomas Howard, *Evangelical Is Not Enough* (Nashville, 1984), p. 104. Sadly Howard, who converted to the Roman Catholic Church, is describing a liturgy that no longer exists in modernized Roman Catholicism.

[17]Richard John Neuhaus, *The Naked Public Square* (Grand Rapids, MI, 1986).

theory of evolution without being allowed to make any reference to Darwin or fossils. It is as futile as trying to understand the Byzantine mosaics at Ravenna, Handel's *Messiah* or Shakespeare's *Macbeth* without the Bible or a knowledge of Holy Tradition.

The Christian West cannot be understood, let alone strengthened, outside of a moral discourse whose foundation is Jewish and Christian religion. Dean C. Curry makes this point when he writes,

> The (religious) moral prerequisites and purposes of democratic capitalism are rarely articulated, and are frequently ignored, even by the religious leaders of free societies. This is tragic. For democratic government cannot endure apart from a common understanding that liberty is not an end in itself, but means toward the fulfillment of humanity's deepest quest for personal and communal meaning.[18]

If all Conservatives have to offer is a promise of a higher Gross National Product, a smaller welfare state, a better anti-missile defense system or a smaller computer chip, they may make a little money, win a few debates, even an election or two, but I do not believe that they will ultimately prevail over the secular utopians who are inexorably forcing their coercive social engineering programs on our society. Contemporary conservatism will fail to reform and protect the last vestiges of the humane institutions in this society if the only arguments for moral regeneration it can muster are secular ones. These rationales draw different conclusions than the theses of the utopian Left, but, nevertheless, use the same secularized intellectual methodology.

Nothing better illustrates the problematic nature of the secular world view more than the growth of prenatal testing. Without a religious belief system to guide it, modern science is adrift in a world in which everything that is possible becomes permissible. The secularized Conservative who wishes to cling to "traditional values" or "family values" without making a commitment to religious first principles, has his work cut out for him in the face of the late twentieth century revival of the

[18]Dean C. Curry, *First Things* (April, 1991).

eugenics movement. With ultrasound imaging, chorionic villus sampling (CVS) and cordocentesis now becoming routine procedures in the search-and-destroy mission being waged by doctors against "imperfect" babies, the glaring inability of scientists to guide themselves without the benefit of religious faith and moral absolutes has become evident.[19]

In a society in which the pursuit of happiness is the only "ethic" and in which the purpose of life is to be "happy" and in which religion has been relegated to the nether world of subjective opinion, what defense against the barbarity of a wholesale Nazi-style eugenic program is there, given the bright lure of the expansion of genetic knowledge? And on what moral grounds, other than religious faith, can the Neo-Conservative or Conservative plead with a woman to not kill her less than perfect child? And, if religion is to play no part in setting the human agenda, how can one logically argue that an "expensive," "worthless" human life is worth saving or bringing to term? Conservatives and Neo-Conservatives might be squeamish about the modern eugenics movement but, absent religious conviction, what good argument is there against Nazi-style eugenics?

The idea of the sanctity of life, let alone freedom from state intrusion, makes little sense if life and free will are no longer understood as gifts from God. From a historical Christian point of view, the secularist vision of life falls short of describing the reality of the human condition. As St. John Chrysostom writes, "To say that things which exist were gotten out of existing matter and not to confess that the Creator of all things produced them out of what did not exist would be a sign of extreme mental derangement."[20]

LIVING IN THE PAST

Some Neo-Conservatives and Conservatives sense their moral dilemma — the problem of trying to find a meaning to life without religion.[21] Thus they occasionally make vague appeals to "tradi-

[19]Elizabeth Kristol, "Picture Perfect: The Politics of Prenatal Testing," *First Things* (April, 1993).

[20]St. John Chrysostom, *Homilies on Genesis*, 2, 2, A.D. 388, in *The Faith of the Early Fathers*, vol. 2, trans. W. A. Jurgens, p. 102.

[21]For instance, since about 1987, one has read an increasing number of pieces in

tion," "Western values," "family values," even generic "religious values." But these rather contentless appeals amount to little more than nostalgia and hardly represent a challenge to the secularistic juggernaut. As Fr. Richard John Neuhaus writes,

> . . . There are those [conservatives] who . . . do not themselves believe, but they recognize the importance of religion as a 'useful lie' essential to securing . . . public order. . . . It is sad because they do not believe, and it is sadder because they are prepared to use, and thereby abuse, the name of the God whom they do not honor.[22]

Nostalgic appeals for a return to past beliefs do not meet the huge task of moral reconstruction at hand. Nor do they provide a bulwark against the rampant and craven inhumanity of our age. Sentimental Conservatives' attachments to other people's religiosity is no substitute for actual religious faith. In the end, the secular conservative can articulate no convincing argument for the self-denial and sacrifices that are necessary for people to make in order for our society to remain civil. If our recent history is any indication, the lure of unlimited selfishness is too seductive for most people to resist. The pleasures of illiterate barbarism seem to make perfectly good sense if God is dead, or at least is understood to no longer demand a change in the content of our characters and love for others, including "the least of these."

Some Conservatives recognize their intellectual dilemma and have tried to make appeals to religious feelings without making a commitment to specific religious faith. For instance, historian Page Smith, at the end of his important book, *Killing*

Commentary about Jewish faith but usually only in terms of an academic or abstract interest in that faith. On the other hand, some writers for Commentary have begun to address the problem more forthrightly; Irving Kristol writes, "When we look at secularization . . . I would describe it as the victory of a new, emergent religious impulse over the traditional biblical religions that formed the framework of Western civilization . . . Pure reason can offer a critique of moral beliefs but it cannot engender them . . . the Western world has been leading a kind of schizophrenic existence, with a prevailing moral code inherited from the Judeo-Christian tradition and a set of secular-humanist beliefs about the nature and destiny of man to which that code is logically irrelevant." Irving Kristol, "The Future of American Jewry," *Commentary* (August, 1991).

[22]Richard John Neuhaus, "The Public Square," *First Things* (September, 1991).

the Spirit, can do no better than propose a very general and exceedingly vague solution to our problems. He makes only a feeble attempt to offer an alternative to the harshly secular "academic fundamentalism" he so rightly deplores.

> A new consciousness representing a synthesis of the two prior consciousnesses, the Classical Christian (thesis) and the Secular Democratic (antithesis) must take shape. I do not presume to say just what form this new consciousness will take. I am confident that it must include the enduring elements of both traditions, powerfully reanimated and enthusiastically reconstructed.[23]

Robert Nisbet, in his book, *History of the Idea of Progress*, concludes his masterful study as follows: ". . . it seems evident from the historical record, (that only) in the context of a true culture in which the core is a deep and wide sense of the sacred are we likely to regain the vital conditions of progress itself and of faith in progress — past, present, and future. . . ."[24] Neither Page Smith or Nisbet makes mention of the content of "the sacred" nor do they provide any clue about *which* "religious tradition" it can be drawn from. And, of course, they make no personal declaration of faith of the kind that would draw hoots of derision from their secular colleagues in academia.

Some light has been shed by the Neo-Conservative camp on the need for a more specific affirmation of religious faith. Roman Catholic Michael Novak writes,

> If those who live under democratic capitalism lose sight of the moral foundations of the system, a loss of morale is likely to occur. . . .It is no accident that democratic capitalism arose first in Jewish-Christian lands.[25]

And yet, as Michael Novak and other Conservatives pay their respects to the fruits of Christian truth, the robust defense of that truth, and the Holy Tradition that guarded it, is woefully neglected. One has a hard time believing that the Conservatives' lack of specific affirmations of faith, does not have something to

---

[23]Page Smith, *Killing the Spirit*, pp. 304-305.
[24]Robert Nisbet, *History of the Idea of Progress*, p. 357.
[25]Michael Novak, *The Spirit of Democratic Capitalism* (New York, 1982), pp.334-35.

do with their desire to avoid embarrassment in a secular academic world that tolerates all "faiths" except traditional Judaism and Christianity.[26]

Dostoevsky wrote that once people stop believing in God, they will believe in anything. The failure of the conservative movement to provide effective leadership toward a moral restoration of our culture is the futile story of trying to combat moral decay without an authentic commitment to historical Christian religious truth. St. Neilos observed a similar problem in the fifth century. He writes,

> Both Jews and Greeks fell short of this, for they rejected the Wisdom that is from heaven and tried to philosophize without Christ, who alone has revealed the true philosophy in both His life and His teaching.[27]

Peter L. Berger, Professor of Sociology at Boston University writes,

> Religious faith is possible only on the basis of the insight that religion satisfies certain needs, either collective or individual. . . . (The) sociologist might conclude that religion is wanted for social order, (the) psychologist that religion springs from profound needs of the soul, but neither of these propositions can lead to an affirmation beginning with the

---

[26]Unfortunately, the younger generation of conservative thinkers are as thoroughly secularized as their elders. Anyone who reads such conservative publications as *The American Spectator or Commentary*, is aware of the fact that few of the younger conservative writers, who so cleverly analyze the failures of the Left, give any religious perspective to their social critique.

Typical of this secularized conservatism is a collection of essays by various leading young conservative and neo-conservative writers. In a book titled *Beyond the Boom; New Voices on American Life, Culture and Politics* (New York, 1990), many young intelligent conservative writers have written really nothing more than a well-written but rather obvious critique of our liberal culture. As D. G. Myers wrote in his review of this book, "Although *Beyond the Boom* is crammed with derision for (Liberal) quacks . . . it includes no sustained defense of a single artist or intellectual figure." (*Commentary*, February, 1991) In other words, according to these young conservatives, we live in a world without heroes, no one to show us the way out of our moral quagmire. Like their leftist secular peers, most young conservatives only know what they stand against but they seem unable to articulate what they stand for beyond a secular vision, different in detail, but similar in its secular technocratic presuppositions to the Left's.

[27]St. Neilos the Ascetic, *Ascetic Discourse*, vol. 1, *The Philocalia* (New York and London, 1979), p. 201.

words, "I believe."[28]

The Conservatives and Neo-Conservatives have done us an invaluable service in exposing for all to see the bankruptcy of secularism, particularly as manifested in its socialist statist stepchild, big government utopianism. They have helped us to know what we are against. But inasmuch as the Conservatives have proposed only economic, political, nationalistic or technocratic solutions to what are fundamentally religious-moral problems, they have not told us what we can be *for*.

Most of our conservative leaders have failed to finish the sentence, "I believe . . ." with a convincing declaration of faith.

[28]Peter L. Berger, *Commentary* (April, 1991).

CHAPTER FIVE

THE ROOTS
OF THE
CULTURAL WAR

Like all wars, our cultural war has its roots in certain ideas.
It seems to me that the roots of our cultural war, or rather the
war on our culture, go back to three crucial events of intellectual, historical and religious import: the Great Schism between
the Eastern and Western branches of the historical Church,[1]
the failed attempt to reform the Roman Catholic Church in the
fifteenth and sixteenth centuries, and the Enlightenment-
Romantic movements of the eighteenth and nineteenth
centuries.

---

[1] "The most serious division in the medieval Church was that which came to separate
its two most important branches, the great Church of Old Rome and the great Church
of New Rome which is Constantinople and of her sister Patriarchates. There had been
differences in outlook from the earliest times. The Christological controversies of the
fourth and fifth centuries had increased a spirit of rivalry between the Patriarchates,
lasting until the Arab conquest of Syria and Egypt left Constantinople the one free
Patriarchate of the East and the spokesman for Eastern Orthodoxy. Meanwhile the
collapse of the Roman Empire in the West had made the Roman Church the surviving
representative of unity and order. Western Christendom with its numerous rival lay
rulers began to look on the Roman Pope as the head of the Christian commonwealth,
whereas in the East the Emperor remained the Viceroy of God. There had always been
a difference in language between the two halves of the old Empire; and language tends
to influence thought. Greek, with its rich vocabulary, its subtlety and its flexibility,
induced a different philosophical outlook from that induced by Latin, with its legalistic
precision; and, as time went on, it became rare for anyone to speak or understand
both tongues. Inadequate translations increased misunderstandings. Political needs
and problems differed. Quarrels, even schisms, occurred from time to time throughout
the Dark Ages; and, if none of them was final, it was because neither side wished for
a definite breach and because contact between East and West was not too close, and
divergences could be tactfully ignored. (For the rivalry between Rome and the Eastern
Patriarchs see S. Runciman, *The Great Church in Captivity* (New York, 1968), p. 21,
n. 1. For the later disputes between Rome and Constantinople see S. Runciman, *The
Eastern Schism*, pp. 1-27), pp. 81-82.

58

THE SCHISM

In the first event, the schism between the Eastern Orthodox Church and its Roman Western counterpart, the unity of Christendom was shattered largely because of claims of absolute authority — of Papal authority — made by various bishops of Rome that included political temporal power.[2] Popes had aligned themselves with the Germanic Latin emperors of Western Europe against what had been the legitimate center of Christendom in the Byzantine East. This overt politicizing of a church office had dramatic consequences.

There were of course also theological grounds for the schism, for instance, the well known dispute over the Filioque. The "Filioque" refers to a phrase the Spanish Roman Catholic Church added to the Nicene Creed (in a well-intentioned attempt to correct Arianism), wherein they said that the Holy Spirit "proceeds from the Father *and the Son*," rather than "from the Father," as the Creed had always stated before.[3]

Had the argument over the wording of the Creed, the "Filioque," been the only bone of contention between the historical Church of the East and the West, it probably would not of itself led to schism. In fact numerous attempts were made to repair the theological breach from both sides.[4] But the gradual absolutizing of the office of the Papacy in the Western Church, and the intransigent, often arrogant, behavior of some of the Eastern bishops and emperors, created insurmountable obstacles to reunion.[5]

---

[2]"Historians have shown that the exact date of the Schism cannot really be established. There were conflicts as early as the 4th century and the break in 1054 was followed by centuries of union attempts." Fr. John Meyendorff, editor, *The Primacy of Peter* (Crestwood, 1992), p. 70.

[3]" . . . in the Cappadocian conception of the Trinity, the Father is seen as personal (or 'hypostatic') origin of divine existence. In the Middle Ages this was the major theological objection of the Orthodox East to the Western interpolation of the Creed by the words 'and the Son' (Filioque) . . . . Latin arguments made it appear that the existence of the Spirit is not, primarily, a hypostatic, personal reality, proceeding from the person of the Father and the Son." (Ibid. p. 18.)

[4]See S. Runciman, *The Great Church in Captivity*, pp. 90–91.

[5]"As always in the controversy between East and West, the matter of authority in the church seemed to be the most important and to lie at the bottom of the other matters. If it could have been resolved, other questions (like the Filioque) would have become negotiable; until it was resolved, other questions remained hopeless." Jaroslav Pelikan, *The Christian Tradition*, vol. 2, *The Spirit of Eastern Christendom* (Chicago, 1974), p. 272.

Professor of History Harry J. Magoulias at Wayne State University explains that primacy of honor among the other bishops having long been conceded, the growing demands by successive bishops of Rome for supremacy and jurisdiction overturned the precedent of six centuries of more or less collegial fraternity among all the bishops of Christendom.

> During (the) first six centuries (of the Church), despite the growing of animosity between Constantinople and Rome, the pope was (still) a citizen of the (Byzantine) empire . . . (then) in 568 the barbarous Lombards moved into Italy from the north and occupied large areas, . . . Ravenna, the imperial capital of Italy, was now cut off from Rome, and the pope became responsible for the military defense and political administration of that key city. The pope, by virtue of political accident, had become a secular ruler, a fact of tremendous historical consequence. . . . Since the actions of both Frankish King and Roman pope (who together were usurping the authority of the Byzantine emperor and the Patriarch of Constantinople) were illegal vis-à-vis the legitimate Christian empire of Byzantium, a forgery was conveniently drawn up . . . to support the pope's (new) . . . claims. According to this document, the *Donation of Constantine*, all ecclesiastics were subject to the bishops of Rome.[6]

Orthodox scholar, historian, and philosopher Charles Ashanin has pointed out that one reason for the formation of the papacy was that it represented the Western Church's attempt to control history in order to ward off the threat of the Church being overwhelmed by secular political forces. Thus the Roman Church gradually became a powerful secular force itself. Professor Ashanin writes that the Eastern Church, the Orthodox Church, came up with a very different solution to the problem of history. It defined itself as the Christ-bearing community within the world led, not by a pope, but by the Holy Spirit working through the collegial, fraternal association of *all* the bishops.

Also see p. 275 on the liturgical context of the debate on the Filioque. Also see George Ostrogorsky, *History of the Byzantine State* (Rutgers, 1969), pp. 336-337.

[6] Harry J. Magoulias, *Byzantine Christianity* (Detroit, 1982), pp. 91-94.

Thus Eastern Christianity protects the nature of Christianity from losing its personal revelatory character . . . Doctrine as we find it in Western Christianity . . . acquires an authoritarian character.

. . . Papacy is a compromise between Christianity and history . . . and all the decisions of the Vatican Council of 1870 which gave the principal of the papacy the status of dogma could not overcome this fact.[7]

At the heart of the schism was the politicizing of a church office, the Roman papacy, and the new historically illegitimate claims of supreme power by the popes, over and above the other Christian bishops.[8] As historian and Orthodox scholar John Meyendorff writes, "The early church did not have a central administration."[9]

Eusebius, the fourth-century bishop, writing in his famous *History of the Church*, relates several telling incidents in which the early Church's bishops confronted schism or heresy by *collectively* presenting a united front. By letter or in person, the bishops would present their views at great councils to reconcile problems *collectively and collegially*, rather than by papal decree. No one bishop had any greater ecclesiastical authority than another,[10] although the doctrinal purity of the bishops of Rome had long been admired and deferred to. Nevertheless the decisions of the ancient church councils were arrived at by vote and collegial debate, not by papal pronouncement.[11]

[7]Charles Ashanin, *Essays on Orthodox Christianity and Church History*, 1990, pp. 32 and 43. (Available from the author by writing to: 5319 Boulevard Place, Indianapolis, IN 46208.)

[8]"The conflict between East and West was not over the authority of the church fathers . . . but over the relation between the authority of bishop of Rome and all the other authority of the church. Strictly speaking, the conflict was not even over the issue of primacy, since all Eastern theologians conceded this to Rome. The question was, however, how it was that Rome had obtained the primacy." Jaroslav Pelikan, *The Spirit of Eastern Christendom*, p. 272.

[9]John Meyendorff, *Imperial Unity and Christian Divisions*, (Crestwood, 1989), p. 33.

[10]In the early church in Jerusalem it was James, not Peter, who was the first bishop. "The community led by James, the brother of the Lord, is the earliest, chronologically, of all the local churches to be revered by all, but without any direct authority over the other churches: these, later in the first century, are gradually to follow the new pattern and turn into local churches, each with one sovereign bishop as leader." Nicholas Koulomzine, *The Primacy of Peter*, p. 28-29.

[11]"That was the real issue between East and West: the refusal to submit matters in controversy to a general council, the refusal to arrive at a solution in accordance with the ancient practice of the fathers in such matters." (Nil. Cab. Caus. Diss. P.G. 149:685) Jaroslav Pelikan, *The Spirit of Eastern Christendom*, pp. 273-74.

Eusebius' ancient history of the early Church seems to contradict modern Roman Catholic claims about the early Church's government, especially as regards papal authority. G. A. Williamson, the classics scholar who translated the 1965 Dorset Press edition of Eusebius' *History*, writes,

> Dogmas which those who are not members of the Roman Communion reject, we shall not find in the pages of Eusebius; papal infallibility, the Immaculate Conception . . . belong to a later age . . . The word 'Pope' is applied only to the bishop of Alexandria (at that time the center Eastern Orthodox scholarship and theology before the rise of Constantinople in the fourth to sixth centuries), which shares with Rome the primacy of the churches and is no wit inferior to her.[12]

Eusebius wrote about an early controversy concerning the Easter festival, about how Lent was to be celebrated, and how it was resolved by the early Church. This serves as an excellent example of how the Church reconciled its debates in a collegial manner before the evolution of the Roman papacy.

> The Asian dioceses thought that in accordance with ancient tradition they ought to observe the fourteenth day of the lunar month as the beginning of the Pascal festival. . . . But no where else in the world was it customary to arrange their celebrations in this way. . . . So synods and conferences of bishops were convened, and without a dissenting voice (in about the year A.D. 180) drew up a decree of the Church, in the form of a letter addressed to Christians everywhere. . . . Thereupon Victor, head of the Roman Church, attempted at one stroke to cut off from the communion . . . the Asian dioceses, together with the neighboring churches . . . But this was not to the taste of all the bishops: they replied with a request that he would turn his mind to the things that make for peace. . . . We still possess the words of these men, who very sternly rebuked Victor.[13]

[12]Eusebius, *Introduction to the History of the Church*, trans. G. A. Williamson (New York, 1965), p. 10.

[13]Ibid. Book 5, pp. 230-32.

When successive heads of the Roman Church refused to submit to the collegial authority of their brother bishops, and the break was formalized between Rome and Byzantium, far more was at stake than mere politics. In the East the historical Church's traditions were maintained, including the mutual collegial shared authority, established by the Apostles, of all the bishops of the world. In Rome, a powerful "papacy" evolved in which the natural checks and balances of a collegial system of Church governance gradually eroded.[14]

The consequences of the politicizing of the bishopric of Rome, and the accumulation of political power by one Roman Pope after another, had devastating results for the historical Church as a whole. Its final result was the Reformation and the shattering of Christian unity that followed in its wake.[15]

Unlike the Patriarchate in Constantinople, which was balanced by — not to say in competition with — the power of the Byzantine Emperor and the other bishops of the Eastern Church, the Roman Pontiff was both the head of the Roman Catholic church and the Papal States. Stripped of the collegial system of church governance the bloody, chaotic competition for the throne of Peter finally culminated in a divided papacy — between Avignon and Rome — which took on the murderous trappings of a struggle to control lands, armies and cities. The results were predictable; the degradation of both Church and state and finally a backlash — the Reformation.[16]

THE ROOT OF THE DIVISION
BETWEEN EAST AND WEST

Yet beyond the politics of the moment, geographical distance and language barriers, there was, I believe, a much

---

[14]"The assertion of an authority alongside that of Scripture and tradition (by the Popes) led to a claim of prerogatives over all other structures in the church." Jaroslav Pelikan, *The Spirit of Eastern Christendom*, p. 274.

[15]One of the great corrupting events in the life of the western Roman Church was the internal schisms in the Roman Church that occurred because of the claims by multiple popes to indeed be *the* pope: "There appeared to be no historical precedent, in the West . . . for such a schism. The very orthodoxy of 'the entire catholic faith' (All. Ep. Jo XX111.1) was in jeopardy, and mass apostasy became a genuine threat." Jaroslav Pelikan, *The Christian Tradition*, vol. 4, *Reformation of Church and Dogma* (Chicago, 1984), p. 72.

[16]E. R. Chamberlain, *The Bad Popes* (New York, 1969).

deeper cause that contributed to the growing schism between the Eastern and Western Church. It seems to me that at the heart of the growing apart lay two different visions of Christianity or even of God, differences which persist to this day.

The late eminent Orthodox theologian, and Professor of Eastern Church History at the Harvard Divinity School, George Florovsky writes,

> It has been recently suggested that basic division in the Christian Word was not so much between 'Catholics' and 'Protestants,' as precisely between East and West. This opposition is not of a dogmatic nature: neither the West nor the East can be summed up in one set of dogmas applying to it as a whole . . . . The difference between East and West lies in the very nature and method of their theological thinking, in the very soil out of which their dogmatic, liturgical and canonical developments arise, in the very style of their religious life. [17]

The Roman Church in the West was dominated by the theology of St. Augustine, the East by a very different teaching best represented by St. Maximus. [18] The differences between these

---

[17] Georges Florovsky, *The Collected Works of Georges Florovsky*, vol. 1: *Bible, Church, Tradition: An Eastern Orthodox View* (Belmont, 1987), p. 116.

[18] "No less striking was the contrast between the Augustinian tradition (in the West) and the Greek tradition (in the East) in the understanding of grace and salvation. An epitome of the contrast is the formula of Maximus: 'Our salvation finally depends on our own will' (Max. Ascet. 42. PG. 90:953) . . . The dichotomy represented by the antithesis between Pelagianism and Augustinianism was not part of Maximus' thought. Instead, his doctrine of salvation is based on the idea of participation and of communion that excludes neither grace nor freedom but supposes their union and collaboration, which were re-established once and for all in the incarnate Word and his two wills.' (Meyendorff (1969) 114)." Jaroslav Pelikan, *The Spirit of Eastern Christendom*, pp. 182-83.

Another Orthodox Saint, Gregory Palamas, also typifies the difference between Augustinianism and Western predestinarian rationalism as Fr. Florovsky writes: "Actually the whole teaching of St. Gregory presupposes the action of the Personal God. God moves toward man and embraces him by His own "grace" and action, without leaving that (light unapproachable), in which He eternally abides. The ultimate purpose of St. Gregory's theological teaching was to defend the reality of Christian experience. *Salvation is more than forgiveness. It is a genuine renewal of man.* And this renewal is effected not by the discharge, or release, of certain natural energies implied in man's own creaturely being, but by the "energies" of God Himself, who thereby encounters and encompasses man, and admits him into communion with Himself. *In fact, the teaching of St. Gregory affects the whole system of theology, the whole body of Christian doctrine. It starts with the clear distinction between 'nature' and 'will' of God* . . . . Already St. Augustine diverged at this point from the Eastern tradition. Under

two figures of history illustrate the profound differences between Eastern and Western Christianity. The Schism cannot be understood at all, nor the Roman Catholic roots of Protestantism fathomed, without an understanding of the vast difference between the Augustinian tradition and the Eastern Orthodox world view that was best expressed by St. Maximus, the "Eastern Augustine," as he has been called.

St. Augustine's own early writings tend to contradict his later works. It is therefore almost impossible to sum up Augustine's theology with any accuracy. But whatever Augustine the man intended, one can speak about what *Augustinianism* became.[19] *Augustinianism* became a rationalistic system of belief that, building on certain isolated elements of St. Paul's writings, and the influences of pagan philosophy, evolved into a rationalistic dualism — a closed system of theology — stripped of mystery and awe.[20]

Fr. John Meyendorff writes,

> . . . The Augustinian doctrine of original sin . . . is based upon (an) incorrect Latin translation of Romans 5:12 (which adds) a juridical character to the Augustinian interpretation of original sin. . . . The New Testament doctrine of justification, which is to be understood in the context of the Pauline concept of the old law — showing the sin to be a sin, but also fulfilled in Christ, in whom we are justified for the Law — is thus taken out of the proper New Testament context . . . overwhelming all the other concepts with which the Bible describes salvation: sanctification, new life, union with God, participation in the divine nature.[21]

Augustinianism teaches predestination and election. Funda-

Augustinian presuppositions the teaching of St. Gregory is unacceptable and absurd." Georges Florovsky, *The Collected Works of Georges Florovsky*, vol. 1: *Bible, Church, Tradition: An Eastern Orthodox View*, pp. 117-18.

[19] "Even though the century following the death of Augustine saw his predestinarianism attacked by his critics . . . the Augustinian understanding of original sin and of grace continued to shape Western theology." Jaroslav Pelikan, *The Spirit of Eastern Christendom*, pp. 182-83.

[20] "When (Augustine) came to speak of the divine essence, it was usually defined in relation to absoluteness and impassability rather than on the basis of the active involvement of God in creation and redemption." Jaroslav Pelikan, *The Christian Tradition*, vol. 1: *The Emergence of the Catholic Tradition*, p. 296.

[21] John Meyendorff, *Catholicity and the Church*, p. 67.

mentally, Augustinianism teaches that so-called original sin has stripped people of their intrinsic value; that they are ir-redeemably "fallen." This fallenness includes people's free will. Thus for God to save "The Elect," only grace will suffice. This grace is not chosen by the sinner, but conferred upon him by God regardless of the sinner's wishes.[22]

God, according to Augustinianism, has created one sinner to be saved and another to be damned. God does not do this for any particular reason, such as His knowing who will choose to love Him or not, but capriciously for unknown reasons.[23]

Following the logic of Augustinianism, one comes in-escapably to believe that some people have been created *solely* to be eternally damned. This so-called Double Predestination, became the creed of some of the rationalistic scholastic theologians of the Western Middle Ages and was carried to its extreme in the Reformation by Martin Luther and John Calvin — a reductionist rationalism that came to full, detailed and ex-cruciating fruition in the Calvinist Reformed wing of the Pro-testant denominations.[24]

As historian William Manchester writes,

> Perhaps the most popular Protestant dogma . . . was predestination: the tenet that God, being omniscient and

---

[22]"What was distinctive about (Augustine's) version of (the church's creed of faith) was his awareness of the sovereignty of divine power and divine grace. This awareness took the form of a doctrine of predestination more thoroughgoing than that of any major orthodox thinker since Paul. (Augustine) defined predestination as 'God's ar-rangement of his future works in his prescience, which cannot be deceived and changed.' (Aug. Persev. 17. 41 PL 45:1019) As part of the apologetics of his *City of God*, Augustine sought to distinguish the Christian-Pauline understanding of predestination from pagan fatalism . . . but even in this book he came eventually to include the human will in the order of effects of the divine predestination." Jaroslav Pelikan, *The Emergence of the Catholic Tradition*, p. 297.

[23]"Human history was the arena for this demonstration, in which the 'two societies of men' were predestined, the one to reign eternally with God and the other to undergo eternal suffering with the devil. Double predestination applied not only to the city of God and the city of earth, but also the individuals. Some were predestined to eternal life, others to eternal death; and among these latter were infants who died without baptism." Ibid. pp. 297-98.

[24]"Since grace was sovereign, those whom God had predestined would be saved. 'As the one who is supremely good, he (God) made good use of evil deeds, for the damnation of those whom he had justly predestined to punishment and for the salva-tion of those whom he had kindly predestined to grace.' (Aug. Enchir. 26.100.CCSL 46:103) even in the case of the damned, the omnipotence of God achieved its pur-pose and the will of God was done. . . .Why then did God create those whose fall he foreknew? To manifest his wrath and to demonstrate his power." Ibid. p. 297.

omnipotent, is responsible for every action, virtuous and vile, and man is without choice. Luther, the ultimate determinist, could not grasp the concept of moral freedom. In *De Servo Arbitrio* (1525) he wrote: 'The human will is like a beast of burden . . . God foresees, foreordains, and accomplishes all things by an unchanging, eternal, and efficacious will. By this thunderbolt free will sinks shattered in the dust.'[25]

The Pre-Reformation Roman Catholic Church — infected at times as it was by Augustinian fatalism — nevertheless taught that salvation, though it came by God's grace, had to be chosen or rejected by individuals. Moreover, a sometimes harsh theology was mitigated by liturgical, sacramental worship, beauty and pastoral care.[26]

But Luther, the one-time Augustinian monk, was as resolutely at war with the notion of free will as he was with the Western historical Church. Luther writes,

The human will stands like a saddle horse between the two. If God mounts into the saddle, man wills and goes forward as God wills . . . but if the devil is the horseman, then man wills and acts as the devil wills. He has no power to run to one of the other two riders . . . but the riders fight to obtain possession of the animal.[27]

The Lutheran position is straightforward. It degrades man to the level of a beast; it contradicts Holy Tradition and Scripture and it flies in the face of human experience, which is faced everyday with choices between good and evil. It is also self-contradictory. It condemns sin, and yet asserts the will is not free to choose to resist sin. Sometimes this contradiction led

[25]William Manchester, *A World Lit Only By Fire: The Medieval Mind and the Renaissance* (Boston, 1992), p. 176.

[26]A good example of the essential spiritual unity between the Eastern and Western Church, where the rationalism of Augustinian ideas was absent, can be seen in the spiritual classic *Unseen Warfare*. Originally written by Lorenzo Scupoli, a sixteenth century Roman Catholic monk, it was re-edited by Nicodemus of Mount Athos and Theophan the Recluse, famous Orthodox monks. It embodies the canon teaching of both Eastern and Western Christianity, a tradition that transcends Augustinian rationalism.

[27]Martin Luther, *De Servo Arbitrio* (11784.B), A.D. 1524-25.

to tortured illogic. For instance, Leonhard Koppe, friend of Luther and co-reformer with him writes, "You should be quite certain that God foreordained what happened and that it is not a result of your own actions or plans."[28]

To understate the case, the Augustinian-Lutheran theory of a capricious, judgmental God, who created some men *expressly for eternal damnation* is *not* the view of the Eastern Church Fathers or even of most of the pre-Augustinian Fathers of the Western Church.[29]

THE GOD OF HISTORY

As expressed by St. Maximus, the vision of the Orthodox Church is of a loving God who desires all men to be saved. Moreover, the Church teaches that God respects Mankind's free will.[30]

In the East, because of the Church's fundamental belief in the awesome mysterious, unknowability of the loving God, no attempt was made to rationalistically balance free will and God's omnipotence in a precise theological "system." The Orthodox Church taught that finite man could never describe, let alone understand, the essence of God or exactly how salvation worked. Rather, the Church taught, people could use their free will to choose to love God, just as Holy Tradition had taught that God had chosen to love mankind by sending His Son to us. The Orthodox view of God, salvation and judgment is one fraught with a deep sense of God's love for all creatures, His goodness and the mystery of faith.[31]

[28] As cited by E. Michael Jones, *Fidelity*, May, 1991.

[29] "The chief idea of St. Maximus, as of all the other Eastern theology, (was) the idea of deification.' (Max. O. derm. PG. 90:873) . . . there were two principal passages of the Bible in which the definition of salvation as deification was set forth: the declaration of the psalm, 'I say, You are gods,' which was quoted in the New Testament; and the promise of the New Testament that believers would 'become partakers of the divine nature,' " Jaroslav Pelikan, *The Spirit of Eastern Christendom*, p. 10.

[30] "(Maximus') repeated and unequivocal insistence upon grace . . . was not intended to exclude the free will of man from participation in the process. For 'the Spirit does not generate a will that is not willing, but he transforms into deification a will that has the desire (for salvation)' (Max. Qu. Thal.6 PG. 90:280) Thus the antithesis between divine grace and human freedom, which dogged Western theology for many centuries, did not present a problem in that form for Eastern Christian thought." Ibid. pp. 11-12.

[31] "At the root of the conflict between dualism and orthodox monotheism was the

In the Augustinian West, dogma was added to dogma in an almost "scientific" attempt to define and categorize, or even to explain God. In the East the temptation to use the rational mind to try to explain the inexplicable was by and large avoided. In fact such innovations were rejected as evil and pointless.[32]

This then, I believe, is the real underlying reason for the persistent division between Eastern and Western Christendom. The East wanted to retain the faith of the early church. The West wanted to build "creatively" on the apostolic tradition following the lead of Augustinian innovation, rationalism and dogmatic pronouncement. The East remained opposed to a rationalistic, intellectualized approach to Christian truth. The West added layer upon layer of scholastic "explanations" of the faith (including the inventions of Purgatory, Limbo, and detailed, almost "scientific," explanations of Transubstantiation, Grace, Predestination, etc.). The East saw God as standing *outside* of time and space, *outside* of rationalistic description, *outside*

---

question of the relation between evil and the God of love. . . . If, as Orthodoxy maintained, there was one God of love who was the Creator, 'whence came diseases and death and other evils like those?' (a.p. Joh. D. Dialex. PG 96:1325) A basic element of the (Eastern) Orthodox response to such questions was a reassertion of the patristic and classical definition of evil as the privation of good rather than a positive form in its own right. . . . Darkness was not a reality but only the absence of light. . . . The loss of (men's) appointed purpose had made them evil. . . . Much of the problem of evil was an attempt to resolve the (Augustinian) connection between foreknowledge and predestination . . . . The very presence of sin and evil and the capacity of a creature to transgress the divine commandments was grim proof for the freedom of the will (to the Eastern Orthodox theologians)." Ibid. pp. 221-22.

[32]"The drifting apart of the Eastern and Western branches of Christendom is clearly marked in their respective attitudes towards mysticism. Since the later middle ages the Church in the West, with its superb organization and its taste for philosophical systems, has always been a little suspicious of its mystics. . . .

"In the Eastern tradition theology and mysticism were held to be complementary. Outside of the Church personal religious experience would have no meaning; but the Church depended for its very life on the experience granted in varying degrees to each one of the faithful. This is not to say that dogma is unnecessary. Dogma is the interpretation of the revelation that God has chosen to give us. But, within the framework thus provided, each man and woman can work out his or her own way towards the ultimate end which transcends all theology and which is union with God. 'God became Man that men might become Gods." (For the best account of the Eastern mystical outlook see V. Lossky, *Mystical Theology of the Eastern Church*, especially pp. 7-22. See also P. Sherrard, *The Greek East and Latin West*, pp. 31-4.) . . .

"The mind must learn to refuse to form concepts about God. It must reject all intellectual and abstract theology and all attempts to adapt the mysteries of God to human ways of thought. According to Gregory of Nazianzus, anyone who imagines that he has come to know what God is has a 'depraved spirit.' " S. Runciman, *The Great Church in Captivity*, pp. 128-30.

of the necessity to conform to some mathematical human equation between predestination and free will. In the West theologians became philosophers and spent centuries endlessly worrying the subject of God's sovereignty like dogs with a troublesome bone.[33] In the East, the Holy Mysteries of God and Church were allowed to remain Holy Mysteries. In the West, the Church became a political, dogmatic institution, corrupt and stripped of mystery and awe.

In the Calvinism of the later years of the Reformation, Roman Catholic scholastic rationalistic dogma became entrenched beyond anything the Augustinian Scholastics of the High Middle Age had even dreamed of.[34] Protestantism stripped away the Roman Catholic sacramental tradition that had balanced and kept the extremes of Augustinianism at bay, for instance, softening St. Thomas Aquinas' juridical rationalistic pronouncements with the spirituality of a Lorenzo Scupoli or St. Francis of Assisi. In the Reformation sacramental faith was replaced with a non-sacramental theology that was as cold as Dutch winter sunlight.

The Reformation "God" emerged as a, if not *the*, Devil; a Supreme Being that created some people for the *express purpose* of damning them and chose a few, the "Elect," to save. The stark reality of the Reformers' views were dressed up, rationalized, explained, padded, even lied about, but nevertheless, in the end, good and evil were joined in this force they called "God."[35]

---

[33] In Jaroslav Pelikan's masterful *The Christian Tradition* series, vols. 1-5 (Chicago, 1974-1989). The theme of the debate over predestination and free will that followed in the wake of Augustinianism, dominates almost every age of Christian thought up to our own in the Western Church.

[34] "The gulf between faith and reason, between God and fallen human nature, which was inherited from Augustine, maintained in Thomism, and even widened in the Nominalist Scholasticism of Occam, remained the common denominator of Western Christianity before and after the Reformation." John Meyendroff, *Catholicity and the Church*, p. 69.

[35] "Calvin referred to Augustine to make clear that . . . God's image was now 'extinguished' and replaced by 'guilt, unrighteousness, and unholiness.' (Blngr. Dec. 3. 10. (1552;169r)) . . . To Reformed theology, this Augustinian consensus of all the Reformers, that works were not a factor in salvation, must imply no less consistently that works were not a factor in damnation, either; the rejection of works (and free will) and the exaltation of . . . grace . . . did not only apply to the reconciliation of man to God . . . but to the eternal will of God by which he had chosen some and condemned others . . .

Sharing Augustine's complete doctrine meant also sharing the criticism's of that doctrine. . . To Costellio, 'Predestination' in Calvin's usage seemed interchangeable

In the Orthodox Church of the East, God was understood to be *wholly good*. Above all, He was the being that stood *above* creation and was not bound by it. God was not the creator of evil, let alone a vengeful being who desired some people to be lost. Evil was understood to be the *absence of good*, not a self existing reality. This even included the Devil, who as a real person was created as an angel of light. It was the Devil's perverse desire to be God, apart from God, which led to the absence of God's grace from him and his followers, and then to evil. God never used evil means, even to bring just results. All things and choices that rejected God were evil. All things and choices that conformed to God who is love were good. Those who were lost, were those who deliberately *chose* not to follow God and who persisted in this choice to the end of their lives. They were not capriciously doomed (let alone expressly created for damnation!), but made their own hell by willfully separating themselves from a loving God who desired their salvation in this life and the next. God honored free will. To teach otherwise, the Eastern Church believed, made it seem as if God were the agent of evil. In the mind of the Eastern Church this was heresy and blasphemy.[36]

The Orthodox East has at its core an understanding of a mysterious, loving God.[37] In the Augustinian West a vision of

---

with 'fate.'

By having sentenced the reprobate to eternal damnation before they were born, 'that God of Calvin's' was forcing them to sin . . . From the Roman Catholic side too, Calvin's predestinarianism was equated with fatalism." Jaroslav Pelikan, *Reformation of the Church and Dogma*, p.227.

[36]The East found Origen heretical because he said all men would be saved, *no matter what they chose*. Similarly, the East regards Augustinianism in its extreme form as a heresy because it teaches that men will be saved (or lost), *no matter what they choose!* The Orthodox Church rejects both the extremes of Augustinianism and Pelagianism.

[37]Salvation, in Scholastic theology, is conceived along Augustinian lines and interpreted in increasingly juridical terms. . . .

. . . In the East the relations of God and man are conceived by the Greek Fathers differently than in the line of thought which started with Augustine.

On the one hand, the distinction between the Creator and the creature is maintained with full strength, especially since Athanasius: divine essence and human nature can *never* mix or be confounded or be participated by each other. God is *absolutely* transcendent in this essence, which can never be known or seen even in the life to come. The divine transcendence is not due, as in Augustine, to the limitations of our fallen state or to the imperfections of our bodily existence, disappearing when our soul is liberated from material bonds: God, in His very being, is *above* creature; He is always free in His relation with the created world, and nothing created can either possess Him or see Him. The whole negative (or apophatic) theology of the Fathers expresses precisely this and reflects the fundamental, biblical view of the transcendent God.

a juridical, vengeful capricious god-devil emerged, leading in the end to a rebellion against religion altogether by the bitter secularists of the seventeenth to twentieth centuries, who looked at and rejected the historical results of such theology, from the dictatorial corruptions of the papacy, to the cruelties of Calvin's theocratic Geneva, to the evils of Calvinist-inspired South African apartheid.

From the Eastern Church's point of view, atheism is a logical, perhaps even desirable, choice if God is presented as the sort of "God" that the Scholastics, like Thomas Aquinas, of the Middle Ages believed in or as the god-devil of Calvin.[38]

CONCLUSION

To understand the roots of the chaos of our own era it is necessary to understand the origins of the division between the Eastern and Western historical Church. As we have seen, this division has far deeper grounds than simply a series of political or ecclesiastical misunderstandings or contests for power. At its heart the Great Schism is not an historical event but a continuing battle between Augustinianism and scholasticism, on the one hand, and the tradition of the historical Church, on the other. At stake is the most important religious question of all: the nature of the character of God. The difference of opinion, between the Eastern Orthodox Church and the Western Roman Church came, I believe, to glaring fruition approximately five hundred

---

However, the existence of man as a creature of God is not viewed as a *closed* existence: man has been created in order to share in the life of God, in order to be *with* God. Man, therefore, is conceived dynamically not only in what he is — a creature — but also in what he is called to be, "a partaker of the divine nature" (2 Peter 1.4).

There is no question of *adding* human acts to the divine act, which otherwise would be insufficient for man's salvation. The whole problem is not a juridical and utilitarian one — what is sufficient, and what is not — but rather a question of the original human destiny, which is to be *with* God and in God. John Meyendorff, *Catholicity and the Church*, pp. 68-73.

[38] "The gravest of all objections (to Calvinism, Reformed doctrine and Protestant Augustinians) was the question of consolation, hope, and the certainty of election . . . Calvin's 'fictitious fate of predestination was hostile to religion' (Conf. Remon. pr. (1622. C3v) because it managed to undercut both the free will of God and the free will of man." Jaroslav Pelikan, *Reformation of Church and Dogma*, pp. 229-33.

years after the Schism of A.D. 1054. The date was A.D. 1517, and the "new Augustine," Martin Luther, was about to complete what Augustine began.

CHAPTER SIX
THE
REFORMATION

In 1517 the unity of Christians was further and perhaps irreparably eroded with Martin Luther's effective declaration of independence from the corrupted Western Latin Roman Church. What began as an effort to reform the Roman Church in the West soon devolved into the most devastating schism the Church had ever suffered. The Reformation in the end reformed little in the Roman Church. It rather created a rival Augustinian religion of its own.

A spirit of revolution against historical Church authority (protest being, after all, the root of *Protest*antism) soon came to be seen as the accepted state of affairs in the new Protestant denominations.[1] From the very beginning of the Reformation it became evident that its leaders, following the model of Martin Luther, were much more revolutionaries than reformers.[2] They were prepared to cast away the most important elements of the Holy Tradition in favor of what soon developed into a new religion.

From the beginning the Reformers behaved in an authori-

---

[1] 'I frankly acknowledge,' wrote Josse Clichtove, 'that there are very many missteps in such areas of church life as fasting, penance, celibacy, and monasticism; and it was the duty of the church officials to clean up such abuses. There was 'superstition,' 'immoderate ambition among monks,' excessive 'credulity' in the cult of saints, 'crass ignorance' about Scripture, and need for instruction of the people (and by better educated clergy). By 'boldly passing judgment' on such abuses, the Reformation had performed a useful service, but its demand for 'pure doctrine and uncorrupted morals' was no justification for 'overthrowing all the authority of all the ages of history.'" Jaroslav Pelikan, *Reformation of Church and Dogma*, p. 248.

[2] "... before the arguments (of the Reformation) were over, no article of faith had been left unscathed." Ibid., p. 249.

tarian manner as harsh as that of the Popes they were attacking. Luther, Calvin and the other Reformers did not believe in free will. God had, according to them, predestined everything. They saw themselves as the instruments of God's will and therefore needed to brook no dissent or opposition. Theirs, they believed, was a "manifest destiny." They were no less than the "instruments of the Lord." The fatalistic character of the Reformer's theology soon colored the historical events that followed in the wake of their embrace of deterministic, Augustinian ideas.

Having rejected the teaching authority of the Roman Church, Protestantism was divided at its birth between the Lutheran Church and the Reformed, a collection of denominations even more fatalistic in their theology than the Lutherans. New sects formed, each with its own views of worship, each as intolerant of the others as it was of Rome. Each was as repressive as the worst of the Roman Catholicism it was "reforming." Anabaptists, Mennonites, Bohemians, Congregationalists, and Presbyterians all began to compete, one against the other. They often celebrated their spiritual rebirths violently.

> Tirades led to recriminations, then to public executions. . . .
> Peasants would walk thirty miles to hoot and jeer as a fellow
> (Protestant) Christian, enveloped in flames, writhed and
> screamed his life away.[3]

The warning signals of just how far such "reforms" would eventually go should have been clear for all to see because of several startling developments very early in the Reformation. For instance, in 1529 Martin Luther and his fellow Reformer, the Swiss theologian Ulrich Zwingli, came to intellectual blows over the Sacraments and soon split one from another over the meaning of the Communion — the central sacrament of Christianity. When Zwingli was killed, Martin Luther rejoiced and in a letter to a friend called Zwingli's death "a triumph for us." The Eucharist whose celebration had been taken for granted for the whole life of the Church as manifesting the real presence of Christ in sacramental form had never before been questioned

---

[3] William Manchester, *A World Lit By Fire*, p. 177.

by *any* persons calling themselves Christian. It was no more questioned than the divinity of Christ.[4] Yet now Western Christendom was so divided over the basic sacraments that one "Reformer" rejoiced when one of his *own number* was killed!

Barely eighty years after the beginning of the so-called Reformation, the various Protestant sects had already split into more than 280 denominations. Even the most committed Protestant must have been grieved to see the one thousand five hundred years of essential sacramental Christian unity, destroyed in less than eighty.[5]

Martin Luther's boundless revolutionary zeal was clearly manifest in his willingness to put fellow Christians to death, for instance, in advocating death sentences for rebellious Anabaptists. He unleashed far more severe persecutions of his fellow Protestant believers than had been used by the corrupted Roman hierarchy against the original Reformation. But even more shocking from the point of view of those concerned with the continuity of the historical Church was Luther's extraordinary radical suggestion that the first and second letters of John, James and the Book of Revelation be dropped from the New Testament Canon. Luther also wanted the books of the Old Testament to be revised as well. He discarded the writings that subsequently came to be known as the Apocrypha, and adopted the Hebrew Old Testament, instead of the Greek Septuagint, the Scriptures the authors of the New Testament had used and which they quoted.

Luther took the opportunity afforded him in his self-appointed role of translator of the Bible into German, to add and delete words, from the Bible to bolster his ideological-theological revolutionary agenda.[6] For instance, he decided to strengthen some of his favorite passages, like Romans Chapter 3, and weaken others. He added the word "only" to key Biblical

[4]"From the logic of the Protestant arguments it was . . . becoming manifest that a denial of the legitimacy of communion under one kind would head to a denial of the real presence itself." Jaroslav Pelikan, *Reformation of Church and Dogma*, p. 249.

[5]"As they watched the Reformation advance from one heterodox deviation to another, adversaries could discern the complete fulfillment of the predictions of the divinely inspired Paul' (Orat. 4.2. (Mylius 2:345) about the rise of 'heresies'. . .

"While there had been heresies and schisms before, it soon became clear that the Protestant Reformation represented a threat that was in many ways unprecedented; unprecedented also was the sheer range of doctrines in dispute." Jaroslav Pelikan, *Reformation of Church and Dogma*, p. 245-246.

[6]Please see George Florovsky, *The Byzantine Ascetic and Spiritual Fathers* (Belmont, 1987), for a detailed study of the Reformation interpretation of the writings of St. Paul.

passages in which he revised such sentences as: you are saved only by faith, or you are saved by faith alone. These essential forgeries provided Luther with the "proofs" he needed to bolster his evolving and creatively innovative theology.[7]

In 1529, Dr. Link, the pre-eminent German language scholar of the day, wrote to Luther asking him why he had been inserting words into the German Bible. Luther's astonishing written answer nicely sums up the heart of the Protestant problem of individualistic subjectivity, "It is so because Dr. Martin Luther says it is so!"

The Reformation was a far more grievous blow to Christian unity, Church discipline, the continuity of apostolic succession and sacramental worship than the Great Schism had been. In the rivalry between the Eastern and the Western Church, political power was at stake, and while there were theological debates, as well as a growing division over the papacy and the Augustinian view of God, a great unity of sacramental practice, doctrine and spirituality had prevailed throughout the Church as a whole, at least in the ranks of the common people. In both East and West the historical Church maintained apostolic continuity, wherein the bishops could trace their historical lineage back to the Apostles and Christ. And in both East and West, the Canon of Scripture was faithfully upheld. Moreover, the whole Church understood the sacred character of the Eucharist. But with the advent of the Reformation, the very foundations of historical apostolic legitimacy, the Canon of the Bible, Christian faith, life, and sacramental worship — even the Eucharist — were challenged and finally overthrown in a welter of schism, apostasy, even warfare. In the end, before his death, Zwingli went so far as to dismiss the presence of Christ in the Eucharist altogether as a mere "figure of speech!"[8]

[7]"Luther went so far as to insert the word 'alone' into his translation of Romans 3:28 making it read: 'that man is justified without the works of the law, through faith alone'. While he defended the insertion . . . his critics attacked him for 'lacerating and falsifying' (Ec. Enchir. 5 C Cath 34: 97-98)) not only the biblical text but the biblical doctrine." Jaroslav Pelican, *Reformation of Church and Dogma*, p. 252.

[8]" 'We must understand first of all,' Zwingli argued in 1526, 'that throughout the Bible there are to be found figures of speech, (which are) . . . to be understood in another sense' (Zwingli. Gen. 17:10 (CR 100:105)) . . .

'Truth it is indeed, that the words (This is my body, this is my blood) be as plain as may be spoken; but that the sense is not plain.' (Cran. Gard. f3 (PS 15:103)) To Calvin it was an 'axiom' that 'whenever sacraments are being dealt with, it is usual for the name of the things signified to be transferred by metonymy to the sign.'

To recapitulate, the schism between Eastern Orthodox and Western Roman Catholic Christians set the stage for Roman Catholic excesses, including claims of supremacy, and later even "infallible," papal authority that led to an extraordinary corruption of the Latin Church. The growing corruption of the Papacy fueled the reactionary rebellion against historical Christian authority and Holy Tradition by the Protestant Reformers. In turn the Reformation unleashed a debunking of all hierarchy and sacramentality.[9]

PANDORA'S CHURCH

The failed attempt to reform the Roman Church opened up a Pandora's box of unintended consequences. Rather than reforming the historical Church in the West, the Reformers soon broke away or were excommunicated, and ended up starting new "churches" which then evolved into whole new religions each in turn splitting and re-inventing itself into countless sects and cults. Schism digressed first into warfare, then into denominationalism. The modern age of pluralistic, cultic "Christianity" had been born.

There were many unfortunate results following the Reformation. The Protestants smashed religious images and desecrated religious art, perceived by the Reformers to be "idols." They invoked the Biblical commandment against graven images, not infrequently stoning to death monks, nuns or lay people who tried to prevent the desecration of their churches. This modern iconoclastic movement — the anti-cultural, anti-liturgical, anti-traditional, finally, anti-sacramental, subjective

---

(Calv. West. (CR 37:36))

Therefore it followed, according to Calvin, that 'believers have, outside the Lord's Supper, what they receive in the Supper itself.'

Zwingli (went so far as to express) the wish 'that the word sacrament had never been accepted in German' (Zwingli. Unt. pr. (C.R. 91:789)" Ibid. pp. 189-194-195.

[9] "Luther's revolt . . . began in the spirit of reform . . . (But) in emphasizing faith alone, the Bible, and the calling, Luther opened the door to the democratic ideal of a priesthood of all believers, an ideal that the radical reformation took far more literally than did Luther himself." E. Digby Balltzell, *Puritan Boston and Quaker Philadelphia* (New York, 1979), p. 60.

and reductionist Protestant movement — contributed much
to the decline of Christian culture and the rise of an accordingly
anti-art, even anti-reality pietism which still dominates most
of Protestantism today. As a result, Protestants often became
thoroughly disengaged from their own culture, leaving the stage
bare in the arts, humanities and politics for the aggressively
anti-Christian secularists to take possession of the levers of
cultural power.

The Reformation also opened the door to a renewed spirit
of Manachaeism, the ancient heretical belief that the spirit
world is superior to the physical world. The Protestant prejudice
against the flesh, virtually a denial of the Incarnation, is still
with us today as manifested in Protestantism's anti-
sacramentality, in favor of "pure spiritual" worship, in its bias
against the arts, icons, imagery, incense, vestments, nature
and beauty and its false dichotomy between evangelism and
the rest of life's "worldly" activities.

Making the best of a bad job, and putting a bold face on
their failure to reform the Roman Catholic Church, the first Protestants attempted to make a virtue out of what had for over
one thousand five hundred years been thought to be a self-
evident vice — division among Christians. They began to ignore the precedent of Church history as their own battles
became an embarrassment in the light of centuries of Christian unity.

Yet the leaders of the Reformation were not altogether ignorant of Church history. They were well aware that in the early
Church the authority of Holy Tradition and apostolic continuity was treasured above all else. For instance, the Reformers
had access to documents such as Dionysius', bishop of Alexandria, writing to Novatus (in approximately A.D. 166),
reprimanding him in this way.

> You ought to have been ready to suffer anything whatever
> rather than split the Church of God, and martyrdom to
> avoid schism would have brought you as much honor as
> martyrdom to escape idolatry — I should say more. For in
> the latter case a man is martyred to save his own single
> soul, in the former to save the whole Church.[10]

The Reformers also would have known that St. Irenaeus,

---

[10]Eusebius, *The History of the Church*, Book 6, p. 285.

writing in the year A.D. 180, in his work titled *Against Heresies*, had this to say: "A truly spiritual Disciple shall judge those who make schism and are destitute of the love of God, who look to their own advantage rather than to the unity of the Church, who for any kind of trifling reason cut apart and divide the great and glorious body of Christ, and destroy it insofar as they are able."[11]

Luther, Zwingli, Calvin and company were not unfamiliar with St. Cyprian of Carthage who wrote in A.D. 251,

> If someone does not hold fast to this unity of the Church, can he imagine he still holds to the faith? If he resists and withstands the Church, can he be confident that he is in the Church, when the blessed Apostle Paul teaches this very thing and displays the sacred sign of unity when he says: 'One Body and One Spirit, One hope of your calling, One Lord, One Faith, One Baptism, One God?' . . . The Episcopate is one, of which each bishop holds his part within the undivided structure. The Church is also one . . . the Bride of Christ cannot be defiled . . . whoever is separated from the Church and is joined to an adulteress is separated from the promises of the Church; nor will he that forsakes the Church of Christ attain rewards of Christ. He is an alien, an enemy. He cannot have God for his Father who does not have the Church for his Mother. . . . [12]

Ironically, while many of the first Protestant sects claimed that they were "returning to the simple faith of the early Church," the *actual* Fathers of the historical Church resoundingly and even with great ferocity denounced *all* schismatics; those who divide the Body of Christ — the one Holy Catholic and Apostolic Church for whatever reason. The Reformers must have known this to be the case and, to the extent they did, their actions cannot be excused.

In hindsight, however, it is abundantly clear that the Reformers like Wycliffe, Huss, Luther, Calvin, Zwingli and company started a historical process of revolutionary proportions,

[11]St. Irenaeus, *Adversus Haereses* 4, 33, 7, A.D. 180, in *The Faith of the Early Fathers*, vol. 1, trans. W. A. Jurgens, p. 221.

[12]St. Cyprian of Carthage, *Treatise on the Unity of the Catholic (Universal) Church*, in *The Faith of the Early Fathers*, vol. 6, trans. W. A. Jurgens, p. 221.

the consequences of which they could never have understood nor to which they would have ultimately subscribed. The Reformers certainly had no idea that the Protestant Reformation, with its unintended pluralistic impulse, would eventually become the principal engine of secularization in Western culture. Nor did they know that the ideas of the Reformation would eventually make an unholy alliance with the humanistic philosophy of the ultimate "Scholastic" movement — the Enlightenment. Moreover, it is doubtful that the Reformers could have foreseen the fact that in destroying Western Christian unity they were simultaneously destroying the ability of the Western Church to exercise discipline. In the world of the Reformation, a Protestant who did not want to be disciplined by his or her church or its teaching could walk down the street to another church, or even begin one of his or her own. Thousands of Protestants bent on self-styled quests for "purity" of doctrine did that very thing.

THE BEGINNING OF THE END

Early in the process that led to the Reformation, Lorenzo Valla, exposed (A.D. 1440) as a forgery the *Donation of Constantine*, upon which spurious claims of papal authority had, up to that time, partialy rested. Valla was no reformer but was merely clearing up the historical record of the Roman Church. He had no intention of creating a new religion or of destroying the unity of Western Christendom. He was no more than a pioneer in philology — the study of words to determine their meaning.[13]

By contrast, what Luther began as a quest for the purity of the visible Church soon devolved into little more than debunking, demythologizing and deconstruction of the Holy Tradition. In our own day, this process has finally reached its logical, if unintended, conclusion in the near total abandonment of the Christian ethos by our desacralized secular cultural leaders and the demotion of man to "lower than the cockroach" by our

---

[13] Jeremy C. Jackson, *No Other Foundation: The Church Through Twenty Centuries* (Westchester, 1980), Chapter 11.

academic elite. It seems that when Zwingli and company debunked the sacredness of the sacraments, much more than the communion bread and wine lost its sacramental meaning.

If the authority and the sacraments of the historical Church could be debunked under the guise of "reform" in one generation, then the received wisdom of the ages regarding man's place in the order of things could also be debunked several generations later. The process of delegitimization was easier to begin than to stop. Things regarded as sacred for millennia were, in the Reformation, declared to be "mere symbols." In one generation the Eucharist was "debunked," later humanity itself was found to be nothing more than a collection of atoms, a "blob of tissue," full of sound and fury signifying nothing.

Seen in the best light, the leaders of the so-called Reformation began their process of reform with a desire to eradicate rampant corruption from the Latin Church. But then they and their followers, went much further and opened a door to a permanent state of skepticism and even atheism that has been the hallmark of our inhumane, individualistic Western culture ever since.

CALVIN

The person who most thoroughly wedded the reductionist Augustinian rationalism of medieval Scholasticism to the Protestant cause was the Swiss Reformer John Calvin. Since Calvin's philosophy was influential with the Puritan founders of America, and since Calvin's theology created the Presbyterian doctrines out of which so many American sects evolved, his influence on Protestant thinking and, by extension, American culture is important to understand.

In Calvinism, the tradition of harsh scholastic rationalism that had always found expression in the Roman Catholic Church since Augustine was given a new voice.[14] Calvin defined his Augustinian doctrine of predestination in his *Institutes*.

---

[14] "If Scripture alone was to decide what was authentically apostolic, and if the church (in the Reformers opinion) had fallen away from the apostolic norm . . . it was difficult to avoid the conclusion that the Nicene Creed . . . itself had been a product of (the) 'fall of the church' (Soc. Cat. fr (BFP 1:684)) . . . rather than a valid sum-

Predestination we call the eternal decree of God, by which He has determined in Himself, what He would have become of every individual of mankind. For they are not all created with a similar destiny; but eternal life is foreordained for some, and eternal damnation for others. Every man, therefore, being created for one of the other of these ends, we say, he is predestined either to life or death.[15]

In reply to the charge that his fatalistic doctrine would destroy the incentive to obey the commands of God, Calvin answered that nothing in the doctrine of predestination excused "reckless indulgence." The divine will could be clearly read in Scripture, Calvin taught, and all people, whether "elect" or not, should shape their behavior accordingly.

Calvin applied this line of reasoning with strict logic to all of society. Since a person's behavior had nothing to do with his or her salvation, there was a temptation to disobey God's law. Regardless of whether one was elect or not, what one did would not effect the outcome of one's salvation. Since one's moral choices naturally had no bearing on one's salvation, Calvin believed that to compensate for the lack of motivation to moral and orderly behavior the Church and State should collude to subject all people to close moral scrutiny. The legislated morality of Puritanism was thus a social discipline borne of Calvin's belief that people had no free will. He wanted the behavior of all people, especially Christians, monitored.

To Calvin, God was a demanding judge under whose searching eye Christians should conduct themselves soberly, if not because of a fear of the Lord, then because of a fear of the Church's and State's ability to coerce morality, down to the tiniest detail, and to punish deviant behavior ruthlessly.

Calvin's own life and work was consistent with service to his harsh "God." When Calvin's sermons failed to convince, he resorted to force in prohibiting "unseemly acts" or words. Since, in Calvin's Geneva, virtually all entertainment was proscribed

---

mary . . . of the apostolic faith." And, as if in substantiation of the (Roman Catholic) warnings of the 'domino theory' (both) the doctrine of the sacraments (and) the dogmas of Nicea and Chalcedon . . . would be . . . repudiated." Jaroslav Pelikan, *Reformation of Church and Dogma*, pp. 321-24.

[15]*Institutes* (vol. 3, A203 Trans: Walter.)

as "unseemly" and even dozing in church was a punishable offense, a very dreary, self-righteous religion emerged that came to be called "Puritanism."

The slightest criticism enraged Calvin. Those who questioned his theology were dismissed as "pigs," "asses," "riffraff," "dogs," "idiots," and "stinking beasts." One morning Calvin found a poster on his pulpit accusing him of "Gross Hypocrisy." Since Calvin indirectly ruled his city state of Geneva as well as being its chief theologian and grand inquisitor, he did not have to accept this "scandalous affront" lying down. A suspect was arrested. No evidence was produced, but he was tortured day and night for a month until he confessed. Then his feet were nailed to a stake by which he hung in public for a day. Ultimately he was decapitated.

Since Calvin's "God" allowed no free will, Calvin saw no reason to, either. Calvin's justification for the execution of the unfortunate, alleged "mocker," who had left the offending message on Calvin's pulpit, reveals the shamelessly self-righteous mindset of all the Reformation's tyrannical inquisitors. "When the papists are so harsh," wrote Calvin, ". . . are not Christ's magistrates shamed to show themselves less ardent in defense of the sure truth?"

Historian William Manchester writes,

> In Calvin's Orwellian theocracy . . . the Consistory, (Calvin's thought police) . . . made no distinction between religion and morality . . . legislation specified the number of dishes to be served at each meal and the color of garments worn. What one was permitted to wear depended upon who one was, for never was a society more class-ridden. Believing every child of God had been foreordained, Calvin was determined that each know his place . . .

> Abortion was not a political issue because any single woman discovered with child was drowned . . . (along with her unborn child and her lover, if he could be found).

> The ultimate crime, of course, was heresy. . . . Holding religious beliefs at odds with those of the majority was no excuse in (Calvin's) Geneva or, for that matter in other Protestant theocracies. It was the consummate irony of the Reformation that the movement against Rome, which had begun with an affirmation of individual judgment, now

repudiated it entirely. Apostasy was regarded as an offense to God and treason to the state. As such it was punished with swift, agonizing death.[16]

Calvin held no official political office. He had no need to. The town council of Geneva saw its duty to be the protector of Calvin's church, ideas, theology and authority. For Calvin, the purpose of government was to regulate society according to the will of God as he, Calvin, interpreted it. For some twenty years, Geneva served as a model of theocracy — a church-controlled state. Calvin taught that the organized church was essential for the supervision of the state. Ironically, his view paralleled the worst of the papal pronouncements from Rome.

The idea of dependence on the church by church members for their salvation seemed to contradict Calvin's teaching on Predestination. If people were already elect, or damned, what difference did belonging to or obeying a church make? This was a perplexing question for both Luther and Calvin, since logically it seemed to undermine their positions of political and ecclesiastical power. Their very doctrine seemed to make them not essential. Yet "inner voices" told them that this could not be. Calvin's explanation was simple: it was God's will that the elect be saved *through* the true — in other words, Calvin's — church! Through its inspired teaching and discipline the ways of Heaven might be reflected on earth. An "inner voice," he wrote, had made this clear to him. Thus, absent Holy Tradition, Calvin's final legitimization of his own authority did not rest on apostolic succession, or faithfulness to doctrine, but on personalized — and thus highly subjective — revelation.

Ironically, Calvin began to re-create the authority of his new "church" to imitate that of the Roman Church he was rebelling against. He replaced the Pope with himself, the Roman Church with what eventually became the Presbyterian denomination, the Roman bishops with presbyters, the Inquisition with the Consistory.[17]

Calvin borrowed heavily from Augustine, Thomas Aquinas and the Scholastic Roman Catholic rationalistic tradition, in which theology had been stripped of mystery and reduced to

[16]William Manchester, *A World Lit Only By Fire*, pp. 190-93.

[17]T. H. Greer, *A Brief History of the Western World*, 6th ed. (New York, 1991), pp. 364-67.

cold, theological formulas and in which the teaching of Augustinianism became far more extreme than that of Augustine
himself. Calvin also borrowed from the humanism of the
Renaissance, which had stripped theology and religious art of
its sacred mystery and opened everything to "scientific,"
naturalistic scrutiny, as if there were no longer sacred, non-
negotiable truths, and as if all of the Church's sacraments were
mere symbols open to rationalistic examination, rather than
Holy Mysteries, and as if iconography was mere biblical illustration which should be "up-dated" and "improved."

Calvin's followers soon went even further than their men-
tor in giving formal expression to a wholly novel theology
unrelated to the main body and practice of historical Christianity, East or West. "Calvinism," otherwise known as "Reformed
theology," went further in breaking with the past traditions of
the Church than anyone could have imagined was possible even
during the early days of the Reformation. It was no coincidence
that almost the only Father of the Roman Church the Reformed
theologians selectively quoted was Augustine. The Western
Church's most problematic Father soon became the Calvinists'
one link with the Christian past.

THE FIVE POINTS

The proponents of Calvinism met at Dort in Holland in 1618.
There they formulated what are called the "Five Points of
Calvinism." The Five Points were based on isolated, occasionally
mistranslated, Pauline statements taken out of the context of
Scripture, and the context of the interpretation of the ancient
Holy Tradition; for instance, Romans 5.10, 2 Corinthians
5.18-19, Ephesians 2.15-16, Colossians 1.21-22, Romans
3.24-25. The Five Points were also based on the early writings
of St. Augustine about predestination, many of which he subsequently either repudiated or clarified.[18] But principally, those
who led the Council of Dort relied on the reductionist or even
deconstructionist theological theories of John Calvin in for-

---

[18]Please see George Florovsky, *The Byzantine Ascetic and Spiritual Fathers* (Belmont, 1987). Especially Ch. 1.

mulating their new Protestant "Summa."

The authors of the Five Points borrowed from the spirit of medieval Scholasticism in that they reduced God's relationship to man, salvation, creation and Christ's Incarnation to five easy-to-remember, rationalistic, theological formulas stripped of liturgical, sacramental meaning. Just as the early Reformers had stripped their churches bare of images and tinkered with the New Testament Canon, at Dort the mystery of salvation, of God's interaction with mankind was stripped bare and "clarified." At Dort, Protestantism's final break with the spirit of the historical Church was achieved. The loving, mysterious God, who desired all people to be saved became, in the hands of the Reformed theologians, nothing more than a confused memory.

Ironically the "God" the Calvinists invented was also reduced to near impotence by theoretically being portrayed as monstrously omnipotent. The Calvinist "God" was a great unfathomable Zeus-like computer in the sky who arbitrarily saved some while damning others — an irrational, perhaps berserk, Augustinian phenomenon no more loving or predictable than a forest fire. The "God" of Calvinism emerged as inexplicably less merciful than most of his human creatures.[19]

The Five Points of Dort were:

1. *Total Inability — or — Total Depravity*: The sinner is dead, blind, and deaf to the things of God. His will is not free; indeed, he or she cannot choose good over evil. Thus one can never choose to love God or to do right. Faith is not something one contributes to salvation, it is God's gift to those He has chosen to be saved. This must be so, since, at the fall, man fell *completely*, he lost his free will and became totally depraved.

2. *Unconditional Election*: God's choice of certain individuals unto salvation, before the foundation of the world, rests solely in His sovereign will. His choice of certain individual sinners to be saved is not based on any criterion that is humanly knowable. He does not even choose to save those He foreknew would love or obey Him. Election, therefore, is not determined by or conditioned upon, what a man will do. On the con-

---

[19]"It necessarily followed (from the council of Dort's proclamations) that 'Christ has not reconciled the world,' (Synod of Dort, Session 143 (Act Syn. Dort. 1:343)) but only the elect." Jaroslav Pelikan, *Reformation of Church and Dogma*, p. 238.

trary, God gives faith to individuals He selects. God's choice of the sinner, not the sinner's choice to follow Christ, is the only cause of salvation. This must be so since humanity has no capacity to choose since the will and the intellect are utterly depraved.

3. *Particular Redemption — or — Limited Atonement*: Christ's work was intended only to save the Elect who were already chosen before creation. It secured salvation for the Elect by paying the penalty of sin for those chosen in the process of Unconditional Election. There was no reason this should be so since all men are sinners and should be damned. Nevertheless, for reasons known only to Himself, God chose out a handful to be saved. The lost (the "Vessels of Wrath," as Calvin called them) and the Elect equally deserve damnation but God saw fit to save a few for His own unfathomable reasons.

4. *Irresistible Grace*: The Holy Spirit's work can be understood as that of extending a special call to the Elect. This call inevitably brings the Elect to salvation. Just as the Elect are chosen by God, not saved by choosing to become like Christ, so they cannot resist God's Irresistible Grace — the call of the Spirit. His call cannot be rejected. There is no choice in the matter on the part of the sinner. The Spirit forces the sinner not only to believe but to cooperate with the will of God.

5. *The Perseverance of the Saints*: The Elect are eternally saved. Nothing they do can ever remove them from the Book of Life. They had no choice in the matter of coming to God and neither can any action, thought, or desire remove them from God's plan to make them persevere to the end. However, The Elect can never know if they are the Elect for certain in this life, so that there is no ultimate assurance of salvation for the individual. Even so, the "Vessels of Wrath," those chosen by God to be damned from before the Creation, can take no action to come to God. Repentance, the content of their character, good works or faith in Christ will avail them nothing.[20]

With God portrayed as a fatalistic, cruel force of nature, with the Incarnation reduced to nothing more than play acting, since "The Elect" were already chosen before Christ came to earth, with Christ's death reduced to a sacrifice to an angry,

---

[20]David Steele and Curtis Thomas, *The Five Points of Calvinism* (Phillipsburg, 1963), pp. 16-19.

vengeful "God," with man reduced to a creature without free will, Calvinist Reformed theology logically, if unintentionally, opened the door to the Enlightenment's demotion of humanity and religion.[21]

Since the truth about God could apparently be reduced to a few, almost Darwinian, dogmatic propositions and since God could be stripped of His mystery, not to mention His loving character, and since humanity was seen as having no particular consequence and, ironically, at the same time, such power as to be able to debunk all the Church's Holy Tradition and *to describe the character of God*, then why not complete the circle of reductionist rationalism? Why not systematically attempt to explain *everything*? Why not follow science and progress to some new utopian future unencumbered by old-fashioned religious tradition? Why not overthrow *all* hierarchy? And, if one took the Augustinian theological proponents of the Dort council at their word, why not reject their easily explained and monstrous "God" with his cruel natural selection of the fittest "Elect," and lead mankind beyond the constricting belief that it need be subject to an arbitrary system of cosmic triage? Since God had ordained everything beforehand, so that what mankind did was "right," in the sense it existed as part of God's will (since humanity had no free will and no choice), then why not dispense with moral absolutes altogether, stop playacting, as if moral choices had consequences, and just do whatever it was one wanted to do in the first place and call *that* "God's will?" This was precisely the logic that, I believe, gave rise to the Enlightenment.

THE ENLIGHTENMENT

After the Great Schism of 1054 and the Reformation, the third event responsible for the creation of our modern post-Christian era was the Enlightenment. The new Renaissance-Protestant habit of mind, of questioning the authority of the historical Church, and the rationalist excesses of Calvinism,

---

[21]The five heads of doctrine of the Synod of Dort fixed the Reformed understanding of the will of God for the world in a form that was to become normative." Jaroslav Pelikan, *Reformation of Church and Dogma*, p. 239.

were taken to their logical, secularized conclusion by the eighteenth century philosophers of the Enlightenment. Alexis de Tocqueville speaks revealingly about the impact that Protestantism had on one of the fathers of the Enlightenment, Voltaire:

> Voltaire's three-year stay in (Protestant) England had familiarized him with political freedom, but failed to make him like it. What delighted him in that country was the *skeptical philosophy* so freely voiced there.[22]

In the seventeenth and eighteenth centuries, certain English and French philosophers began to debunk all religion, even the idea that the supernatural existed, and to replace such religious concepts with what they called "reason." It was in the explosive environment of shattered historical Christian religious certainties, rationalistic Roman Catholic Scholasticism, new Protestant dogmas, and harsh rationalistic Calvinistic determinism, that the Enlightenment was born. What the Enlightenment philosophers did was to secularize the Protestant revolution and complete it, in much the same way that Darwin later secularized the theological concept of election and called it the survival of the fittest, and Marx secularized the Augustinian-Calvinist idea of predestination and called it the inevitable march of history.

It seems to me that the Enlightenment can only be understood as the secularized bastard child of three reactionary movements, all of which came about because of the corruption of the Latin Western Church: the Scholastic Movement, the Renaissance and the Reformation. As such the Enlightenment was a movement led by men who rejected the teachings of the Roman Catholic historical Church and, borrowing a rationalistic rebellious page from the Renaissance and the new religion of Protestantism, began to question all authority, even the idea of the divine order itself.

What Renaissance scholars began in their questioning of the Holy Tradition ended as a rejection of that Tradition. What the Protestants began as a revolt against papal corruption ended as a rebellion against God. What started as a rejection of the sacramental authority of the Church ended in a rejection of the sanctity of human life. What began as the debase-

---

[22]*The Ancien Regime and the French Revolution,* trans. Stuart Gilbert (Manchester, 1955), p. 178. (emphasis mine)

ment of Holy Mystery, by the rationalistic Scholastic movement, ended in the setting up of mortal men and women as new "gods." At the end of the Reformation, Western culture stood on the brink of loosing its sense of the sacred. The Enlightenment philosophers gave people the final shove over the precipice of doubt to the brink of which they had been led by a corrupt, Scholastic Roman Church and the Protestant Reformers.

In the Enlightenment, several French philosophers, Voltaire and Turgot, among others, rejected the traditional world view of Christian religion altogether, and adopted the anti-Christian, anti-traditional beliefs that are still prevalent today. The philosophers taught that people did not need transcendent, God-given truth, nor the guidance of historical Christian Holy Tradition. They believed that people could better decide moral questions unaided by religion, Church authority or God. They held, moreover, that those who embraced a traditionally religious view of life were in fact an impediment to human progress and reason. They believed secular reason was the only necessity for human understanding and progress. Human reason, not God, would be a sufficient "progressive" foundation for the society of the future.

The Reformers had rejected the ancient Holy Tradition of the Church and replaced it with the slogan of "Sola Scriptura!" They said that they needed no tradition by which to interpret the Scriptures. They held that by using their reason alone, the Bible was intuitively self-explanatory. The philosophers of the Enlightenment took the ideas of the Reformers further — they rejected not only the historical Church, liturgical worship, the Holy Mysteries, the sacraments and the Holy Tradition, but the Bible as well. All they were left with was the Reformers' faith in the individual's intuitive ability to interpret life's big questions unaided. They reduced the Reformers slogan "Sola Scriptura," to merely, "Sola!"

The Marquis de Condorcet, Voltaire's friend and co-laborer in the rationalistic Enlightenment vineyard, wrote his famous summary of the Enlightenment's principal creed:

> We have witnessed the development of a new doctrine which is to deliver the final blow to the already tottering structure of (religious) prejudice. It is the idea of the limitless perfectability of the human species.[23]

---

[23]Marquis de Condorcet, *Sketch for a Historical Picture of the Human Mind* (Paris, 1933 edition).

Such a statement might at first seem to be the opposite of the Five Points of Calvinism. But with the door opened to the mad impulse of reductionism by the Scholastics, with God "explained" by the Reformers, with the sacramental unity of the Church smashed by the Calvinists, with the "God" of the Council of Dort presented as a capricious monster, Condorcet's ideas were the next logical step.

If reality could be reduced, to no more than a game of predestined election — survival of God's fittest — why not dispense altogether with a god who was looking more like a devil every day? Why not elect man to preside over a paradise of his own making? Indeed why not invent a whole new world and redeem mankind through art, social engineering and science rather than spiritual renewal?

CHAPTER SEVEN
AMERICAN HUMANISM

The ideas of the Enlightenment philosophers were embraced in the New World as well as in Europe.[1] Thomas Jefferson, Thomas Paine, Benjamin Franklin and many others of the American founding fathers, were heavily influenced by the new Protestant-Enlightenment faith in human reason so well expressed by Condorcet. The idea of the limitless perfectibility of the human species, *not historical Christianity*, was the overriding ideology of the founders of the American experiment.[2]

Because, in the early days of American history, the transition from Christian belief to secular materialism was not yet complete, some of the American founders continued to lace their speeches and writing with references, often fervent and personal, to Christian ideas and teaching. Nevertheless, as our subsequent history makes so abundantly clear, the nation that grew on the foundation they built is an aggressively secular nation that now opposes itself to almost every single one of the basic moral, hierarchical and sacramental teachings of the ancient historical Church.

From the beginning of American history, the influence of two strong secularizing anti-Christian forces were at work in

---

[1] "Americans . . . enthusiastically embraced the utopian elements in Enlightenment thought. They believed that it was possible to establish a more or less perfect human society . . ." Page Smith, *The Shaping of America: A People's History of America*, vol. 3 (New York, 1989), p. 36.

[2] "We find . . . major themes of the new American consciousness—the new utopian vision, a democratic fervor religious in its intensity. . . . It was thus often unclear whether the 'new Jerusalem' was a secular city inhabited by mortal men . . . or the earthly paradise . . . a utopia created with a minimum of assistance from the Almighty." Ibid. p. 37.

shaping the American ethos.[3] The first was found in the theology of Calvinistic Puritanism which stood on the twin ideological pillars of Augustinian fatalism and "Sola Scriptura," crying out against church tradition, liturgical worship, icons, bishops, and the sacraments, as well as the princes and kings against whom the Puritans revolted politically. The second anti-Christian force was shaped by those such as Jefferson, who had wholeheartedly embraced the European Enlightenment and were busy applying it to the founding documents of America in large utopian, humanistic doses.

Calvin's concept of the "Elect" was conveniently secularized by the American founders, and extended to political systems through which *nations* could become "Elect." Thus the early Americans, both Puritans and Enlightenment humanists, saw themselves as the citizens of an Elect nation—a covenant people—a "city set on a hill."[4]

While becoming thoroughly secularized, Protestant America nevertheless retained a sentimental attachment to a sort of watered-down, comfortable and socially acceptable "Christiani-ty."[5] Americans rejected the more crude forms of anti-religious bigotry of the French Enlightenment philosophers, some of whom had even stood by and applauded the beheading and persecution of scores of priests in the French revolution.[6]

---

[3] "Perhaps the most crucial element of the Enlightenment to enter the mainstream of American Protestantism was the notion that human society could be perfected . . . . That curious mixture of piety and millennial utopianism that developed in the United States." Ibid. pp. 319-323.

[4] "The practical activities of Americans in the first decade of the new nation were in large part dictated by . . . the manner in which the Classical-Christian Consciousness was being eroded . . . transmuted into the Secular-Democratic Consciousness. . . .

Calvin . . . (had) propounded the doctrine of predestination. God had, ... determined which souls were to be saved and which to be damned, and there was no escape from this destiny." Ibid. pp. 310-311.

[5] "The notion of a God was almost universally accepted (in early America), hence deism. Christ was thought of as a wise and good man, . . . the supreme moral teacher . . . Benjamin Franklin, Benjamin Rush, and John Adams are helpful in measuring the changes in Christian doctrine . . . in the (early American) period. (Franklin's) 'First Principals' were consistent with an effort to describe . . . a 'rational' Christianity. . . . There is no mention of Christ, the Son or of the Holy Spirit. Underlying Franklin's theology is the notion that anyone can pretty much make up his own religion to suit himself." Ibid. pp. 315-317.

[6] "The anti-religious spirit of the age had various consequences, but it seems to me that what led the French to commit such singular excesses (was that) . . . religion was expelled from their souls. . . .

Firmly convinced of the perfectibility of man, they had faith in his innate virtue . . . They had that arrogant self-confidence which often points the way to disaster

Nevertheless, American humanists enthusiastically embraced the utopian elements of Enlightenment thought and the Romantic movement that followed it. America, they believed, was to be "paradise anew, . . . another Canaan (that) shall excel the old," as the poet laureate of the French revolution, Philip Freneau wrote in his poem, *The Rising Glory of America*."[7]

The new American consciousness lauded by Freneau was the child of the French Enlightenment, not the historical Church.[8] However secular it was in its essence, it nevertheless embodied a utopian vision of democratic fervor religious in its intensity. This utopian dream was unconsciously cross-bred with the millennial aspect of Protestantism and fatalistic Calvinist determinism, thereby allowing Americans to conveniently combine, in the words of historian Page Smith: "earthly utopian expectations with Christian dogma . . ."[9]

Increasingly in the new American "utopia," sin was banished as the moral source of human problems, and materialistic—finally consumeristic—"progress" was increasingly venerated as the new "God" that would save the American "Elect" not from sin, but from economic and political backwardness.[10] It came to be believed that prosperity would lead to goodness without the need to address questions of sin or repentance. Education, economic plenty, perpetual growth and entrepreneurship would create an environment so pleasant as to dispense with the need for repentance since educated, well-fed, democratically represented people would be too happy to indulge in anti-

---

. . . They had a fanatical faith in their vocation—that of transforming the social system, root and branch. . . . This passionate idealism was . . . in fact a new religion. . . . The attack that then was launched on all (traditional) religious faith had disastrous effects. . . . Both religious institutions and the whole system of government were thrown into the melting pot, with the result that men's minds were in a state of total confusion . . . they knew neither what to hold on to, nor where to stop." Alexis de Tocqueville, *The Ancien Regime and the French Revolution*, translated by Stuart Gilbert (Manchester, England, 1955), pp. 177-178.

[7] *Sketch for a Historical Picture of the Human Mind* (Paris, 1933 edition; trans. Morag).

[8] "Adams himself was certainly a child of the Enlightenment. . . ." Page Smith, *The Shaping of America*, p. 321.

[9] Ibid. p. 37.

[10] "Rush noted with pleasure 'the progress of reason and liberty.' . . . He saw them 'as preludes to a glorious manifestation upon the hearts of men.' What had begun as a movement designed to bring 'liberty to the whole world' would . . . bring something even better, 'the salvation of all mankind.' Ibid. p. 318.

social or self-destructive behavior.[11] In other words, virtue and goodness would be created out of thin air without benefit of any old-fashioned Holy Tradition.

Rarely in the crusading moralism of the new lexicon of American ambition could one detect an echo of the ancient Church, which taught that the folly of riches and self-esteem is the root of evil and that free will and choice make us morally accountable for our actions, not only before man, *but before God*. And that God desires us to be sinless and to love our neighbors as ourselves. Much less did the majority of the utopian founders seem to realize the hopelessness of thinking that by our own efforts, much less by a secular political system, we can create a heaven on earth through material gain, social engineering or right-thinking politics. Whomever the deist, humanistic American founders were influenced by, it certainly was not the desert Father, Saint John Cassian who, in the fourth century wrote,

> A clear rule for self-control handed down by the Fathers is this: stop eating while you are hungry and do not continue until you are satisfied. When the Apostle said, 'Make no provision to fulfill the desires of the flesh,' (Romans 13.14), he was not forbidding us to provide for the needs of life; he was warning us against self-indulgence . . . self esteem and pride. . . .[12]

Both the parent, Protestantism, the child, the Enlightenment and the Enlightenment's derivative, the Romantic movement, were dominant in early American thinking, in which a climate of rebellion against Holy Tradition, sacramentality, hierarchy, community, patriarchy, the teaching of the historical Church, repentance from greed and self-indulgence and finally God, thrived.

It seems to me that the real focus of the American Protestant spirit soon became one that held that no authority exists outside of the individual. Luther and Calvin had successfully

---

[11]"Writing to Jefferson . . . Adams assured the president that 'The proud oppressors over the Earth shall be totally broken down and those classes of Men who have hitherto been victims of their rage . . . shall perpetually enjoy perfect peace and Safety till time shall be no more.'" Ibid. p. 323.

[12]*The Philokalia*, vol. 1: *On the Eight Vices* (London, 1979), p. 74.

challenged the Western Roman Church and created a new individualistic theology. The individual was understood, by the American Protestants of the eighteenth to twentieth centuries, to be able to sweep back the veil of the Holy of Holies and to apply Calvinist-style reductionist and subjective methods of biblical exegesis to all of life's questions.[13] After all, Zwingli had declared the historical Church's Eucharist to be essentially a fraud, the Council of Dort found that the mystery of God's interaction with man could be explained, even reduced, to the Five Points of Calvinism and, of late, faith had been reduced to the "rational Christianity" of Unitarianism. The individualized, subjective "born again experience" of the nineteenth century frontier cults and "revivals" would dispense with the essential need for baptism, confession and communion altogether, since the Christian experience was reduced to simply "getting to know Jesus as your personal Savior." Finally, in our own century, psychology explained spirituality and replaced it, just as political solutions to moral problems replaced the traditional Christian call to repentance.

In the end it was the rationalism of Augustinian-Calvinist Protestantism, combined with the emerging utopian American addiction to material progress, that became the true religion of America. In comparison to the ancient sacramental apostolic Church, this new "religion" was a wholly self-made, secularized phenomenon. However elaborate its ecclesiastical trappings, in the end it became thoroughly relativistic—a creature of its age cut off from any meaningful continuity with the historical, liturgical sacramental Church.[14]

Orthodox scholar Fr. Thomas Hopko writes: "References to religious doctrine and practices in America are (now) virtually

---

[13]"Many New Englanders felt as did Abigail Adams, who chafed at listening to sermons 'that I cannot possibly believe' . . . She wished to hear 'liberal good sense . . . true piety without enthusiasms, devotion without grimace, and religion upon a rational system.' So John and Abigail became Unitarians. Hundreds and then thousands of their fellow New Englanders followed them into the new denomination, which soon became the established church of 'rational Christianity.' " Page Smith, *A People's History of America*, vol. III: *The Shaping of America*, p. 324.

[14]"We speak of this fragmentation (which was to go on and on) as American religious pluralism. John Adams viewed it . . . as a salutary development. What it meant sociologically was that it was always possible to devise a new variation of the Christian faith to meet the needs of every group. . . . Indeed it soon appeared that one of the 'rights' of Americans was to establish new religions whenever the spirit moved them." Ibid. p. 324.

never references to what is true or false, to what is right or wrong, to what is meaningful or senseless. They are almost, without exception, in terms of what is modern or backward."[15]

ABANDONMENT OF REASON

Having drunk deep at the well of skepticism, those who had abandoned the teaching of the prophets, Christ and the Apostles, now began to even question their own Enlightenment assumptions. Rationalism began to digest itself. The inheritors of the Enlightenment began to doubt their own faith in reason, which had replaced traditional faith in Christian dogma.[16] For instance, the Swiss philosopher Jean Jacques Rousseau taught that truth is adrift on an ocean of relativism. He came to eventually believe that for mankind to be "saved" it must abandon civilization, founded on rationality and return to a more "natural state."

In fact, Rousseau's alternative to Christian Holy Tradition and civilization, which came to be known as the Romantic Movement, was almost a parody of it. Mankind needed salvation, Rousseau believed, not from sin, but from the constrictions of Jewish and Christian civilization. Thus, "primitive," nonrational intuition, feeling and subjective experience were now understood by the Romantic movement's adherents to be good, whereas reason, empirical evidence, Christian sacramental spirituality or scientific discovery were held to be evil.[17] This anti-Christian philosophy, in which choice, freedom and personal autonomy are all but worshipped, continues to shape our hedonistic present.[18]

The Enlightenment had provoked its own demise. Now, in

---

[15]Thomas Hopko, *All the Fullness of God* (Crestwood, 1982), p. 152.

[16]This is what Herbert Schlossberg has described as, "The return of Western culture to its pagan past . . ." Herbert Schlossberg, *Idols for Destruction: Christian Faith in its Confrontation with American Society* (Nashville, 1983), p. 268.

[17]Rousseau's cry was, "back to nature!"

[18]"Of all the misleading interpretations of this complex age, few are more so than the common one that secularism means the replacement of a world-view that is religious with one that is not. . . . The religious character of human ideas . . . is all-pervasive . . . the much vaunted secularization process means the flourishing of anti-Christian religions." Herbert Schlossberg, *Idols for Destruction*, p. 273.

the climate of doubt, with even the god of reason debunked, the debunkers became the debunked. The Enlightenment's extreme secularism, its rationalism, its cynicism, its reliance on science and material progress, led some, like Rousseau, to call for a return to mystical, quasi-religious ideas. But the eighteenth and nineteenth century modern-era Rousseauian return to mysticism was not a return to the Holy Tradition of Orthodoxy, rooted in the historical Christ. Far from it. What Rousseau's Romantic movement proposed was the worship of *irrationality*, feeling and intuition for *its own sake*. What was to be worshipped now was primitive human instinct, not the God of Abraham.

The Romantic movement became a perverse mirror image of Calvinism. Mankind was now placed at the center of the universe. Where Calvinism found human beings to be utterly depraved, the Romantics found people to be utterly good. For the Romantics, a strange new religious faith in the will of the people became the guarantor of morality. It came to be thought that democracy could exist independently of Christian moral philosophy and the Jewish and Christian religious absolutes that had underwritten human dignity or millennia.[19] The "people's will" replaced what had once been understood to be the Law of God as the guiding principle of human history in the lexicon of secular Romantic movement icons. In America, this idea was given further expression by those who began to give the same kind of reverent treatment to the American Constitution that had once been reserved for the Holy Tradition. Thus if something could be said to be constitutional or legal it came to enjoy the same moral standing that was once exclusively accorded to teachings understood to represent apostolic truth.

The Romantic movement's abandonment of tradition, hierarchy and even the fundamentally religious concept of communitarian civilization, in favor of various forms of unbridled individualism, finds its echoes in twentieth century feminist calls for abandoning what is regarded as "male-oriented rationality" in favor of so-called female intuition. It echoes as well in feminist experiments in "new family units" of single-parent households

[19]"Humanism has become the most messianic of the . . . religions of the West. . . . It should be clear . . . that what is widely regarded as a struggle between the religious and the secular is really a struggle between religions." Ibid. pp. 273-75.

or lesbian "parents" replacing traditional families, in "liberated" men abandoning their dependent children, and in the abandonment of esthetic values in art in favor of political propaganda.[20] Literary deconstructionism, the final expression of the Romantic movement's intuitive style of "feeling" the world, has even gone so far as to challenge the very idea that words can have *any* rational, commonly understood meaning.[21]

It is ironic given the fact that Christian Holy Tradition was at first rejected in the name of reason, by *both* the Reformers *and* the Enlightenment philosophers, that today we live in a climate of studied *irrationality* in which, even in our universities, we find evidence of a growing departure from traditional academic subjects in favor of what is now a post-Enlightenment and even post-Romantic culture of dogmatic anti-reason. All around us is post-modern evidence that Protestant-Enlightenment rationalism has failed—has turned inward and devoured itself. Just as Protestantism originally failed to reform the Roman Western Church, and dissolved into schismatic, self-defeating denominationalism, so the faith in reason that was supposed to replace Christianity altogether, has been replaced with a faith in irrationality! One now finds university courses on "New Age" magic and occult studies, on sexual-fertility rites and pagan deities, and homosexual or feminist "life-styles," not taught as history or science but as a "life-style option."[22]

We see that Western intellectual man has come full circle. The smashed stained glass windows of the churches of Geneva, Zurich, Amsterdam and elsewhere that were metaphorically replaced by the clear plain glass of reductionist Calvinist reason, were in turn smashed and replaced by the harsh void of pure secular rationalism. However, people being what they are — spiritual, sacramental creatures — this state of affairs could not persist. The spiritual void created by reductionist Protestantism and Enlightenment secularism has been filled, the "stained glass windows" of mystery and spirituality restored. But the new mystical images in these windows are not Chris-

---

[20]Peter Shaw, *The War Against the Intellect* (Iowa City, 1989), pp. 67-88.

[21]"Deconstructionist attitudes, especially skepticism about the existence of any firm knowledge and the replacement of rationality by subjectivity, have spread beyond literary theory to virtually every corner of literary study." Ibid. p. 64.

[22]"Sex and magic are now academic growth industries," Peter J. Leithart writes. *First Things*, September, 1991.

tian—they are thoroughly pagan.[23]

Martin Luther's, John Calvin's, Jean Jacques Rousseau's and Thomas Jefferson's utopian, deterministic, religiously secularized great-grandchildren are alive and well. The inheritors of the Protestant-Enlightenment whirlwind have formed a distinct and separate nation within what remains of Western culture. They have made war on the last vestiges of Holy Tradition. It is they who have prosecuted the cultural war to its conclusion. This "war" of ideas rages about us and has reduced more and more of life to mere politics. It has replaced the teachings of Holy Tradition with new dogmas of secular academic fundamentalism, irrationality and selfish demands for unlimited self-realization. Special interests groups abound, and there is a new tribalism emerging in American society. We now even have a newly-revived neo-paganism, of the kind feminists, with their worship of female pagan deities and their revival of child sacrifice to the god of "self" through abortion, have begun to practice.[24]

CONCLUSION

The modern Knowledge Class was largely forged in the crucible of the Reformation and the Enlightenment-Romantic movements. Today the revolt against history continues, now against the very culture that gave it birth. The intellectuals of our day have disavowed their former "God," reason, that was to have replaced what they held to be the "silly superstitions" of Christian faith with "enlightened" ideas. Instead of promoting some alternative to Christianity, they now worship doubt itself and have given up their grandiose schemes for mere selfish programs of self-fulfillment.[25]

---

[23]For a study on how the Romantic movement has affected modern education in America, as one example of the re-emergence of paganism in the West, see William K. Kilpatrick, *Why Johnny Can't Tell Right From Wrong: Moral Illiteracy and the Case for Character Education*, pp. 103-104.

[24]"Thus social and political propaganda comes disguised as social research." Herbert Schlossberg, *Idols for Destruction*, p. 152.

[25]"Of late, behaviorists in university psychology departments have been forced to make room for what Paul Vitz calls 'selfist' psychologies, emphasizing emotional satisfactions and mystical states that can only be called religious. In all this, the irrational is not only tolerated but cultivated as beneficial. See Paul Vitz, *Psychology as Religion: the Cult of Self-Worship* (Grand Rapids, 1977) cited in Herbert Schlossberg, *Idols for Destruction*, pp. 159-60.

CHAPTER EIGHT
THE PROTESTANT DILEMMA

The Protestant dilemma is one that is shared by all revolutionaries who find that once the old order is overthrown, constructing a "new society" on the rubble of the old is a harder task than they had anticipated. The dilemma of American Protestantism was foreshadowed by what took place in the early years of the European Reformation. Mildly revolutionary groups begot extremists who in turn begot even more extreme separatists. These last then denounced the original Reformers as no better than collaborators with the *ancien regime*. Neverending fragmentation has led Protestantism, according to Professor of Sociology Steve Bruce at Queen's University in Belfast, to be the chief, if unwitting, force behind the secularization of Western culture.

> What has rarely been given sufficient weight, . . . is the role which Protestantism inadvertently played in its own collapse. Particularly overlooked are the organizational consequences of core reformation ideas."[1]

I believe that the philosophical children of Protestantism were conceived when Western Christians consorted first, with rebellion against Holy Tradition, and secondly with political power and materialistic greed. In the final pages of his *Institutes* Calvin wrote, "I am so far from prohibiting them (the subjects of a King) in the discharge of their duty (revolution) . . . that I affirm, that if they connive at kings in their oppression of their people, such forbearance involves the most nefarious perfidy,

---

[1]Steve Bruce, *A House Divided: Protestantism, Schism, and Secularization*, p. 1.

because they fraudulently betray the liberty of the people, of which they have been appointed protectors by the ordination of God."[2] In this passage is to be found the basic rationale for the pious Protestant New Englanders' revolutionary sentiments leading to the bloody American Revolution several generations after Calvin published his *Institutes*.[3]

In Calvin's Protestant revolutionary zeal is also to be found the partial inspiration of the Enlightenment philosophers who made a virtue of questioning all authority, hierarchy and established human order.[4] Calvin might have been shocked to learn just how far his theological and political ideas would be taken beyond what he may have intended, but the fact remains that what, in its individualistic revolutionary impetus, he began in one context—theocratic Geneva—has gone so far in another—twentieth century America—as to actually undermine the very first principles Calvin stood for.[5]

The fragmenting logic of schism, within Christendom, has been inexorably secularizing in its consequences. As Professor Steve Bruce writes,

> Once you recognize the variety of ways to truth (through dividing Christendom into thousands of denominations each claiming to be "the church") you are part of the way to accepting the right to be wrong and the idea of one inclusive church (or truth) is undermined.[6]

DEVOLUTION

Much as many politically conservative Protestants may say they long for a renewal of "traditional values," and deplore the

---

[2] John Calvin, *Institutes of the Christian Religion*, vol. XX, 10-23, CB 8.

[3] "Calvin's first edition of the *Institutes* . . . (were regarded as) the Protestant Summa. . . . History, for Calvin, was the theater of God's judgment. . . . God's design, Calvin taught, was determined . . . the elect were predestined by God to carry out His (historic revolutionary) design." E. Digby Baltzell, *Puritan Boston and Quaker Philadelphia*, p. 63.

[4] "The philosophical conceptions of the eighteenth century have rightly been regarded as one of the chief causes of the Revolution . . ." Alexis de Tocqueville, *The Ancient Regime and the French Revolution*, translated by Stuart Gilbert, p. 37.

[5] "Writers like Michael Walzer have . . . seen the Calvinists and the Puritans as the Bolsheviks of the Reformation." E. Digby Baltzell, *Puritan Boston and Quaker Philadelphia*, p. 65.

[6] Steve Bruce, *A House Divided: Protestantism, Schism, and Secularization*, p. 3.

moral anarchy typical of our age, they are now unable to contain the continuing social devolution their own rebellious forefathers contributed to. This is due to their having rejected the concept of one authoritative historical Church, with its Christian unity centered on sacramental worship, the Holy Tradition and apostolic continuity.

Protestants lost control of the process of subjective biblical interpretation. This in turn led to open ended rationalistic inquiry of the modern variety.[7] Protestant religion seems to have been reduced to just one more component of monolithic mainline relativism.[8] The Protestant spirit of revolution in our culture, and the overthrow of traditional structures of authority on all fronts, can be clearly traced to the philosophical ideas that led to the French, American and even Russian revolutions.[9]

As Charlotte Allen writes,

It was not long into the sixteenth century when the Protestant reformers discovered that they had . . . 'sown the wind.' Once the initial break with Rome occurred, there was no stopping the proliferation of Protestant sects, some far more millennial, utopian and radically egalitarian than the fundamentally conservative Luther could have ever imagined. . . . Luther's doctrine of the 'two kingdoms' rigorously separating the spheres of ecclesiastical and secular authority, led eventually to the thorough secularizing of Western society, the privatizing of religion, and . . . the draining of

---

[7] ". . . in American Protestantism, or the pessimistic Calvinistic remembrance of sin still holding humanity . . . it remains that the life of the Christian in the Church does not participate in God's life. Hence, of course, in both the 'neo-orthodox' and in the 'liberal' camp of Protestantism, many hold as indifferent the essential Christian Kerygma whether Christ was God or not, whether His Resurrection was or was not a historical fact. And one is bound to ask oneself what is left of the biblical and patristic sythesis and of Christianity in general." John Meyendorff, *Catholicity and the Church*, p. 81.

[8] "The result (of the Protestant denominational fragmentation) was a person who had learned to live . . . by his own will. He proved capable of forming endless new combinations and permutations, political, social and religious. Like recombinant DNA, (the new Protestant American) went on mutating with bewildering speed and facility. In one lifetime such an 'individual' might encompass half a dozen careers . . . changing his religion as often as his occupation." Page Smith, *The Shaping of America*, vol. 3, p. 325.

[9] "The Enlightenment had adapted the Christian notion of perfection achieved in the afterlife and applied it to man's earthly existence." Ibid. p. 316.

the sense of the sacred out of everyday life. Not surprisingly, Protestants were the first Western Christians to lose their faith en masse to modernity. . . .[10]

Martin Luther's revolt against the authority of the Roman Church began in the spirit of reform. He did not intend to found a new religion, but was concerned mainly with purifying the Roman Church and rendering faith more accessible. Luther's most crucial departure from the liturgical tradition of the historical Church was his reinterpretation of the Mass, which he changed to call "the Lord's Supper." As we have seen, other reformers like Zwingli took this impulse much further and reduced "the Lord's Supper" to a little practiced, little understood symbol.[11]

The Reformers replaced the visible Church and its hierarchy of bishop and priest with the so-called invisible church, a loose association of all those calling themselves Christians. In emphasizing faith and the Bible alone, Luther opened the door to the democratization of the "priesthood of all believers," an egalitarian ideal that the radical Reformation took much further than even Luther intended. Thus was manifested the first impulse of modern pluralism and the slide toward a denominational plethora of diversity which finally reached a crescendo in the total moral relativism of our own age.[12]

The tendency of Protestantism to lead toward secularization via its own style of theological anarchy has been well documented. As James Joll writes, "There are movements (like Protestantism) in the history of all religions which reject all authority, whether temporal or spiritual, and claim complete liberty to act in accordance with the Inner Light."[13]

---

[10]Charlotte Allen, "The Protestant Ethos: A Review," *First Things*, September, 1992, p. 48.

[11]See Steven Ozment, *Protestants: The Birth of Revolutions* (New York, 1992), a comprehensive study of Protestantism's unintended secularizing consequences.

[12]"Principally those challenges came form the left wing of the Reformation, which, as its leading scholarly interpreter has put it, was not a 'reformation' . . . but 'a radical break from the existing institutions and theologies . . .' (Williams (1962) 846) In many ways that radical break was an anticipation of the very critiques of orthodoxy and apostolic continuity that were to come from modern thought in the eighteenth, nineteenth and twentieth centuries, so that the full implications of these challenges did not become apparent until (much later)." Jaroslav Pelikan, *The Christian Tradition*, vol. 4, p. 305.

[13]James Joll, *Anarchists* (New York, 1978), p. 18.

Luther, it has been said, had "all the ingenious enthusiasms of the anarchist."[14] Through his enthusiasm for personal biblical interpretation and pietism, Luther opened the door to the Anabaptist movement, which replaced the authority of the sacraments, and even the Bible, with a new and extremely individualistic religion.[15]

ANABAPTIST ANARCHY

Almost from its beginning, Protestantism invented two competing traditions. One was a reforming impulse of building upon the Roman Church. The second embodied a spirit of iconoclastic anarchy exemplified by the Anabaptists, and later by the Quakers and hundreds of derivative sects, which rejected most forms of social contract, responsibility and even civil government. Christ, to the Anabaptists, was the great liberator, the greatest Lenin-Mao of all time, not the founder of a sacramental, historical institution known as The Church.

Various Anabaptist sects sought to return to what they thought was a "primitive Christianity," taking the Sermon on the Mount out of the context of Scripture and applying it in a subjective manner. They became pietistic perfectionists who, like Calvin, denounced all adornment, drinking or the practice of any entertainment. They were committed to egalitarianism to a degree that was virtually communistic as they began to withdraw to segregated "holy" communities.[16]

The world, the Anabaptists believed, was hopeless—totally evil—and would remain so until the Second Coming. From the

---

[14]R. H. Tawney, *Religion and the Rise of Capitalism.* As cited by E. Digby Baltzell, *Puritan Boston and Quaker Philadelphia,* p. 69.

[15]"Luther's indifference to the traditional issues of church structure . . . helped to make it possible for his followers to accommodate themselves to systems of ecclesiastical organization ranging from state church to free church and from a retention of the historic episcopate to . . . congregationalism." Jaroslav Pelikan, *Reformation of Church and Dogma,* p. 313.

[16]"Anabaptists insisted on enforcing the sole authority of Scripture and implementing . . . to baptism the same definition of 'sign' that Zwingli had applied to the Lord's Supper. . . . Luther and Calvin both charged that the pope and the Anabaptists were essentially alike in this subjectivism. . . . What had perverted the sacraments . . . among 'Evangelicals' (as the Anabaptists began to call themselves,) Calvin charged was no less among the 'papists,' (and was) . . . an apostasy from 'the pure and chaste doctrine of the holy apostles' (Menn. Nw. Geb. (Harrison 126)" Ibid. p. 315.

Anabaptist perfectionist, and apocalyptic point of view, the only hope of Christians was to withdraw into ghettos made up exclusively of converts who had seen the "Inner Light" and were marked by "rebaptism" and "rebirth."[17]

In Europe, as the radical Reformation spread, there were startling manifestations of the exponential growth of schism and anarchy. For instance, in 1534 the Count of Munster was seized by a group of radical Anabaptists, under the fanatical leadership of Jan Beuckels of Leiden. Beuckels and his followers stormed the city hall and destroyed all records of debts and legal contracts in order to show their contempt for private property. They burned books and manuscripts, that they believed represented un-Christian "worldliness," and instituted polygamy and communism in the name of "Christian love."

The new Anabaptist amalgam of radical communist-style egalitarianism, combined with polygamy and violence, horrified the less radicalized Protestant community. After all, Martin Luther and the other Reformers had largely followed the traditional Roman Catholic means of "converting" people to their cause; they converted the princes, kings, lords and dukes and the people were expected to follow the example of their betters. The radical democratization of the Anabaptists was as alien to Luther as it was to Roman Catholicism.

---

[17]The almost xenophobic exclusivist pietism of the Anabaptist foreshadowed the pietism of American fundamentalists particularly in their idea of withdrawal from "the world" and the subjectivity of faith. Jaroslav Pelikan outlines some of the main points of the Anabaptistic rejection of Christian tradition as follows:

"Truly 'apostolic' was whatever was laid down in 'the teaching of Jesus Christ and the apostles' (Menn. Doop. (Harrison 414-15)) regardless of 'all the doctors and learned men,' (Menn. Fund. 5. (Meihurzen 39)) who might have taught otherwise 'ever since the time of the apostles.' (Menn. Doop. (Harrison 420)) Despite the supposed authority of these 'many hundreds of years,' (Drk. Phil. Enchiv. 4. (BRN 10;95)) it was necessary to identify the 'natural light' of human reason, not the Word of God, as the source of such tradition. (True Christian doctrine) had been 'lost for a long time.' (Hub. Bn. (QERG 29;369)) so had all the articles of true apostolic doctrine. . . . For fourteen hundred years (the Anabaptists held) there had existed no gathered church or sacrament.

The true church was a 'little flock' and had always been a minority. From the time of the apostles the church had 'gradually degenerated' into a reliance on 'outward works,' of which . . . 'ceremonies' . . . blatantly manifested their idolatry . . . The true church, 'gathered in the Spirit,' had to separate from the 'carnal church.' " Ibid. pp. 314-17.

REVOLUTIONARIES BECOME THE ESTABLISHMENT

In reaction to the Anabaptists, and their revolutionary actions, the first generation of Protestant Reformers, including Calvin and Luther, began to reverse their earlier revolutionary rhetoric. Where Calvin had once called for uprisings against kings and popes, he and other Protestants began to beg for the maintenance of the status quo. The Protestants drew up several declarations, such as the Augsburg Confession, to stop the chaos they had unleashed. For instance, article Sixteen of the Augsburg Confession reads,

> It is taught among us that all government in the world and all established rules and laws were instituted and ordained by God.

In reaction to the Anabaptists' embrace of polygamy, the Reformed theologians pled in the Augsburg Confession for civil order: "For the Gospel does not destroy the state or the family, but rather approves them."

But the Reformers' sudden discovery of the need for civil order came too late. The Protestant revolution continued apace and Luther and Calvin had to resort to force to maintain order in their ranks. In 1536 Luther signed a memorandum recommending the death penalty for any of the Anabaptist persuasion.[18] Ironically, the schism of the Protestants issued in an era of tyranny, of one group of Protestants against another, more forceful, and certainly just as virulent, as any against which Luther had objected as practised by the Roman Catholic hierarchy.[19]

PIETISM — THE RETREAT FROM REALITY

But far more serious in regard to the future consequences

---

[18]E. Digby Baltzell, *Puritan Boston and Quaker Philadelphia*, p. 61.
[19]Ibid. p. 60.

for Western society were the conclusions that Luther drew because of his fear of the political violence his "Reformation" had spawned. Luther was forced, by the logic of events of his own time, to a kind of schizophrenic conclusion. In the secular "sphere of sin" the use of force might be necessary, in the name of law and order. In the Church, however, only matters of the "Spirit" should be addressed. Therefore, the Church should only be involved with the "inner life."

Luther introduced the idea of the separation of "ordinary life" from the "life of the Spirit." This provided a theological rationale for Luther to duck responsibility for the anarchy, war and rebellion that his "Reformation" had unleashed. In Luther's convenient separation of church and state is found the birth of Protestant pietism, which was formulated as a separation of life into compartments in which "worldliness" could be dealt with in one way and the "life of the Spirit," in another.

Almost from its inception to our own day, Lutheranism tends to leave secular and even ecclesiastical authority to the state and limits its denomination to the role of preaching to the faithful.[20] This pietism was thrust on the Lutheran denomination by its own failure to come to grips with the anarchic external reality it had helped to create.

Calvin, too, ran into the inherent problem of Protestantism, as was so tragically evidenced by his use of violence against those who questioned his character or theology. Without an authoritative body to rule on doctrinal disagreements schism fomented further schism. In emphasizing the importance of the Bible at the expense of the historical Church, Calvin fomented a spirit of rebellion which caught up with him. So he began to stress the need for a highly educated ministry to interpret the Bible.[21] Here then we see the final irony of the Reformation: Calvin's need to create a new theological "tradition" to replace the old, and Luther's flight to pietism, after his forceful oppres-

---

[20]A fact that led to some Lutherans, Schliermacher for instance, to teach that to "be a good Christian is to be a good German." A pietistic philosophy of life that many have said contributed to the passivity of the German church to Hitler's rise and one that no doubt formed the philosophical basis for such twentieth century Protestants, like Billy Graham, who refuse to speak out on issues like abortion because, in Graham's words, "I only preach the Gospel."

[21]"Schism . . . had the tendency to go on spawning new schisms, for even the new sect would not be pure enough for some, who would separate themselves yet again in their quest for a truly holy church." Jaroslav Pelikan, *Reformation of Church and Dogma*, p. 86.

sion of his theological opponents. The Reformers' retreat from idealism to pietistic authoritarianism presents us with a vivid example of the inherent contradiction of simultaneously rebelling against order and tradition, yet insisting on the rightness of one's *own*, new "tradition."

In theory, Calvin stressed the need for people to attempt to understand God's design by themselves and follow God's will individually. But in practice this free-for-all "intuitive" approach produced anarchy, so Calvin began inventing a new Protestant "Reformed tradition" for men to follow. The official confessions of the Lutheran and Reformed Protestants show them rather pathetically scrambling to restore order, even to impose it.[22]

DISASTER

According to Calvin, history was the stage upon which God arbitrarily paraded His capricious works. By the inexorable logic of his theology, Calvin taught that God's design was predetermined, preordained and unmovable. Some, "The Elect" were predestined by God to carry out His design in His theater: the earth. All others were expressly created to be damned. Calvinism seemed to leave mankind mired in its sin, alienated from God and anxious about its own election, yet driven by this alienation and anxiety to carry out God's predestined designs.[23] It was the ultimate "Catch 22" theology.

The fact that Calvin was no longer interested in reforming the historical Church, but wanted to invent a new one, is illustrated by the reality of Calvin's Geneva. Calvin organized Protestant Geneva to become a school for political leadership,

---

[22] *Article XVI of the Augsburg Confession. The Apology of the Augsburg Confession,* Article XVI. *The Formula of Concord,* Chapter XII. *Erroneous Articles Against the Anabaptists,* ff18-14. *Anglican Thirty-Nine Articles of Religion,* Article XXXVI. *The Second Helvetic Confession,* Chapter XXX. *The Belgeic Confession,* Article XXXVI. *The Scots Confession,* Chapter XXIV. *The Westminster Confession,* Chapter XXIII—for a growing and futile body of Reformed and Lutheran confessions that attempted to restore order by proclamation to the disorderly ranks of the rebellious, warring, fractious Protestants to some semblance of unity.

Peter J. Leithart writes: "Having dismissed the Roman view of ritual, the Reformers were faced with the challenge of the Anabaptists . . . they had to resist the apparent logic of Anabaptism without abandoning their principals of 'Scripture alone' and 'faith alone.' " *First Things,* January, 1993.

[23] E. Digby Baltzell, *Puritan Boston and Quaker Philadelphia,* p. 63.

dedicated to training capable and successful men, convinced that they were the elite of the new religion. As "The Elect," it was their duty to lead lesser men in forming the "New Zion."[24]

With the quest for a new moral authority as the intellectual impetus, a gradual shift took place from Holy Tradition to academic and political pursuits—from the ethics of changeless, non-negotiable morality to the ethics of scholarship and the secular ethos.

The Protestants' dilemma of having abandoned the Western Holy Tradition on the one hand, and yet having a desire to maintain order and community on the other, is nicely illustrated by the work of the 17th century scholar, Thomas Hobbes. In an increasingly individualistic and revolutionary Protestant era, Hobbes was obsessed with society's need for authority, security and order. Hobbes, and others like him, began to try and combat the revolutionary free-thinking anarchy they saw in the universities and other intellectual centers of life, a movement that was replacing the historical Church's teachings.

Hobbes recognized the threat of unbridled skepticism. He wrote in his book *Leviathan* (1651), "The universities have become to this nation (England) as the wooden horse was to the Trojans." Hobbes, in the same work, noted that "the chief leaders (are now) ambitious ministers and ambitious gentlemen, the ministers envying the authority of the bishops, whom they thought less learned, and the gentlemen envying the privy council whom they thought less wise than themselves."[25]

Hobbes saw clearly that Protestantism had simply replaced the Holy Tradition with hundreds of new fractured "traditions" of its own. But short of recommending a return to the historical Church, Hobbes could do little more than identify the terrifying slide toward moral chaos. Hobbes proposed various authoritarian social engineering programs to compensate for the loss of the old moral order. Hobbes' resort to social engineering was to become the wave of the future.

[24]Ibid. p. 65.
[25]Thomas Hobbes, *Leviathan*. London, 1651-1968 edition.

CHAPTER NINE

THE BIRTH OF THE AMERICAN CIVIL RELIGION

The Puritans, following John Calvin, gave America's early history its crusading covenant pietism. The Quakers, on the other hand, contributed to our nation's subjective "touchy-feely" quality, perhaps a religious equivalent to Jean Jacques Rousseau's back-to-nature Romantic movement.

The inheritance of the Anabaptist's impulse to anarchy, and to the near complete subjectivizing and privitizing of the spiritual "calling" as an "Inner Light," was popularized by the Quakers. From the Quaker point of view, there was no need even for magistrates, ministers or any kind of formal church or secular authority. They believed that God and His will are to be found only in the prompting of the "Inner Light," within the spirit and heart of each individual Christian as he or she sees fit.[1] Ideally, each individual was to be his or her own "Holy Tradition," "bishop" and "priest." Doctrine, liturgy and instruction were replaced by personal conscience and intuition guided by each person's subjective reading of Scripture "as the Spirit led."

Together, Puritans and Quakers, directly and indirectly, shaped the American Christian consciousness. And while they were superficially opposed to each other on some points of doctrine, nevertheless, they shared many of the same revolutionary aims. Both were anti-episcopal, both opposed the historical Church's authority structures (whether from Canterbury, Rome or Constantinople), both were anti-monarchist and adamant disbelievers in the real presence of Christ in the sacrament of

---

[1] E. Digby Baltzell, *Puritan Boston and Quaker Philadelphia*, pp. 92-93.

112

Holy Communion. Both the Puritans and Quakers stripped their worship of liturgical tradition. Both believed in free-form, make-it-up-as-you-go-along, non-liturgical religious worship. Both rejected, even despised, organized ritual and liturgy, vestments, stained-glass, written prayers, creeds and what they regarded as "idolatrous" statuary or icons. In short, both the Calvinist Puritans and the Quakers were thorough iconoclasts — anti-aesthetic, anti-material and, in the end, I believe, anti-reality. Between them they created an era of American iconoclasm — a new Manichaeism — which revived the old heresies that once plagued the early Church, pitting the flesh against the spirit and the created world against God.

Both Quakers and Puritans were also subjectivists. The Puritans pursued their "calling," the Quakers their "Inner Light." Each had no place in their theologies for the Holy Tradition let alone an objective historical apostolic succession. Both would have argued that the Bible, not the individual, was absolute; but since it was up to the *individual* to determine *what* the Bible said, in effect, the individual became autonomous. The ancient Holy Tradition was traded for thousands of subjective, individual "Holy Traditions."

In Puritan and Quaker Protestantism, the Protestant problem is seen in its glaring totality. Without the guiding principles of Holy Tradition, Protestant Christians had to fall back on their varying interpretations of Scripture. In the end there were practically as many interpretations and intuitions as there were people claiming to be Christians.

Puritans emphasized grace while they were still in England, but defended works after settling in the new world when they themselves became the new establishment. (In this the Puritans followed the lead of Luther and Calvin, whose revolutionary pronouncements had been moderated in the light of the Anabaptist civil unrest.)

In the New World, the Quakers tried to remain true to their early revolutionary ideals and thus developed a whole theology of disownment. Much like today's "progressives" and "liberals," they were determined to remain outsiders, even in the society of their own making. The egalitarian religious ethic postulated by the Quakers was associated with a lack of social authority and created a climate in which extreme individualism could flourish.

The belief in the authority of the historical Church had been rejected by both Quakers and Puritans. It was a short next step to the loss of faith in the authority of all institutions.

TOTAL WAR ON TRADITION

In both Eastern and Western pre-Reformation Europe, the definition of Christendom was one replete with images of one Holy, Catholic and Apostolic Church, centered in the timeless authority of the bishops and priests that administered changeless sacraments and led worshippers in venerable liturgies. Christians held the Church to be the mystical body of Christ, organized by a universal hierarchy of priests and bishops.[2]

What the sectarian movements of the Reformation did was to abolish the authority of bishop, priest, Church and sacrament. New terms not found in Holy Tradition or the Bible, such as "the twice-born fellowship of all believers," were invented to sanctify what was in fact a *secularizing* movement away from the historical Church's religious authority. Intuitive feelings and subjective interpretations of Scripture began to replace the apostolic Holy Tradition as the guiding principle for Biblical understanding. The words, "I believe," began to replace the ancient declaration of faith: "This is what the Church has always taught."

These developments stood in stark contrast to the Church's understanding of Christianity in which, for instance, the average layman in Byzantium and pre-Reformation Western Europe understood his sinfulness but nevertheless was able to lead a life focused on the sacraments. The Christian was confident of salvation because sin could be dealt with in a systematic way by regular use of the sacraments of Confession and Communion, in a liturgical cycle of worship which fostered a mystical

[2]"From very early times an episcopal polity, presumed to stand in unbroken succession from the apostles, had been taken to be one of the criteria of apostolic continuity, in conjunction with the authoritative canon of Scripture and the creedal rule of faith . . . Christ . . . had vouchsafed his protection against the gates of hell only to that church which could legitimately claim this foundation of apostolic polity." Jaroslav Pelikan, *The Christian Tradition*, vol. II, *The Spirit of Eastern Christendom*, pp. 157-58.

relationship with a loving God.[3] The individual Christian looked to the working out of his or her salvation within the context of the larger whole: the historical Church which was visibly present as the Christ-bearing community on earth as well as in Heaven, and gave the Christian the sacramental tools whereby he or she could gradually work out his or her salvation.

In the new landscape of Quakerism and other Protestant sects, however, a stark, inward-looking individualism developed. One's relationship with God was largely defined by one's own feelings about God; one's salvation was secure only to the degree one felt the presence of an "Inner Light" or felt "born again." Nothing external, sacramental, measurable or necessarily apparent to others was of any use in developing one's relationship with God.[4]

Quaker anti-authoritarianism and anti-sacramentalism came directly out of the Anabaptist doctrines of perfectionism. These ideas led the Quakers to abandon most social, political and secular responsibilities, to preach pacifism and, in the end, even to refuse public office or to take an oath of office — even to vote.

It fell to the Quakers to play out the end game of a confused Lutheran reductionist pietism. Luther had separated the idea of being a citizen of the world from being a citizen of Heaven to such a degree that he could advocate the armed suppression and violent persecution of his fellow believers, on one hand, and pietistic non-involvement by Christians in the affairs of government on the other. The anti-authoritarian passivity of the Quakers soon transmuted into an anti-intellectual and anti-

---

[3]"(To the medieval man) the apostolic and catholic faith was 'one faith' because it was a faith that had been delivered once and for all and had been transmitted by apostolic tradition. Therefore it was unchanging and unchangeable, and the very suggestion that it had undergone change or development or growth seemed to strike at the foundation of apostolic continuity." Jaroslav Pelikan, *The Christian Tradition*, vol. 3: *The Growth of Medieval Theology*, pp. 44-45.

[4]This personalized inward-looking religion, which began to replace historic external worship reached it zenith in the pietistic movement lead by such people as Count Zinzindorf who wrote: ". . . As soon as the Savior takes possession of the heart, . . . he immediately tells it about the difference between right and wrong." (Zinz. Beth. 2. (Beyreuther 6 IV. :23)) Jaroslav Pelikan writes: "In the effort to replace 'the external evidence of Christianity, . . . with an appeal to men . . . to look into themselves .. the moral dimension of conversion . . . provided an indispensable component of the new (Protestant) apologetics." Jaroslav Pelikan, *The Christian Tradition*, vol. 5: *Christian Doctrine and Modern Culture*, p. 146.

cultural tradition as well. Whereas the Calvinists and Puritans
were essentially Augustinian rationalists, and produced highly
complex intellectual bodies of dense dogmatic theology in the
Scholastic Western tradition, the Quaker movement produced nothing of the kind.[5] As a result, it became an article of
faith that the social identity of the Quakers should be guided
by no intellectually binding dogma or theology and had to rest
instead on a series of petty personal experiences or, as they
called them, "testimonies," which became as absolute in the
Community of Friends as Calvinist theology was of the Puritan
denominations.

As Historian E. Digby Baltzell points out in his classic *Puritan
Boston and Quaker Philadelphia*, Alexis de Tocqueville was the
first to discover of American democracy that *equality* and *individualism* are two sides of the same coin. Tocqueville showed
how, far from producing creative individuality, both were more
likely to lead to stultifying uniformity in manners as well as
ideas.[6] Today in our secularized churches and schools, in the
best of the Puritan and Quaker "tradition," politically correct
thinking takes precedence over freedom of expression —
ironically, in the name of "sensitivity" to individualism and diversity. Subjective feelings and self-realization have replaced rational discourse, not only in theology, but now even in the
politics of victimization.

The Puritans, Quakers and other Protestants in America had
abandoned kings, popes, princes and hierarchy. They no longer
held the Bible to be interpreted by a non-negotiable, changeless
Apostolic Holy Tradition — part of a living sacramental life that
pre-dated the formation of the Canon of the books of the New
Testament itself. Instead they held the Bible to be a progressive
"self-evident" revelation whose meaning was il-

---

[5]E. Digby Baltzell, *Puritan Boston and Quaker Philadelphia*, pp. 92-105.

[6]See *The Journal of John Winthrop*, (New York, 1908 edition).

In the Bay Colony, governed by the Puritan leader John Winthrop, utopianism was
soon undone by the sectarianism inherent in Protestantism. Winthrop described the
Bay Colony as a "City set on a hill," yet one is struck in reading his account of the
day-to-day events in the Puritan Colony by the fact that at least half of the events
he reports are of the sectarian squabbles between believers. The colony was almost
split in the case of Anne Hutchinson, wherein she took issue with the other colonists
over the "indwelling of the Holy Spirit." There was a move to "banish" one minister,
Roger Williams, over theological differences. Only ten years after their arrival, the
Puritan community was riven by dissent, shaken by one split after another, and
threatened with ecclesiastical anarchy.

luminated, not by changeless, apostolic, historically-rooted Holy Tradition, but by the individual whims of each Christian who read it, as God "spoke" to his or her heart, and as he or she "stood on the word."[7]

THE NEW MULTIPLE PERSONALITY

As American history moved beyond its short-lived Puritan and Quaker era, most Americans seemed not to have been troubled by the fact that they now held fast to two contradictory intellectual and religious systems. On the one hand they nostalgically believed in a residual, biblical Christianity that still purported to be concerned with salvation, if no longer with history, worship or sacrament. Yet, on the other hand, they seemed to be living by the inspiration of Enlightenment secularism of the kind that taught that man was perfectible without God and that sin was a figment of the imagination.

As I have remarked earlier, Americans came to believe that all human problems could be cured by the right laws, good feeling, enlightened economic policies and scientific inventions.[8]

In this context, Protestants began to view the Bible as merely a source of personalized, rather than universal, truth. The historical Church had always held the Bible to be a part of an *external* sacramental Holy Tradition. The Bible was to be interpreted by the mind of the Church, not by the whims of individuals or self-proclaimed leaders, let alone to have its meaning determined by the intuitive feelings of those who read it. Protestants reversed this and increasingly used the Bible as a mirror with which to look inward. In radical contradistinction, Protestantism placed individuals' feelings about God, the Bible and morality at the heart of Christian teaching.

The philosophers of the Enlightenment borrowed from Prot-

[7] "The fundamental issue, as it had been in the Reformation and in the Enlightenment, was authority. 'We are,' Keble lamented, 'practically without a court of final appeal in doctrinal causes.' " Jaroslav Pelikan, *The Christian Tradition*, vol. 5: *Christian Doctrine and Modern Culture*, p. 242.

[8] "But if Americans, for the most part, rejected the anti-religious bias of the French philosophers, they enthusiastically embraced the utopian elements in Enlightenment thought. They believed that it was possible to establish a more or less perfect society in which freedom, justice and equality would prevail and everyone would be happy according to his or her deserts." Page Smith, *The Shaping of America*, p. 36.

estantism's subjective utopian expectations. They translated the idea of heavenly perfection into earthly expectations of material and political progress. They also borrowed from the Calvinists in adopting a "scientific" reductionist approach to reality.[9] The "enlightened" Americans expanded upon the ideas of the French philosophers. No longer was perfection to be achieved in Heaven but rather now, here on earth by whatever means were necessary, not excluding bloody revolution.

FRANKLIN AND JEFFERSON

Benjamin Franklin was typical of the new American secularists. He took the Quaker-Rousseaunian style of personalized "intuitive" faith to its logical conclusion. He dismissed the notion of historical Christianity and sin altogether and attempted to achieve humanistic perfection in this life by his own efforts and with no reference to Christ. He made his own list of what he called his "twelve virtues" and tried to live by them. To do this, he devoted one week to each and tried to achieve perfection by living by the rule of his own weekly "beatitude."[10]

Christ was demoted by Franklin and Jefferson (as well as others such as Benjamin Rush) to a "wise" and "good" man, a supreme "moral teacher." As for God, He might be an active principal in the universe but He was certainly no longer on any personal or intimate footing with mortals. American Deism might be said to have represented no more than French Enlightenment-Romantic movement humanism, with a nostalgic whiff of Calvinist and Quaker Protestantism thrown in for good measure.

The Incarnation of Christ was seen by the American Deists as unnecessary. Historian Page Smith writes of Benjamin

---

[9] "In all the annals of recorded history we find no mention of any *political* revolution that took this form of the French Revolution: its only parallel is to be found in certain *religious* revolutions. Thus when we seek to study the French Revolution . . . it is to the great religious revolutions we should turn." Alexis de Toqueville, *The Ancien Regime and the French Revolution*, p. 41.

[10] Page Smith, *The Shaping of America*, pp. 315-17.

Franklin's theology: "There is no mention of Christ, the Son or of the Holy Spirit. Underlying Franklin's theology is the notion that anyone can pretty much make up his own religion to suit himself."[11] This making up religion to suit oneself was, of course, what Protestants since Luther had been doing all along, albeit dressing up their intuitive assertions as "Biblical."

Jefferson, in particular, was a devout missionary for the French Enlightenment. He religiously believed in reason, science and progress as alternative social foundations to the historic Christian faith. There came into being through the influence of Jefferson and other prominent American founders what Page Smith has called the "secular democratic consciousness." Encouraged by Jefferson, this secular democratic consciousness soon became the predominant political force in American life, as it had already become the mainstay of European post-Christian countries before. Religion, at least of the hierarchical, sacramental, liturgical and traditional kind, was relegated to the sidelines.[12]

The Last thing the far-off "God" of American Humanism embodied was any set personality or doctrine that would run counter to modern ideas of "progress" or the rationalistic materialistic and individualistic spirit of the age. The "Christ" or "God" that "lived within" each individual's heart could be individually tailored to each person's taste. What was needed to conquer the great American landscape unfolding to the West

---

[11]Idem. *A People's History of America*, vol. 3, p. 317.

[12]Jefferson represented the paradigm of the American secularism that came to full fervor in the nineteenth and twentieth centuries. He would not expose his children to the Bible, which he regarded as "demoralizing" (with all its sordid stories of sin, repentance, suffering, depravity, and realism), but selectively taught instead, "the useful facts" of Greek, Roman, European and American History. Children, Jefferson said, should be taught the first elements of morality, so that they could achieve happiness, the pursuit of which Jefferson had guaranteed them. By "morality" Jefferson did not mean the morality of Moses or Jesus of Nazareth, or the Christian Holy Tradition that had been passed down from one generation after another, but the secular civic virtue of the new world order espoused by Samuel Adams in which "Men of science and virtue" would create "perfect peace" by their own politically enlightened efforts.

"Perfect peace" and "happiness," it soon became evident, could much more easily be provided by a benevolent modern super-state than by the backward-looking historic Church that believed that sorrow comes from sin and that peace only comes from sacrificial holiness, and that political "solutions" to moral problems are counterproductive and usually coercive.

Nowhere in the Jeffersonian-American secularized civic virtue ideal is a statement found that true happiness, i.e., the peace that passes understanding, can only be acquired in a restored relationship to God through Christ, in a life lived as a sacramental act of worship and in a realization that mankind is not perfectible but rather morally teachable only by virtuous example.

was optimistic political and religious harmony. Since there were thousands of competing denominations, this unity could only be achieved by relativizing all of them as "equally true" and by rendering religion into a purely "personal matter." In the New World, the last thing anyone wanted to hear about were claims of spiritual religious truth, especially of the kind that would impose limits on economic growth, call the American experiment into question or exclude any lucrative economic activity whatever. Christianity was reduced to little more than a pep talk in favor of the power of positive thinking. People were exhorted to get their "hearts right with God." But they were never called to hearken to the wisdom of the patristic Fathers of the Church.

It surely was not a coincidence that the American enterprise came to be described as a "dream": the "American dream!" Reality, let alone ancient history, was not welcome to intrude into the exhilarating American experiment. Whatever was new was seen as good and progressive; the term "old-fashioned" became a pejorative expression.[13]

Thus was formed that curious mixture of moralistic piety, individualism, pluralism, ruthless materialism and millennial romantic utopianism that is so uniquely Protestant and American in character. Samuel Adams, writing to Jefferson, embodied this new generic pseudo-Christianity perfectly.

> The principles of democratic republicanism are already better understood than they were before. . . . By the continued efforts of Men of science and virtue . . . (the) turbulent and destructive spirit of war shall cease . . . and those classes of men who have hitherto been the victims of their age . . . shall perpetually enjoy perfect peace and safety till time shall be no more.[14]

Samuel Adams' rosy utopianism was later echoed by both Marx and Hitler. Man *could* be the master of his own destiny, so long as he disencumbered himself of "old prejudices" and found the "correct" historic, political, racial, eugenic, economic,

---

[13]Upon his inauguration to the Presidency in 1993, Bill Clinton nicely summed up the utopian-millennial American expectation: "There is nothing wrong with America that what is right with America cannot cure."

[14]as cited by Page Smith, *The Shaping of America*, vol. 3: *The Shaping of the Young Republic*, p. 323.

scientific or technical solutions to his shortcomings. *Science,* and political right-mindedness, would usher in a "new society," a "new man" and a new millennial age of "perfect peace and safety till time shall be no more." In America, the words "change" and "new" began to take on the aura of sacred creeds in much the same way as the word holiness had once epitomized the aim of monastic life.

If the outmoded past held any meaning for Samuel Adams, Thomas Jefferson and company, it was chiefly as a yard stick against which the "New Canaan" could measure its future successes. Reason, the American founders believed, could create a better world. In this new world order such ideas as sin, repentance, grace, the apostolic succession or "old fashioned" changeless sacramental liturgies, were mere impediments to creating a bright, new, free future. As Professor Steve Bruce writes,

> Religious beliefs were not abandoned because they were suddenly thought to be wrong. They simply became less and less important. . . . The consequence of the spread of (Protestant-Enlightenment) rationality from the economic sphere (to the heretofore religious sphere) can be summarized as the replacement of ethical by technical concerns, of moral constraints by practical problems: A modern social system . . . increasingly conceived as operating without (historic religious) virtues.[15]

Religion came to be seen as only one more useful political-psychological component with which to build an economically prosperous secular state. The adherents of the new American civil religion of progress held that the real key to fulfillment was not to be found in old-fashioned religion, but in the future of secular science and pluralistic democratic civic virtue. Religion's chief purpose was seen to be a "useful tool" to provide peace of mind and social order, while people could be helped toward a man-made utopia. The quest became one of self-fulfillment, not obedience to God, much less Christ, who had instructed His followers to "take up your cross and follow me," and who had given His disciples and their successors in the Church special priestly authority.

[15]Steve Bruce, *A House Divided,* pp. 19-20.

By encouraging the idea of autonomy from sacramental worship, Holy Tradition and ultimately from God, Protestantism had promoted the idea that the here and now was a good deal more important than the hereafter. This idea was expanded upon by the American Deists in imitation of the other Enlightenment thinkers. While maintained in the popular religious imagination as a transcendent entity, the jealous God of Abraham began to lose His importance in the American scheme of things.

CHAPTER TEN

PERSONALIZED TRUTHS

If the old shoe of traditional Christian faith and liturgical-sacramental creedal worship no longer was comfortable, America's Protestants would make a new one that would better fit the spirit of the age.

As Page Smith writes,

> A people capable of devising a better plow or more efficient wagon proved equally ingenious in inventing new religions. These were New Lights, Universalists, . . . Swedenborgians, Spiritualists. . . .[1]

As the pluralistic American Protestant frenzy for self-realization built to a fever pitch in the eighteenth and nineteenth centuries whole new frontier cults, sects and religions were invented practically out of thin air in ever increasing numbers in order that the American enterprise might be dignified with a sense of religious mission. Seventh Day Adventism had its prophetess in Ellen G. White. The principles of Christian Science were "discovered" by Mary Baker Eddy. Joseph Smith founded Mormonism. The "born again experience" replaced historic forms of sacramental worship as the new "sacrament" of frontier fundamentalism. Tent-meeting style Protestantism became a way of life. When services moved from the tent to the church, constant exhortations to become "born again," rather than to enter into the life of the historical Church, became normative.

[1] Page Smith, *The Shaping of the Young Republic*, vol. 3: *A People's History of America*, p. 755.

As the conquest of the frontier proceeded, the American penchant for creating new religions to suit every taste, and to assuage every troubled conscience continued apace. As Peter J. Leithart, pastor of Reformed Heritage Presbyterian Church, writes,

> Protestant Evangelicalism, it seems, has a symbiotic relationship with American denominationalism. Evangelicals trace their deepest roots to the Protestant Reformation, which was, among other things, a church split. In America, experiential revivalism and disestablishment have combined to liquidate churchliness and encourage sectarianism.[2]

Professor Steve Bruce writes concerning the results of this explosion of denominational sectarianism,

> Even those sociologists who explain secularization as a result of industrialization, urbanization and the increased rationality of the modern world, would have to recognize that Protestantism was importantly implicated in its own fate. . . . One has the image of reformed Christianity as its own grave-digger . . . Protestantism hastened pluralism and hence secularization, . . . the fragmentation of Protestantism was a sufficient cause of its own demise. . . .
>
> Claimed reliance on the Bible as the sole source of authoritative knowledge, despite the best efforts of its promoters, has consistently failed to produce coherence, consistency and uniformity. Instead, it has generated schism. . . . The essence of reformed Protestantism may be described sociologically as individualistic. The inevitable . . . consequence was the rise of religious pluralism and the expansion of the secular state.[3]

Protestants eagerly embraced the secular religion of Rousseau, whose basic dogma was that the voice of the people, or the voice of "nature" and "history," was the voice of "God." Democracy, which was held to be the "wave of the

---

[2] Peter Leithart, "A Review of *Evangelical Reunion*," *First Things*, October, 1992.

[3] Steve Bruce, *A House Divided*, p. 23 and pp. 229-30.

future," was soon given the aura of a "sacred tradition."[*] Conveniently, this new American "sacred tradition" held that the "American dream" — in other words, the pursuit of individual autonomy, wealth and happiness without moral limits — was the same thing as the thirst for righteousness.

Increasingly this secular American "tradition" or "dream" became unrelated to any underlying religious or moral first principles. The right to happiness and prosperity gradually came to be as unquestioned as the Holy Tradition of the Church had once been, before the Reformation. Public buildings and coinage might bear the inscription "In God We Trust," but the "God" being trusted was an American god invented to suit contemporary and materialistic tastes and to provide a sense of purpose for a vulgar, theologically illiterate people.

THE NEW AMERICAN "RELIGION"

The free-for-all of skepticism ushered in by the rationalists of the Renaissance, Reformation and Enlightenment soon gave way to a new dogma of secularized orthodoxy in which the vulgarities of politics and science run amok replaced religion as the final source of moral values. Thus the "voice of the people," the "voice of history," the "march of progress," was understood increasingly as the sacrosanct guiding principal of political change and revolution against convention. For "progressive" people, being on the "right side of history" or "scientific progress" began to have the same importance that being on the right side of God once had for traditional Jews and Christians. Inevitably, public opinion became confused with morality, and poll-takers with prophets.

Instead of Holy Tradition, Americans, who felt the psychological need for religious support systems, could turn to the various personalized expressions of devotional internalized "faiths" now multiplying in the Republic. Each person, denomination or sect, was free to interpret their "Christianity" as they saw fit. Chaos came to be seen as the "normal" state

[*]The promise of a "utopia" is found throughout the *Federalist Papers*. "A republic. . . promises the cure for which we are seeking." *Federalist Paper* No. 10, Madison (New York, 1961 edition).

of affairs in the burgeoning denominations. The idea that the words "The Church" meant more than a collective description of all denominations, whether a day, a decade, or millenia old, was abandoned.

The right to believe and do anything one wanted to, whether good or bad, true or false, trivial or profound, no matter the consequences of one's beliefs or actions, was held up as proof that the "American dream" worked.[5] The idea that there were certain sacred *non-negotiable* moral-religious truths which were *above* political debate or personal opinion — for instance, the sanctity of human life, including "imperfect" human life — was also gradually abandoned along with fixed forms of liturgical, creedal and sacramental Christian worship. All that remained of the Christian faith was an experiential, nostalgic, personalized and non-communitarian exercise in selfish, often bizarre religiosity and sentimentality.

The historic understanding of what Christian life, worship, faith and sacramental practice had been for nearly two thousand years was all but abandoned. The inheritors of the legacy of the council of Dort and the Protestant ahistoric Anabaptist denominations began to manufacture their own religious reality, worship and theologies, regardless of historical legitimacy or precedence.

Just as the eighteenth and nineteenth century patent medicine manufacturer was free to advertise any noxious concoction as a cure-all, so the self-proclaimed religious leaders of the Protestant sects in America were free to label any and all theology as "Christian," no matter how unrelated to the faith of the historical Church it was.

In America, by the late nineteenth century, politics had replaced religion as the great motivater in human affairs. And by the late twentieth century science had replaced God as the search-and-destroy mission against "imperfect" babies so startlingly illustrates, wherein genetic discoveries, amniocentesis and abortion have resurrected the Nazi eugenic program, repackaged as "pre-natal testing."

The Protestant experiment has run its course. The Protes-

---

[5] "The danger of rights being overridden by abstractions is the danger posed by a 'secular' approach that is typically utilitarian in its calculation of interests. In that approach . . . all values and all truth claims are reduced to the status of individualistic 'interests.' " Richard John Neuhaus, *The Naked Public Square*, pp. 120-21.

tant churches have been fragmented, their influence replaced by the state, priests have been replaced by self-proclaimed "pastors" who now, in turn, give way to the "New Canaan's" politicized "priests": bureaucrats, politicians, scientists, doctors, social engineers, geneticists and their media "prophets."[6]

THE "THREE-LEGGED STOOL"

The new eighteenth and nineteenth century pluralistic American do-it-yourself religions could scarcely have been farther from the ancient Christian faith and Holy Tradition of the historical Church. Once it had been held *by all Christians* that one's Christian life rested on three *equally important* sustaining legs, much like a three-legged stool. The first was adherence to changeless *doctrine*. The second was *moral behavior*. The third was participation in *sacramental worship*.[7] These three interlocking facets of the Christian life were understood to provide the basis for how one went about *being* a Christian, as opposed to merely saying how one *became* a Christian.

Protestants incrementally sawed off one leg of the stool after another. For a start, any idea that how one worshipped was important — let alone absolute — was abandoned wholesale since the competing Protestant sects could not agree on what worship was, let alone on how to celebrate it. In America, even to suggest that certain forms of worship, creed or sacrament were better than others branded one as un-American, anti-pluralistic, even anti-democratic. Like Cain, the Protestants felt free to make up new forms of "worship." They also felt free to abandon any sacramental traditions that they no longer found "useful," sufficiently "progressive," or even "fun."

---

[6] "We are living now in an age of intellectual chaos and disintegration. Possibly modern man has not yet made up his mind, and the variety of opinions is beyond any hope of reconciliation." Georges Florovsky, *The Collected Works*, vol. 1: *Bible, Church, Tradition: An Eastern Orthodox View*, p. 10.

[7] "The source of this changeless truth was to be found in 'the dogmas of the evangelists and apostles and prophets' (Maximus. Pyrr. (P.G. 91:328)) . . . the foundation of faith was the authority of the apostles . . . the clarity of Scripture certified it as the supreme authority of Christian doctrine." Jaroslav Pelikan, *The Spirit of Eastern Christendom*, pp. 16-17.

[8] . . . Religious emotionalism carried the day on the (eighteenth and nineteenth century American frontier . . . We speak of this fragmentation . . . as 'American religious pluralism.' " Page Smith, *The Shaping of America*, pp. 314 and 324.

In eighteenth, nineteenth and twentieth century America, ancient Christian worship was jettisoned in favor of various home-grown revivalist expressions on the one hand and Unitarian reductionism on the other. Any type of religious carousing, which appealed to whatever passing religious taste was now labeled as "Christian" worship. If your heart was "right with the Lord," who cared how you worshipped? That was entirely up to you. After all, "America is a free country and who's to say one person's idea of worship is better than another's?" "We'll have no elites, popes or princes in America!" "Who cares about history and precedent?" "Isn't the whole idea to create a *new* and *better* world?" "As for religion, it's a personal matter!" "One church is as good as another!" "Didn't President Kennedy get elected *because* he promised his Roman Catholic faith would *not* influence his decision-making? Isn't *that* the American way?"

Next to be abandoned was the second leg of the stool — traditional moral teaching and behavior. Easy divorce, toleration of adultery, acceptance of materialistic greed as a national "right," racism, legalized abortion on demand, the search-and-destroy mission for "imperfect" babies through pre-natal testing, are some of the more dramatic departures from the teaching of the historical Church by the Protestant-Enlightenment "Christians" that have made up their own rules of worship, and morals, regardless of Christian Holy Tradition. And how could any right-minded Protestant protest? Is it "any business of ours" what "consenting adults choose to do" any more than its "our right to interfere with how people choose to worship?"

As Episcopalian Bishop John Spong writes in a typical expression of American religious moral inventiveness,

> (We are called) not only to repentance . . . but also to inclusiveness. (We are called) to set aside our fear and be open to . . . those who do not fit the church's narrow definition of sexual morality . . . (If the church) wishes to have any credibility as a relevant institution, (it) must look at the issues of single people, divorcing people, post-married people and gay and lesbian people from a point of view removed from the patriarchal patterns of the past.[9]

[9] John Spong, *Living in Sin? A Bishop Rethinks Human Sexuality* (San Francisco, 1988), p. 39.

Finally, the last leg was jettisoned. The historic Christian creedal doctrines confirmed by the seven ancient ecumenical councils, were gradually abandoned. The Greek root of the word heresy means to pick and choose. Protestants began to pick and choose mightily over many doctrinal issues.[10] This again should have been anticipated as the natural result of the way in which the Reformers went about delegitimizing the Holy Tradition, the Canon of the Bible and the Holy Sacraments.

As we have seen, Reformers like Zwingli had largely abandoned or reduced the Eucharist to a mere symbol. Later modern theologians like Bishop Spong took Zwingli's deconstructionist Reformed logic a step further and deconstructed such areas of traditional faith as the belief in the Virgin birth and the sacramentality of marriage. By the late twentieth century, even some so-called Evangelical Protestants had come to accept materialistic greed as "moral." They even developed a whole cult of wealth aptly called the "Prosperity Gospel." At the other end of the ideological spectrum, liberal Protestants began openly "ordaining" women and homosexuals to the priesthood and openly proclaiming the virtues of legal abortion on demand, fetal experimentation, euthanasia and prenatal testing, as well as appointing women to "edit" the text of Scripture to suit the new politically correct, "inclusive" gender politics of the moment.

If Luther, Zwingli or Calvin were to come back from the grave and protest that things had now gone too far, the modern American Protestant, perhaps a woman Episcopalian "priest" or a Presbyterian homosexual "pastor" could answer with perfect reasonableness that he, or she, merely "interpreted" certain passages of Scripture "differently" than the Reformers. And who could say which "interpretation" was correct?

Tearing out the first leg of the three-legged stool — Holy Tradition, Church authority, and historic Christian sacramental worship — resulted in the other two legs being torn out as well. What began as a challenge to traditional liturgical wor-

---

[10]"John Milton was speaking for a growing number of (Protestant) individualists . . . when he explained that he had 'decided not to depend upon the belief or judgment of others in religious questions,' but 'to puzzle out a religious creed for myself by my own exertions' (Milt. Doct. ep. (Patterson 14:4)) . . . Milton's biographer identified 'the imposers of creeds, canons, and constitutions' as, 'the common plagues of mankind.' (Tin. Chr. 11 (1730 163-64))" Jaroslav Pelikan, *Christian Doctrine and Modern Culture*, pp. 30-31.

ship and apostolic continuity, ended up as a challenge to Christian morality, even basic doctrine itself. In other words, nothing was regarded as sacred by the end of the twentieth century in this best of all possible "New Worlds."[11]

[11]"Whereas Europe became secular by people leaving the churches, American churches retained members while themselves becoming secular . . . pluralism has a delegitimating and hence corrosive effect on religion." Steve Bruce, *A House Divided*, pp. 179 and 181.

CHAPTER ELEVEN

THE NEW REALITY: POLITICS AS RELIGION

Paul Johnson, the famous British historian, writes,

> By the turn of the century politics was replacing religion . . .
> the political zealot offered New Deals, Great Societies and
> Welfare States. . . .[1]

By the late twentieth century, the only real absolute in European and American life became the faith that there are *no moral absolutes* other than the obligation of each citizen to realize his or her "full potential."[2] Once the idea took hold in the West that there were no rules, no limits and no natural laws, the only obstacle to a brighter future was understood to be backward religious ideas. A modern example of this mentality is found in the homosexual movement wherein "homophobia" is understood to be the "sin," not homosexual behavior. Secularized America came to believe that reality was anything one wanted it to be. Everything could be changed or negotiated through political action to enhance one's personal "choices." Even biology could be legislated. If you said something was true, and repeated the idea

---

[1] Paul Johnson, *Modern Times* (New York, 1983), p. 729.

[2] "Today we seek 'salvation' by 'realizing ourselves,' 'expressing ourselves,' 'getting what is due us out of life,' extracting from the pressures and anxieties produced by the need to achieve and 'get ahead' in American society some precious essence of happiness and indulgence." Page Smith, *A People's History of America.* vol. 3: *The Shaping of America*, p. 760.

often enough, or made laws to force people to act as if it were so, then you could make even reality conform to ideology. Square pegs *could* be forced through round holes, given a sufficient politically correct pounding. The biological, spiritual and psychological differences between men and women could be overturned by court decisions. Mere facts would not be allowed to stand in the way of political ideology. Women *would* be found to be suitable for combat roles in the military, whether they were or not. Abortion *would* be promoted as the solution to unwanted pregnancy — whatever biology, genetics and fetology told us factually about the humanity of the fetus. Men and women who abandoned their spouses to pursue careers or other lovers *would* be encouraged in their selfish pursuits, whatever common sense or scholarly study showed about the adverse effects on their children. "Homophobia" *would* be "discovered" to be abnormal, not homosexual behavior. Pre-natal testing *would* be encouraged at the very same time as the law was cosmetically changed to force communities to build facilities for handicapped people. Damn reality — full speed ahead! We *will* have our cake and eat it too! Moreover, we *will* "feel good about ourselves" *no matter what!*

UNWELCOME REALITY

Modern Americans discovered that although reality had supposedly been rearranged to suit them, some people still inexplicably seemed to need some sort of religion. So it was tacitly decided to be religious and secular at the same time. Americans worked hard to have the feelings of "good, God-fearin' folks" while doing bad things. Above all, Americans learned to "feel good" about themselves, no matter what they did. No matter how contradictorily Americans arranged their lives to give the impression to themselves of virtue; for instance, installing special access ramps for the handicapped in the very hospitals in which a search-and-destroy mission for "imperfect" babies was being aggressively waged, through a program of pre-natal testing to identify all future handicapped persons, Americans were told to "feel good about yourself." Reality was not allowed to spoil a good time! Disneyland could co-exist with the revival of Nazi eugenics, abortion with motherhood, families with divorce. The word "choice" became the watchword. *What* you chose did not matter.

America developed into a secularized state that was nevetheless highly "religious" in a non-traditional, aggressively materialistic, egocentric sort of way.[3] A hunger and thirst for "self-esteem," "empowerment," "productivity" and "happiness" replaced the desire for sacrificial faith in a nation now irredeemably adrift from any fixed concept of reality or a higher, non-negotiable moral order.

America is now a nation in which Christianity is thought to be just one more item on the consumerist menu of special interest offerings that may help some individuals prosper and succeed in the never ending American past-time — the quest for self-realization without limits and without feelings of guilt or responsibility for the ultimate consequences of one's actions.

Modern America is a nation in which over 90 percent of the people say they "believe in God" and over 60 percent say they have had a "born again" experience.[4] But evidence of the fact that these beliefs are purely personal, subjective and internal is overwhelming. The divorce rate, the crime rate, the abortion rate, the wide acceptance of pre-natal testing for "defective" babies, the incidence of illegitimacy, the venereal disease epidemic, the disintegration of our cities: all of these give us a precise idea as to just how internalized, non-sacramental religion fails to effect external realities and behavior. We Americans may say we "believe in God," but apparently this "God" merely calls us to enjoy ourselves.

FOR THE SELFISH, BY THE SELFISH
OF THE SELFISH

With Christian religion reduced to the level of a sectarian

---

[3]"In the Puritan town salvation was thought of as something that happened within the community of the faithful. . . . When the older covenanted communities began to break down under the pressure of increasing social and religious diversification, the emphasis came to be on the individual's search for salvation. . . . The disestablishment of the original denominations . . . hastened the shift to what we might call personal Christianity." Ibid. p. 759.

[4]Gallup polls, 1988-91.

squabble in America, a hedonistic, secular-revolutionary world view dominates our culture in spite of our rather superficial, non-sacrificial religiosity and sentimental philanthropy. The American people like to style themselves "good" and "generous" at heart. But with the actual reality of American life taken into account, one wonders what real meaning these words now have. After all, the word "good" was once used to denote a certain standard of virtuous behavior, not just a feeling about one's self.

Sometimes the secular-revolutionary American vision has been dressed up as authentic, even "fundamentalist" religion, by Evangelical revivalist Protestants in our recent past as well as in our own day. But judged by behavior, the true ideology of America — "born-again" or otherwise — has become that of the classic Enlightenment-Romantic movement a vision of: a new aristocracy of materialistic success rather than apostolic authority, of high self-esteem and personal satisfaction, rather than holiness. This pseudo-religious vision has emerged to dominate education, the humanities, big-time religion, government and politics. It is thought that reason, and large doses of experiential non-traditional, individualistic religion, will produce "goodness" in America, and no leader of the old moral order need apply. Emerson, the high priest of American individualism, expressed this sentiment as follows: "Nothing is sacred but the integrity of your own mind . . . the highest revelation is that God is in every man."[5]

POLITICS REPLACES RELIGION

The seeds of the modern secular, super-state big, government without moral limits — what has been called the "nanny-state" were sown by French, then American humanists who believed in the power of reason and science to solve all mankind's

[5]"The Protestant Reformation had invented the individual, but he or she was an individual closely bound up in a community of the faithful. . . . The new (American) version of the individual of which Emerson became the prophet was the free-floating, autonomous individual." Page Smith, *A People's History of America*, vol. 4: *The Nation Comes Of Age*, pp. 522-23.

problems.[6] Protestants had created a vacuum of moral leadership by abandoning the ancient sacramental liturgies, apostolic hierarchy and Holy Tradition of historical Christianity. Their nihilistic work was completed by their secularized disciples, the leaders of the French, then the American Enlightenment and Romantic movements. Having begun by abandoning Holy Tradition and patriarchal authority in the name of "individual liberty," the Protestants and their Enlightenment followers ironically ended up by shaping a world in which, absent Church authority, absolute power was inexorably vested in the ever-expanding, insatiable, secular state.

Since rampant limitless individualism soon degenerated into chaos — divorce, abortion, crime — people increasingly turned to the government — taxes, social programs, welfare — to keep order and to provide solutions to social problems that grew exponentially following the breakdown of the old moral order.[7] As we have seen, this is not to say that a wholly atheistic culture was created. Indeed, lip service to God abounded — and abounds — in the New World. But the "God" now worshipped is a god wholly circumscribed by a larger reality, i.e., the secularized, materialistic, statist "American Dream," the politics of pleasure, self-realization and entertainment, and the worship of economic growth are now understood to be ends in themselves.

"God" has His place in American society, but He is reduced to one more component of the glorious new whole — the "American Dream" — in which Protestants, and protestantized Roman Catholics, and not a few secularized materialistic Orthodox can continue to claim the mantle of "Christianity" and at the same time devote most of their attention to what they regard as the only real game in town: economic prosperity and

---

[6]". . . Eighteenth century philosophers attacked the Church with a sort of studious ferocity . . . they sought to demolish the very foundations of Christian belief. . . . No previous political upheaval, however violent, had aroused such passionate enthusiasm, for the ideal of the French Revolution . . . it was not merely a change in the French social system but nothing short of a regeneration of the whole human race. It created an atmosphere of missionary fervor and, indeed, assumed all the aspects of a religious revival." Alexis de Tocqueville, *The Ancien Regime and the French Revolution*, translated by Stuart Gilbert, pp. 39 and 43-44.

[7]"Those who had once filled the ranks of the totalitarian clergy would become totalitarian politicians. And, above all, the Will to Power would produce a new kind of messiah, uninhibited by any religious sanctions whatever, and with an unappeasable appetite for controlling mankind." Paul Johnson, *Modern Times: The World from the Twenties to the Eighties*, p. 48.

political, ideological, crusades to reshape mankind in a new utopian image in order that the human race may become even more "prosperous."

In this selfish, secular quest, some Roman Catholic and Orthodox bishops, priests, and theologians seem to have been infected with the utopian, Protestant-Enlightenment sickness. They, too, appear to seek *political* (for instance, feminist), not spiritual, solutions to people's problems. They, too, call on the state to expand its programs, bureaucracies and initiatives to bring "justice" which they now understand almost wholly in political-economic or gender terms. In particular, the agenda of many American Roman Catholic bishops seems to be no more than the agenda of the statist-big government American Left with mere nuances of Christian ethics added as an afterthought.[8]

Some Roman Catholics and some Orthodox in America may now be irretrievably politicized. However, they became so in imitation of Protestant, "liberal" theologians of the kind who dominate the World Council of Churches. Thus, Protestants have poisoned the well from which they were drawn and have, as Professor Bruce writes, learned to,

> . . . accept the assumptions and agenda of the modern secular world. Although the Bible is still accorded pride of place in the rhetoric of . . . Protestants, it is interpreted in the light of modern reason and culture . . . (there is) a continual impulse to modernize the faith, to abandon the confines of the historic creeds, and to accommodate the thought and practice of the churches to those of the secular world.[9]

In their abandonment of Holy Tradition, religious truth was individualized by "Conservative" and "Liberal" Protestants alike. In reality, in the American context the labels of "Liberal" and "Conservative" are meaningless. There is no such thing as a Conservative Protestant any more than there were "Conservative" Bolsheviks. The history and continued existence of Protestantism is an ongoing revolution against the Christian precedent. This is so even though many Protestants claim that the

---

[8]". . . There is a perceptible pattern in the postures of politically liberal Christians. The pattern involves political agreement with secularists who make no secret of their contempt for religion." Richard John Neuhaus, *The Naked Public Square: Religion and Democracy in America*, p. 34.

[9]Steve Bruce, *A House Divided: Protestantism, Schism and Secularization*, p. 102.

Bible is their ultimate moral base. Since the interpretation of the Bible is no longer subject to the Holy Tradition, to the Church from which the Bible came or to the mind of the Church of the ages, and is no longer part of the daily discipline of liturgy, prayer and worship, it transpires that the Bible is made to say whatever one likes. Therefore the only voice in society that speaks with authority is the state, since its laws alone are seen to be absolute, not open to personalized revelation.[10]

Morality is increasingly the sole preserve of the state in America. Whether something is "legal," "constitutional" or even merely scientifically possible has become, for many Americans, more important than religious questions of right and wrong. Above all, it seems that the bottom line for most of the American public, religious or secular, of the political Left or Right, is whether the state can deliver economic prosperity which the Left calls "justice" and the Right calls "growth" and both claim to be a "fundamental right."

Perhaps unwittingly, our founders left us in a condition in which political power has increasingly become absolute and unchallenged. Since religious truth has been relativized and personalized, real human rights — the rights to life and to free speech, for instance — have slowly diminished. This trend has been amply demonstrated by the militant intolerance shown toward "politically incorrect" speech on our university campuses, and the intolerance of unwanted unborn Americans, the "defective" unborn, poor, black, sick and elderly people, and others who are perceived to stand in the way of economic self-realization. There seems to be little room in our society for those who might once have been called "the least of these."

Since religion and the traditional hierarchical institutions of family and church are now subordinate to the state, all spheres of life have tended to become politicized. Politics, especially in its most popular form that is, economic, medical,

---

[10]Paul Johnson describes the ultimate expression of twentieth century godless secularism: "[Lenin] had systematically constructed, in all its essentials, the most carefully engineered apparatus of state tyranny the world has ever seen. . . . And there was [no] notion of an external, restraining force in the idea of a Deity, Natural Law, or some absolute system of morality. Lenin's new despotic utopia had no such counterweights or inhibitions. Church, aristocracy, bourgeoisie had all been swept away. Everything that was left was owned or controlled by the state. All rights whatsoever were vested in the state." Paul Johnson, *Modern Times*, p. 84.

and social engineering, is increasingly the only game in town. From the halls of academia to the declarations of modernized American Roman Catholic bishops, everyone seems to be turning to the state for "social justice." When we speak of "morality" today, more often than not, we are talking about social, economic or political "morality," in the now familiar rhetoric of "rights." We are not talking about sin, repentance or individual accountability.

Religion has not escaped this politicization. It has been relegated to the role of providing weak-minded people with the motivation for civic virtue, or personalized, psychological well-being. In this new context religion no longer deals with questions of objective truth, but only with what makes its followers feel good or with what helps them to live productive, i.e., materially "successful," "happy" lives.

Like everything else, religion today is merely an extension of our quest for the secular, material and psychological happiness which the state now guarantees as a "right" of its citizens, without which its citizens are described as "victims." We consume happiness as we do any other product. Like psychology, the product of modern religion is meant to make us feel "whole." It does not demand any kind of sacrifice, much less a hard walk along a life-long, difficult road toward God as we choose to follow Him day by day.

American religion is thus the opposite of the historic Church's vision of salvation as expressed by Greek Orthodox Archbishop Iakovos: "The ultimate hope for every Christian (is) of being one with Christ, completely conformed to His image. . . . True faith comes only after years of searching, testing and experiencing God's love in the practical situations of life."[11]

CONCLUSION

The so-called born again experience of Fundamentalist Protestantism is the perfect expression of the consumerist religion of our times. It demands no more of us than we wish to feel saved. In Protestant circles, "salvation" has become a

---

[11]Archbishop Iakovos, *Faith for a Lifetime* (New York, 1988), p. 14.

self-willed instant cure, a state of mind rather than an objective, sacrificial, long-term journey toward God achieved through sacramental, orderly worship. Spirituality is thus cut off from the external, measurable, actual sacramental life in the Church and now exists only in its own internalized world of emotional feeling. In the climate of private pietism on one hand and politicized Christianity on the other, the ancient spiritual truths of the Church, which once encompassed inward *and* outward manifestations of spiritual growth, have withered.[12] Worldly life and religion are now separated into water-tight compartments.[13] Amongst other reasons, this is because the traditional meeting point between the world and religion, between the flesh and the Spirit — *in other words, the Eucharistic feast* — has been abandoned.

---

[12]For instance, in the American Roman Catholic bishops' embrace of Leftist causes and in the embrace of the politicized, even pagan, World Council of Churches by some bishops in the Orthodox Church, the politicization of even the historic Church progresses apace. As Paul V. Mankowski notes:

"(There is) a crisis affecting American religion: the profound . . . gap between ordinary churchgoers and the administrative *nomenklatura*. (T)here has been talk in American Catholic circles of a 'party of change,' that, 'dominates the fields of liturgy, religious education, justice and peace offices, campus ministry, Catholic higher education . . . this new clerisy is by and large contemptuous both of the beliefs of the faithful and of the tradition in which beliefs are nurtured. Indeed, the prime effort of this detachment of the knowledge class is precisely to insulate the common man from authentic religious tradition so as to render him more easily manipulable by conventional political pressure. . . . The struggle is to insure that those who control the rhetoric by which power is exercised are fully enlightened individuals, those who can be relied upon to insure that correct politics will triumph." "Academic Religion: Playground of the Vandals," *First Things*, May, 1992.

[13]"False religions perpetuate a great divide between flesh and spirit, rather than between good and evil where (historic) Christianity says it lies." Thomas Howard, *Evangelical Is Not Enough* (Nashville, 1984), p. 31.

CHAPTER TWELVE
THE LAST STEP

Our American founders naively failed see where their new faith in reason, science, personal freedom and utopian individualism would lead. They thought a new "Golden Age" of man could be achieved without the moral authority and teaching of the Holy Tradition, beyond an invocation of the name of God, or Jesus, from time to time to lend more authority to what was essentially a humanistic exploit. Learning and science were to be the keys to human progress, not righteousness. And none believed this more than the utopian Protestants who were setting out to build their new world in the field of education.

EDUCATION, PLAYGROUND OF
THE SECULARIZERS

In the early years in our nation's life, there was an attempt made in our universities to balance the new Protestant-Enlightenment secular vision with some of the older teachings of historic Christianity.[1] But from around 1800 onward, what little religious traditionalism remained was constantly challenged in academic circles. The new emerging state colleges of the early twentieth century never even made a pretense of

---

[1] "Such colleges were animated by the Protestant passion for the redemption of the world. The centerpiece of their curricula was a course on 'Moral Philosophy,' often taught by the president of the institution, who was invariably a minister." Page Smith, *Killing the Spirit*, p. 40.

traditional religious affiliation and were decidedly secular from their beginnings.² These secular universities were the first institutions of their kind in the history of any known civilization: schools started with the express purpose of educating students in a purely secular fashion.

Colleges like Yale and Harvard, which once had religious affiliations, quickly became battlegrounds between a dwindling band of defenders of Protestant religion and the so-called liberal forces who soon won the secularist versus religionist battle, and began to dominate higher education. "Practical curricula" replaced curricula with a traditional religious or classical orientation. In reaction to the aggressive secularization of the universities, various Protestant denominations, still paying lip service to the civic usefulness of religion, began founding their own universities. Such colleges were, as Page Smith writes, animated by the Protestant passion for the redemption of the world in the here and now, through being "born again," through scientific and civic virtue — the kind of Christian virtue that helps to foster a healthy economy and a happy, care-free life.³

Yet even though some new religious institutions were established to mitigate the so-called practical curricula of the secular schools, the utilitarian revolutionary Protestant spirit that pervaded them, in turn, led these institutions into the same moral uncertainty as their secular counterparts.⁴ By the early twentieth century, in America, the crusading secular drive for material self-improvement animated almost all institutions of higher learning. From this time on, education was largely seen as a purely *secular* enterprise, a turn of affairs that would have shocked not only the Fathers of Christendom but Plato, Aristotle, Confucius and Martin Luther as well. For the first time in the history of the world, the links between education and

---

² "Religion, Protestantism specifically, suffered a serious erosion. Educated young men like Oliver Wendell Holmes announced their skepticism. . . . The dominant intellectual current of the time was Transcendentalism, a credo of which Ralph Waldo Emerson was the principal prophet. . . . Darwinism was (also) welcomed by the Secular Democratic Consciousness as an ally, in the fight against religion and on behalf of science." Ibid. p. 46.

³ "The political consequences of these events was the formation of the Populist Party, the most radical political party of our history, whose heart and soul was the radical, evangelical, fundamentalist Protestantism of the farmer of the Midwest." Ibid. p. 52.

⁴ "In the new (religious) universities as well as the old, the clergy, who had dominated the boards of trustees of colleges, were replaced by businessmen, lawyers, bankers and railroad tycoons." Ibid. p. 59.

character formation through religious moral teaching had been deliberately severed.

The idea of changeless truth was abandoned by the academic secularists and the Protestant crusaders alike. Self-improvement, through man's own efforts, was seen as the true path to enlightenment. The predominant view was that religion was sometimes "useful" only because, ". . . the conversion of the individual was a precondition for social improvements."[5]

The utilitarian ideas that formed modern concepts of educational philosophy further secularized what little remained of the Christian witness. The notion that the improvement of social conditions was the purpose of evangelism, instead of salvation from sin, came to be widely accepted.[6] Social action became the alternative to traditional religion, just as the practical curriculum replaced the teaching of moral philosophy.

As Professor Steve Bruce writes,

> The general point worth emphasizing here is that it was not just the liberals who were being influenced by new currents in their culture. Those who were later dubbed fundamentalists were not motionless in the cultural sea change . . .
>
> In the 'progressive' and optimistic elements which they incorporated . . . the conservatives were also very much products of their times.[7]

Professor William H. Willimon of Duke University writes: "Fundamentalists deplore all things modern, yet their theology is a ringing endorsement of the modern American nation-state."[8] The Protestant "born-again" experience of instant, easy and magical religious "conversion" was put to the service of new world utopian optimism in American society. New self-proclaimed Christian leaders emerged to try and fill the vacuum created by the new secular onslaught in education. These leaders' pastoral call was exercised wholly outside of the context of the historic Church with its ancient apostolic succes-

---

[5] Steve Bruce, *A House Divided*, p. 103.

[6] "Charles Grandison Finney was the virtual inventor of this form of active Christianity, which he adapted from the frontier revival . . . adding generous amounts of 'social conscience.' " Page Smith, *The Nation Comes of Age*, p. 510.

[7] Steve Bruce, *A House Divided*, p. 103.

[8] *First Things* (August, 1991).

sion. Thus a new "hierarchy" of individualistic charismatic church leaders, each a kind of self-proclaimed sectarian "Moses," was born in America, as it had been before in the Europe of the Reformers.[9] The final blow against the orderly apostolic succession of the ancient Church had been struck in reaction to the final encroachments of secularism into American education and life. Now religious leadership would also be merely an extension of popular opinion. Self-proclaimed "patriarchs" would lead the "church." Their legitimacy would rest on their popularity and their talent for entertaining the flock.

FINNEY AND COMPANY

Charles Finney was one of the pre-eminent self-proclaimed leaders in the nineteenth century American Protestant movement. A minister and revival meeting preacher, Finney was the religious-political father of the prohibition movement and one of the first of a long line of solitary, empire-building revivalists.

America had seen its first "great awakening," led by Jonathan Edwards, in the eighteenth century. But Charles Finney's revival in the first quarter of the nineteenth century was the first of a whole line of uniquely Americanized "revivals" that combined self-proclaimed non-apostolic leadership with the popular post-Victorian passion for middle-class civic virtue and "good," or rather polite, feminized public behavior — Puritanism of the lace-hanky, women's-home-Bible-study variety.

The seeds of Protestant devolution were contained within these so-called great awakenings. Each successive wave of "revival" had less impact on the surrounding culture. Wholly secular agencies began to fulfill the social needs of the nation even more efficiently than the revivalists and their largely feminized, para-church agencies could. In the first awakening, large numbers of people were involved and patterns of social behavior changed visibly. These changes included temperance and anti-slavery agitation. By the third awakening far fewer

---

[9] The techniques of the first self-anointed "evangelists" were so successful that they spawned hundreds of imitations, such as Lyman Beecher, David Macrae, John Humphry Noyes, and many others.

people were involved and the social changes were less measurable.[10] By the time of Billy Graham in the 1950s and the televangelists of the 1970s, a wholly personalized individualistic brand of "Christianity" was being espoused that amounted to little more than religious psychotherapy.[11] This internalized religion of the subjective "born again" experience had little impact on the general culture or its continuing love affair with materialistic relativism, individualism and hedonism — the American way of life.[12]

Nothing illustrates the cultural futility of the nineteenth and twentieth century revivalistic Protestant movements, more than the rise of the so-called Religious Right of the 1970's. Supposedly a movement which was to "bring America back to God" (which or whose god was not clear), the Religious Right's ascendancy took place at the very time the incidence of abortion, divorce, racism, illegitimacy, homelessness, drug abuse and illiteracy were skyrocketing. The social pathologies of the day were apparently unaffected by the drum beat of the Religious Right's politicized, repackaged nineteenth century revivalism. The millions of new "converts," the Religious Right (and the televangelists) boasted, seemed to be more adept at pursuing the "American dream" than ever, but they seemed largely oblivious to any sense of the sacred beyond personal experiences of the "God made me prosperous" variety. The call to journey toward Christ through suffering, discipline, hard work and a sacramental life of liturgical-Eucharistic worship, in which the content of one's character gradually changed for the better, had been wholly replaced by the easy "born again" experience;

---

[10]Steve Bruce, *A House Divided*, pp. 209-27.

[11]Typically, even the Protestant Churches got short shrift. After one made a "personal commitment to Jesus," one was largely on one's own. Billy Graham was typical of the new individualism when he exhorted the newly-converted to "attend the church of your choice next Sunday" after they had "come forward" at his crusades. Given the immense and self-contradictory number of "churches" in America, ranging from Unitarian churches that did not even acknowledge the existence of Billy Graham's God, to the charismatic denominations, the fact that Graham added church attendance at any "church" as an afterthought to the main business at hand — becoming "born again" — is a perfect example of the contemporary evangelical movement's low view of Church, sacrament, apostolic succession and the place of worship, confession and priestly guidance in the life of the Christian.

[12]"Since the advent of pluralism made the church type of religious organization impossible, believers have had the choice of the denomination or sects. The denomination's lack of definitive differentiation from the surrounding culture makes it precarious . . ." Steve Bruce, *A House Divided*, p. 232.

a little nostalgic sentimental political sloganeering about "traditional family values," and the jingoistic drumbeat of American nationalism.

The whole of the Religious Right's enterprise petered out in a morass of infighting, between various politico-religious groups, scandal, money grubbing and empire building by various leaders of the movement. The final debacle was the failure of the Religious Right's president, Ronald Reagan, to realize even *one point* of the Religious Right's social agenda during an eight-year presidency. His successor, George Bush, also refused to use the prestige of the presidency on behalf of any of the Religious Right's moral concerns, beyond expedient political grandstanding on the sanctity of life and prayer in school issues. Pathetically, the Religious Right's ascendancy ended with a rather ludicrous presidential campaign by Pat Robertson, one of the empire-building televangelists of the day.

In 1992, the election of Bill Clinton, whose first initiatives as president were to expand the power of the state and push the New Left's social agenda in areas from abortion "rights," including fetal experimentation, to "homosexual rights," only underscored the Religious Right's failure to engage the wider culture effectively when it had a chance to do so.

AMERICAN HYPOCRISY

Whereas in Europe, Protestantism led to secularized people leaving the churches, in the sentimental anti-reality climate of American utopian optimism the "Conservative" Protestant denominations retained members while themselves becoming secularized in conformity with the prevailing materialistic consensus. This secularization process was achieved by personalizing faith into nothing more than a subjective internal private experience.[13] This slow, but sure, unraveling of the historic mission of the American Protestant denominations was one that began with a call to a "born again" experience instead of sanc-

---

[13]"The 'scandal' of American Protestantism — its ceaseless fragmentation — meant that a new version of Christianity could be invented to meet the needs of every subdivision or faction in American society." Page Smith, *The Nation Comes of Age*, p. 510.

tity, and ended with a "prophetic" call to consumeristic well-being in order that a certain "lifestyle" could be maintained at any cost. This consumerist lifestyle was understood to be the evidence of "God's special blessing" of Americans as an "almost chosen people."

This is not to say that many a fervent Protestant was not on a journey toward God, or that all contemporary Roman Catholic bishops and parishes were the hopelessly politicized dupes of the political New Left, or that all the hard social work of many dedicated Protestants in the 1970's was in vain, or that such movements as the pro-life crusade did not bear good fruit, not least of which were the compassionate acts of charity toward pregnant women by the Protestant-led Crisis Pregnancy Center movement. Yet in spite of these mitigating factors, it seems to me that Protestantism was increasingly cut off from the roots of the historical Church.

Increasingly, Protestantism has become a part of its surrounding culture. It is now being molded rather than molding. It has become the religion of sentimental convenience and rationalistic self-improvement. It seeks to accommodate and finally imitate society's trends. Protestant "faith" has therefore gradually become indistinguishable from the secular civil culture. Its leaders tend to be just another set of celebrities running corporations called "churches," "ministries" and "charities," whose business is self-perpetuation and whose very lucrative "product" is good spiritual feelings.

Protestantism not only destroyed itself, but to some extent, it has spread its relativistic, modern contagion to the leadership of the historical Church as well. In America, under the corrosive influence of Protestantism, many Roman Catholic bishops and priests have become more akin to politicians, bureaucrats and social planners than to men of holiness. Even the Orthodox Church has suffered. Some of its bishops and priests have been seduced into a one way "dialogue" with largely apostate Protestant denominations in the so-called ecumenical movement, the sort of "dialogue" that the Fathers called "theology without prayer," which St. Maximus the Confessor referred to as the "theology of demons."

Part Two:

Authentic Orthodox Faith

CHAPTER THIRTEEN
THE HISTORICAL CHURCH

The late Georges Florovsky, the great Orthodox scholar who was Professor of Eastern Church History at Harvard University, wrote,

> The Church is Christ's work on earth; it is the image and abode of His blessed Presence in the world . . .

> Outside the Church there is no salvation. All the categorical strength and point of this aphorism lies in its tautology. Outside the Church there is no salvation because *salvation is the Church*. For salvation is the revelation of the way for everyone who believes in Christ's name. This revelation is to be found only in the Church . . .

> The realm of the Church is unity. And of course this unity is no outward one, but is inner, intimate, organic. It is the unity of the living body, the unity of the organism. The Church is a unity not only in the sense that it is one and unique; it is a unity, first of all, because its very being consists in reuniting separated and divided mankind. . . . In the Church humanity passes over into another plane, begins a new manner of existence. A new life becomes possible, a true, whole and complete life, a catholic life, "in the unity of the Spirit, in the bond of peace." A new existence begins, a new principle of life, "even as Thou, Father, art in Me, and I in Thee, that they also may be in Us . . . that they may be one even as We are one."[1]

[1] Georges Florovsky, *Bible, Church, Tradition: An Eastern Orthodox View*, pp. 37-39.

147

According to the writings of the Fathers, the confusion which surrounds us is not what God intended for His Church.[2] The lawlessness of our culture need not have infected the historical Church with relativism.[3] Indeed, the culture itself need not have been degraded by false Christianity and the secularism that followed in its wake, because the authentic historical Orthodox Church is still present on earth. The Christ-bearing community, against which the gates of hell have not prevailed, survives to this day.

According to the Church Father and martyr, St. Ignatius of Antioch, writing in A.D. 110, the Church is to be a place of order, unity and apostolic authority.

> Take care to do all things in harmony with God, with the bishop presiding in the place of God, and with the presbyters in the place of the council of the Apostles, and with the deacons, who are most dear to me, entrusted with the business of Jesus Christ, who was with the Father from the beginning and is at last made manifest. Do not be led astray by other doctrines nor by old fables which are worthless.[4]

St. Ignatius of Antioch was the bishop of that city, succeeding St. Evodius who was ordained by St. Peter. St. Ignatius wrote a number of letters to the churches in Asia, all of which confirmed apostolic authority and succession as the foundation of the one Holy Catholic and Apostolic Church. These remarkable letters, written on St. Ignatius' way to a cruel martyrdom in the arena, defend the order and discipline indispensable to the practice of authentic Christianity. St. Ignatius was killed in Rome, but not before his letters were delivered to the seven

---

[2] "For Jesus Christ, our inseparable life, is the will of the Father, just as the bishops, who have been appointed throughout the world, are the will of Jesus Christ. It is fitting therefore, that you should live in harmony with the will of the bishop . . ." St. Ignatius of Antioch, *Letter to the Ephesians*, 3, 2, A.D. 110, in *The Faith of the Early Fathers*, vol. 1, trans. W. A. Jurgens, p. 17.

[3] ". . . The relationship between religious fragmentation and secularization can be summarized . . . fragmentation produced by Protestantism was central in that a monolithic and hegemonic religious culture, (as existed prior to the Reformation) would have provided greater resistance to secularization." Steve Bruce, *A House Divided*, p. 27.

[4] St. Ignatius of Antioch, *Letter to Magnesians*, Ref. 44 and 45, A.D. 110, in *The Faith of the Early Fathers*, vol. 1, trans. by W. A. Jurgens, p. 19.

churches.[5]

Many denominations claim to be churches. But if the words "The Church" are to retain any meaning, we have to ask ourselves what we mean by them. Is "The Church" merely the general collection of people who say they are Christians?[6] Or does the word "Church" have a historical meaning in the same way that words like "France" or "Great Britain" indicate actual places, not just an idea or a feeling of being French or British in spirit?

Well known author and Orthodox priest Anthony M. Coniaris writes,

What do we mean when we use the word 'church?' Look at the tremendous variety of groups that call themselves churches. In fact, anyone can (now) establish a church for himself. . . . But are they truly churches? Were they founded by Jesus and the Apostles? What kind of historical connection do they have with the apostles. . . . We Orthodox Christians mean by Church the Body through which Jesus is present in the world today. It was founded by Christ through the Apostles and has maintained a living, historical connection with the Apostles through the ordination of clergy. The fact that the bishop who ordains an Orthodox priest today can trace his ordination historically all the way back to the Apostles and through them to Christ is a guarantee that the Orthodox Church was not founded by someone called Joe Smith a few centuries ago but by Christ Himself and traces its existence back to Jesus.[7]

For the words "The Church" to have more than a relativistic meaning, they cannot be understood outside of the context of

[5] Because his letters are so early in date and so clearly definitive in their call to Apostolic authority, Holy Tradition and hierarchy, schismatics, heretics and Protestants, particularly those such as the Anabaptists, have at various times tried to discount the legitimacy of them. However the authenticity of these letters has been long since established by various scholars including J.B. Lightfoot, Adolf Van Harnack and Theodore Zahn. Their authenticity is now universally accepted and accepted with it is the knowledge that as early as A.D. 110, a mere 60 or 70 years after Christ's death, and within living memory of the Apostles themselves, apostolic authority was vigorously being defended by the Fathers of the Church.

[6] Anthony M. Coniaris, Introducing the Orthodox Church (Minneapolis, MN, 1982), p. 1.

[7] Ibid. p. 1.

the Church's own well-documented history and her consistent teaching about herself and the secular historic record. The Church has always taught that in order to be authentically apostolic, those claiming to be bishops or priests must be able to show an unbroken historical continuity with the early apostolic Church that was founded by Jesus.[8] As St. Paul wrote, "For no other foundation can anyone lay than that which is laid, which is the Christ." (1 Cor 3.11).

The outstanding and distinguishing feature of the historic Church is its changelessness, its continuity, its faithfulness from age to age and its orderly apostolic succession.[9] According to Holy Tradition, the Church's mission, to carry on what was begun by Christ, did not come about by coincidence but was deliberately established by Christ Himself.[10] According to Scripture, we are told that,

> When Jesus came into the region of Caesarea Philippi, He asked His disciples, saying, "Who do men say that I, the Son of Man, am?" And Simon Peter answered and said, "You are the Christ, the Son of the living God!" Jesus answered and said to him, "Blessed are you, Simon Bar-Jonah, for flesh and blood has not revealed this to you, but My Father who is in heaven. And I also say to you that you are Peter, and on this rock I will build My church, and the gates of Hades shall not prevail against it. And I will give you the keys of the kingdom of heaven, and whatever you bind on

[8]"One of the principal concerns of the apologists (of the Christian faith in the early Church, A.D. 100-300) was to demonstrate the continuity of the gospel with the history of God's revelation in the world . . . the presupposition . . . was that the primitive deposit of Christian truth had been given by Christ to the apostles and by them in turn to the succession of orthodox bishops and teachers. . . . In its earliest Christian use, the term 'heresy' was not sharply distinguished from 'schism'; (1 Cor. 11:18-19) both referred to factiousness . . . Factiousness . . . 'discussions and difficulties, in opposition to the doctrine which you have been taught' (Romans 16:17)" Jaroslav Pelikan, *The Christian Tradition*, vol. 1: *The Emergence of the Catholic Tradition* (100-600), pp. 68-69.

[9]St. Paul rebukes any who would stray from the unity of the Church and follow after self-proclaimed leaders. "For when one says, 'I am of Paul,' and another, 'I am of Apollos,' are you not carnal?" (1 Corinthians 3.4)

[10]"The preaching of the Church truly continues without change and is everywhere the same . . . constantly it has its youth renewed by the Spirit of God. . . . In the Church, God has placed apostles, prophets and doctors, and all the other means by which the Spirit works . . . For where the Church is, there is the Spirit of God . . ." St. Irenaeus, *Against Heresies*, A.D. 180, in *The Faith of the Early Fathers*, vol. 1, trans. W. A. Jurgens, p. 94.

earth will be bound in heaven, and whatever you loose on earth will be loosed in heaven." Then He commanded His disciples that they should tell no one that He was the Christ (Mt 16.13-20).

THE FIRST BISHOPS

The Jews alive during Jesus' time were confused about who Jesus was. They thought that perhaps He was a dead prophet returned to earth. The disciples had shown several times that they were as capable of misunderstanding Jesus as His crowd of followers. Jesus told Peter that the difference between Peter's understanding and the crowd's blindness was not Peter's intelligence, nor even his faith or his goodness; it was that God had chosen to reveal the truth to Peter and the other Apostles before it was revealed to others. Peter and the others had a special task to do and they were given special knowledge.

God chose Peter and the other Apostles in a unique way to establish His eternal Church on earth. Christ spent most of his ministry training and teaching the Apostles for this historic mission. Far from being egalitarian in the use of His time, Christ dedicated the majority of His energies to training a select, hand-picked group of future leaders. In other words, according to the Gospel accounts, most of Christ's ministry was spent establishing and training the men who would lead the Church rather than teaching a mass of individuals.

Jesus promised conflict and triumph for His Church. Hades itself would make war on the Church but it would "not prevail against it" (Mt 16.18). Just as the Father anointed the Son, so Jesus chose the Apostles who would carry on His work. This was evidently the Apostles' understanding of their mission, since the historic record of the early Church unequivocally shows the Apostles began appointing successors before they died.[11]

[11]"The earliest Christians were Jews and in their new faith they found continuity with the old . . . From the early chapters of the Book of Acts we get a . . . picture . . . the members of the church at Jerusalem, which Irenaeus called 'the Church from which every church took its start' (Iren. Haer. 3.12.5.) . . . (This church) followed James, who as 'the brother of the Lord,' was a kind of 'caliph' . . . (Stauffer, 1952, 193-214)." Cited in Jaroslav Pelikan, *The Emergence of the Catholic Tradition*, p. 13.

Jesus gave the Apostles special power to bind and loose on earth and in heaven (Mt 16.19). If we believe the writings of the New Testament and in the truthfulness of the Fathers, Christ Himself established the authority of the Church and its ministry on earth. From the very beginning, the Fathers of the Church respected and diligently followed Christ's pattern of authority in Church governance.[12] And, as we have seen in St. Ignatius' letters, the Fathers vigorously defended the Church's authority, just as Peter, Paul, and the other apostles had.

The historical record shows that the early Church was of one mind in regard to apostolic authority, and legitimacy. In the Didache, the teachings of the Apostles, (A.D. 80-140) we read,

> Elect for yourselves, therefore, bishops and deacons worthy of the Lord, humble men and not lovers of money, truthful and proven; for they also serve you in the ministry of prophets and teachers. Do not, therefore, despise them, for they are your honorable men, together with the prophets and teachers.[13]

At an even earlier date (A.D. 75-80) well within the living memory of the Apostles, St. Clement of Rome, who had been ordained by the Apostle Peter, and who had been appointed and taught by him personally, wrote in the most specific terms about the orderly succession of the bishops.

> (Christ) has commanded the offerings and services to be celebrated, and not carelessly or in disorder, but at fixed times and hours. He has, moreover, by His supreme will, determined where and by whom He wants them carried out so that all may be done in a Holy manner, according to His good pleasure and is acceptable to His will. . . . To the high priest, indeed, proper administrations are allotted, to the priest the proper place is appointed, and upon the Levites

[12]"Those, indeed, who belong to God and to Jesus Christ — they are with the bishop . . . if anyone follow a schismatic, he will not inherit the kingdom of God . . ." St. Ignatius of Antioch, *Letter to the Philadelphians*, A.D. 110, in *The Faith of the Early Fathers*, vol. 1, translated by W. A. Jurgens, p. 22.

[13]*Didache*, Ref. 9, A.D. 140, *The Faith of the Early Fathers*, vol. I, translated by W. A. Jurgens, p. 4.

their proper services are imposed. The layman is bound by the ordinance of the laity. Let each of us, brethren, in his own rights, be well-pleasing to God and have a good conscience, not overstepping the defined rules of His administration in dignity. . . . The Apostles received the gospel for us from the Lord Jesus Christ; and Jesus Christ was sent from God. Christ, therefore, is from God, and the Apostles are from Christ. Both of these orderly arrangements, then, are God's will. . . . Our Apostles knew through our Lord Jesus Christ that there would be strife for the office of bishop. For this reason, therefore, having received perfect foreknowledge, they appointed those who have already been mentioned, and afterwards added the further provision that, if they should die, other approved men should succeed to their ministry.[14]

St. Ignatius of Antioch is counted as an apostolic Father by reason of his having been a student of the Apostle John. As we have seen, on his journey to martyrdom from Antioch to Rome Ignatius wrote seven letters in which he outlined and defended not only the Apostolic succession, but God's order given to the true One Holy Catholic and Apostolic Church.

At the hour of his martyrdom, St. Ignatius held the orderly continuity of the apostolic Church in such high regard that he spent his last days on earth diligently defending the form of Church governance established by Christ. In A.D. 110, he wrote,

For Jesus, our inseparable life, is the will of the Father, just as the bishops, who have been appointed throughout the world, are the will of Christ. It is fitting, therefore, that you should live in harmony with the will of the bishop.

. . . Let us be careful, then, if we be submissive to God, not to oppose the bishops.

. . . It is clear, then, that we must look upon the bishop as the Lord Himself. Indeed, when you submit to the bishop as you would to Jesus Christ, it is clear to me that you are

---

[14]St. Clement of Rome, in *Letter to the Corinthians*, Ref. 19, 19A, 20, 21, A.D. 80, *The Faith of the Early Fathers*, vol. 1, trans. W. A. Jurgens, p. 10.

living not in the manner of men, but as Jesus Christ, who died for us, that through faith in His death, you might escape dying.

. . . In like manner let everyone respect the deacons as they would respect Jesus Christ, and just as they respect the bishops as a father, and the presbyters as the council of God and college of Apostles. Without these it cannot be called a Church.

. . . He that is within the sanctuary is pure; but he that is outside the sanctuary is not pure. In other words, anyone who acts without the bishop, the presbyters and the deacons does not have a clean conscience.[15]

St. Irenaeus, the second bishop of Lyons and a pupil of Polycarp, who was the disciple of St. John the Evangelist, in A.D. 180 wrote,

For the Church, although dispersed throughout the whole world even to the ends of the earth, has received from the Apostles and from their disciples the faith in one God. . . .

The Church, having received this preaching and this faith, although she is disseminated throughout the whole world, yet is guarded, as if she occupies but one house. . . . She, harmoniously, proclaims (the truth) and teaches it and hands it down as if she possessed the one mouth. For, while the languages of the world are diverse, nevertheless, the authority of the tradition is one and the same. . . .

Nor will any of the rulers in the churches, whatever his power of eloquence, teach otherwise, for no one is above the teacher; nor will he who is weak in speaking detract from the tradition.[16]

It is foolish to suppose that those such as St. Ignatius and St. Irenaeus — the direct inheritors of the teaching of the Apostles — misunderstood the Christian faith and the godly

---

[15]St. Ignatius of Antioch, *Letter to the Ephesians*, A.D. 110; *Letter to the Magnesians*, A.D. 110; *Letter to the Trallians*, A.D. 110, in *The Faith of the Early Fathers*, vol. 1, trans. W. A. Jurgens, pp. 37-55, pp. 17-23.

[16]St. Irenaeus, *Against Heresies*, Ref. 191-192, A.D. 180, in *The Faith of the Early Fathers*, vol. 1, trans. W. A. Jurgens, pp. 84-85.

order of church government that had been preached to them. It is supremely arrogant to suppose that we, some two thousand years later, have a better idea of God's plan for Church order than did the actual hearers of the Apostles and the second generation of Christian bishops, many of whom were martyred for their faith. And yet, all historical evidence to the contrary, it is just this supposition we are asked to swallow by those who say that Protestant, make-it-up-as-you-go, individualistic, schismatic "Christianity" is the Christianity of the early Church.[17]

There are those today who trivialize the special authority given to James, who was the first bishop of the Church in Jerusalem, and to Peter, as well as the other Apostles and bishops they appointed, by saying that it was given to "all believers." This belief was, of course, the basis of the Anabaptist anarchy and the Quaker privatization of the faith.[18] This makes nonsense of Christ's specific words (Jn 20.21-23), not to mention the practical understanding of Church government by the first generation of Christians, and all those who followed them, until the rebellious Protestant era of the very recent past. It also makes nonsense of Paul's letters to the churches. In the Epistles, we see that Paul, Peter and the others expected to be obeyed. Unless there was an orderly structure and Church discipline in the early Church, the very existence of the Epistles makes little sense.

THE MALE HIERARCHY

There are also those who say that the male hierarchy of the

---

[17]The extreme expression of this is found in the Anabaptist teaching that, except for themselves, there had been no "true church" for the 1700 years preceding them after the first generation of Christians died. Even today most Evangelical groups ignore church history altogether, or at best mention only Luther, Wycliff, or perhaps St. Augustine. The impression given is that Christianity magically appeared in about the year 1510 and only came to its full flowering in the 19th century with the revivals of Finney, Moody, etc.

The most propagandistic, anti-historical fabrication by a Protestant author of recent memory regarding the historical Church is *The Open Church* by James H. Rutz. This book typifies the Protestant myth of a "simple" non-hierarchical "early church."

[18]See Chapter 3 and footnotes.

Church was a mere "cultural phenomenon," a mere reflection of the "patriarchal" society in which Christ lived. They say that we must move beyond the boundaries of an ancient civilization and "update" Christ's teaching to suit the modern taste for politically correct religion. This assertion logically raises an interesting question. If Jesus is the Son of God, the Creator, who "made them male and female" (Gen 1.27), then why did God not foresee the need to instruct the Church to model itself on the gender politics and changeable sexual fashions of each successive age? Female leadership was not unknown in Christ's time. He made reference to the Queen of the South coming to hear Solomon's wisdom. Moreover, the Hebrew Scriptures are full of women heroes, just as the historical Church is full of Holy Mothers and women saints equal in spiritual standing with Holy Fathers and male saints.

As writer Sheldon Vanauken notes,

> One of two things must be true if women can actually become priestesses: Either God the Father made a mistake and has now changed His mind. Or Jesus who was God incarnate did not do the will of the Father. The first is nonsense. The second amounts to a denial that Jesus was the incarnate God.

> Any argument for the priesting of women that is based upon the Holy Spirit leading the Church into new truth *must* also account for old error — the sixty wronged generations of women. I submit that it *cannot* be done without denying the Incarnation.[19]

If Jesus was "limited" by the culture in which He lived, then how can He be God? And if He is not God made flesh through the free choice of a woman, blessed Mary, Mother of God, then what does it matter what His Church does? It becomes just another cult whose faith is in vain "scriptures"; one, moreover, flawed by sexism and homophobia. Furthermore, how is it that those who demand the "updating" of the Church, whether through the debunking of apostolic continuity, by accepting

---

[19]Sheldon Vanauken, *Under the Mercy* (Ignatius Press, 1988) as cited in "Since God Doesn't Make Mistakes: Women's 'Ordination' Denies the Incarnation," *AGAIN Magazine* April, 1993.

abortion, or by denouncing the male priesthood, claim to be part of the "historic continuity" of the Church when the *changelessness* of Christian truth has been one of the central claims of the Church throughout its history?[20] If Christ is the Son of God, as the Church teaches He is, and He established His One, Holy, Catholic and Apostolic Church to last till "the end of this age," how is it that schismatic Protestants, modernized Roman Catholics and even a few protestantized "Orthodox," do not acknowledge the importance of apostolic succession, Church order and the hierarchical authority that makes Church discipline and purity of doctrine possible?[21]

[20]"To identify the orthodox doctrine of the catholic (universal) church meant to hold to that which the fathers had handed down by tradition. . . . 'Let us,' said Maximus, 'guard the great and first remedy of our salvation. (I am referring to the beautiful heritage of faith.) Let our soul and mouth confess it with assurance as the fathers have taught us.' (Maximus. Ep. 12. PG 91:465 'We do not invent new formulas . . . for this is a presumptuous thing to do, the work and invention of a heretical and deranged mind.' (Maximus. Opusc. 19 PG 91: 224-25)." Jaroslav Pelikan, *The Spirit of Eastern Christendom*, p. 20.

[21]As well-known Orthodox author and Dean of St. Vladimir's Seminary Thomas Hopko explains, "Leadership in the Church, especially in regard to the priesthood, is much more analogous to a family relationship than to a societal relationship. My question would be: Is there such a thing as fatherhood? Is there such a thing as the husband? . . .

All through Church history until now, you find very powerful men and women living the spiritual life. You find very strong monastic life. You find incredible theological arguments and articulations over a wide array of issues. When you take what is given, how the formulation of the Faith was articulated, how people actually lived, how men and women really related — and I'm talking about the saints; I'm not talking about what happened in society, because ecclesiastical history is very different from the Holy Tradition of the saints — you have to ask the question: Why is it that you have women canonized as saints, monastics, missionaries, prophets, teachers, ascetics, healers, evangelizers, but never through that whole period was a woman ordained to be a presbyter or a bishop in a particular Christian community?

But the key question is: Is that really what the priesthood is? Is it not a particular function for the edification of the Body in relation to all the people, which only certain members of the Body are able to adequately carry out, because they happen to have certain qualifications? And if it is in fact the paternal function, the sacramental calling to be a *father* in the community, then do you not have to be a man in order to be a father? Can a woman be a father? Can every man be a father?

Saint John Chrysostom, who said that the office of the presbyter-bishop excludes all women and most men, had in his Church in Constantinople several hundred women deacons, the head of which was Saint Olympia, who was his best friend and co-worker. But it never entered his mind to ordain her to be a presbyter or bishop. And I don't think that she felt that she was being particularly discriminated against by not being one. . . .

I don't think this is simply a question of management or a matter of who gets to serve the Eucharist or preach the sermon. I believe it's a much deeper issue. I believe the very Faith is at stake here, one way or another. And I think that much of what has happened elsewhere proves this to be the case. Wherever you have the issue of women's ordinations being introduced, you also find compromises concerning issues of inclusive language in the liturgy, family life, sexual relations, and the issue of homosexuality and how that's to be interpreted and related to pastorally and spiritually. All this enters the picture immediately.

I think women's ordinations is one of those key issues around which there is a constellation of all the issues. I think the very Faith is at stake here." Fr. Thomas Hopko, "Women's Ordination: An Orthodox Response," *AGAIN Magazine*. April, 1993.

In the Church of the ages the rejoinder to critics, "This is how it has always been done," is in fact a legitimate answer. The Church holds that certain truths are changeless and cannot be improved upon. This is especially true, in the matter of the ordination of women.

One of the fundamental Orthodox objections to the ordination of women is the same as the Church's case against the iconoclasts; Christ has come in the flesh. To Orthodox Christians the Incarnation is not an "idea" or "symbol," it is a historical fact. Everything in the life and worship of the Orthodox Church is designed to underline the historicity of the Incarnation. This is why we have icons; Christ came in the flesh and His icon, and the icons of His saints, martyrs, and apostles, as well as of His mother, bear testimony to the historicity of His coming.

We also have living icons. In the liturgy the priests and bishops stand as representatives of Christ before the altar. The priest and the bishop are not pictures of an abstract idea, they are icons of an historical person who came to earth; the Son of God.

God, the Orthodox Church holds, is outside of time and space. However, this does not change the historical fact that when He manifested Himself in the flesh, He came as a human man, not as an androgynous symbol of "humankind." We do not paint female icons of Christ because Christ was a man. We cannot have priestesses represent the historical Son of God any more than we could tolerate male representations of the blessed Theotokos, the Mother of God, and still claim that she was an historic person, an actual woman who chose to be the God-bearer.

Naturally Protestantism (and modern liberal Roman Catholicism) has tended to be iconoclastic because modernized, secularized "Christianity" no longer affirms the historicity of the New Testament account. In fact, it has actively sought to turn the content of Holy Tradition and Scripture into nothing more than vague religious symbolism. This is what "liberal" theology is all about. But Orthodoxy rejects the iconoclastic position of liberalism and the deconstruction of religion by "higher criticism." While Orthodox Christians affirm the mysteries of faith we also affirm the historical Christ and His incarnation. While Orthodox Christians believe that in Christ there are "neither male or female," since salvation has come equally to all, we nevertheless believe that Christ Himself rightly established the orderly hierarchy of the Church. This is why the Church rejects iconoclasm in whatever guise it comes, whether as the smashing of icons, the deconstruction of Scripture, or the "androginizing" of living icons: the priests and bishops that St. Ignatius tells us stand in the place of Christ at the altar. By ordaining women, "liberal" Protestants are in effect saying, "Christ did not come in the flesh, his maleness does not matter, he is a mere symbol of something larger."

But to the Orthodox Christian, Christ's maleness *does* matter, just as Mary's femaleness matters. Christianity is nothing if not an historical faith. We do not believe that Christ magically appeared. We believe that He grew as a human male fetus in a human female womb, that God came in the flesh, in reality, into time and space, and that nothing God does, including the gender He took upon Himself, is a mistake, in vain or meaningless.

The destruction of icons, the adulteration of the priesthood and the demotion of the sacraments to mere symbols, destroys the Christian witness to the fact of the Incarnation. People seem to mysteriously, instinctively know this is true whether they have thought through these issues or not. How else to explain the attrition that has resulted in the loss of scores of members to the denominations that have ordained women? People know that something scared has been polluted when mere gender politics overwhelms religion. And people know that a modernized "religion" that tries to "keep up with the times" has lost the moral high ground. They vote with their feet.

Seen in this light the feminist movement's ideological crusade for legitimacy must be stopped at the Orthodox Church's door. The Church cannot allow herself to become the plaything of the "political correctness" movement. Nor can the Orthodox Church allow a tiny minority of academics in its own seminaries, or a few politically self-conscious priests or bishops, to squander two thousand years of moral certainty for the pyrrhic respectability offered by today's politicized academic elite, to those who will march in lock-step with them in their anti-hierarchical crusade.

The crusade to make the Church conform to the gender ideology of the present is a crusade to make the Church bow to today's Caesar. Perhaps it is well to remember that one can gain the whole world, including academic respectability, yet lose one's soul. Perhaps it is also wise to remember that the issue of women's ordination and the issue of "inclusive" language, must be seen in a wider context: the feminist and homosexual assault on nature itself. The attempt to reverse the teaching and witness of a continuous male priesthood is the attempt to androgynize not only the Church but God. God, the Orthodox Church teaches, for His own mysterious reasons, has chosen to reveal Himself as a Father. To accept the ordination of women or to force so-called inclusive, gender-neutral, liturgical language on the Church is not only the rejection of God's choice to reveal Himself as *Father* and to send His *Son*, but it is also a not-so-subtle rejection of Christ's real and continuing presence in His Church.

"Inclusive" liturgical language and the ordination of women is no less outrageous to the Christian conscience, and sense of history, than would be the painting of icons of Mary as a man. It is a form of liturgical graffiti which defaces the idea of transcendent, mysterious permanence. It is the smashing of the past without offering anything of permanence to replace the lost certainties of millennia.

The fact that even a few "Orthodox" have been caught up in the feminist crusade, and have begun to play political volley ball with the irreplaceable treasures of the Church, is tragic. The Orthodox faithful and the vast majority of priests and bishops have unanimously resisted the ordination of women. But a tiny vocal minority of "Orthodox" academics, infiltrated by the spirit of the age, have attempted to begin a "dialogue" on the issue of "women in the church" in much the same way that certain Anglican and Episcopalian feminists insinuated a feminist call for women's ordination into their communion in the early 1970's. Such "Orthodox" scholars as Elisabeth Behr-Sigel (*The Ministry of Women in the Church*), and Susan Ashbrook Harvey have openly called for overthrowing the Church's ancient tradition on this matter.[22]

---

[22]Perhaps out of misplaced ideas about "academic freedom," otherwise stalwart bastions of Orthodoxy such as St. Vladimir's Seminary, have seen fit to promote and publicize these anti-Orthodox, anti-traditional views. (See Susan Ashbrook Harvey's glowing endorsement of the ordination of women in her review of *The Ministry of Women in the Church*, St. Vladimir's Theological Quarterly, vol. 37/1 1993). See *The Christian Activist* vol. 3, 1994, *Women Priests, History, and Theology*, for an examination of this issue by scholar Patrick Henry Reardon.

The Orthodox Church has historically been the guardian of the iconography of Christendom and the guarantor of the historical continuity of the apostolic, hierarchical witness of the Christ-bearing community on earth. To squander this inheritance with politically inspired, academic, "theological" games is to hand the modern iconoclasts a hollow victory. To allow the "gender-politics" of the moment — a passing fad at best, a fascist tyranny of coerced "political correctness" at worst — into the Orthodox sanctuary is to pollute and desecrate the altar, to offend the faithful, to divide the Church and to diminish the moral authority of Orthodoxy.

APOSTOLIC CONTINUITY

The first Protestants admitted the importance of apostolic succession and the historic continuity of the male priesthood.[23] However, looking at the Protestant community today, one would not know that apostolic succession had been one of the overriding concerns of *all* figures in Church history; even a concern of the first Reformers as they desperately tried to rationalize and legitimize their new "traditions" to fill the void created by the abandonment of ancient Holy Tradition.[24]

---

[23]Almost one quarter of Calvin's 22-volume *"Institutes"* deals with questions related to apostolic order and church authority. John Calvin, taught that the Kingdom of God, to be revealed in its fulness in the future, is present today in the Church.

Commentary on Amos 9:13 (CO XLKIII, 172): "The Kingdom of Christ shall in every way be happy and blessed, or that the church of God, which means the same thing, shall be blessed, when Christ begins to reign."

Commentary on Psalm 18:43 (CO XXXI, 190): ". . . his kingdom which is the church."

Commentary on Isaiah 65:20 (CO XXXVII, 430): ". . . in the kingdom of Christ, that, in the church."

Commentary on Ephesians 4:8 (CO LI, 193): "The noblest triumph which God ever gained was when Christ, after subduing sin, conquering death, and putting Satan to flight, rose majestically to heaven, that he might exercise his glorious reign over the church."

Commentary on Matthew 5:18 (CO XLV, 172): "The kingdom of Heaven means the renovation of the church, or, the prosperous condition of the church."

[24]"Continuity with the apostles was . . . a standard since the ancient church. . . . To the Eastern Orthodox of Byzantium, this (apostolic continuity) was the changeless truth of salvation. The first history of the church, that of Eusebius (4th century), opened its account with the words, 'the succession from the holy apostles' (Eus. H. e. 1.1.1 GLS. 9:6) affirming the apostolic continuity of the institutions and teachings of the true churches. . . . Each of these assumptions came into question in the period in the Reformation.
.   .
Principally those challenges came from the left wing of the Reformation which . . . was not a 'reformation' . . . but 'a radical break from existing institutions and theologies' . . .

The Fathers of the Church taught that only through the un-broken continuity of the witness of the Church and Her Scrip-tures can we have any certain or historically verifiable knowledge of who Christ is or how to worship Him. St. Irenaeus writes,

> We have learned the plan of our salvation from none other than those through whom the gospel came down to us. In-deed, they first preached the gospel, and afterward, by the will of God, they handed it down to us in the Scriptures, to be the foundation and pillar of our faith. . . . It is possible, then, for everyone in every (local) church who may wish to know the truth, to contemplate the tradition of the Apostles which has been made known throughout the whole world. . . . We are in a position to enumerate those who were instituted bishops by the Apostles, and their suc-cessors to our own times: men . . . to whom they were com-mitting the self-same churches. . . . They wished all those and their successors to be perfect and without reproach, to whom they handed their authority.[25]

If Jesus *is* indeed Lord, if Peter was correct in saying, "You are the Christ, the Son of the living God" (Mt 16.16), then, ac-cording to Holy Tradition, the Church is bound to worship Christ in the manner He required and the Apostles, authors of the Scriptures, and Fathers taught. "The cup of blessing which we bless, is it not the communion of the blood of Christ? The bread which we break, is it not the communion of the body of Christ? For we, being many, are one bread and one body; for we all partake of that one bread." (1 Cor 10.16-17)

Writing well before the Canon of the New Testament was even finalized, St. Irenaeus knew exactly what the Church taught and on whose authority his faith rested.

> When, therefore, we have such proofs, it is not necessary to seek among others the truth which is easily obtained from the Church. For the Apostles, like a rich man in a bank, deposited with her most openly everything which pertains

(Williams 1962. 846) . . . the full implications of these challenges did not become apparent until (long after)." Jaroslav Pelikan, *Reformation of Church and Dogma*, pp. 304-05.

[25]St. Irenaeus, *Against Heresies*, Ref. 208-09, A.D. 180, in *The Faith of the Early Fathers*, vol. 1, trans. W. A. Jurgens, p. 89.

to the truth; and everyone whosoever wishes draws from her the drink of life. For she is the entrance to life, while all the rest are thieves and robbers. . . . If there should be a dispute over some kind of question, are we not to have recourse to the most ancient Churches in which the Apostles were familiar, and draw from them what is clear and certain in regard to that question? What if the Apostles had not in fact left writings to us? Would it not be necessary to follow the order of tradition, which was handed down to those whom they entrusted the Churches?[26]

The historic record of the Church, and the writings of the early Church Fathers, demonstrate that long before the Canon of the New Testament was closed, even before some of the books of the New Testament were written, the authority of the apostolic hierarchy in the Church was well established. This being so, one can legitimately wonder if today's calls for change in the Church, particularly vis-à-vis gender politics and "empowerment," do not rest more on modern fashion than on scholarship, let alone traditional concepts of spirituality. Demands for feminist "empowerment" ring hollow in the service of the One Who said, "The first shall be last."

THE HISTORICAL CHURCH AND SCRIPTURE

Even better established than the authority of the apostolic hierarchy were the basic forms of sacramentalism that survive until today in the Orthodox Church. Indeed, as we shall see, the oral part of the Holy Tradition *preceded* the written New Testament. St. Irenaeus wrote in A.D. 180, over 200 years before the Councils of Hippo, A.D. 397, Laodicea, A.D. 363, and Carthage, A.D. 393-97, at which the New Testament books were finally collected into one book: "What if the Apostles had not in fact left writings to us? Would it not be necessary to follow the order of tradition. . ."[27]

[26]Ibid. ref. 213, pp. 90-91.
[27]Ibid. ref. 213. pp. 91.

It was just this, "order of tradition" that was the apostolic tradition which was handed down to us, that the early Church followed, continuing steadfastly for almost four hundred years before the Canon of the New Testament was universally recognized. And while hundreds of "Holy Writings," epistles and other documents competed for the attention of the Church, the Church itself was not mired in confusion but passed on the Apostolic inheritance of truth from one generation to the next (Acts 2.42).[28]

The Church teaches that it is only within the context of this orderly, living apostolic tradition of Eucharistic worship that the Scriptures can be fully and accurately understood and interpreted. The interpretation of Scripture, the rule of faith, has always been understood to only make complete sense within the context of the whole Church. As Prosper, Bishop of Aquitane said, "The rule of faith is established by the rule of prayer." In other words, the ancient forms of worship in the Church pre-date its dogmatic theology.

According to the Fathers, the Holy Tradition and Scripture are one in their message — neither separate nor competing. They are one and the same, just as Christ and His Church are one and Christ is one with us in the Sacrament of Communion. As Georges Florovsky writes,

> Loyalty to tradition does not mean loyalty to bygone times and to outward authority; it is a living connexion with the fulness of Church experience. . . .
>
> The Church bears witness to the truth not by reminiscence or from the words of others, but from its own living, unceasing experience, from its catholic fulness. . . .

---

[28]"Scripture needs to be explained. It is revealed in theology. This is possible only through the medium of the living experience of the Church. . . .

If we declare Scripture to be self-sufficient, we only expose it to subjective, arbitrary interpretation, thus cutting it away from its sacred source. Scripture is given to us in tradition. It is the vital, crystallizing centre. The Church, as the Body of Christ, stands mystically first and is fuller than Scripture. This does not limit Scripture, or cast shadows on it. But truth is revealed to us not only historically. Christ appeared and still appears before us not only in the Scriptures; He unchangeably and unceasingly reveals Himself in the Church, in His own Body. . . .

This experience has not been exhausted either in Scripture, or in oral tradition, or in definitions. *It cannot, it must not be, exhausted.*" Georges Florovsky, *Bible, Church, Tradition: An Eastern Orthodox View*, pp. 48-49.

It is quite false to limit the 'source of teaching' to Scripture and tradition, and to separate tradition from Scripture as only an oral testimony or teaching of the Apostles. In the first place, both Scripture and tradition were given only within the Church. Only in the Church have they been received in the fulness of their sacred value and meaning. In them is contained the truth of Divine Revelation, a truth which lives in the Church. This experience of the Church has not been exhausted either in Scripture or in tradition; it is only reflected in them. Therefore, only within the Church does Scripture live and become vivified, only within the Church is it revealed as a whole and not broken up into separate texts, commandments and aphorisms.[29]

The New Testament came out of the Holy Tradition of worship and is inseparable from it. Unwittingly, many Protestants *act* as if this is true even if they do not acknowledge it to be so. When a Protestant accepts the doctrine of the Trinity, or the doctrine of the two natures of Christ, as both fully God and fully Man, he is accepting the teaching of the Fathers, the oral tradition, the Creeds and the dogmatic definitions of the seven historic ecumenical councils.[30] And when any Protestant refers to the books of the New Testament as "the Word of God" he is accepting the common practices of the Church and the decision of the Councils of bishops as to which books were included in the New Testament and which were rejected.[31]

---

[29]Ibid. pp. 46-47.

[30]Most Protestants are painfully unaware of how it is that Christians have come to believe certain things. They do not seem to realize that the history of doctrine *is* the history of the Church. Nor do they understand that without the ecumenical councils — especially the first four — central doctrines assumed to be "Biblical," such as that of the Trinity, would not have been effectively defended against heresy since they are not clearly specified in the Bible.

[31]"The history of the New Testament canon and its development is a fascinating subject — and crucial to the understanding of both the Bible and the Church. For over two hundred years a number of books we now take for granted as being part of the New Testament were disputed by the Church before being included. Many other books were considered for inclusion, but eventually excluded. . . . The earliest complete listing of all twenty-seven books of the New Testament was not given until A.D. 367, by St. Athanasius, a bishop in Egypt.

"This means that the first complete listing of New Testament books as we have them today didn't appear until over 300 years after the death and Resurrection of Christ. . . . If the New Testament were begun at the same time as the U.S. Constitution, we wouldn't see a final product until the year 2087! . . .

"With the passage of time the Church discerned which writings were truly apostolic and which were not. It was a prolonged struggle taking place over several centuries

The understanding of the centrality of the Holy Tradition was the same in the East and the West until the time of the Reformation. Tertullian, who has been called the Father of Western theology, wrote in A.D. 200,

> Although the (individual local) Churches are so many and so great, there is but the one primitive (i.e., original, ancient) Church of the Apostles, from which all others are derived. Thus, all are primitive, all are Apostolic, because all are one. . . . Indeed, every doctrine must be prejudged as false if it smells of anything contrary to the truth of the Churches and of the Apostles of Christ and God. . . . Moreover if there be any (heresies) bold enough to plant themselves in the midst of the Apostolic age, so that they might seem to have been handed by the Apostles because they were from the time of the Apostles, we can say to them: Let them show the origins of their Churches, let them unroll the order of their bishops, running down in succession from the beginning, so that their first bishop shall have for author and predecessor some one of the Apostles or of the Apostolic men who continue steadfast with the Apostles. For this is the way in which the Apostolic Churches transmit their lists; like the church of the Smyrnians, which records that Polycarp was placed there by John; like the church

---

in which the Church decided what books were her own. As part of the process of discerning, the Church met together in council. These various Church councils met to deal with many varied issues, among which was the canon of Scripture.

"These councils sought to proclaim the common mind of the Church and reflect the unanimity of faith, practice, and tradition of the local Churches represented.

"The Church Councils provide us with specific records in which the Church spoke clearly and in unison as to what constitutes Scripture. Among the many councils that met during the first four centuries, two particularly stand out:

"1. The council of Laodicea, which met in Asia Minor, around AD 363. This council stated that only canonical books of the Old and New Testaments should be used in the Church. It forbade reading other books in Church. It enumerated the canonical books of our present Old and New Testaments, with the exception of the Apocalypse of Saint John. This is the first council which clearly listed the canonical books. Its decisions were widely accepted in the Eastern Church.

"2. The Third Council of Carthage, which met in North Africa, around AD 397. This council, attended by Augustine, provided a full list of the canonical books of both Old and New Testaments. The 27 books of the present day New Testament were accepted as canonical. It also held that these books should be read in the Church as Divine Scripture to the exclusion of all others. This Council was widely accepted as authoritative in the West." Fr. James Bernstein, "Who Gave Us The New Testament?" *AGAIN Magazine*, vol. 15, no. 3, 1992.

of the Romans where Clement was ordained by Peter. . . . Then let all heresies prove how they regard themselves as Apostolic, when they are challenged by our Churches to meet [these] tests. . . .[32]

Tertullian, writing in A.D. 200, in answer to the heretics of his day, addressed them in the same manner in which we might address today's modernized "Christians" who claim to be "apostolic." Tertullian denounced anything that was contrary to, or outside of, the historical Church. His appeal was not to Scripture, but to the tradition of Christ and the Apostles out of which the Holy Writings themselves came. The claims of heretics, he argued, called into question the legitimacy of their Christian faith because they were made outside of the context of the authentic Church. "Show us your list of bishops," is the question the historical Church legitimately asks of those who are outside of her.

We who walk in the rule which the Churches have handed down through the Apostles, the Apostles from Christ, and Christ from God, admit that the reasonableness of our position is clear, defining as it does that heretics ought not to be allowed to challenge an appeal to the Scriptures, since we, without using Scripture, prove that they have nothing to do with the Scripture. . . . They cannot be Christians, because it is not from Christ [through the Apostolic succession] that they have gotten what they pursue of their own choosing. . . . Not being Christians, they have acquired no right to Christian literature; and it might be justly said to them, 'Who are you? When and from where did you come? Since you are not of mine, what are you doing with what is mine?' I am the heir of the Apostles. As they carefully prepared their will, as they committed it to a trust, and as they sealed it with an oath, so do I hold the inheritance.

You, certainly, they always held as disinherited, and they rejected you as strangers and enemies.[33]

In the year A.D. 200, Tertullian provided an answer to those

---

[32]Tertullian, *Against Heretics*, Ref. 292-97, A.D. 200, in *The Faith of the Early Fathers*, vol 1, trans. W. A. Jurgens, p. 123.
[33]Ibid. Ref. 297-98, pp. 122-23.

Protestants who centuries later would attempt to argue for the right to break with the Church by saying "the Bible says." To them Tertullian answers, "(you) have acquired no right to Christian literature." Again he asks, "Who are your bishops? Show us your list."[34]

MORAL AUTHORITY

As if anticipating both the Protestant chaos of schismatic opinion and the illegitimate power vested in a single "pope," Cyprian of Carthage wrote in A.D. 250,

> From that time (Jesus' appointing of the apostles) the ordination of bishops and the plan of the Church flows on through the changes of times and successions; for the Church is formed upon the bishops, and every act of the Church is controlled by these same rulers. Since this has indeed been established by divine law, I marvel at the rash boldness of certain persons who have desired to write to one as if they were writing their letters in the name of the Church. Far be it from the mercy of the Lord . . . to permit

[34]"The Gospels are written within the Church. In this sense they are the witness of the Church. They are records of church experience and faith. But they are no less historical narratives and bear witness to what had really taken place, in space and in time. . . .

Revelation is preserved in the Church. Therefore, the Church is the proper and primary interpreter of revelation. It is protected and reinforced by written words; protected, but not exhausted. Human words are no more than signs. The testimony of the Spirit revives the written words. We do not mean now the occasional illumination of individuals by the Holy Ghost, but primarily the permanent assistance of the Spirit given to the Church, that is 'the pillar and bulwark of the truth' (I Timothy 3:15). The Scriptures need interpretation. Not the phrasing, but the message is the core. And the Church is the divinely appointed and permanent witness to the very truth and the full meaning of this message, simply because the Church belongs itself to the revelation, as the Body of the Incarnate Lord. . . .

But this witness is not just a reference to the past, not merely a reminiscence, but rather a continuous rediscovery of the message once delivered to the saints and ever since kept by faith. Moreover, this message is ever re-enacted in the life of the Church. Christ himself is ever present in the Church, as the Redeemer and head of his Body, and continues his redeeming office in the Church, but precisely enacted. The sacred history is still continued. The mighty deeds of God are still being performed. . . . And only within the experience of the Church is the New Testament truly and fully alive. Church history is itself a story of redemption. The truth of the book is revealed and vindicated by the growth of the Body." Georges Florovsky, *Bible, Church, Tradition: An Eastern Orthodox View*, pp. 26-27.

the ranks of the lapsed to be called the Church.[35]

As the many early writings of the Church Fathers make abundantly clear, the Church has *always* held that it is both a hierarchical and an ontological reality. As George Florovsky writes,

> The Fathers did not care so much for the *doctrine* of the Church precisely because the glorious *reality* of the Church was open to their spiritual vision. One does not define what is self-evident.[36]

The Church has never seen itself as a chaos of spiritual individualism, let alone as a maelstrom of twenty-three thousand denominations battling for turf, each armed with its own subjective reading of Scripture and its self-invented "traditions." Nor has the historical Church seen itself as under a dictator or "infallible" pope.

The historical Church teaches that it has a head who is Christ. It teaches that Christ has appointed human, apostolic leaders under Him. Just as a family has a mother and father who keep order among their children, authentic Church leaders are not self-proclaimed, any more than were the sons of Aaron in the Old Testament. Rather, their authority is passed from one spiritual generation to the next as a mother and father pass on their heritage to their children.[37]

The early Church kept careful count of exactly how many bishops there had been "from the Apostles" in each bishopric.

[35]Cyprian of Carthage, *Letter to the Lapsed*, Ref. 55-556, A.D. 251, in *The Faith of the Early Fathers*, vol. 1, trans. W. A. Jurgens, p. 221.

[36]Georges Florovsky, *Bible, Church, Tradition: An Eastern Orthodox View*, p. 57.

[37]"From very early times an episcopal polity, presumed to stand in unbroken succession from the apostles, had been taken to be one of the criteria of apostolic continuity, in conjunction with the authoritative canon of Scripture and the creedal rule of faith." Jaroslav Pelikan, *The Spirit of Eastern Christendom*, p. 157.

"The hierarchs have received this power to teach, not from the church-people but from the High Priest, Jesus Christ, in the Sacrament of Orders. But this teaching finds its limits in the expression of the whole Church. The Church is called to witness to this experience, which is an inexhaustible experience, a spiritual vision. A bishop of the Church must be a teacher. Only the bishop has received full power and authority to speak in the name of his flock. The latter receives the right of speaking through the bishop. But to do so the bishop must embrace his Church within himself; he must make manifest its experience and its faith. He must speak not from himself, but in the name of the Church. This is just the contrary of the Vatican formula: from himself, but not from the consensus of the Church." Georges Florovsky, *Bible, Church, Tradition: An Eastern Orthodox View*, pp. 53-54.

For instance, Eusebius, in his fourth century *History of the Church*, always refers to a bishop as being twelfth, twentieth, or whatever number, "from the Apostles" in order to show that a particular bishop was legitimate, or a certain teaching was authentically apostolic.

By A.D. 393, the canon of the New Testament Scriptures was approximately fixed.[38] The Church Fathers rejected many hundreds of early Christian writings competing with the books ultimately agreed upon as constituting the New Testament. When the Fathers rejected certain writings it was on the basis of Holy Tradition — "the apostles' doctrine" referred to by St. Luke, the writer of Acts. And it was the bishops of the Church, not a "pope," who determined which books to include and which to reject — just as it was the bishops who defended Christian doctrine at the ecumenical councils by answering heretics who had departed from the teachings of the Apostles.

Within only a few years of Christ's ascent to Heaven, the Apostolic succession of bishops was not only the Church's practice, as is demonstrated by the installation of St. James, the "brother" (i.e., relation) of Christ, as Bishop of the Jerusalem Church, but it was also defended by the Church Fathers as an essential of Christian teaching and life.

As Eusebius writes,

> After the martyrdom of James, and the capture of Jerusalem which instantly followed, there is a firm tradition that those of the apostles and disciples of the Lord who were still alive assembled from all parts together with those who, humanly speaking, were kinsmen of the Lord — for most of them were still living. Then they all discussed together whom they should choose as a fit person to succeed James, and voted unanimously that Symeon, son of the Clopas mentioned in the gospel narrative (Jn 14.25; perhaps Lk 24.18) was a fit person to occupy the throne of the Jerusalem see.[39]

[38]Several books remained suspect, primarily the book of Revelation which was not accepted in some quarters until St. Athanasius fought to make it so in the mid-fourth century.

[39]Eusebius, *The History of the Church*, Book 3, translated by G. A. Williamson (New York, 1965), p. 123.

Polycrates, Bishop of Ephesus, wrote to Bishop Victor of Rome in A.D. 180 concerning St. John the Evangelist, who ended his days as a bishop himself.

Again there is John, who leant back on the Lord's breast, and who became a sacrificing priest (the bloodless sacrifice of the Eucharistic feast) wearing the miter, (The bishop's distinguishing hat) a martyr (he had been imprisoned for Christ) and a teacher; he too sleeps in Ephesus.[40]

Moreover Eusebius writes,

There was one power of the divine Spirit coursing through all the members, one soul in them all . . . and our leaders (the bishops) performed ceremonies with full pomp, and ordained priests (and performed) the sacraments and majestic rites of the Church; . . . If we may put it so, . . . with our very eyes we see that the traditions of an earlier age were trustworthy and true.[41]

To circumvent the facts of the Church's early history, accepted, until A. D. 1054, by the Church, East and West, one needs to jump through many torturous, hermeneutical hoops. Calvin and Luther well understood this. They spent much of their lives selectively quoting certain Western fathers, like St. Augustine, in order to try and prove themselves "apostolic." Only later did Protestants like the Anabaptists dispense altogether with even a pretense of being part of the historical Church. To avoid working within the framework of the Church's hierarchy of authority, in which the bishops and priests of the Church are in direct unbroken continuity with the Apostles, we must ignore the clear teaching of Jesus, the action and teaching of the Apostles, the Church Fathers and the witness of the very well-documented history of the early Church, as recorded by historians like Eusebius.

According to the teaching of the Holy Tradition, the Bible

---

[40]As cited by Eusebius, *The History of the Church*, Book 3, p. 141.

[41]Eusebius was writing in the third to fourth centuries. The "earlier age" he referred to was the first and second century Church of the Apostles. Ibid. Book 10, pp. 383-84.

is a sure witness to the Church and its historic apostolic tradition. This must of course be so; the Biblical authors were inspired by the same Holy Spirit Who has subsequently led the Church. It was out of apostolic Holy Tradition that the New Testament and doctrines of the Church emerged.

The historical record is unequivocal. It was through the Church that the books deemed as false were not included in the New Testament Canon. It was out of the living Tradition of Eucharistic worship that the New Testament emerged, not out of some cold-blooded biblical science of the kind that is practiced by many modern "theologians." It was by those bishops and martyrs who defended the Holy Tradition that the New Testament canon was passed intact to us. And it was from the bishops, beginning with James, that the doctrinal pronouncements accepted by all Christians were formulated in response to the heretics departing from the Holy Tradition of the Church. This is what we read in the book of Acts. And this is what the historical record shows. If Protestants answer that all this may be so but that it does not matter, then they must also acknowledge that they are the first people claiming to be Christians who believe that the existence of the Church is irrelevant to the individual pursuit of holiness and salvation. And if modern Roman Catholics wish to maintain that the "infallible" papacy is a "fact of history," they will be hard-pressed to find early accounts of the Church, such as Eusebius', to support them. Indeed, all the evidence seems to point to a collegial Church government from the beginning. In a way, the problem of an "infallible" papacy is similar to the Protestant problem of an "infallible" Bible. Both errors discount the importance of the leading of the Church by the Holy Spirit.

CONCLUSION

Eusebius underlines the fact that the collegial Church preceded the New Testament. He writes concerning "Scriptures" deemed false, and therefore not included by the Church Fathers in the sacred Canon of the New Testament,

These would all be classed with Disputed Books . . . (dis-

tinguished from) those writings which according to the tradition of the Church are true, genuine, and recognized. . . .[42]

In another place Eusebius dismisses the books left out of
the Canon as "irreconcilable with true orthodoxy." In other
words, if the witness of the Church which depends on the orderly succession of bishops is not trustworthy, then neither is the
New Testament account. The living tradition of the historic
Church was faithfully passed down from one generation to the
next in the form of the continuity of an apostolic appointment
of bishops who defended the oral and written living Holy Tradition.[43] As St. Irenaeus wrote to Eleutherius, Bishop of Rome,
(A.D. 170), concerning the lists of the bishops of Rome,

> Having founded and built the church, the blessed apostles
> entrusted the episcopal office to Linus, who is mentioned
> by Paul in the epistles to Timothy (2 Tim 4.21). Linus was
> succeeded by Anencletus: after him, in the third place from
> the apostles, the bishopric fell to Clement, who had seen
> the blessed apostles and conversed with them, and still had
> their preaching ringing in his ears and their authentic tradi-
> tion before his eyes.[44]

Irenaeus then goes on to list the remaining bishops right
up to "the twelfth . . . from the apostles," Eleutherius, to whom
he was writing.

Clement of Alexandria in A.D. 90 in his Book 1 of
Miscellaneis speaks of the bishops of the Eastern Church and
their direct continuity from the Apostles.

> These men preserved the true tradition of the blessed teach-
> ing straight from Peter, James, John and Paul, the holy
> apostles, son receiving it from father. . . . By the grace of
> God, they came right down to me, to deposit those ancestral
> apostolic seeds.[45]

The Church teaches us that these "ancestral apostolic

---

[42]Ibid. Book 3, p. 135.
[43]See vol 1, The Ante-Nicean Fathers, (Edinburgh, 1867, and Grand Rapids, 1993).
[44]As cited by Eusebius, *The History of the Church*, Book 5, p. 208.
[45]Ibid. p. 214.

seeds," this continuity, is miraculous because the individual members of the Church, even including its bishops, at times do things which are far from God's will, Christ's teaching and the spirit of the Holy Tradition. But the Church prevails nevertheless, even if it takes many hundreds of years to confront its failures and correct its errors. As St. Irenaeus writes,

> That in which we have faith is a firm system directed to the salvation of men; and, since it has been received by the Church, we guard it. Constantly it has its youth renewed by the Spirit of God, as if it were some precious deposit in an excellent vessel; and it causes the vessel containing it to be rejuvenated. For where the Church is, there is the Spirit of God; and where the Spirit of God, there the Church and every grace. The Spirit, however, is truth.[46]

According to the historic Church, heresies come and go, fashions change, evil, corrupt or politicized bishops may rise and fall. But in the end, as the seven ecumenical councils of the Church demonstrate, the Church prevails and heresy is vanquished. The sure knowledge of right and wrong moral principal is preserved. In the words of St. Justin Martyr, "And to all who wish to learn, we pass on intact what we have been taught."[47]

---

[46]St. Irenaeus, *Against Heresies*, Ref. 226, A.D. 180, in *The Faith of the Early Fathers*, vol. 1, trans. W. A. Jurgens, p. 94.

[47]St. Justin Martyr, *First Apology*, Ref. 113, A.D. 148, in *The Faith of the Early Fathers*, vol. 1, trans. W. A. Jurgens, p. 51.

CHAPTER FOURTEEN

UNITY IN THE CHURCH

The Church teaches that it is inevitable that Christians will give offense to one another. Christ foresaw this and established a means through which differences of opinion could be resolved without threatening the unity of the Church.

Moreover, if your brother sins against you, go and tell him his fault between you and him alone. If he hears you, you have gained your brother. But if he will not hear you, take with you one or two more, that by the mouth of two or three witnesses every word may be established. And if he refuses to hear them, tell it to the church. But if he refuses even to hear the church, let him be to you like a heathen and a tax collector. Assuredly, I say to you, whatever you bind on earth will be bound in heaven, and whatever you loose on earth will be loosed in heaven. Again, I say to you that if two of you agree on earth concerning anything that they ask, it will be done for them by My Father in heaven. For where two or three are gathered together in My name, I am there in the midst of them (Matthew 18.15-20).

Taken in context, Jesus was speaking to the disciples, the future leadership of the historic Church. Jesus established an orderly way for resolving the disputes that the Church teaches are the consequence of sin even within the authentic and legitimate historic Body of Christ.

Jesus Himself respected precedent. He built on the Old Testament law in laying down His own rule of Church discipline.

175

Jesus quoted the book of Deuteronomy 19:13, "by the mouth of two or three witnesses every word may be established," as the basis of settling disputes between believers in the Christian era.[1] What Christ established was a *collegial system*, not a "papacy."[2]

The Church teaches us that a Christian who feels some other believer has wronged him or her, or has a doctrinal difference of opinion with that believer, is not free to pursue personal vindication, let alone have recourse to the secular courts. Nor is he or she free to create a schism by splitting from the Church, or starting his or her own "church."

Jesus established an orderly approach to settling disputes in the Church. Jesus' method of establishing justice between believers does not rest on some experiential basis of good feelings or special "words of knowledge" from God. Nor does it rest on the magical or "infallible" pronouncements of a "pope." It is rooted in the Old Testament Jewish legal system. Everything is to be argued before witnesses, that "every word may be established" in an orderly conciliar manner.

ORDER IN THE CHURCH

The Church, according to Orthodox Holy Tradition, is not a one-man dictatorship, nor is it a chaotic anarchy of private interests. Its authority rests in a collegial body of bishops who are in direct historic succession from the Apostles.[3] This has been the pat-

---

[1] "This struggle over the authority of the Old Testament and over the nature of the continuity between Judaism and Christianity was the earliest form of the quest for a tradition that has . . . recurred throughout Christian history . . . . What the Christian tradition had done was to take over the Jewish Scriptures as its own . . . . The growth of . . . hierarchical and ethical structures of Christianity led to the Christianization of many features of Judaism . . . Clement spoke of 'priests' and of 'the high priest' and significantly related these terms to the Levitical priesthood . . . . " Jaroslav Pelikan, *The Emergence of the Catholic Tradition*, pp. 13-25.

[2] See *The Primacy of Peter*, edited by John Meyendorff (Crestwood, 1992). See in particular Nicholas Koulomzine's essay, "Peter's Place in the Primitive Church," pp. 11-34, for an excellent explanation of the Roman Catholic errors.

[3] "The Christian adoption of Abraham as 'father of the faithful' and the Christian identification of the church, the city of God, with the heritage of Abel illustrates this quest (for Old Testament continuity). . . . When the church formulated its quest for a tradition in a doctrine of correction — and fulfillment, it was enabled to claim as its own all the saints and believers back to Abraham and even to Adam." Jaroslav Pelikan, *The Emergence of the Catholic Tradition*, pp. 14-15.

tern of Church governance since Christ. Unfortunately this divine order was partially squandered, in the Latin Church, through the exaggeration and corruption of papal authority that led the Roman Church into grave errors and has diminished its witness. These errors in turn bred the reaction by Protestants against the historical Western Church.

Nevertheless, these tragedies could have been avoided. The Church has taught that when internal differences of opinion arise and if rational argument before a collegial body of witnesses fails, then the next step is to go before an even more formal deliberative body of Church authorities — the bishops. There the authority of the full apostolic hierarchy will come to bear on the issue in question and the case will be heard again. This was so in the seven ecumenical councils when the claims of heretics were heard, argued, measured against the Holy Tradition and resolved. If someone is excommunicated, disciplined or confesses his sins and repents, the Church's decision is binding. But if one of the disputants will not follow Christ's system of Church government and refuses to submit to the authority vested in the Church, then that person is to be "like a heathen and a tax collector" (Matthew 18:17). He is to be anathema.

St. John Chrysostom writes,

> Priests have received a power which God has given neither to angels or to archangels. It was said to them: 'Whatsoever you shall bind upon earth shall be bound in heaven; and whosoever you shall loose, shall be loosed.' Temporal rulers have indeed the power of binding; but they can bind only the body. Priests, however, can bind with a bond that pertains to the soul itself and transcends to the very heavens.[4]

Jesus instructed His Church that Christian order depends on the authority He had given to the apostolic Church leaders, and to the priests and bishops who followed them. "I say to you, whatever you bind on earth will be bound in heaven, and whatever you loose on earth will be loosed in heaven" (Matthew 18.18). Jesus was speaking of the fact that He had given

[4]St. John Chrysostom, *On the Priesthood*, Ref. 1119-20, A.D. 386, in *The Faith of the Early Fathers*, vol. 2, trans. W. A. Jurgens, pp. 89-90.

real spiritual authority to the Church hierarchy, represented at the time by the Disciples. "Then Jesus said to them again, 'Peace to you! As the Father has sent me, I also send you . . . If you forgive the sins of any, they are forgiven them; if you retain the sins of any, they are retained' " (John 20.21-23).

The Church and its authorities, bishops and priests, have a special authority given to them by Jesus (James 5.14-15). As we see, from the earliest writings of the Fathers, and Luke's account of the early Church in the Book of Acts, this has been the understanding of the Church since its beginning. The Church is not an egalitarian free-for-all, let alone a "democratic" system. Its authority does not rest on its ability to govern according to people's wishes. Its standard of morality is not the result of a public opinion poll. The Church's task is not to make everyone happy.

In the historical Church, authority is vested by God the Father in the head, Christ, then in the Apostles, Christ's delegates, and the bishops and the priests who are the Apostles' successors. Like the family, the Church is a hierarchy (1 Peter 5.1-4). It is an institution that was made by God, not mankind.[5] Its Head is Christ alone, not an all-powerful bishop, pope or patriarch. It is part of a non-negotiable, external heavenly order. It is not a human institution that can be tampered with, any more than the Ark of the Covenant could be desecrated with impunity by the Philistines. The structure of the historical Church is not some modern, politically expedient, or "politically correct" invention but was established from the beginning as an orderly, changeless, institution, as all the Scriptures and the other writings of the early Church confirm.

Cornelius, Bishop of Rome in A.D. 249, wrote describing the orderly structure of the Church in Rome in his day,

> There can be only one bishop (in each locality) in a Catholic (i.e., universal historic) Church, in which (in Rome for instance) there are forty-six presbyters, seven deacons, seven subdeacons, forty-two acolytes, . . . readers, and door-keepers.[6]

[5]"The Apostles received the gospel for us from the Lord Jesus Christ; and Jesus was sent from God. Christ, therefore, is from God, and the Apostles are from Christ. Both of these orderly arrangements, then, are by God's will." Clement of Rome, *Letter to the Corinthians,* A.D. circa 80-98, in *The Faith of the Early Fathers,* vol. 1, trans. W. A. Jurgens, p. 10.

[6]Letter from Bishop Cornelius to Fabius, A.D. 249. Eusebius, *The History of the Church,* Book 6, p. 282.

Eusebius describes how the early Church dealt with the actions of the errant bishop Novatus. Novatus had taken unilateral action, not approved by the other bishops of the Church. He was excommunicating Christians who had renounced their faith under torture by their Roman persecutors but, who later had repented and asked for re-admission to the Church.

> To deal with the situation a synod of the largest scale was convened at Rome, and was attended by sixty bishops and a still greater number of presbyters and deacons . . . . The result was a unanimous decree that Novatus, his companions . . any who thought fit to approve his attitude of hatred and inhumanity to brother Christians, should be regarded as outside the Church, those brothers who had had the misfortune to fall should be treated and cured with the medicine of repentance.[7]

In the authentic historical and apostolic Church, there is a permanent system of Church government. This is clearly illustrated by Eusebius' example of the disciplining of Novatus. According to Christ, this system is ratified by heaven's authority. It has been functioning since the days of the early Church.

St. Peter recognized the special authority entrusted to the bishops and priests in the Church. He even wrote to the elders, bishops and priests, saying that if they discharged their duties of leadership well that they would be specially rewarded in heaven.

> The elders who are among you I exhort, I who am a fellow elder and a witness of the sufferings of Christ and also a partaker of the glory that will be revealed: Shepherd the flock of God which is among you, serving as overseers . . . and when the Chief Shepherd appears, you will receive the crown of glory that does not fade away. (1 Peter 5.1-4)

Peter put the new elders on an equal footing of authority with himself. "I who am a fellow elder" is the way Peter identifies himself. Clearly Peter is exhorting the new bishops and priests to carry on the work of Christ in the same manner in

---

[7] Ibid, p. 280.

which Christ instructed him. Clearly, Peter, "a fellow elder," is no "pope."

> Shepherd the flock of God which is among you, serving as ourselves, not by constraint but willingly, not for dishonest gain but eagerly; nor as being lords over those entrusted to you, but being examples to the flock. (1 Peter 5.2-3)

If the shepherds of the flock, to whom Peter is writing, did not have real power, Peter's exhortation would make no sense. The potential abuses Peter warns them to avoid — dishonest gain or being "lords" over the flock, rather than the flock's leaders by example — are only possible if the shepherds are in authority. Peter obviously had the authority to command. He knew the other elders (bishops and priests) likewise had real authority that they needed to be careful not to abuse. And the very kind of thing Peter warned his fellow elders about — lording it over other believers — is in fact ironically the sin of an "infallible," politicized papacy whose historic basis lies in Peter's authority.[8]

Interestingly enough one of the strongest denunciations of the abuse of the bishop of Rome's power comes from one of the most revered "popes" of all; St. Gregory the Great, bishop of Rome, writes:

> ". . . the prelates of this Apostolic See, which by the providence of God I serve, had the honor offered them of being called universal by the venerable Council of Chalcedon. But yet not one of them has ever wished to be called by such a title, or seized upon this ill-advised name, lest if, in virtue of the rank of the pontificate he took to himself the glory of singularity, he might seem to have denied it to all brethren. . . ."[9]

SCHISM

One reason schism, or abuse of power, was regarded as such a dreadful sin in the earliest Church and is still held in that light today by Orthodox believers, is that it undermines

---

[8] For an excellent series of essays refuting the Western and Latin-Roman claims about the papacy, see John Meyendorff, editor, *The Primacy of Peter*, especially Chapter 1, "Peter's Place in the Primitive Church," by Nicholas Koulomzine.

[9] St. Gregory the Great, Book V, Epistle XVIII.

the collegiality of the bishops and their ability to exercise the authority James and the other bishops vested in their successors (1 Corinthians 1.10-17).

It does not take much insight to understand that God's plan for His Church does not include the unrepentant chaos of twenty three thousand new Protestant denominations whose competitive anarchy has rendered claims of absolute truth ridiculous in the eyes of the world. Nor does one have to be a theologian, or jurist, to understand that in a divided Church, there can be no ultimate Church discipline. In a Church divided either by Protestant chaos or papal dictatorship, Christians cannot obey Christ's explicit teaching on how to resolve their disputes. On the one hand there is no Church to whom they can appeal. On the other, there is only an earthly monarch.

According to Holy Tradition, there can be no Christian order unless there is Christian unity. Moreover, historically legitimate hierarchy still exists with unbroken and verifiable ties back to the Apostles. This is why the continued existence of the Protestant denominations is an affront to the claims of the historic Church. This is why the rebellion of Protestantism is a great and tragic sin. And this is why the politicized papal monarchy is a continuing stumbling block between the Churches of the East and West, whether any given "pope" is a "good pope" or not.

Protestants and Roman Catholics have somehow read the First and Second Epistles of Peter, the Second Epistles of John and Jude, yet have not heard the repeated warnings against those who "Promise them liberty (yet are) themselves slaves of corruption." (2 Peter 2.19) The warnings against division, strife, lording it over others and schism in the New Testament are so frequent that the call for Church unity, order and humble collegiality might be described as the main theme of the epistles. Yet it remains one that Protestants and supporters of a dictatorial, "infallible" papacy have been conditioned not to discern.

Protestantism has abandoned the historical Church and its apostolic authority. That is why its worship is desacralized and its doctrine is such a chaotic scandal. The very existence of this movement is an invitation to anarchy, just as the Roman Catholic papacy is an invitation to cycles of corruption and rebellion. The history of the Western Church since 1054 unequivocally demonstrates this.[10]

Protestantism has no excuse for its existence, and the clear witness of history rebukes the Western invention of an "infallible," politicized papacy. The alternative, the true historical Orthodox Church is still present, *as it always has been without interruption since Christ.* Protestants are free to become Orthodox Christians and graft themselves into the root and branch of the apostolic Church. Roman Catholics are free to come home. Only misplaced sincere belief, pride, the protection of vested interests or ignorance stand in their way.[11]

UNIQUE AUTHORITY

When Christ said, ". . . If two of you agree on earth concerning anything they ask, it will be done for them by My Father in heaven" (Matthew 18.19), He was speaking very specifically to the Disciples and their apostolic successors, as is obvious by even a casual study of the context of His teaching, especially as seen in the light of John 20.21-23. Paul recognized the authority of the Apostles when he went up to Jerusalem to present himself to them after his dramatic conversion on the road to Damascus.

Bishops and priests may agree over a decision of Church discipline, or doctrine, or accept repentance as someone confesses their sins. The model of Church government established by Christ is not based on the decision of one powerful "pope," speaking *ex cathedra* or infallibly, be he in Rome or in Tulsa, Oklahoma, in the form of an Evangelical mini-pope presiding over a one-man denomination or para-church empire, or interpreting his "infallible" Bible outside of the context of the Church.

---

[10]"The distinction between what individual theologians held and what was believed, taught and confessed by the church or churches was itself rendered increasingly ambiguous by the schism of the fourteenth and fifteenth centuries and above all by the Reformation of the sixteenth. . . ." Jaroslav Pelikan, *Reformation of Church and Dogma,* p. 6.

[11]The well-known Lutheran theologian Richard John Neuhaus, who converted to the Roman Catholic Church in 1991, said that the Lutherans were now "just one more Protestant denomination" since the original reforms demanded by Luther had been achieved in the Western Church so that there was no longer any logical reason, besides human empire-building, to remain outside of the historical Church. Dramatic conversions are possible, even in our day. Increasing numbers of *both* Protestants and Roman Catholics are in fact becoming Orthodox in America and around the world.

As we have seen from Eusebius, Orthodox Church authority is collegial; when "two or three," in positions of legitimate apostolic authority, decide something, it will be "bound on earth and in heaven." In such matters what they, the Apostles, and their successor bishops in the Church decide will be binding. This is the way in which the seven great ecumenical councils defended the doctrines, of the Church — doctrines most Protestants still accept while naively rejecting the authority of the men who defended them against error. And this is the way the historical Orthodox Church has functioned since Christ. "This was done to remedy schism, lest anyone rend the Church of Christ by drawing it to himself."[12]

ORDER IN THE HISTORIC CHURCH

Jesus therefore said to them again, 'Peace be with you; as the Father has sent Me, I also send you.' And when He had said this, He breathed on them, and said to them, 'Receive the Holy Spirit.' 'If you forgive the sins of any, their sins have been forgiven them; if you retain the sins of any, they have been retained." (John 20.21-23).

The great Church Father, St. John Chrysostom, reflecting Christ's words of instruction, articulated the position of the Orthodox Church of the ages: "Priests have received a power which God has given neither to angels nor to archangels."

It may come as a surprise, especially to those of us who were raised in the Protestant denominations, that according to Holy Tradition, Christ's plan for the Church was not chaos, individualism or schism. "Knowing this first, that no prophecy of Scripture is of any private interpretation . . ." (2 Peter 1.20-21)

As St. Cyprian of Carthage wrote, private interpretation of Scripture proves that a person or local congregation is *not* a part of the true Church of Christ. He said, "We know that only in the Church, where prelates have been established by the gospel law and by the ordinance of the Lord it is permitted to baptize and give the remission of sins. Beyond the pale,

---

[12]St. Jerome, *Letter to Evangelius*, Ref. 1357, circa A.D. 415, in *The Faith of the Early Fathers*, vol. 2, trans. W. A. Jurgens, p. 187.

however, nothing can be bound and loosed, where there is no one who is able to either bind or loose."[13]

THE NATURAL LAW OF ORDER

The Church teaches that God is a God of order, not chaos. We read that, "The earth was without form, and void; and darkness was on the face of the deep. And the Spirit of God was hovering over the face of the waters" (Genesis 1.2). God brought order from chaos (1 Corinthians 3.4). God created humankind as male and female (1 Corinthians 7.1-16), each with a unique, orderly, equal but different and synergistic role to play (1 Corinthians 14.34-35). God established parents as heads of the household (Ephesians 5.22-33 and 6.1-4). God chose the Jews to be His people and He used them to bring the order of His truth to the chaos of pagan disorder (Romans 4.1-25). God sent One Son — not competing sons — to establish *one* Holy Catholic and Apostolic Church (John 1.1-5). ("I believe in One Holy Catholic and Apostolic Church. I acknowledge one Baptism for the remission of sins.") God chose twelve specific Apostles. When Judas was replaced by Matthias it was in the orderly manner mandated by God. (Acts 1.23-26). Paul was confirmed and sent out by the authority of the apostolic Jerusalem Church, in which James presided as bishop. Paul did not get a personalized call no one else heard: "the Lord laid thus and such on my heart. . ." Ananias *also* heard the call from God and he presented Paul to the Disciples in Jerusalem. Only then was Paul sent out by the Church (Acts 13.2-3).

In Acts 13.1-4 we read that "As they (the apostolic leaders of the Church) ministered to the Lord and fasted, the Holy Spirit said, 'Now separate to Me Barnabas and Saul for the work to which I have called them.' Then, having fasted and prayed, and laid hands on them, they sent them away. So, being sent out by the Holy Spirit they went down to Cylicia. . . " Saul (St. Paul), and Barnabas did not get some private call from the Holy Spirit

[13]St. Cyprian of Carthage, *Letter to Bishop Jubaianus*, Ref. 594, A.D. 554, in *The Faith of the Early Fathers*, vol. 1, trans. W. A. Jurgens, p. 237.

to become evangelists. It was the Church's leaders who heard the call. In fact, their act in sending out Paul is presented as an act of the Holy Spirit who alone guides the true Church. The voice of the Jerusalem hierarchy and the voice of the Spirit are presented as one and the same.

Paul continued as he began. He did not set out to convert people to a chaotic self-created "Pauline church," unlike Luther who founded the "Lutheran church" or Calvin, whose followers came to be known as "Calvinists." Rather, Paul preserved the unity of apostolic authority given to him. Indeed much of St. Paul's writing is taken up with rebuking schismatics. Before leaving a locality in which he had made new converts, we read that Paul "appointed elders, in every church, and prayed with fasting. . . ." (Acts 14.23). In other words, he appointed others to become leaders, bishops, of the Church in apostolic continuity, in the same way as he had been sent out.

The orderly authority of the Apostles and the newly appointed elders, priests and bishops in the Church was well-established from the beginning. We can see that the order Christ ordained in the Church, (Matthew 16.18-19), was indeed followed from the earliest days of the Church. For instance, in the case of how the dispute over circumcision was resolved.

> But some of the sect of the Pharisees who believed rose up saying, 'It is necessary to circumcise them, and to command them to keep the laws of Moses.' So the apostles and elders came together to consider this matter. And when there had been much dispute, Peter rose up and said . . ." (Acts 15.5-7)

What *is* clearly recorded is that disputes in the Church were not settled in an atmosphere of egalitarian congregationalism. After everyone had a say, it was an Apostle, in this case Peter, who rose up and spoke. And it was to his authority that the disputants deferred, not because of any revelation by some "Inner Light," but because of the external, authority structure of the Church hierarchy put in place by Christ. And since James was the first bishop of Jerusalem we can see by the fact that Peter "rose up and spoke" that James was no "pope," that the Apostles shared their authority. This point is made even more forcefully when we look at how the Jerusalem Decree was arrived at, proclaimed to the churches and worded: ". . . it seemed good to the Holy Spirit, and to us, to lay upon you no greater burden than these necessary things. . . ." (Acts 15.22-29) The Apostles and the elders whom they had appointed, spoke not only with authority but as *co-directors* of the Church along with the Holy Spirit. And they spoke collegially as "us."

Christ established one Church, gave it a specific hierarchy, specific sacraments and a specific, orderly, collegial way in which it should govern itself. This is less a theological statement than an historical observation. In fact, as we have seen, where schism and chaos reign, or where there is a dictator speaking "infallibly," that place is by definition *not* the Church. This is true even though many true believers may be found within the gates of a myriad of well-meaning, but nevertheless sadly confused, Protestant denominations, and in the increasingly chaotic Roman church, doing the best they can by the feeble light they have been given.

The Fathers of the Church speak with one voice. In A.D. 304 Lactantius wrote,

> Many heresies have come about, and because the people of God have been cut apart by the instigation of demons, the truth must be briefly marked out by us, and must be placed within its own proper domicile. Thus, if anyone wishes to draw the water of life, he will not be turned aside to broken cisterns which hold no supply.
>
> . . . It is, therefore, the Catholic Church (i.e., historic and universal) alone which retains true worship. This is the fountain of truth; this, the domicile of faith; this, the temple of God. Whoever does not enter there or whoever does not go out from here, he is a stranger to the hope of life and salvation. . . . Because, however confident all the various groups of heretics are, that they are the Christians, and think that theirs is the Catholic Church, let it be known: that (it) is (in) the true Church (alone in), which there is confession and penance.[14]

Jesus did not establish a Church whose hopeless destiny was to split into ever tinier warring fragments. In fact Jesus

---

[14]Lactantius, *The Divine Institution*, Ref. 637, A. D. 304, Ibid. p. 267.

taught that schism was a sign of the coming of the Anti-Christ. "And then many will be offended, will betray one another, and will hate one another. Then many false prophets will rise up and deceive many. And because lawlessness will abound, the love of many will grow cold. But he who endures to the end shall be saved" (Matthew 24.10-13).

All the Fathers, including St. Basil the Great, speak as one against schism.

> Because their separation (is) initiated through schisms, . . . those who (have) separated themselves from the Church no longer (have) in themselves the grace of the Holy Spirit. . . . Nor could they any longer confer on others that grace of the Holy Spirit from which they themselves had fallen away.[15]

HOPE

The sense of frustration felt by some sincere godly Protestants because of the fact that they have no legitimate historical Church authority to appeal disputes to need not have been there at all. In fact, there *is* such a thing as the historical Church and against all odds and in spite of the imperfections of its people and leaders, it is still in existence today. Its altar is undefiled, its doctrine is pure, its sacraments are holy, and its Holy Tradition has been preserved.

The Orthodox Church's hierarchy is made up of sinful men who have made many terrible mistakes. Yet collectively, in spite of themselves, they have miraculously preserved the faith, doctrine, teaching, Holy Tradition, and Holy Sacraments established by Christ, the Apostles, and Fathers, and paid for with the blood of the martyrs.

The changelessness of the Orthodox Church has been its hallmark. The living continuity of two thousand years remains intact — an extraordinary and observable fact that can be seen to exist in time and space independent of theological speculation. This is a fact that is documented and preserved in the bones of the Fathers, Saints and Patriarchs, bones which lie

---

[15]St. Basil the Great, *The First Canonical Letters*, Ref. 919, A.D. 374, in *The Faith of the Early Fathers*, vol. 2, trans. W. A. Jurgens, p. 6.

side by side in, amongst other places, Jerusalem, Antioch, Constantinople and Moscow. They are a historic witness to the sure unbroken continuity of the faith and the practical answer to the demand, "Show me the list of your bishops."

That the preservation of the historic Church is a fact of history should not surprise those of us who believe in the Christ of miracles or the leadership of the Holy Spirit. Today if St. Irenaeus were to ask to see the lists of the bishops of the faithful and historical Orthodox Church, we could still oblige him. Moreover if he, or any other Church Father, came into an Orthodox church to worship they would recognize the liturgy and prayers as belonging to the same historical body in which they worshipped hundreds of years before.[16]

The Church of the Apostles, that Jesus said the very gates of hell would not prevail against, has indeed been preserved. Whether in Boston, St. Petersburg, Constantinople or Jerusalem, its historic continuity is observably intact. Every Orthodox liturgy performed bears faithful witness to this fact. The unbroken continuity of the Orthodox Church is open to study. It is well-documented.[17]

---

[16]"There are three main Orthodox Liturgies; St. Chrysostom's (fourth century), St. Basil's (third century), and that of St. James, the Brother of the Lord (first century)." *A Dictionary of Greek Orthodoxy* (Pleasantville, 1984), pp. 234-35.

[17]See Eusebius, *The History of the Church*; Jaroslav Pelikan, *The Spirit of Eastern Christendom*; Timothy Ware, *The Orthodox Church* (London and New York, 1974); and Runciman, *The Great Church in Captivity* (Cambridge, 1968) for just four of the many hundreds of works on the Orthodox Church's history.

CHAPTER FIFTEEN

FALSE AUTHORITY

The sins of heresy, schism and rebellion are not new to the Church of the East or West. St. Ambrose of Milan wrote in A.D. 389: "Even the heretics appear to have Christ, . . . none of them deny the name of Christ; yet, anyone who does not confess all that pertains to Christ does in fact deny Christ."[1]

Some people in the denominational "churches" also "appear to have Christ." Perhaps coveting some special, almost magical authority for themselves, they take Jesus' very specific teaching on church authority out of context, and apply it to themselves personally.[2] Thus one might hear some earnest Evangelical Protestant pray, "Oh Lord, we just come to You and pray for so and so and we just bind in heaven what we are asking for, that it may be done here on earth for You have said, Where two or three are gathered together. . . . "

There is a curious flaw in such "prayer." It is as mistaken as if someone read the American founding documents out of context and began to borrow the trappings of governmental authority and to lace their personal speech with phrases such as, "I the court rule that . . ." or "In this case my motion is passed by a majority vote and is now law" or "I veto this argument and, exercising the authority vested in me . . .," or "in the name of the Constitution of the United States I command you to do the dishes!"

---

[1] St. Ambrose of Milan, *Commentary on the Gospel of Luke*, Ref. 1304, A.D. 389, in *The Faith of the Early Fathers*, trans. W. A. Jurgens, p. 163.

[2] Sometimes this goes to extremes, as in the case of the Jonestown and Waco, Texas, cults and ensuing tragedies.

A question would arise as to the sanity of an individual who seriously spoke like this in everyday conversation. The same is true of many well-meaning religious people who borrowing inappropriately from the Scripture, vest in themselves personally the trappings of the special authority clearly reserved by Christ for the whole of the Church's hierarchy in its orderly and unique apostolic authority. "For these are wells without water, clouds carried by a tempest. . . . For when they speak great swelling words of emptiness . . . it would have been better for them not to have known the way of righteousness, than . . . to turn from the holy commandment. . . . " (2 Peter 2.17-21).

In the book of Acts we read of confusion similar to that experienced by today's Protestants and Roman Catholics. Certain Jewish leaders tried to use Christ's name as if it were a magic talisman which would give them automatic power and authority outside of the context of the Church. But just as today's Protestant denominations fail in any reasonable test of historic legitimacy, and the papacy fails the test of observable history, so we read in the Book of Acts of the failure of those who used Jesus' name outside of the context of His Church.

> Then some of the itinerant Jewish exorcists took it upon themselves to call the name of the Lord Jesus over those who had evil spirits, saying, 'We adjure you by the Jesus whom Paul preaches.' Also there were seven sons of Sevea, a Jewish chief priest, who did so. And the evil spirit answered and said, 'Jesus I know, Paul I know; but who are you?' Then the man in whom the evil spirit was leaped on them, overpowered them, and prevailed against them so that they fled out of that house naked and wounded. (Acts 19.13-16)

TRUE AUTHORITY

The hierarchy established by God in the historical Church can be traced in the Holy Tradition as well as in many biblical passages, including Matthew 16.18-19, Ephesians 2.20, John 21.15-17, John 20.21-23, 1 Timothy 3.15, Revelation 21.14,

Acts 1.21-26, Acts 8.14-18, and Acts 13.2-3. The Fathers of the Church, many writing *well over two hundred years before there even was a New Testament,* bear unanimous witness to the Orthodox understanding of Church order. In A.D. 95 Clement, Bishop of Rome, who had known the Apostles and had, as Eusebius said, the Apostles' words "still ringing in his ears," wrote,

> The Apostles received the gospel for us from Jesus Christ . . . So Christ from God, and the Apostles from Christ . . . So they preached from country to country . . . they appointed their first converts, after testing them by the Spirit, to be the bishops and deacons of the future believers.[3]

In A.D. 69 St. Ignatius of Antioch, second from the Apostle Peter wrote,

> . . . be eager to do everything in God's harmony, with the bishop presiding in the place of God. . . . .[4]

In A.D. 180, St. Irenaeus of Lyons in *Against Heresies* wrote, "We are in a position to reckon up those who were by the Apostles instituted bishops in the Churches and (to demonstrate) the succession of these men to our own times."[5] Like Eusebius, Irenaeus, who was the disciple of Polycarp and pupil of St. John the Apostle, counted the exact number of bishops who had passed on the authority of the Church to their successors since the Apostles. He did so in order to establish their credentials. By this means Irenaeus was able to successfully challenge the heretics of his own day as being outside of the legitimate inheritance of the Church.

Thus if the heretics were to say "Irenaeus, by what authority do you condemn our teaching as false," he need not reply, "By my own" or, "by my personal interpretation of Scripture" but rather "By the authority vested in me by Christ through the laying on of hands in direct unbroken apostolic continuity back to Christ Himself!" And he could also respond, "because my

---

[3] Clement of Rome, *Letter to the Church at Corinth,* the *Ante-Nicene Fathers,* vol. 1, (Edinburgh, 1867, Grand Rapids 1993), pp. 1-26.

[4] Ignatius of Antioch, *Ignatius to the Magnesians,* 6.1. *The Faith of the Holy Fathers,* p. 12.

[5] Eusebius, *History of the Church,* vol. 3, Chapter 3.

teaching is in conformity to the teaching of the Apostles preserved by Holy Tradition and faithfully passed on, unchanged, from
one generation to the next!"[6]

The mandate of history aside, perhaps the best argument
against the Roman Cathoic and subsequent Protestant abandonment of the collegial authority of the Apostles can be found
in the horrific schismatic *results* engendered by those have
turned their backs on the historical Church. We see the
evidence of these results around us everywhere in the trivialization of worship, the abandonment of moral discipline,
authority and unity, and a horrid counterfeit "spirituality" that
is a force of reactionary secularism in our religiously pluralistic
society.

DELUSION

There is a delusion shared by even those Protestants who
call themselves "conservative" or "traditional" or "evangelical."
They too have reduced faith to an individualized experience.
They have even gone so far as to reduce their concept of the
Church to a subjective interpretation. In this regard one often
hears Protestants say things like, "Well, isn't the church just
the whole body of Christ, made up of all people who call
themselves Christians?" Or, "The Church lives in my heart. It's
not a place or thing, it's the faith I have inside of me. I carry
my own church inside of me." Or, "Apostolic continuity is just
a spiritual continuity." The historic writings of the Fathers of
the historic Church denounce all such personalized pieties with
a resounding "No!"[7]

If Christianity is true, then its truth exists independently of
our feelings about it. It is rooted in history, not simply in

---

[6]This is the line taken by St. Maximus: "As a confessor and theologian, Maximus
was obligated to preserve, protect and defend the doctrine that had been handed down
by the fathers; for to 'confess with soul and mouth' meant to affirm 'what the fathers
have taught us.' (Maximus. Ep. 12. P.G.91:465) In any theological argument,
therefore, it was necessary to produce 'the voices of the fathers as evidence for the
faith of the church.' (Maximus Ep. 13. P.G. 91:532)" Jaroslav Pelikan, *The Spirit of
Eastern Christendom*, p. 8.

[7]"You shall not make a schism. Rather, you shall make peace among those who are
contending . . . you shall keep what you have received, adding nothing to it nor taking
anything away." *Didache*, A.D. 140, trans. W. A. Jurgens (Collegeville, 1970), p. 2.

theological ideas or subjective feelings. Similarly, if there is a historical Church, it exists not in our hearts, but in *fact*, in *history*, *time* and *space*, just as Christ did when He walked on earth. Seen in this light, the Church's purpose on earth is to be the Christ-bearing community in the real world, not a personal, inward-oriented feeling.

Suppose Jesus had given anyone claiming to be a believer the authority to bind or loose in heaven what is bound or loosed on earth. Suppose each believer could proclaim *himself* a "church." Believing Christians brought before the Church for judgment, or to resolve their theological or doctrinal disputes, could render the whole process utterly meaningless by simply saying, "I disagree with your decision; I'm right and you are wrong. I bind my own will in heaven as on earth. Jesus has promised me personally that whatever is decided by me, along with a couple of like-minded friends, will be backed up by God. Who elected you? This is a democracy! I decide I'm right and you're wrong. God will support me and you are now judged and found wanting. Verse so and so in the Bible says. . . ."

This is, in fact, what many Protestants have done in one way or another since the Reformation. And it is the sort of argument one hears made by protestantized democratized Roman Catholics and even some secularized "Orthodox" who wish to "democratize" or "modernize" the historical Church or to make it more "relevant," "open" or "politically correct." We have twentythree thousand Protestant denominations to show us where this type of judgmental pietism, this individualistic, holier-than-thou, secularized and thoroughly arrogant mentality leads.

Professor Steve Bruce writes about this Protestant death wish.

> Liberal Protestantism can be fairly simply identified. It is a tendency which regards human reason as paramount and which begins its theologizing from the agenda of the secular world. It thus appears as a continual impulse to modernize the faith, to abandon the confines of the historic creeds, and to accommodate the thought and practices of the churches to those of the secular world. . . . In many ways, liberal Protestantism was (an) . . . attempt to create an intellectually supportable version of Christianity, in the face of massive (Reformation-Protestant) divisions within the body

of those who claimed to worship the same God.[8]

As Professor Bruce notes, the differences between "conservative" Protestants and "liberal" ones is superficial. Both equally reject the authority of the historic apostolic Church established by Christ. Without the guidance of Holy Tradition, both are left with little more than personalized, deconstructed and subjective readings of the Scripture on which to base competing theological and moral claims. "Both were certain that God's unfolding truth (was) richer and fuller than ever before. . . ."[9]

In other words, "liberal" and "conservative" Protestants *both* pride themselves on moving *beyond* what they regarded as the unnecessary constrictions of Holy Tradition and apostolic authority, into a utopian world of individualistic Biblical interpretation, social change, millennial prosperity and personal freedom, based on the idea of "Sola Scriptura."[10]

It was, after all, in the name of Scripture that Anabaptists became anarchists as they searched the Word and received "messages" direct from God which told then to burn property deeds in the name of a new, improved, egalitarian Christianity. It was Scripture that convinced Quakers to abandon baptism, Eucharist and sacramental church weddings in favor of do-it-yourself desacralized, "hand-fast" marriages. It is in the Bible that today's rapacious T.V. "evangelists" find verses with which to confuse people into giving them money. It was in the Bible that David Koresh found arguments to convince his followers to obey him, even to burn themselves to death in the Branch Davidian compound in Waco, Texas, on April 19, 1993. The Bible is the primary witnessing tool with which Mormons confuse ignorant Protestant, Roman Catholic and Orthodox Christians into abandoning Christianity and joining their nineteenth century cult. And the "liberal," secularized leaders of the

---

[8]Steve Bruce, *A House Divided*, pp. 102-18.

[9]Ibid. p. 103.

[10]In this regard the work of the twentieth century Protestants on the political and theological Right, like Carl Henry, J. F. Packer, and others, is just as ahistorical as the theology of the Protestant Left. While being "conservative" in the details of their social critique, in the end the writers in question can only fall back on, "I think" or "the Bible says," never, "This is what the Church has always taught." When Protestants do make reference to church history, or quote a church father, it raises the question of why they feel the need to bolster their theological arguments at all if "Sola Scriptura" is enough.

World Council of Churches, that colluded with the Communist persecutors of Christians, often quote the Bible to justify their coercive, utopian political crusades.

SCRIPTURE

Today, confused and well-meaning Protestants of all denominational persuasions, having little or no historic foundation at all, take Scripture — in other words, *their* interpretation of Scripture — as their only source of spiritual authority. They replace the historic Church's Holy Tradition with themselves — personally. Each individual becomes his or her own "ecumenical council," "bishop" and "priest." Each is a law unto himself as he reads the Bible and claims, "God is speaking to me." This fervor of individualized faith is practiced outside of the context of the historical Church. Each Protestant claims to base his or her ideas — which are often contradictory one of another — "on Scripture." The battle cry, "Sola Scriptura" often turns out to be nothing more than the first verse to the song "I Did It My Way!"

Unfortunately Protestants do not read the Bible in the context of Christian history. They more often than not study it in a historical, liturgical and spiritual vacuum. Yet it is the historical Church, out of which the Bible came, that *alone* provides us with the contextual key to begin to understand the meaning of the Scriptures. And it is only in the context of the living continuity of *sacramental worship*, through which all Christians in all ages of the Church are bound into one family, that the Gospel comes to life and is given its proper place.[11]

---

[11]"What is the Bible? Is it a book like any other intended for any occasional reader, who is expected to grasp at once its proper meaning? Rather, it is a *sacred* book addressed primarily to believers. . . . St. Hilary put it emphatically: Scripture is not in the reading, but in the understanding. Is there any definite message in the Bible, taken as whole, as one book? And again, to whom is this message, if any, properly addressed? To individuals, who would be, as such, entitled to understand the book and to expound its message? Or to the community, and to individuals only in so far as they are members of that community?

Whatever the origin of particular documents included in the book may have been, it is obvious that the book, as a whole, was a creation of the community, both in the old dispensation and in the Christian Church. The Bible is by no means a complete *collection* of all historical, legislative and devotional writings available, but a *selection* of some, authorized and authenticated by the use (first of all liturgical) in the com-

A high price has been paid for egocentric, self-centered, individualistic Protestant style of "spirituality" which has ignored the wisdom of the ages. Protestant "Conservatives" and "Liberals" have not succeeded in achieving agreement, even among themselves, as to what the Bible "says." What began with the brave cry "away with bishops, Sola Scriptura!" ends in the realization that the Bible, taken out of the context of Holy Tradition, liturgy, sacramental worship and prayer "means" whatever each person says it does.

Ironically, Protestant theologians are the fathers of deconstructionism. It is they who abandoned both the historic and spiritual context from which the Bible came. Modern Protestantism has rendered the meaning of the text unintelligible beyond individual emotional responses. And so the circle of subjectivity is completed. Faith is now personalized into a "born-again experience." The Church "lives in our hearts," the sacraments are "mere symbols," and finally the Bible's "message" turns out to be a message of the sort madmen "hear" in their minds when secret voices "speak" things to them that no one else can hear.

According to the historical Church, the questions we should ask before reading the Scriptures are: "To whom were these remarks addressed? In what context were they spoken? What preceded them? What came after?" And most important of all, *"How are these teachings interpreted by the Church Fathers, the men who were closest to the source —* men who, in many cases, knew the Apostles?

---

munity, and finally by the formal authority of the Church. . . . The message is divine; it comes from God; it is the Word of God. But it is the faithful community that acknowledges the Word spoken and testifies to its truth. The sacred character of the Bible is ascertained by faith. The Bible, as a book, has been composed in the community and was meant primarily for its edification. The book and the Church cannot be separated. The book and the Covenant belong together, and Covenant implies people. It was the People of the Covenant to whom the Word of God had been entrusted under the old dispensation (Romans 3.2), and it is the Church of the Word Incarnate that keeps the message of the Kingdom. The Bible is the Word of God indeed, but the book stands by the testimony of the Church. The canon of the Bible is obviously established and authorized by the Church. . . . Tertullian's attitude to the Scriptures was typical. He was not prepared to discuss the controversial topics of the faith with heretics on the Scriptural ground. Scriptures belonged to the Church. Heretics' appeal to them was unlawful. They had no right on foreign property. Such was his main argument in the famous treatise, *De praescriptione haereticorum.* An unbeliever has no access to the message, simply because he does not receive it. For him there is no message in the Bible." Georges Florovsky, *Bible, Church, Tradition: An Eastern Orthodox View,* pp. 17-19.

We should ask how we might understand the Bible in the context of sacramental, liturgical worship, rather than as an egocentric exercise in "Bible study." Unfortunately many well-meaning Christians seem to read their Bible only as a mere personalized "devotional" or "inspirational" book, not as a book of truth to be interpreted consistently in the light of the Church's Holy Apostolic Tradition, Sacraments, liturgies and teaching. They seem to superstitiously believe that each verse, word and line, whether in or out of context, correctly translated or not, meant as history or allegory, is addressed to them *individually* in some magical way. The Church has taught that Bible study without prayer and outside of the context of authentic sacramental worship is, as St. Evagrios the Solitary taught, the "theology of demons."

This type of spiritually arrogant, anti-communitarian, "intuitive" reading of the Bible, without regard for history, liturgical worship, context or interpretation by the historic Church reduces the Bible to personalized mush, not very different from the astrological charts printed daily in the tabloid newspapers.

Such astrological devotional reading treats the Bible not as a book of truth, history, allegory, mystery and spirituality, with a long and distinguished history of authoritative interpretation, but rather as a sort of fortune cookie in which we get personal, magical messages. It seems to me that the motivation for this kind of star-gazing "Bible study," and the sort of "prayer" that accompanies it, may be the same one that drives tens of thousands of misguided spiritualists to mediums and palm readers. It is the total privatization of religious truth. It may be, in fact, the final blow to claims of the historicity of Christianity. It is the sort of "Bible study" of which Jean Jacques Rousseau and the Romantics would have approved. It is also the most damning testimony available to the secularistic scoffer; Biblical Christianity is an irrational religion for the emotionally unstable and gullible.

Worst of all, such a personalized, subjective approach to the Bible removes its reading from the context of the community of believers. When the Bible is studied outside of the context of the Church, when each person expects God to address them *individually* the practice of such religiosity sinks to the level of just one more selfish exercise all too typical of our selfish world.

Ironically, some Protestants, including those who call themselves "Fundamentalists," while paying lip service to "biblical inerrancy" and while believing they are sincerely "looking to the Bible" as their "sole source" of spiritual guidance, nevertheless, by taking verses out of the historic context of Holy Tradition and liturgical worship, de-historicize the Bible. Thus fundamentalist Protestants are in this sense no less liberal than the Liberal Protestants they loudly denounce and loathe. Both manage to effectively reduce the Bible's historical authority to zero by removing it from the context of the community of faith: the Orthodox Church.

Let us remember the roots of this type of subjective Biblical interpretation go back to the very beginning of the Protestant rebellion. It was Martin Luther who wanted to drop various books of the Bible not in accordance with his personalized, subjective theology. These included First and Second John, James and Revelation. And it was Calvin in his *Institutes*, who wrote that intuitive feelings, rather than Consensus Fidelium (the Holy Tradition), are the hermeneutical principles by which sacred tradition must be replaced.

Just as Martin Luther had the audacity to add words to the Bible in his German translation, and to suggest the elimination of whole Biblical books, so today's Protestants continue in Luther's unholy anarchy by further personalizing Bible study and further removing it from the context of sacramental communal worship. As a result, Protestants routinely misinterpret verses about healing, prosperity, blessing and priestly authority. Blinded by faulty self-serving "Bible study," of the kind Calvin said was better than dependency on Holy Tradition, Protestants have traveled far from historic Christianity. In fact, many Protestants have removed themselves so far from the context of ecclesiastical accountability, that it is very difficult to even begin to explain to them that what they now believe bears little resemblance to the faith or worship of the historical Church.

FALSE LEADERS

Unfortunately what is true for individuals is also true of the teaching in the schismatic denominations as a whole. Cut off from historical tradition and precedent, legitimate apostolic

Church hierarchy and God-given, legitimate sacramental worship, Protestant pastors have become their own self-appointed individual "popes." They have assumed the mantle of the teaching authority of the whole Church without being answerable to the doctrines of the historical Church of the ages. They have, on an individual basis, repeated the mistake of the Roman Catholic Church. They have turned the study of Scripture into a cold, biblical science, removed from the context of living sacramental worship. They are subject to no ecclesiastical checks and balances. Thus they go off on any and all imaginable tangents. Unwilling to personally submit to the discipline of spiritual fathers, they can hardly call others to moral accountability. They are the unfortunate, often historically ignorant, sometimes egomaniacal inheritors of the Protestant revolution that has engulfed us. Some may call themselves "Conservative," but such claims ring hollow in the context of a reactionary Protestantism that has failed to honor — let alone conserve — the essentials of Christian worship, order, unity, discipline and Holy Tradition.

The spiritually impoverished parishioners in most Protestant congregations have no one to appeal to and thus can either abide the make-it-up-as-you-go-along teaching of their mini-popes — the Protestant empire-building "pastor" or leader — or find another local "church." Once again, this "church" will be just one more island of Protestant individualism adrift from historical Christianity. If they do not like any "local church," Protestants can start their own "churches," even whole denominations. If they desire to go to confession, they find a psychologist. If they wish to hear God's will for their lives, they flip open the Bible, at random, and let God "speak," or conduct an emotionally charged, seance-style "prayer meeting" or turn on the television set and hope that some empire-building televangelist will enlighten them with an electronic "word of knowledge."

APOSTOLIC ACCOUNTABILITY

All such individualistic anarchy in the name of "spirituality" is foreign to the authentic historical Church. Personal accountability is exercised through confession to a priest. There is accountability to the hierarchy and its collective wisdom, which represents not just the subjective opinions of those alive now, but the wisdom of the Church of the ages going back to the Fathers, Christ and the Old Testament Prophets. In this way we may gradually come to discern the mind of the Church.

At times there may arise individual excesses, even false teachings in the historical Church. These can be judged and corrected on the basis of the continuing living Holy Tradition. One bishop or priest's fall from grace, or the mistakes or heresy of one part of the Church, is eventually corrected by the whole. In the end the mind of the Church is quite definite and consistent on all important matters of salvation, prayer, morals, sacrament and apostolic authority: those things that have been believed by all Christians everywhere, since the beginning.

In the Orthodox Church, congregations are not simply set adrift with their individual pastors, high-powered individual "gurus," their denomination's self-appointed "leaders," and their changeable interpretations of Scripture. In the historical Church the priest's authority is derived both from being in the apostolic succession and from being faithful to the Holy Tradition. The priest's authority derives from the authority of his bishop and the bishop's authority is subject to the precedent of changeless truth and history established by Christ and the Apostles that is called the Holy Tradition.

Schism is inherently evil within the Orthodox Church because by its very nature it denies the work of the Holy Spirit Who guides the One Holy, Catholic and Apostolic Church.[12] As such, schism is the ultimate unforgivable sin — the sin against the Spirit which cannot be forgiven because the damage done is eternal and irreparable. It denies the universal truth of Christianity as each person becomes his or her own measure of all things sitting in judgment on the Church, armed only with a purely subjective reading of Scripture. Holy Tradition teaches that schism is a re-crucifixion of Christ. Division among believers, according to Christ, is part of the anti-Christ's program, not that of God (Matthew 24.3-13).

---

[12]"He that is within the sanctuary is pure; but he that is outside the sanctuary is not pure. In other words, anyone who acts without the bishop and the presbyter and the deacons does not have a clean conscience." St. Ignatius of Antioch, *Letter to the Romans,* A. D. 110, in *The Faith of the Fathers,* vol. 1, trans. W. A. Jurgens, p. 18.

FORGIVENESS WITHIN THE CHURCH

How patient are we to be with what we perceive as the day-to-day failings of the historical Orthodox Church? How forgiving are we to be of other Christians in the historical Orthodox Church? How long-suffering of the weaknesses of our Orthodox bishops and priests? When do we shake the dust off our shoes and go off and start our own "churches," as Protestants repeatedly have done, and as many American Roman Catholics seem to be doing as they are becoming more and more insubordinate in their rejection of Holy Tradition? How many times must we forgive the Church Her torn skirts before we do what some isolated "Orthodox" groups have done, who have fallen out of Communion with the Orthodox Church in the name of "purity?" When do we "excommunicate" the Orthodox Church rather than submit to its historic and apostolic authority and Holy Tradition even when its human leaders are far from perfect? How long do we wait before we leave, rebel, cause schism or try and manipulate or bully our apostolic leaders? Or, as Peter, to whom apostolic heavenly authority was given, said, "Lord, how often shall my brother sin against me, and I forgive him? Up to seven times?" Jesus said to him, "I do not say to you, up to seven times, but up to seventy times seven" (Matthew 18.21-22).

Forgiveness between believers in the Orthodox Church is not left to chance. Nor is it reduced to score-keeping. Christ taught us to pray "Forgive us our sins as we forgive the sins of others!" Jesus gave the Church's hierarchy special authority to bind in Heaven, to discipline believers and offer God's forgiveness for sins on earth. He also taught forgiveness within the Church. It is in the spirit of Christ's teaching to Peter that the Orthodox Church in Her wisdom and love welcomes back the repentant sinner. And it is in the spirit of long-suffering that we in the historic Orthodox Church forgive our leaders, priests and bishops, their human failings. In this we must choose to follow Christ's example, who forgave Peter when he did the work of Satan, becoming "mindful of the things of (men) but (not) the things of God" (Matthew 16.22-23).

The merciful character of the Church is revealed in its prayers. After confession, in the Orthodox Church, the penitent sinner hears these tender words from his or her priest.

My spiritual child, who has confessed to my humble self, I, humble and a sinner, have not power on earth to forgive sins, but God alone; yet through that divinely spoken word which came to the Apostles after the Resurrection of our Lord Jesus Christ saying: 'Whosesoever sins ye remit, they are remitted, and whosesoever sins ye retain, they are retained,' we too are emboldened to say: Whatsoever thou has said to my most humble self and whatsoever thou has not succeeded in saying, either through ignorance, or through forgetfulness, whatever it may be; God forgive you in this present world, and in that which is to come.

These words embody the eternal mercy of Christ mysteriously extended to us through His historic, apostolic Orthodox Church. In the priest's response to the repentant sinner, we see the historical Church obey Christ's teaching to Peter, in which He gave him authority to judge his flock, but tempered it with mercy, telling Peter to forgive seventy times seven.

CHAPTER SIXTEEN
SALVATION

"The arena, the field of battle, the site where the fight actually takes place is our own heart and all our inner man. The time of battle is our whole life."[1]

We have been looking at the fact that, contrary to Protestant-secularist mythology, the Church is a historical reality. Now we shall see that the Augustinian-Scholastic, and Protestant concept of salvation is not the same as that taught by the Orthodox Church.

FREE WILL

St. John of Damascus (674 - 749 A.D.) wrote,

For as we are composed of soul and body . . . our soul does not stand alone, but is, as it were, shrouded by a veil, it is impossible for us to arrive at intellectual conceptions without corporal things. Just as we listen with our bodily ears to physical words and understand spiritual things. . . . [2]

For the Byzantine Orthodox theologians like St. John of Damascus, there was not a contradiction between faith and

---

[1]Lorenzo Scupoli, *Unseen Warfare*, edited by Nicodemus of the Holy Mountain and revised by Theophan the Recluse, translated by E. Kadloubovsky and G. E. H. Palmer (Crestwood, 1987).

[2]As cited by H. J. Magoulias. *Byzantine Christianity* (Detroit, 1982), p. 48.

reason, or between God and mankind's free will. "Some may say that it is not necessary to study nature," he wrote. "We ought to know that these are the words of the indolent and lazy. The study of nature, which is the basis of theology, proves theological truth. The student will see the spirit of God in nature."[3]

In the time of the Byzantine empire, it was believed, as expressed by St. Symeon the New Theologian, that human nature is "mutable and changeable." Human beings were not condemned to live "forever bound by the iron chain of an immutable nature."[4]

The great message of the Christian Fathers, like St. Maximus the Confessor, St. Gregory of Sinai and St. Symeon the New Theologian, was that our human and sinful nature is alterable. In contrast to the rigidity of the Augustinian view of predestination and original sin, the Eastern Church believed that free will is God's greatest gift to His creatures.[5]

Irenaeus, bishop of Lyons, expressed this idea well in A.D. 180.

> For God made man free from the beginning, so that he possessed his own power just as his own soul, to follow God's will freely, not being compelled by God. For with God there is no coercion; but a good will is present with Him always. He, therefore, gives good counsel to all. . . . Not merely in works, but even in faith, man's freedom of choice under his own control is preserved by the Lord, who says: "Let it be done to you according to your faith."[6]

---

[3]Ibid. p. 48.

[4]Ibid. p. 77.

[5]"In Scripture we see God coming to reveal himself to man, and we see man meeting God, and not only listening to his voice, but answering him too. We hear in the Bible not only the voice of God, but also the voice of man answering him — in words of prayer, thanksgiving and adoration, awe and love, sorrow and contrition, exultation, hope or despair. There are, as it were, two partners in the Covenant, God and man, and both belong together, in the mystery of the true divine-human encounter, which is described and recorded in the story of the Covenant. Human response is integrated into the mystery of the Word of God. It is not a divine monologue, it rather a dialogue, and both are speaking, God and man. . . . Yet, all this intimacy does not compromise divine sovereignty and transcendence. God is 'dwelling in light unapproachable' (I Timothy 6:16). This light, however, 'lighteth every man that cometh into the world' (John 1:9). This constitutes the mystery, or the 'paradox' of the revelation." Georges Florovsky, *Bible, Church, Tradition: An Eastern Orthodox View*, p. 21.

[6]St. Irenaeus of Lyons, *Against Heresies* A.D. 180, in *The Faith of the Early Fathers*, vol. 1, trans. W. A. Jurgens, p. 98.

According to Holy Tradition, we can choose to change our ways. We may exercise our free will and flee the slavery of sin "according to our faith." We are not locked into a path of election or damnation. Far from it: we can choose to love God as He loves us. We can even spend a lifetime in trying to become like God ourselves. St. Symeon taught that in our efforts to flee sin, we are not left as orphans unaided, for "within all of human nature He (God) placed a loving power so that the rational nature of man might be helped by the natural power of love."[7] Love, according to the Church, is the power of mercy by which God draws us back to Himself.[8]

NEW HOPE

It seems to me that the root problem of our culture is that we have looked for salvation in the wrong places.[9] The secularists have looked for salvation from sin by turning to the works of political action, as if coercive government programs could eradicate evil. The American Protestant also looks for a magical instantaneous "silver bullet" solution to sin. He calls this the "born-again" experience. But, according to the Holy Tradition, just saying that one is "born-again" is meaningless. It does not entail the necessary repentance, ascetic struggle, hardship, sacramental worship and the use of our free will to choose God's way again and again, which the historical Church has taught is the only way we can become like God, strive to become "deified" — in other words imitate Christ and through imitation to become God-like ourselves. As the Psalmist expresses the desire to be saved: "I shall (only) be satisfied when I awake in Your likeness" (Psalms 17.15).

The witness of the historical Church contradicts both secular idolatries *and* Protestant delusions of simplistic solutions to our moral problems. Instead, it holds out the hope of a spiritual

[7] H. J. Magoulias, *Byzantine Christianity*, p. 48.

[8] As St. Clement of Rome writes: "Let us fear Him. . . so that through His mercy, we may be protected from the judgment to come." The first Epistle of Clement: *The Ante-Nicene Fathers*, vol. 1, (Edinbourgh, 1867, and Grand Rapids, 1993).

[9] "Western civilization . . . has departed from the faith . . . history is now seen as the vehicle of salvation. Whether in the form of . . . the Enlightenment type of progress . . . Marxism . . . or Western social engineering . . . it places salvation within the institutions of history and thus fulfills the biblical definition of idolatry." Herbert Schlossberg, *Idols for Destruction* (Nashville, 1983), p. 13.

journey toward the end of becoming God-like, of awakening one day in His likeness.

In A.D. 270, St. Basil the Great wrote,

> I would say that the exercise of piety is rather like a ladder, that ladder which once was seen by the blessed Jacob, at which one end was near the earth and reached to the ground, while the other end extended above and reached to Heaven itself. What is necessary is that those who are being introduced to the virtuous life should put their feet on the first steps and from there mount ever to the next, until at last they have ascended by degrees to such heights as are attainable by human nature.[10]

As St. Basil the Great teaches, salvation is not a matter of instant experience, nor is it one of cosmic fate or election. Rather it is like everything else — a process, a struggle, a climbing of a spiritual ladder.

How are we saved? How can we some day awake in God's likeness? Some Protestants will give a simplistic and incomplete answer to this question: "By believing that Christ died on the cross for us." According to Holy Tradition, that answer is, at best, only partially correct. An answer, more in keeping with Holy Tradition, to the question, "How are we saved?" is simple but difficult: *by struggling to become like Christ*. Orthodox author and priest Anthony Coniaris writes,

> Salvation is not static but dynamic; it is not a completed state, a state of having arrived . . . but a constant moving . . . toward becoming like Christ, toward receiving the fullness of God's life . . . it can never be achieved fully in this life.[11]

According to St. Basil the Great, to become like Christ we must obey Him and imitate Him.

The design of our God and Savior in regard to mankind is

---

[10] St. Basil the Great, *Homilies on the Psalms*, A.D. 270, in *The Faith of the Early Fathers*, vol. 2, selected and translated by W. A. Jurgens, p. 16.

[11] Anthony M. Coniaris, *Introducing the Orthodox Church* (Minneapolis, 1982), p. 48.

a calling back from the fall and a return to familiar friendship with God from the alienation brought about by disobedience. This is the reason for Christ sojourning in the flesh, for the model of His Gospel actions, the suffering, the cross, the tomb, the resurrection: that man, who is being saved through his imitation of Christ, might receive that old adoption as Son.[12]

Whether we call it a born again experience, election, an Inner Light, or some other short cut or explanation, no magic formula exists that can provide us with automatic salvation if we do not practically follow Christ. Indeed, the Church teaches that even being convinced that one is of the elect does not assure one of salvation. As St. Mark the Ascetic wrote in the early fifth century,

Everyone baptized in the orthodox manner has received mystically the fullness of grace; but he becomes conscious of this grace only to the extent that he actively observes the commandments.[13]

Holy Tradition teaches that we are not saved by the mere declaration of a formula, let alone by accepting theological declarations and dogmas, however correct or Biblical they are. Nor do works save us. We will be saved when we become *like Christ*. We are gradually saved as we are deified, by doing Christ's teaching and His commandments. Because of our faith in Him and our desire to become God-like, we are not so much saved all at once as slowly changed into the creatures we were created to be. Only then may we return to familiar friendship with God.

St. Paul writes, "Therefore if anyone is in Christ, he is a new creation; old things have passed away; behold, all things have become new" (2 Corinthians 5.17). This has been understood by the Church as both a *prescriptive* and *descriptive* passage. It is not only a definition of what a Christian *is*, but also a description of how to *become* a Christian. One is saved by

---

[12]St. Basil the Great, *On the Holy Spirit*, A.D. 375, *The Faith of the Early Fathers*, vol. 2, trans. W. A. Jurgens, p. 16.

[13]St. Mark the Ascetic, *On No Righteousness by Works: The Philokalia*, vol. 1, trans. G. E. H. Palmer, Philip Sherrard and Kallistos Ware, p. 155.

becoming a new creation. This is not a one-time magical event, nor a black and white state of being "saved" or "elected" but rather a *process* — *a life-long struggle,* one that is at times so hard that it has been described as taking up a cross (Matthew 16.24-25).

Orthodox Archbishop Paul of Finland sums up this timeless journey toward the eventual goal of salvation.

> Our salvation begins when we receive forgiveness for our sins in Holy Baptism, and indeed many times again later in Confession, the sacrament of repentance or washing with tears. This is followed by new efforts, renewed through the Holy Spirit, to live in Christ as a member of His Body, the Church. The goal of this life is to try to be pure in heart and so to "see God" (Matthew 5:8) in the Holy Spirit.[14]

According to the teaching of the Church, Jesus Christ became flesh through the Incarnation. He did so because we human beings chose to depart from God. Death was the result. In His love God desired to restore us to Himself, to defeat death by death through Christ's resurrection. In his classic fourth century work, *On the Incarnation,* St. Athanasius teaches that by choosing sin we chose death rather than life. Therefore we are unable, by ourselves, to find our way back to the love of the Creator, the Author of Life. St. Athanasius writes,

> The Word of God came in His own Person, because it was He alone, the Image of the Father, who could recreate man made after the Image.[15]

Instead of sending us a mere book or a set of theological rules to obey, Christ, "the Lover of Mankind," came to us *in person* to live among us, in order that we might have a real living, breathing example to imitate. Christ taught that we could follow Him back to the Father and become the new creation of which the Psalmist and St. Paul write. This is why the historical Church has spent the better part of two thousand

[14]Archbishop Paul of Finland, *The Faith We Hold* (Crestwood, 1980), p. 23.

[15]St. Athanasius, *On the Incarnation,* translated by a religious of C.S.M. (Crestwood, 1989), p. 41.

years praising God for Christ's Incarnation. As St. Basil the Great wrote in his beloved prayer, "We thank thee that thou hast not destroyed us in our transgressions, but in thy love toward mankind thou has raised us up, that as we lay in despair, we might glorify thy Majesty." St. Mark the Ascetic writes concerning Christ's Incarnation,

> Call to mind who He is, and what He became for our sakes. Reflect first on the sublime light of His Divinity . . . glorified in the heavens by all spiritual beings: angels, archangels, thrones, dominions, . . . cherubim and seraphim. . . . Then think to what depth of human humiliation He descended . . . becoming in all respects like us who were dwelling in darkness and the shadow of death. . . . Being rich, He became poor for our sakes, so that through His poverty we might become rich. In His great love for man He became like us, so that through every virtue we might become like Him.[16]

Before we can even begin to adequately answer the question, "How are we to be saved?" we need to ponder another question first: "Why did Christ come to us?" Did He come only to die for us, to satisfy the wrath of an angry, juridical Augustinian "God," or did He come to us so that we might have someone to show us how to become again the image and likeness of the loving God?

Sin, according to the Fathers, is choosing to *not* be like God. Evil deeds are all those choices and actions that are contrary to the character of the loving God. The Church teaches us that Satan can create nothing: he can only destroy. One of the tragic results of our sin, in other words, our choosing to not be like God, is the reality of physical death. Our model, Christ, chose to die and to be raised from the dead so that we could follow Him through the very gates of death into a new life, "so that through every virtue we might become like Him." Thus He used death to destroy death! He saved us from death, not by magic, but by example.

---

[16]St. Mark the Ascetic, *Letter to Nicholas the Solitary: The Philokalia*, vol. 1, trans. G. E. H. Palmer, Philip Sherrard and Kallistos Ware, p. 155.

But now Christ is risen from the dead, and has become the first fruits of those who have fallen asleep. For since by man came death, by Man also came the resurrection of the dead. For as in Adam all die, even so in Christ all shall be made alive. But each one in his own order; Christ the first fruits, afterward those who are Christ's at His coming" (1 Corinthians 15.20-23).

According to the Church, Jesus not only *told* us how to be reconciled to God, He *showed* us. By following His example, we can imitate, even put on, the loving character of God. Therefore Jesus, the Church teaches, came to us that we might be like Him, even become immortal. St. Athanasius writes:

The Savior of us all, the Word of God, in His great love took to Himself a body and moved as Man among men, meeting their senses, so to speak, half way. He became Himself an object for the senses, so that those who were seeking God in sensible (i.e., visible, ordinary) things might apprehend the Father through the works which He, the Word of God, did in the body.[17]

According to Holy Tradition, Jesus taught that salvation is a journey toward God, not an instant solution to our problems. Jesus described the process of salvation as passing through a narrow gate, so narrow that He likened it to a birth canal, to being born again. "Enter by the narrow gate: for wide is the gate and broad is the way that leads to destruction, and there are many who go in by it. Because narrow is the gate and difficult is the way which leads to life, and there are few who find it" (Matthew 7.13-14).

According to the Church, Christ gave us His teaching, His life and His Church so that we can be like Him and be enabled to travel the difficult, sacramental, narrow path — the way — toward God and away from death. It is this hope of which St. John Chrysostom writes.

Have you sinned? Go to Church and wipe out your sin. As

---

[17]St. Athanasius, *On the Incarnation*, translated by a religious of C.S.M., p. 43.

often as you might fall down in the marketplace, you pick
yourself up again. So too, as often as you sin, repent your
sins. Do not despair. Even if you sin a second time, repent
a second time. Do not, by indifference, lose hope entirely
of the good things prepared. . . . For here (The Church)
is a physician's office, not a courtroom; not a place where
punishment of sinners is active, but a place where
forgiveness of sin is granted.[18]

Jesus taught us that neither belief, nor spirituality, nor even
good works, are enough. He said that we must follow Him
sacrificially, not only believe on Him but *imitate Him*; become
like Him, lest we become indifferent and lose hope.

For I say to you, that unless your righteousness exceeds
the righteousness of the scribes and Pharisees, you will by
no means enter the Kingdom of heaven . . ." (Matthew
5.20). Therefore you shall be perfect, just as your Father
in heaven is perfect (Matthew 5.48).

As Orthodox scholar Fr. Thomas Hopko writes,

In the Orthodox view, deeds are not an end in themselves
for the doer, but are more like a saving instrument in the
transformation of man's corrupted nature into a "new creation" (2 Corinthians 5.17). Therefore Christ's gospel commandments are not law but grace and mercy. They are
medicine given for our use, without which we cannot get
well.[19]

Like the disciples, all of whom made material sacrifices in
order to follow Jesus, we are to act on our faith in practical,
measurable ways in order that, along with the Psalmist, we
might some day say, "I have kept myself from the paths of the
destroyer" (Psalm 17.4). Acting on our faith in Christ will take
us toward God, making us into the creatures He intended and
slowly, painstakingly, making us into the sort of people that
will find God's love blessed instead of terrifying.
Good works, the Church teaches, help in the process of

---

[18]St. John Chrysostom, *Homilies On Penance*, A.D. 387, in *The Faith of the Early
Fathers*, vol. 2, trans. W. A. Jurgens, pp. 96-97.

[19]*The Orthodox Faith*, vol. 1. The Department of Religious Education of the Orthodox
Church in America (New York, 1976), p. 17.

salvation, not because they save us, but because in the doing
of good works, we are trained, through virtuous habits of action, to become the kind of people who will find Heaven heavenly. In order to become like Christ we must learn self-discipline
and good habits. Virtue, the Church tells us, is not *taught* as
much as it is *practiced.* The Church teaches that in order to
be like Christ we must first act like Him — whether we "feel"
like Him all of the time or not.

HEAVEN AND HELL

Fr. Anthony M. Coniaris writes concerning the teaching of
Holy Tradition on the nature of Hell,

> We are the ones who create hell when we use the gift of
> free will that God gave us to say 'No' to Him. To exclude
> God from our lives is to be in Hell. God did not create us
> for hell. He created us for the Kingdom of heaven. We are
> the ones who create hell for ourselves through our prideful
> rebellion and disobedience. Having been created free, man
> cannot be forced into a union with God. He is allowed the
> privilege of facing the eternal consequences of either his
> 'Yes' or his 'No' to God.[20]

According to the teaching of the Church, the persons
deliberately turning away from God will discover the ultimate
revelation of God's love to be not heavenly but hellish, even
if they say they "believe in Jesus." (Matthew 7:21-23)
    The Church teaches that what we actually are (that is, the
sum total of what we have in fact made ourselves into) is what
counts, not what we say we believe, let alone how we feel. This
is what Christ taught us when He said: "Not everyone who says
to Me, 'Lord, Lord,' shall enter the kingdom of heaven, but he
who does the will of My Father in heaven . . ." (Matthew 7:22).
According to Jesus, we may know *exactly* what the will of the
Father is: "Let your light so shine before men, that they may
see your good works and glorify your Father in heaven." (Matthew 5:16)

---

[20]Anthony M. Coniaris, *Introducing the Orthodox Church*, p. 120.

The historical Church has taught that God's love is constant. In A.D. 380 St. Gregory of Nyssa wrote, "He that desires all men to be saved and to come to a knowledge of the truth shows thereby the most perfect and blessed way of salvation, the way, I say, of love."[21] The Orthodox Church has not taught that God seeks revenge on sinners. God is not like a human judge who wishes to punish the wicked; even less does the Church tell us that God is like some vengeful deity of Greek myth, an Augustinian-Calvinist juridical horror who capriciously elects to punish some people. As St. John Chrysostom writes, "Let us therefore take courage at His love of mankind and let us be diligent in showing repentance (which means a change of heart, followed by a change of behavior) before that day arrives which will preclude our benefiting from repentance."[22]

The Holy Tradition of the Church has taught that God is love. "Even so it is not the will of your Father who is in heaven that one of these little ones should perish" (Matthew 18:14). Yet, according to Holy Tradition, God's judgment of sin is real but not vengeful. Rather, God's judgment is a manifestation of His fiery, pure love which He bestows on everyone equally, believer and non-believer alike, just as the sun shines on the just and the unjust. According to Eusebius: "The hungry He has filled with good things and the arms of the proud He has broken. Not only for believers but also for unbelievers has He proved true the record of the ancient narratives."[23]

The reason God's love is felt as judgment by those who reject Him is because some people have grown so far away from Him that they begin to hate any manifestation of His existence. Their own life choices, and habits of behavior, have taken them far away from the Image of God they were created to be. They have chosen self-rule rather than obedience. Sometimes people travel so far away from God that their hatred of His love becomes palpable. As Orthodox Archbishop Paul of Finland writes, "The part played by man's free will in salvation was shown on Calvary in the different fates of the two evildoers who

---

[21]St. Gregory of Nyssa, *Commentary on the Canticle of Canticles*, A.D. 380, in *The Faith of the Early Fathers*, vol. II, translated by W. A. Jurgens, p. 46.

[22]St. John Chrysostom, *Homilies on the Gospel of Matthew*, A.D. 370, in *The Faith of the Early Fathers.*, vol. II, translated by W. A. Jurgens, p. 111.

[23]As cited in *Handbook of the Orthodox Church*, vol. I, Department of Religious Education, The Orthodox Church of America, (New York: 1976), p. 113.

were crucified with Christ."[24]

It is not hard to imagine that a person who derides Christ's life, death and resurrection, will find God's love hellish in the next life. This is the natural consequence of his willing rejection of God's love in the person of Christ in this life. Old habits die hard.

St. Mark the Ascetic writes,

"He who does not make his will agree with God is tripped up by his own schemes."[25]

St. Mark the Ascetic's point is well-illustrated by the parable of the prodigal son (Luke 15:11-32). In Jesus' story we hear that the father loved both his prodigal and his faithful son equally. But because of the resentment of the elder son toward the returned prodigal, the father's love was received very differently by his two sons. The more the father loved the prodigal, the more his other son hated, was "tripped up" by his father and brother. So the father's love had two very different effects on his two sons. For one, the love was heavenly, for the other, it was hellish. The father loved both and was prepared to be equally generous to each. He had certainly not "predestined" one to experience hell and one to be saved. Depending on their attitude toward their father and to each other, each son brought his own judgment or blessing to the father's feast, at which *both* were equally welcome.

Concerning our self-judgment, St. Mark the Ascetic writes,

Just as a thought is made manifest through actions and words, so is our future reward through the impulses of the heart. Thus a merciful heart will receive mercy, while a merciless heart will receive the opposite.[26]

St. Mark's words are not made as a threat, but rather as an observation of how God's law of reciprocal love works. This

---

[24]Archbishop Paul of Finland, *The Faith We Hold*, p. 21.

[25]St. Mark the Ascetic, *On the Spiritual Law: The Philokalia*, vol. I, translated by G. E. H. Palmer, Philip Sherrard and Kallistos Ware, p. 139.

[26]St. Mark the Ascetic, *No Righteousness by Works: The Philokalia*, vol. I, translated by G. E. H. Palmer, Philip Sherrard and Kallistos Ware, p. 112.

is the same truth contained in the Lord's prayer: "Forgive us our sins as we forgive those who sin against us." To the humble, repentant heart of the prodigal son, the father's love brings joy. To the sanctimonious and ungenerous heart of his other son, the father's love brings sorrow and further aggravates his soul-destroying resentment, precisely because the elder son did *not* forgive as he had been forgiven.

The Church teaches that salvation or damnation is the choice of our own free will. This is emphasized by St. Augustine of Hippo: "God makes His sun to rise even on such men (sinners) and bestows his most lavish gift of life and health on them no less than He did before."[27] Augustine writes of the fact that we are responsible for dealing with our sin by choosing to use our free will to journey toward Christ and not away from Him. "Let your sin have you for its judge, not its patron. Go up and take revenge (judgment) against yourself, and put your guilt before yourself. Do not put it behind you or God will put it in front of you."[28]

A PARABLE

Perhaps there is another way to show clearly how what is heavenly to one may be hellish to another. Let us imagine a superb classical concert in which J. S. Bach's Brandenberg Concertos are being performed. In attendance at this concert are two groups of listeners. The first is made up of people who have, from childhood, listened to, studied, loved and enjoyed classical music, particularly the Baroque music of Bach and Handel. They have worked hard all year to save their money to buy tickets to this concert. They are dressed for the occasion. They savor each moment of the event. Some have even brought the score of the music in order to better follow the performance. At that same concert is also a very different group of people in attendance. (Perhaps they are the lumpish "product" of our failed public education system!) They have been taken to the

---

[27]St. Augustine of Hippo, *Letter of Hippo to Macedonius, The Imperial Victor of Africa,* A.D. 413, in *The Faith of the Early Fathers,* vol. III, translated by W. A. Jurgens, p. 7.

[28]St. Augustine of Hippo, *Sermons,* A.D. 391-430, in *The Faith of the Early Fathers,* vol. III, translated by W. A. Jurgens, p. 25.

event by a well-meaning teacher who wants them to "experience the cultural diversity" their city affords them. They dislike classical music and would rather be at a rock concert.

Both groups of people are hearing the same superbly performed, lovingly rendered music. Both are in the same place. Both have the opportunity to enjoy the fruits of the lifelong work of the musicians whose talent is so impressive.

One group of people have cultivated an understanding, love and appreciation of the music — their experience of the concert is "heavenly" because of their deliberately chosen habits of mind. The others have chosen to live in an esthetic wilderness that has dulled their senses beyond repair — their experience is "hellish." Their habits of a lifetime have changed them dramatically into very different people than they would have been had they chosen and cultivated different habits of character. To make the concert enjoyable to the second group, the concert master would have to dismiss his musicians, perhaps hire a rock and roll band, install smoke machines, lights and special effects equipment.

But if the concert master did not want to do this — if he had artistic and/or esthetic standards, desired to serve and uplift those in his audience who had spent years preparing to fully appreciate this moment — then he would have no choice but to continue with the program. If necessary, he might have to eject those who were so bored that they were threatening to reduce the concert to chaos. It seems to me that this is somewhat the nature of the judgment described in Matthew 25:31-46.

JUDGMENT

St. Mark the Ascetic writes of God's judgment,

Every one receives what he deserves in accordance with his inner states. But only God understands the many different ways in which this happens.[29]

[29]St. Mark the Ascetic, *On the Spiritual Law: The Philokalia*, vol. I, translated by G. E. H. Palmer, Philip Sherrard and Kallistos Ware, p. 131.

According to Holy Tradition, God seeks no revenge, but He does allow us to exercise our free will. Those who do not follow Him create their own judgment. The inner state of those who rebel against God and His law of love, is not in accordance with the character of God, or His creation. In other words, it willfully flies in the face of reality. Therefore God's love becomes a self-created hell for those who hate Him.

In the early Church this was the understanding of the nature of God's judgment. St. Justin Martyr wrote in A.D. 198,

> If men, by their works, show themselves worthy of His design, they are deemed worthy, so we are told, to make a bond with Him and reign with Him, being freed of all corruption and passion. . . . Our coming into being in the beginning was none of our doing. But now, to follow those things which are pleasing to Him, and to choose them by means of the rational faculties which He has bestowed upon us; to this He persuades us, and leads us to faith.[30]

The Church teaches that God's constant changeless love, by which He persuades us, is the same toward everyone. In order to make heaven heavenly for those who hate Him, God would have to change His love into something other than what His loving character is.

As C. S. Lewis so brilliantly illustrated with his portrait of the lost rebellious dwarfs in his book *The Last Battle,* those who find God's "concert" hellish have brought their own sullen, unappreciative and rebellious judgment with them. There is no way God can coerce them into Heaven unless he strips them of their free will. To save the rebellious God-hater whose deliberate habits of life have taken him or her far from God's design for human existence, God would have to strip that person of the freedom to choose and render him or her inhuman and unworthy of the title of having been created in "the image of God."

Our "Concert Master" is not vengeful, nor is He coercive. He will not force sullen people to be indoctrinated with music appreciation courses. He leads us to faith; He does not force us. Yet He will not change His tune to suit the debased esthetic or moral standard we may choose to live by. Nor is our eternal

---

[30]St. Justin the Martyr, *First Apology*, A.D. 148, in *The Faith of the Early Fathers,* vol. I, translated by W. A. Jurgens, p. 51.

future sealed by conditioning or fate or some weird conception of predestination or election. It may well be that some of
the people in the second group at our concert will learn to love
God's music, however little they comprehend it. They may (and
often do, in the end, against all odds) even come to enjoy the
concert and thus find the concert truly heavenly. For that matter some in the first group may tire of the concert and walk
out.

Nothing in regard to our salvation is dictated by fate, by
whatever theological name it is called. This is the lesson of the
thief on the cross who chose Christ while his companion persisted in cherishing death over life. And this is the lesson of
the Roman Centurion, whom Christ described as having the
greatest faith He had found in Israel, even though the Centurion
was neither a Jew nor a convert to Christianity.

For those who have traveled toward God by imitating Christ,
knowingly or unknowingly, however late in the day, and
regardless of whether they have been in or out of the historic
Church, God's love will be heavenly. (Matthew 14:47-50). But
for those who have traveled away from God, even if they have
spent their life in Bible study and have paid lip service to Christian doctrine and sacramental observance, God's love will be
hellish. They have not imitated Christ and are, therefore, "Orthodox" or not, opposed to God's character. (Matthew 7:1-23)
Unlike the Psalmist, they have been satisfied with less than
becoming like God. (Psalm 17:15) St. Gregory of Nyssa makes
this very point.

> The doorkeepers at the heavenly kingdom are careful and
> they do not play games. They see the soul bearing the marks
> of her banishment . . . then the miserable soul, accusing
> herself severely of her thoughtlessness and howling and
> wailing and lamenting, remains in the sullen place, cast
> away as if in a corner.[31]

St. Mark the Ascetic writes, "Hell is ignorance, for both are
dark."[32] Those in rebellion against God have grown and pros-

---

[31]St. Gregory of Nyssa, *Against Those Who Resent Correction*, A.D. 379, in *The Faith
of the Early Fathers*, vol. II, translated by W. A. Jurgens, pp. 57-58.
[32]St. Mark the Ascetic, *The Philokalia*, vol. I, translated by G. E. H. Palmer, Philip
Sherrard and Kallistos Ware, p. 114.

pered in God's field but have become self-created and willfully ignorant weeds, not part of the good crop. (Matthew 13:24-30) They are self-condemning because they have chosen to learn the wrong habits. It takes a lot of hard work, and consistent, life-long effort, to create a private hell out of the gift of life. It takes a lifetime of misspent activities to irredeemably alter the Image of God which we each bear — to alter it so drastically that our Creator will not recognize us as His own and will say, "I never knew you."

CONCLUSION

"But He will say, 'I tell you I do not know you, . . . Depart from me, all you workers of iniquity'" (Luke 13:27). The Church teaches that, for those who hate God's works, His Son, His laws, His historical and apostolic Church, His worship, His ecclesiastical servants, His beauty, His Sacraments, His creatures, an encounter with Him, however loving, will be a terrible thing.

St. John Chrysostom writes that God's judgment will be terrible for the people who have spent a lifetime rejecting the love of God.

> Weep for the unbelievers! Weep for those who die in their wealth, and who with all their wealth (including the "religious" wealth of spiritual pride) prepared no consolation for their own souls, who have the power to wash away their sins but did not will to do it . . .[33]

Orthodox theologian Father Thomas Hopko sums up the position of the Orthodox Church concerning salvation and damnation in this way.

> If some men refuse the gift of life in communion with God, the Lord can only honor this refusal and respect the freedom of His creatures which He Himself has given and will not take back. The doctrine of eternal hell, therefore, does not mean that God actively tortures people by some unloving and perverse means. It does not mean that God takes

---

[33]St. John Chrysostom, *Homilies on the Epistles to the Philipians*, A.D. 398, in *The Faith of the Early Fathers*, vol. II, translated by W. A. Jurgens, p. 121.

delight in the punishment and pain of His people whom He loves. Neither does it mean that God 'separates himself' from His people, thus causing them anguish in this separation (for indeed if people hate God, separation would be welcome, and not abhorred!). It means rather that God continues to allow all people, saints and sinners alike, to exist forever.[34]

The historical church — the Orthodox Church — has always taught that Hell is real. But it has also taught that Hell is of our own choosing. God's love is constant. And God is thoroughly good as is manifested in all of His Creation. It is we human beings who sometimes choose to be fickle.

We, the Church teaches, will be judged in the sense that God is God, He is "I AM"; He does not change. We will be judged in the same way we are "judged" if we choose to crash our car into a concrete wall that is immovable; a wall that has been described as an immovable stumbling stone. (Romans 9:32 - 33) God, the Church teaches us, loves all people. His judgment is not a judicial act of revenge, but a result of the consistency of His loving and immutable character.

St. Evagrios the Solitary speaks for the Church when he writes concerning the nature of God's judgment,

> All impure thoughts that persist in us because of our passions bring the intellect down to ruin and perdition. . . . It is not possible for an intellect choked by such ideas to appear before God and receive the crown of righteousness. It is through being dragged down by such thoughts that the wretched intellect, like the man in the Gospels, declines the invitation to the supper of the knowledge of God (Luke 14:18).[35]

St. Peter of Damascus makes the same point.

> If we cling to our disease . . . we will have made ourselves like the demons . . . we will have scorned our benefactor. We do not all receive blessings in the same way. Some, on

---

[34]*Handbook of the Orthodox Church*, vol. I, Department of Religious Education, The Orthodox Church of America, p. 112.

[35]St. Evagrios, the Solitary, *On Discrimination: The Philokalia*, vol. I, translated by G. E. H. Palmer, Philip Sherrard and Kallistos Ware, pp. 51-52.

receiving the fire of the Lord, that is, His Word, put it into practice and so became softer of heart, like wax, while others through laziness became harder than clay and altogether stone-like.[36]

Greek Orthodox Bishop of Oxford, England, Kallistos Ware writes,

If anyone is in hell, it is not because God has imprisoned him there, but because that is where he himself has chosen to be. The lost in hell are self-condemned, self-enslaved; it has been rightly said that the doors of hell are locked *on the inside*.[37]

---

[36]St. Peter of Damascus, *Introduction to The Seven Forms of Bodily Discipline: The Philokalia*, vol. III, translated by G. E. H. Palmer, Philip Sherrard and Kallistos Ware, p. 78.
[37]Kallistos Ware, *The Orthodox Way* (Italics are Ware's) p. 103.

CHAPTER SEVENTEEN
SIN

In contrast to our current secularized political wisdom, Holy Tradition teaches us that sin — all human choices and actions that are un-God-like — is the real root of human anguish (Rom 8.1-8).

Through the Scriptures, we learn that Christ treated cruelty, evil, enmity, injustice, theft, hatred and oppression as a constant in fallen human behavior (Mt 26.11). Christ presented no utopian or millennial agenda on how to bring political, economic or social "peace" and "justice" to the world in this age (Mt 24.6-14). Nor did He outline a political solution to the problem of sin through which we could coerce people into a "new Canaan" through innovative social engineering projects.

Holy Tradition never identifies sin as a matter of collective, societal, political, racial or gender guilt, but always as a result of individual moral choice and responsibility.[1] Holy Tradition identifies all social, political and economic problems as the result, not the cause, of moral or immoral choices for which *persons* are accountable.

In the tradition of the Orthodox Church there is not a dogma of fatalistic inherited guilt as there is in the Augustinian-Scholastic West. Our capacity to exercise love, free will, and choice is understood as the essence of what it means to be "made in God's Image."[2]

---

[1] "So long as we assign the causes for our weaknesses to others, we cannot attain perfection . . ." St. John Cassian, *On the Eight Vices: The Philokalia*, vol. 1, trans. G. E. H. Palmer, Philip Sherrard and Kallistos Ware, p. 85.

[2] "Virtue is not the knowing of good and evil. Rather virtue is the doing of good and not-doing of evil." Lactantius, *The Divine Institutions*, 6,5,10, A.D. 304, in *The Faith of the Early Fathers*, vol. 1, trans. W. A. Jurgens, p. 268.

PERSONAL RESPONSIBILITY

In today's world we tend to speak of justice and injustice almost exclusively in political, legal, social or economic terms. We tend to minimize personal moral responsibility in favor of collective guilt, a kind of political "original sin," which in turn has created the "no fault" mentality. This kind of thinking lets people off the hook concerning their individual actions, often placing the blame for our personal evil behavior on society.[3] For instance, crimes committed by some youths are routinely excused in the popular press, because it is said society is "responsible" for producing the conditions of poverty, or racism, which in turn "produces" juvenile criminals.

Sexually transmitted diseases, such as AIDS, have been described by the media as if moral or immoral behavior was not a factor contributing to their spread. This fiction portrays such problems as merely the result of bad "social policy," perhaps a lack of "sex education" or insufficient funding for "scientific research," rather than often the consequence of irresponsible, sinful behavior for which each person must accept personal responsibility.

Holy Tradition tells us that Christ taught moral responsibility exclusively in personal, non-political terms. His vision was one of people making the right or wrong moral choices for which they were personally accountable (Mt 12.35-37). The Church teaches that those who wish to follow Christ are personally responsible to choose to do good to other people because they are to love them as Christ loved us (Mt 5.7). This is not a sentimental concept. Doing good and showing mercy often involves us in the arduous and unpleasant task of standing against evil, even rebuking sin and depravity, as we try to be the salt and light of the world. Sometimes, the price for doing good is persecution.

Naturally, if many people do good, including being willing to rebuke evil behavior, this produces "social results." But the Church teaches us that seeking social change without first convincing

[3] ". . . The worst utopian temptation is the desire to shift the focus of responsibility from the individual to the institution. . . . An individual governed by the utopian imagination doesn't see moral problems, he sees technical problems, and as a result, his solutions are technical: clean needles, safe-sex kits. . . ." William K. Kilpatrick, *Why Johnny Can't Tell Right from Wrong*, p. 222.

people to alter their moral behavior is futile. Our own history
seems to teach the same lesson. Fr. Georges Florovsky writes,

> The reconversion of the world to Christianity is what we have
> to preach in our day. This is the only way out of that im-
> passe into which the world has been driven by the failure
> of Christians to be truly Christian. Obviously, Christian doc-
> trine does not answer *directly* any practical question in the
> field of politics or economics. Neither does the gospel of
> Christ. Yet its impact on the whole course of human history
> has been enormous. The recognition of human dignity, mer-
> cy and justice roots in the gospel.[4]

Our efforts to "reform society" without demanding individual
moral accountability is at the very heart of the failure of the
twentieth-century Socialism and, in particular, our own big
government's inability to produce non-coercive, humane
change through its many taxation, social engineering and
welfare projects.

The futility of big government's attempt to impose secular
"morality" on society has been demonstrated by the failure of
every utopian, socialist and communist state, including our own
bloated welfare state, to deliver on its social promises.[5] These
failures have at least partly been caused by the secularization
of modern political culture, which has resulted in what the
historian Macaulay has called "the most frightful of all spectacles, the strength of civilization without mercy." It has been
in trying to "do good" without religion that modern super states
have produced the bloodbaths that distinguish ours, the most
bloody, as well as the most secular and statist of all centuries.

Historian Paul Johnson describes the anti-human impulses
that have pervaded the modern secularist attempts to create

---

[4] Georges Florovksy, *Bible, Church, Tradition: An Eastern Orthodox View*, p. 12.

[5] ". . . Socialism is not an improvement upon democratic capitalism but a relapse
into the tyrannical statism from which the latter has emerged. The enforcement of
high moral ideals by coercion of law has been tried before. . . . Running through
(socialist utopian ideals) is a constant thread of statism. In general, the left wishes
to strengthen the political system at the expense of . . . moral-cultural system." Michael
Novak, *The Spirit of Democratic Capitalism* (New York, 1982), p. 334.

godless political utopias wherein questions of morality and meaning have consciously been reduced to mere social engineering, and spirituality and religion have been relegated to the sidelines of culture. Johnson writes,

> The Will to power produce(d) a new kind of messiah, (first in the dictators of the 1920's and 1930's then in the Communist and Socialist super states of the 1940s to 1990s) uninhibited by any religious sanctions whatever, and with an unappeasable appetite for controlling mankind . . . with an unguided world adrift in a relativistic universe (this) was a summons to . . . gangster-statesmen to emerge.[6]

What the bloody lesson of the twentieth century has taught us above all is that idealistic social and political programs which are divorced from transcendent religious values result in little more than coercion.[7] By contrast, Holy Tradition teaches that Christ's way is at odds with our politicized world, and that the effects of sin cannot be repaired by social engineering however sophisticated (Mt 10.34-39).

WHY BE GOOD?

As Christ's life amply demonstrates, to be God-like is not necessarily to always be happy. Those who scavenge through Christ's teaching in order to selfishly find worldly happiness or a declaration of individualistic "rights" will, like the rich young ruler in the gospel account, depart disappointed to seek other more fulfilling gods. Saint Mark the Ascetic writes, "He who believes in the blessings of the world to come abstains of his own accord from the pleasures of this world."[8] Jesus did not hold out any immediate material reward as an incentive for good behavior. He did not sweeten the pill of moral accountability by giving us sympathetic "no-fault" excuses for our bad behavior

---

[6] Paul Johnson, *Modern Times*, p. 48.

[7] "It is a sad commentary on the sociology of knowledge in the Christian churches that so few theologians or religious leaders understand economics . . . Many seem trapped in pre-capitalist modes of thought. Many . . . reduce all morality to the morality of distribution." Michael Novak, *The Spirit of Democratic Capitalism*, p. 336.

[8] St. Mark the Ascetic, *On No Righteousness by Works: The Philokalia.* vol. 1, trans. G. E. H. Palmer, Philip Sherrard and Kallistos Ware, p. 137.

(Mt 11.20-24). He provided no material, political, or psychological motivation to become like Him (Mt 19.16-22). He simply stated that if we imitate Him we could "be perfect," we could eventually become like God, our Creator, and thereby fulfill our purpose, what the Orthodox Church has called deification.

Holy Tradition tells us to do the right thing only because it is the right thing to do. We are told that our true meaning is found in returning to our Creator and worshipping Him. We are told that to do this we must embark on the journey of ascetic sanctity, which means the journey to overcome our passions and become like Jesus.[9] Furthermore we are told that, because we have free will, it is our individual responsibility to imitate Christ and to struggle, through sacramental asceticism, to change the content of our characters. According to the Church, the buck stops with us — personally, whatever our circumstances or excuses for our bad behavior (Mt 25.31-46). This is why the Church provides the sacraments. They enable us to come to Christ, to worship Him, to repent and to become like Him through *doing* the right things, through ascetic perseverance and faith.

THE SACRAMENT OF CONFESSION

I remember trying to explain to a Protestant friend why it was that going to confess to my priest was an indispensable part of spiritual self-discipline, of trying to become more like Christ, of battling against my sin, and of following the teaching of the Church. He remarked that he understood. He had several friends from his Southern Baptist church he went hunting with. They had all agreed to be "accountable" to each other. Twice a year or so they would get together to "rap," "dialogue," "share" in a "mutual support group." He had found this very helpful to his "Christian life." He said he knew just what I meant.

Friendship, talking with one's friends, social fellowship are no doubt all good things, but they have nothing whatsoever to do with the sacrament of confession of one's sin to a priest. In confession, one receives absolution from one who is in direct succession from the Apostles, and Christ—that is, one to whom

[9] ". . . We are . . . foolish if we rely on theoretical knowledge . . . knowledge . . . is not firmly established if unaccompanied by works. For everything is established by being put into practice." Ibid. p. 126.

has been given authority to "bind in heaven" that which he binds of earth (Jn 20.21-23).

What is amazing to me is that otherwise conservative people, in the Protestant denominations, who, for instance, would be horrified by the idea of "alternative lifestyles" replacing traditional families, have themselves replaced the traditional family of God with a self-invented, alternative religion of chaotic personalized experience, in which they are accountable to no one, and in which they "do their own thing" in the best tradition of the 1960s. While they would argue against relativistic chaos in many other areas of life — for instance against an "if it feels good do it" approach to sexuality — they have accepted just such a secularistic state of affairs in their personal spiritual lives when it comes to personal moral accountability. And yet the voice of the Orthodox Church is there for all who wish to heed it. It speaks clearly concerning the unique authority vested in the Church. Saint Basil the Great writes of the special relationship of Christians to their confessors: ". . . diseases of the body are not divulged to all, nor haphazardly, but to those who are skilled in curing them. . . ."[10]

The Church extends the mercy of Christ to its people by obeying Christ's command to the Apostles, which was passed to their successor bishops. "As the Father sent Me, I also send you. . . . If you forgive the sins of any they are forgiven them; if you retain the sins of any, they are retained." (Jn 20.21-23)

In its wisdom, the Orthodox Church has ignored modern psychological explanations of sin, let alone ideas of collective "no fault" societal guilt, and instead teaches us to pray,

O Father, Lord of heaven and earth, I confess to Thee all the hidden and open sins of my heart and mind, which I have committed as to this present day; wherefore, I beg of Thee, the righteous and compassionate Judge, remission of sins and grace to sin no more.

The Orthodox Church does not abandon its flock to be orphans, accountable only to their flimsy changeable feelings and

---

[10]St. Basil the Great, *On Rules Briefly Treated*, Ref. 975, A.D. 370, in *The Faith of the Early Fathers*, vol. 2, trans. W. A. Jurgens, p. 25.

consciences, unguided and deprived of the necessary discipline that comes from regular observance of the sacrament of confession. If some secularized "Orthodox" do not regularly go to confession it is because — to their loss — they willfully choose to not take advantage of their great inheritance. And if some "Orthodox" priests do not insist that their flock come to confession, then it is a mark of their own protestantized corruption. St. Basil the Great spoke for the whole Church, regarding the tradition of confession to a priest, or a monastic spiritual Father.[11]

> It is necessary to confess our sins to those to whom the dispensation of God's mysteries are entrusted. Those doing penance of old are found to have done it before the Saints. It is written in the Gospel that they confessed their sins to John the Baptist; that in Acts they confessed to the Apostles by whom also all were baptized.[12]

In the Orthodox Church, the priest does not claim to forgive sins by his own power, but instead gently helps the sinner to come to God and seek forgiveness, reconciliation and a new start. The priest's special authority lies in his power to pronounce the penitent sinner forgiven by God. In this way, the believer is actively helped to learn good habits and to avoid sin.[13] The believer is also offered the hope of countless new beginnings and the certainty that he or she has indeed been forgiven, as well as a wealth of practical advice and, from time to time, a well-deserved godly rebuke. This was the understanding of confession in the West as well as the East. St. Ambrose of Milan writes,

> The sinner not only confesses his sins, but he even enumerates them and admits his guilt; for he does not want to conceal his faults. Just as fevers are not able to be assuaged when they break, so too the illness of sins burns on while it is hidden, but disappears when it shows itself

---

[11]An Orthodox Christian is free to choose any Orthodox priest as his or her confessor. This may be one's local priest or it may be another priest, retired priest, bishop, monk or archpriest. The important thing is to go to regular confession with the same priest or monk and to do and obey.

[12]St. Basil the Great, *On Rules Briefly Treated*, Ref. 977, A.D. 370, in *The Faith of the Early Fathers*, vol. 2, trans. W. A. Jurgens, p. 26.

[13]See *A Dictionary of Greek Orthodoxy*, pp. 94-96.

in confession.[14]

How precious a sacramental gift confession is becomes abundantly clear to those of us who come to the Orthodox Church from non-Orthodox backgrounds. Our "confessions" once consisted of half-formed, lonely muttered prayers, into our pillows, or occasional sessions of pastoral "counseling" with a physician of the soul who had neither the skill, nor the authority, to pronounce as well.

No priest, no guidance, no accountability and no regular reminder to confess was offered to those raised in most Protestant "churches." We had little opportunity or active regular encouragement to grow, learn and start anew. We had no saint's lives to practically inspire us. We were deprived of the wise mercy of the historical Church. We were deprived of the cumulative pastoral wisdom of two thousand years. Stranded with ourselves, and with whatever theological or psychological whim our pastor used to "therapeutically" modify our behavior, we were bereft of the sacrament of penance that all Christians took for granted for most of the life of the Church. We had the Bible to guide us, but most of our time was taken up arguing about what it "meant" to us. It might have been of us Protestant orphans that St. Mark the Ascetic was speaking when he wrote, "For it is dangerous to isolate oneself completely, relying on one's own judgment with no one else as witness."[15]

Holy Tradition teaches that Christ calls His children to live holy lives. In His mercy, Christ established the Church to help us accomplish the hard life-long task of achieving personal sanctity. So that we might not isolate ourselves, so that we might be accountable, so that we might not have to rely on pietistic or fundamentalist man-made rules, the Church does not expect us to be holy by our own miserable lonely efforts. The Church teaches us that we cannot expect to grow toward God if we harbor unconfessed secret sin. St. Jerome addressed this fact.

If the Serpent, the Devil, bites someone secretly, he infects

---

[14]St. Ambrose of Milan, *On Twelve Psalms*, Ref. 1259, A.D. 381, in *The Faith of the Early Fathers*, vol. 2, trans. by W. A. Jurgens, p. 150.

[15]St. Mark the Ascetic, *Letter to Nicolas the Solitary: The Philokalia*, vol. 1, trans. G .E. H. Palmer, Philip Sherrard and Kallistos Ware, p. 158.

that person with the venom of sin. And if the one who has been bitten keeps silent and does not do penance, and does not want to confess his wound to a brother and to his Master, (his spiritual father and priest), then his brother and Master, who have the Word that will cure him, cannot very well assist him. For if the sick man is ashamed to confess his wound to the physician, medicine will not cure that to which it is not applied.[16]

Today, the counterfeit of authentic confession is offered to people in the form of psychological, or pastoral counseling. This counterfeit of confession can also take the form of self-help group therapy, prayer meetings, home Bible study or times of "fellowship and sharing." But in the view of the Church, these are band-aid solutions to a severe wound — sin!

The failure of psychology to help people change their behavior is in evidence in our desacralized world in which psychotherapy has replaced sacramental confession and secularized social programs have tried to devise coercive, amoral short cuts to a secularized, social utopia.[17] Professor of Psychology William Kirk Kilpatrick shows, in his important book, *Psychological Seduction: The Failure of Modern Psychology*,[18] that there has been an *increase* of social pathologies — divorce, abortion, crime and anti-social behavior of all kinds — at exactly the same time in our history as psychology has replaced religious confession and reduced sin to no more than a "psychological problem."

PERSONAL CONFESSION

As a new convert to Orthodoxy, I found confession embarrassing and frightening. Yet nothing in my spiritual life has been more helpful to me, or has given me more true peace, than

---

[16]St. Jerome, *Commentary on Ecclesiastes*, Ref. 1375, A.D. 388, in *The Faith of the Early Fathers*, trans. W. A. Jurgens, pp. 196-97.

[17]" . . . Though Orthodox Confession intends to be an analysis of the soul, it is not a medical psychoanalysis . . . seeing that sin is a moral failure that results in emotional upheaval, the authority and benefit of Confession is bound to prove more restoring to inner health than corrective procedures deriving from sources other that the word of God." *A Dictionary of Greek Orthodoxy*, p. 96.

[18]William Kirk Kilpatrick, *Psychological Seduction: The Failure of Modern Psychology* (Nashville, 1983).

regular confession to my spiritual father. What began as a terror is of the greatest comfort to me now, even though I still approach confession with fear and trembling. Moreover, in trying to be accountable to my priest I have taken genuine, if small and incremental steps, away from certain evil behaviors which seemed to be beyond hope of change. Being accountable, without excuses, and knowing that I will have to face someone to whom I will have to admit my moral failures, has slowly begun to change my behavior, step by difficult step. In my own life, I have begun to discover the truth that Saint Ambrose and the other Fathers write about — unconfessed sin is unchanged sin. Unchanged behavior is a stumbling block to learning the good habits that will help us to imitate Christ.

The idea of confession is foreign to the people of our day. Ours is an age that has placed a premium on self-esteem, self-realization, self-image, "rights," and egocentric intellectual pride. Ours is an age that has perfected the cult of the feel-good self, that has politicized morality, and that eschews any concept of personal moral accountability to the divine order. Ours is a culture that may be fairly described as having perfected the art of self-esteem for no reason.[19] But the voice of the historical Church is clear on the need for those of us who wish to be saved to see our sinful pride for what it is. Saint Evagrios writes,

> In the whole range of evil thoughts, none is richer in resources than self-esteem; for it is to be found almost everywhere, and like some cunning traitor in a city it opens the gates to all the demons.[20]

This may not be what the "New Age" religions of therapeutic Protestantism, jingoistic Americanism, secularism, user - friendly modernized Roman Catholicism, feminism or psychology teach us, with their constant mind-numbing exhortations to "feel good about yourself," nevertheless, humility has been the beginning of wisdom and the start of the way back to God for all Christians since the beginning of the Church.

---

[19]This trend is perhaps best exemplified by various educational surveys that have found American students testing lower than the rest of the developed world in academic skills, yet testing higher in "self-esteem."

[20]St. Evagrios the Solitary, *On Discrimination: The Philokalia*, vol. 1, trans. G. E. H. Palmer, Philip Sherrard and Kallistos Ware, p. 46.

There is no substitute for confession to a priest in our ascetic struggle to be saved — to *subdue* our self-esteem — to become God-like — to change the content of our characters, to curb our passions in order that we may find Heaven heavenly.

CHAPTER EIGHTEEN
THE ULTIMATE LAWLESSNESS

The concept of privatized religiosity on the one hand, and the loss of a sense of personal responsibility for one's actions on the other has had dramatic and far reaching consequences.[1] It has led to the idea that one's behavior, one's sin, is a purely "personal" affair. This attitude of subjectivity is at the heart of the sexual, criminal and behavioral license now prevalent in our crumbling, divided, tribalized society.[2]

The practice of legal abortion on demand is the most startling example of the ultimate lawlessness inherent in today's style of American individualism. The abortion of 1.6 million babies—almost one third of American children conceived each year—is the most drastic example of an external behavior that is

---

[1] "The invisible church (of the Anabaptists and Quakers) replaced the visible, hierarchical church of . . . bishop, priest and monk. . . . The Anabaptists despaired of the world but had faith in their ability to lead a strict Christian life within small and segregated communities. . . . From the Quaker point of view . . . there (was) no need for . . . any kind of Church hierarchy (or Holy Tradition) since God's authority is to be found through the promptings of the Inner Light." E. Digby Baltzell, *Puritan Boston and Quaker Philadelphia*, pp. 60, 62, and 93, passim.

[2] Philip Tucker, Dean of Berkley Divinity School at Yale University, writes, "If the inner depths of the self are given this sort of authority, it can only mean that the most insistent prompting of the self is always taken as definitive of the self's true nature and good. The self's depths are set up to be judge of the self's depths. Even Locke recognized that it is unsatisfactory to make each 'person' the judge in his own case, and surely the same thing is true of 'selves.' To take this view is to adopt the very dubious proposition that if one has desires and inclinations and they are powerfully presented from the depths of the self, they are, by virtue of the strength of their presentation, both 'natural' and 'good.' To take this view is also to condemn the self to what Auden once called 'promiscuous fornication with its own images.' Apart from the undertakings that present the self with its arena for action and so its true calling, the self inevitably collapses into itself as it chases about panting after its own productions." Philip Tucker, "Sex and the Single Life," *First Things*, May, 1993.

now regarded as a mere "personal choice." It is also evidence of the fact that America has become a thoroughly pagan nation; state sanctioned child sacrifice has returned.

The taking of human life, for the sake of convenience, is now regarded as a mere "choice." Sex between "consenting adults" is viewed as no one else's business, in spite of whatever harm the "consenting adults" do to themselves, the child they conceive, the home they break apart, or their society. Abortion on demand is also a tragic example of the extreme enmity against God that our pagan country now has. It may well represent the final stage, the inevitable conclusion, of the rebellious Protestant-Enlightenment-Romantic movements experiment in selfish individualism.

Legalized abortion on demand is the final fracturing of our social fabric. Now even the primeval community of mother and child has been torn apart. The unborn child is believed to be at war with its mother; his or her interests pitted against its mother's.

It is urgently necessary that we examine the Holy Tradition as it applies to the question of abortion since, in the question of the sanctity of life, we have the most important moral issue confronting the Orthodox Church today.

THE CHURCH'S STAND
AGAINST ABORTION

The stand of the historical Church throughout the ages against the practice of the murder of the unborn serves as a good example of the Church's changeless resolve in upholding the Law of God which, as Eusebius writes, "made the barbarous, uncivilized customs of uncivilized races give place to his own civilized and most humane laws."[3] Since we live in a pagan culture very like the declining Roman Empire in which the Church found itself, nothing could be more timely than a study of the Church's attitude to abortion and child sacrifice.

The early Church taught that the practice of abortion contradicts the law of God, "You shall not murder." It also contradicts the teaching of Christ to do to others as we would have them

[3] Eusebius, *Festival Oration, History of the Church,* Book 10 (New York, 1965), p. 387.

do to us. Since all wish to live and not to be killed, we can assume that everyone also desires life! "Love does no harm to a neighbor. . . ." (Rom 13.10).

Both before and after the tragic division of the Eastern and Western Church abortion was denounced as the murder of innocent children. The early Church was confronted by a society like ours, in which abortion and infanticide were tolerated. From its very inception, the Church mounted a vigorous defense of the innocent life of unborn children. In the Didache (the written summary of the teaching of the Apostles, finished at the end of the first century), the faithful were told that "you shall not procure abortion. You shall not destroy a newborn child."[4]

Significantly, the instructions prohibiting abortion in the Epistle of Barnabas (circa 138 A.D.) were couched in terms of combating lawlessness.

> There are two ways of instruction, as there are two powers, that of light and that of darkness. And there is a great difference between the two ways. One is controlled by God's light-bearing angels, the others by the angels of Satan. And as the latter is the ruler of the present era of lawlessness, so the former is lauded from eternity to eternity. Among the precepts of the way of light is this; do not murder a child by abortion, or commit infanticide.[5]

The Church from its beginning has always been a stern guardian of innocent life. For instance, Dionysius, Bishop of Alexandria in A.D. 244, wrote in his letter to Hermammon about the state of pagan barbarity against which the Church steadfastly stood.

> For (the Church is) able by being present and seen . . . and speaking boldly, to frustrate the schemes of the wicked demons . . . devilish rites, loathsome tricks, and unholy sacrifices, (which) cut the throats of unfortunate boys, use the children of unhappy parents as sacrificial victims, and

---

[4] *Didache*, Ref. 1A, A. D. 80-140, *The Faith of the Early Fathers*, vol. 1, translated by W. A. Jurgens, p. 2.

[5] *Epistle of Barnabas*, A. D. 138, *The Faith of the Early Fathers*, vol. 2, translated by W. A. Jurgens, p. 14.

tear out the vitals of newborn babies cutting up and mincing God's handiwork.[6]

This was the climate of perversity, resembling that of our own day, against which the Fathers of the Church, East and West, unequivocally stood. This was a social climate that included legal infanticide, human sacrifice and abortion. And it was the Church's visible and absolute stand "by being present and seen" that gradually eliminated the public acceptance of these practices as matters of "personal choice." It was the Church that replaced the private evil of human sacrifice, abortion and infanticide with public moral accountability.

Perhaps two things can be learned by today's Christians regarding the Church's stand against abortion. First, it took centuries to change the pagan climate of perversity. Second, because the Church persevered and molded the culture rather than conforming to it, eventually attitudes and laws were changed. Patience and steadfast perseverance seem to be the qualities that wrought change.

The early historic Church very evidently had not separated life into watertight compartments between state and Church, or between private and public moral choice. Indeed, the early Church took a vigorous public stand on the sanctity of life and, as a result, inspired a change in public sensibility and laws.

THE FATHERS AND ABORTION

St. Basil the Great wrote "a woman who has deliberately destroyed a fetus must pay the penalty for murder."[7] He also addressed himself to the status of abortionists within society: "Those also who give drugs causing abortions are murderers themselves, as well as those who receive the poison which kills the fetus."[8]

Tertullian, representing the Western Church as its first great theologian, in A.D. 208 wrote,

---

[6] Eusebius, *The History of the Church*, Book 7, p. 293.

[7] Saint Basil the Great, *Letter to the Bishop of Iconium: The First Canonical Letter*, Ref. 919A, A. D. 374, in *The Faith of the Early Fathers*, vol. 2, translated by W. A. Jurgens, p. 7.

[8] Ibid. Ref. 919F.

How, then, is a living being conceived? Is the substance of both body and soul formed together at the same time, or does one of them precede the other? We do indeed maintain that both are conceived, formed and perfected at the same time, as they are born together; nor is there any moment intervening in their conception, which would give prior place to either. Consider the first events in the light of the last. If death is defined as nothing other than the separation of body and soul, then life, the opposite of death, should be defined as nothing else but the union of body and soul . . . We acknowledge, therefore, that life begins with conception, because we contend that the soul begins with conception.[9]

Writing in A.D. 122, Saint Hippolytus of Rome said, "See, then, into what great impiety that lawless one has preceded, by teaching adultery and murder at the same time! (For the heretic teaches) women . . . to take drugs and render themselves sterile and to bind themselves tightly so as to expel what was being conceived."[10] In A.D. 300, the council of Elvira pronounced the following: "If a woman . . . has killed that which came of her deed, it is determined that she is not to be given communion, even at death; because she has made twins (adultery and murder) of her wickedness."[11] And in A.D. 412 St. Augustine of Hippo wrote, "The soul is mingled with the body so as to form the one person of a man! Just as the soul employs the body in the unity of a person to form a man, so to God makes use of man in a unity of a person to form Christ."[12] One of the most highly regarded Christian writings by the Church Fathers of Alexandria in the second century states: "You shall love your neighbor more than your own life. You shall not slay the child by abortion. You shall not kill that which has already been generated."[13]

---

[9] Tertullian, *On the Soul*, Ref. 249A, A. D. 208, in *The Faith of the Early Fathers*, vol. I, translated by W. A. Jurgens, p. 144. The only deviation from this teaching was that of Thomas Aquinas who, in his scholastic attempt to "explain" life's great mysteries, denounced the Church's historic teaching that life begins at conception and instead tried to teach that life begins at "ensoulment" or "quickening."

[10] Saint Hippolytus of Rome, *On the Refutation of All Heresies*, Ref. 396A, A. D. 122, *The Faith of the Early Fathers*, vol. 1, translated by W. A. Jurgens, p. 173.

[11] Council of Elvira, Ref. 611B, A. D. 300, in *The Faith of the Early Fathers*, vol. 1, translated by W. A. Jurgens, p. 257.

[12] Saint Augustine, *Letter to Volusian*, Ref. 1421, A. D. 412, in *The Faith of the Early Fathers*, vol. 3, translated by W. A. Jurgens, p. 6.

[13] Epistle of Barnabas, XIX, 5.

Athenagoras wrote a letter to the pagan Roman Emperor, Marcus Aurelius, defending Christians from the false accusation that they did not revere human life. He wrote to refute the charge that Christians were "cannibals who drank blood and ate flesh" when they took Communion.

> What reason would we have to commit murder when we say that women who induce abortions are murderers, and will have to give account of it to God? For the same person would not regard a fetus in the womb as a living thing and therefore an object of God's care, and at the same time slay it, since it had come to life.[14]

Here a teaching against abortion was used to support another argument. In other words, at this very early date (approximately A.D. 161-80), the equation of abortion with murder and lawlessness was already such a self-evidently well-known part of Christian ethics, *even to the pagan Romans*, that it could be used as *proof* of the Church's high view of all human life.

St. Clement of Alexandria, writing in the third century, took Athenagoras' defense of the unborn child one step further.

> Those who use abortifacient medicines to hide their fornication are causing the outright destruction, together with the fetus, of the whole human race.[15]

St. Clement of Alexandria places abortion in a universal context in which the murder of one innocent and defenseless person represents the symbolic destruction of the value of all other human lives. Thus he established the inextricable link between the rights of the defenseless unborn and the human rights of all people of all cultures and ages and races — "The whole human race." Clement taught that if one innocent life is held as cheap and expendable, then all life is held in contempt. Clement shows that the human rights of the one are inextricably bound up with the necessity to show mercy to the many.

In the fourth century, two great bishops and theologians spoke on behalf of the Church against abortion. Saint Basil the Great, as we have seen, re-affirmed the teaching of the historical Church: "Those who give potions for the destruction

[14]Athenagoras, *A Plea for the Christians*, XXXV.
[15]Paedogogus, Book 11, 96, 2.

of the child conceived in the womb are murderers, as are those who take potions which kill the child."[16] Saint John Chrysostom even rebuked men who persuaded *prostitutes* to have abortions: "You do not let a harlot remain a harlot but make her a murderer as well."[17]

The Church Fathers were of the opinion that the life of a unique human being begins at the moment of conception. As any one who has read the book *The Concentration Can*, by world-renowned French geneticist Jerome Lejeme, will know, modern science confirms this fact.[18] Saint Basil the Great stated: " . . . we (the Church) do not have a precise distinction between a fetus which has been formed (old enough to recognize) and one which has not yet been formed (at an embryonic stage)."[19]

St. Gregory of Nyssa, in a statement that any modern geneticist would quickly second, also addressed the question of at what point a fetus possesses human life. "Abortion is a precipitation of murder, nor does it matter whether or not one takes a life when formed, or drives it away when forming, for he is also a man who is about to be one."[20] As Orthodox scholar Father John Kowalczyk writes, "It is clear that the Church Fathers believed that a unique human personality was formed at the moment of conception."[21]

The leadership of the present day Western and Eastern historical Church likewise staunchly condemn the practice of abortion. John Paul II has been steadfast on this point as have most other Roman Catholic and Orthodox bishops. On the issue of abortion there is unanimity between the Orthodox and Roman Church, past and present. John XXIII restated the principles of the Western historical Church with his insistence on the evil effect of legalized abortion on the whole of human society. "Human life is sacred. From its very inception the creative action of God is directly operative. By violating His laws, the divine Majesty is offended: the individuals themselves and

---

[16]Saint Basil the Great, Letters, CLXXXVIII, Canon 8.

[17]Saint John Chrysostom, Homilies on Romans, XXIV.

[18]Modern genetics confirms the full genetic humanity of the fetus from the moment of fertilization. Jerome Lejeme, *The Concentration Can* (Harrison, NY, 1992).

[19]Saint Basil the Great, Letters, CLXXXVIII, Canon 2.

[20]Saint Gregory of Nyssa, Apology, IX.

[21]John Kowalczyk, *An Orthodox View of Abortion* (Minneapolis, 1979), p. 19.

humanity are degraded, and the bounds by which members of society are united are severed."[22]

The Second Vatican Council, in its *Constitution Regarding Today's World,* declared that "life from its very conception must be guarded with the greatest care," and that "abortion and infanticide are abominable crimes."

Following the lead of the Fathers and the Holy Tradition, the bishops of the Orthodox Church around the world have taken an unequivocal stand against the evils of taking of innocent unborn human life. The bishops of the Orthodox Church in America (OCA) declared at their convention in 1992: "All men, women and children — young and old, sick and healthy, rich and poor, powerful and weak . . . born and unborn — are eternally precious in God's sight."[23] Archbishop Iakovos, primate of the Greek Orthodox Church of North and South America, writes expressing the historic Church's position as applied to our modern political situation,

> Christ came to liberate us from an old, sinful way of life and to introduce us to a new freedom under God. But legalization of the illegal is not liberation from anything. . . . Many politicians and social activists have gotten involved in promoting abortion in the name of women's rights or freedom of sexual expression. As a matter of fact . . . the United States has spent billions of dollars financing and subsidizing abortion centers. . . . Our moral values . . . have gone completely haywire. To get involved in such a corrupt, trendy way of thinking is testament to abdicating any moral responsibility.[24]

The bishops of the Antiochian Orthodox Church, in January 1993, made a special statement on abortion through a series of articles in their official publication, *The Word:*

> The scope of North America's decadence is beyond any mere recitation of the perversions, violence, mayhem and wickedness currently commonplace in the culture. However, there is one particularly abhorrent act which overwhelmingly exemplifies and defines — *legalized abortion.* . . .

[22] John XXIII, *Encyclical Mater et Magistra,* III, 194.

[23] As cited in *American Orthodoxy,* 4, (Summer, 1992).

[24] Archbishop Iakovos, *Faith for a Lifetime* (New York, 1988), pp. 171-172.

The precepts of the Orthodox Christian Faith mandate the protection of innocent human life, especially that of the unborn child. The Church has always regarded abortion as premeditated murder and very strongly opposes abortion.

The personhood of the unborn is considered to exist from conception and has never been questioned in our theology. Indeed, conception has always been recognized as the time when the soul and body were united. . . .

The position of the Orthodox Church on abortion has not changed one iota since its foundation with Christ and the Apostles.[25]

And speaking from the very heart of the Orthodox monastic tradition Fr. George Capsanis, abbot of the Monastery of Osiou at Mt. Athos in Greece writes,

. . . we cannot accept institutions such as those allowing abortion, which evade the freedom of love and which introduce the 'freedom' of egoism as a way of life.[26]

SCRIPTURE

The Fathers turned to the Scriptures to confirm the Church's stand against aborting babies, sacrificing infants and committing infanticide against unwanted children already born. In the Scriptures, they found that the full humanity of the unborn was constantly reaffirmed, both in general and specifically. The Fathers held that the preciousness of human life — especially the embryonic and fetal life of Jesus Christ — was affirmed. As Tertullian noted, "Therefore, God, as was ever foretold in the past, descended into a certain virgin and was formed flesh in her womb, and was born God and man combined. The flesh, born by the Spirit, is nourished, grows into manhood, speaks, teaches, acts and is the Christ."[27] Saint Cyril of Jerusalem

---

[25]*The Word*, published by the Antiochian Orthodox Church, January, 1993.

[26]Archimandrite George Capsanis, Abbot of the Monastery of Osiou (Mt. Athos, Greece), *The Eros of Repentance*, translated by Alexander Golitizin, (Newbury, 1993), p. 71.

[27]Tertullian *Apology*, Ref. 277, A. D. 197, in *The Faith of the Early Fathers*, vol. 1, translated by W. A. Jurgens, p. 114.

writes, "John the Baptist was sent by the Holy Spirit while yet He was carried in his mother's womb . . . John alone, while carried in the womb, leaped for joy; and there he saw not with the eyes of the flesh, he recognized the Master by the Spirit."[28]

The origin of the Church's faith in Christ rests in the events surrounding His conception and birth. In A. D. 382 Saint Gregory the Theologian wrote,

> If anyone does not agree that Holy Mary is the Mother of God, he is at odds with the Godhead. If anyone asserts that Christ passed through the Virgin as through a channel, and was not shaped in her both divinely and humanly, divinely because without man and humanly because in accord with the laws of gestation, he is likewise Godless.[29]

The Church has always regarded Christ as divine and unique from the moment of His conception and has regarded all human beings, who are icons of Christ, in the same manner—fully human and worthy of love and protection in the womb. A partial sample of several passages of Scripture give some idea of what the Fathers, and all other generations of Christians in the historic Church, have found in the Bible regarding the uniqueness of unborn human life.

"Before I formed you in the womb I knew you; Before you were born, I sanctified you; And I ordained you a prophet to the nations." (Jeremiah 1.5).

"The Lord called Me from the womb, from the matrix of My mother He has made mention of My name." (Isaiah 49.1, 5)

"But when it pleased God, who before my birth had set me apart and had called me through His grace. . . ." (Galatians 1.15-16).

"For thou didst form my inward parts, thou didst knit me together in my mother's womb. . . ." (Psalm 139.13-16).

"Thy hands fashioned and made me . . . Thou didst clothe me with skin and flesh. . . ." (Job 10.8, 9.11).

Evidence of the full human, even spiritual, life of the fetus,

---

[28]Saint Cyril of Jerusalem, *Catechetical Letters*, Ref. 810B, A. D. 350, in *The Faith of the Early Fathers*, vol. 1, translated by W. A. Jurgens, p. 349.

[29]Saint Gregory the Theologian, *Letter to Cledonius*, Ref. 1017, A. D. 382, in *The Faith of the Early Fathers*, vol. 2, translated by W. A. Jurgens, p. 40.

though documented by modern scientific studies — of fetal brain wave activity, genetics, chromosomal studies, and fetology — was recognized by the Biblical authors first.

> In those days Mary arose and went with haste into the hill country, to a city of Judah . . . And when Elizabeth heard the greeting of Mary, the baby leaped in her womb. . . . (Luke 1.39-41).

It is instructive to note, as Fr. John Kowlaczyk points out, "that in this passage the word for the unborn child Elizabeth is carrying is *brephos* ('baby'), the same word used for Christ in the manger in Luke 2.12. In fact, the New Testament has no word for 'fetus.' In the Bible, a fetus is a child."[30]

The ultimate testimony to the Church's high view of fetal life is found in the Church's teaching on the Incarnation.

> Today is the beginning of our salvation, the revelation of the eternal mystery! The Son of God becomes the Son of the Virgin as Gabriel announces the coming of Grace. Together with him let us cry to the Theotokos: Hail, O Full of Grace, the Lord is with You."[31]

The Church has always regarded human life as sacred from conception, centuries before science confirmed the full genetic humanity of the fetus. In addition, the Church also refuses to affix a time when a developing fetus "becomes human," just as Christians, in another battle related to human dignity, refused to determine humanity on the basis of skin color. The Church teaches that passage from a mother's womb is no magical humanizing event, any more than being born a white European male exclusively confers humanity.

COMMEMORATION OF THE UNBORN

In the Orthodox Church calendar there are three occasions in which the Church commemorates three important persons in the womb. This happens in the celebration of The Annun-

---

[30]John Kowlaczyk, *An Orthodox View of Abortion*, p. 20.
[31]The Troparian for the Feast of the Annunciation.

ciation,[32] the feast of the conception of the Theotokos, (Mary), by Saint Anne,[33] and the celebration of the conception of Saint John the Baptist by Saint Elizabeth.[34]

In the feast of The Annunciation, the hymn for the day does not imply that the Virgin Mary, the Theotokos (Greek for God-Bearer), carried a blob of worthless "tissue" in her womb! Nor does it teach us that the fetus in her womb would *someday* become the Christ. Rather the Church celebrates Christ, *as the Christ*, from conception.

> Today is the beginning of our salvation, the revelation of the eternal mystery! The Son of God becomes the Son of the Virgin as Gabriel announces the coming of grace . . .
>
> . . . O marvel! God has come among men; He who cannot be contained is contained in a womb; the Timeless One enters time. . . .[35]

Christ is regarded as, "God . . . among men" *even while He was a fetus*. Christ aborted would have been no less an act of deicide than Christ crucified.[36]

Holy Tradition teaches that the moral nature of the universe itself also speaks against murder. This natural order of things — this Natural Law — is reflected in the Scripture: "Can a woman forget her nursing child, and not have compassion on the son of her womb?" (Isaiah 49.15). "Every wise woman builds her house, but the foolish pulls it down with her hands." (Proverbs 14.1). In the light of Holy Tradition the willful abortion of a baby by its mother is as unnatural a practice as can be imagined. It is a choice which reverses and even attempts to deny both the mother's instinct to protect her child and the genetic and spiritual fact of what fetal human life is. It is the ultimate "pulling down" of our human house with our own hands.

Through modern science, the study of brain wave develop-

---

[32]March 25th.

[33]December 9th.

[34]September 23rd.

[35]*Great Compline for the Feast of the Annunciation.*

[36]One can only speculate with horror at the monstrosity King Herod would have unleashed on the unborn babies of Israel had there been an abortion clinic on every street corner and had he discovered that Mary was pregnant with the Christ Child *before* the birth of Jesus!

ment and fetal development, through fetoscopy, fetology and genetics, we now know that a developing baby has the full chromosomal, genetic and biological attributes of all other human beings. Thus science and Christian ethics confirm a high view of unborn human life. Today it is only in the realm of *political* "theology," *not science,* that any debate exists, as to what an unborn child is.

UNBORN PATIENTS OR VICTIMS?

The factual correctness of the Churches' high view of unborn human life is dramatically reaffirmed by the astounding modern medical practice of surgery on pre-born children. Today life-saving operations are performed on babies in the womb. During such procedures, developed in the late 1980s at the University of California at San Francisco, the baby is temporarily "born": it is exposed through a surgical incision, then is put back into the womb to finish growing after complex life-saving surgery is performed![37] The majority of fetal patients treated in these remarkable life-saving surgical procedures suffer from one of three major conditions: progressive hydronephrosis, congenital diaphragmatic hernia or sacrococcygeal teratoma. Additionally, as Dr. Harry Jacee reports in the Journal of Pediatrics, there have been an encouraging number of reports of successful treatment of fetuses with abnormally rapid heart rates by non-surgical methods.[38]

In a perverse symmetry, at the very same time as new medical techniques for treating babies in the womb have been developed, there have also been a series of scientific "breakthroughs" in abortion methods designed to kill fully developed, completely viable babies of *exactly* the same age as those being treated in the womb.

Journalist Jenny Westburg, in an important article, *D&X: Grim Technology for Abortion's Older Victims,* explains these new "break-throughs."[39] In September of 1992, Westburg reports, a new second and third-trimester abortion procedure

---

[37] *Journal of the American Medical Association*, vol. 265, no. 6 (1991), pp. 737-741.
[38] *Journal of Pediatrics*, vol. 118, no. 2 (1991), pp. 303-305.
[39] *Life Advocate*, February, 1993.

was discussed at the National Abortion Federation (NAF) Risk Management Seminar in Dallas, Texas. Dr. Martin Haskell, A Cincinnati abortionist, presented a scientific paper describing the "procedure." The new technique is called "dilation and extraction." Haskell has coined the term "D&X" for the method, in order to distinguish it from the standard D&E method. ("D&E" stands for dilation and evacuation.) D&X differs from D&E in that the unborn child is removed intact, rather than being dismembered inside the uterus. The child is killed by suctioning the brain tissue through a hole in the base of the skull, which the abortionist makes with blunt surgical scissors. This is accomplished while the living child's head is still inside the mother, after pulling the baby's body out, feet first.

Haskell recommends the D&X procedure for the late second-trimester and third-trimester abortions. Classic D&E presents "technical problems" in late pregnacy because of the "toughness of fetal tissues at this stage of development." Accordingly, most late abortions have traditionally been performed by instillation methods, such as saline and prostaglandin. However, these methods are risky for the mother; moreover, no traditional instillation method entirely guarantees the death of the baby, which to abortionists, is a serious drawback.

Since D&X avoids the problems attendant to late-term dismemberment, it can be employed throughout the second and third trimesters. While Haskell has utilized D&X through 26 weeks' gestation, he cites another physician's experiences as evidence that D&X can be used to perform third-trimester abortions. Dr. James McMahon, of McMahon Medical Center and Eve Surgical Centers in Los Angeles and Tarzana, California, uses D&X to abort children up to 32 weeks "or more," according to Westburg. In order to use D&X in the third trimester, only a few modifications are necessary, including additional cervical dilation and a slower operating time. Haskell, according to Westburg, says he has performed over 700 D&X abortions. The D&X is so similar to infanticide that when a college student observed Haskell perform a D&X abortion in 1989, her reaction was to call the police.[40]

The D&X procedure begins with "dilation (and) *more dilation*." The cervix is initially dilated to 9-11 mm, with mechanical

---

[40]See "Dismemberment and Choice," *Life Advocate*, January, 1993, p. 36.

dilators (synthetic laminaria, or Dilapin), which remain in place overnight. The following morning, the Dilapin are removed and replaced with a second insertion of 15 to 25 Dilapin. Once again, these are left in place overnight. The Dilapin dilation process may cause severe cramping, which is treated with pain relievers when necessary. The operation itself takes place on Day 3. After removing the Dilapin, the abortionist ruptures the membranes (if the patient's water has not already broken) and drains the amniotic fluid. Then the abortionist's assistant places an ultra-sound transducer on the mother's abdomen and locates the child's legs and feet. The abortionist then uses a large forceps to grasp one of the baby's legs. He pulls firmly, forcing the child into a feet-down position. He continues pulling until the baby's leg is drawn into the birth canal.

Next, using his hands instead of forceps, the abortionist delivers the baby's body in a manner similar to vaginal breech birth. First the child's other leg is delivered, followed by the torso shoulders, and arms. The baby's head "usually" remains inside the uterus, too large to pass through the internal cervical os.

The abortionist then performs the next step, which, according to Westburg, Haskell euphemistically calls "fetal skull decompression." Using blunt-tipped surgical scissors, he pierces the child's head at the base of the skull. He then forces the scissors open, enlarging the wound. Removing the scissors, the abortionist inserts a suction catheter into the wound and vacuums out the child's brain tissue: "evacuates the skull contents." With the suction tube still in place, the abortionist then pulls the corpse from the woman's body. He delivers the placenta with forceps, and scrapes the inside of the uterus with a sharp curette, then with a large-bore suction curette. According to Haskell, the woman usually "recovers" quickly: on her feet in thirty minutes; out the door in two hours. Haskell claims a "low rate" of complications, although he does not provide specific numbers. The Dallas conference, at which Haskell described the D&X technique, was entitled "Second Trimester Abortion: From Every Angle." Haskell's presentation included a 10-minute video of an actual D&X.[41]

---

[41]Jenny Westburg, "D&X: Grim Technology for Abortion's Older Victims," *Life Ad-*

The grim irony of our times can be seen in the fact that the unborn child who is the patient in a life-saving fetal surgical procedure could — *legally* — become the unwilling "donor" of its own organs and tissue in the very same hospital. All the mother of the child would have to do is walk down the hallway and demand an abortion. Conversely, if the unborn patient died of complications following a surgical procedure, the mother could sue for malpractice, as could the child, if it was born handicapped. In fact, a case of this kind occurred in New York in 1992. As Richard John Neuhaus writes,

> You have probably read something about "The Butcher of Avenue A," a Dr. Abu Hayat who did abortions on the Lower East Side of New York, and is now convicted of doing them very shoddily. He is facing up to twenty years in jail. Rosa Rodriguez, eight months pregnant, came in for an abortion that was badly botched. Leaving the clinic with the abortion incomplete, Ms. Rodriquez changed her mind and the next day delivered a girl child at a hospital. Ana Rosa is now (as of May, 1993) eighteen months old and is described by the press as a bright, active child "who loves to eat croissants and play with her sister Jenny." The problem is that she has no right arm, it having been sliced off during the abortion process by Dr. Hayat. . . .
>
> Had Ana Rodriquez not survived, and had she not been missing an arm, we would have heard nothing about the Butcher of Avenue A, or the hundreds of abortionists who similarly exploit women in trouble. The pro-choice activists are determined to prevent any regulation of abortion clinics, even the minimal record-keeping mandated by Pennsylvania and upheld in last year's *Casey* decision by the Supreme Court. Oddly enough, and despite *Roe*, New York still has on the books a law prohibiting abortions after "viability." In reality, almost 4,000 abortions per year are

---

vocate, February, 1993.

    Haskell, Martin, M.D., "Dilation and extraction for Late Second Trimester Abortion," paper presented at the NAF Risk Management Seminar, September 13, 1992; in *Second Trimester Abortion: From Every Angle — Presentations, Bibliography & Related Materials*, Washington, D.C.: National Abortion Federation, 1992, p.28. (Note: Except where otherwise indicated, all quotes are from "Dilation and Extraction for Late Second Trimester Abortion," by Martin Haskell, M.D., as cited by Jenny Westburg.)

performed in the state on children beyond the twentieth week. Nonetheless, Hayat was tried and convicted under that law, plus several others related to medical malpractice.[42]

Yet there are still those who maintain the biological-political fiction that what is in a mother's womb is "not alive" and has "no rights" independent the parents', mother's or society's "right to choose." They say that the baby is merely "part of the woman's body." This is a total medical and scientific fiction — the ultimate "old wives' tale."

SANITY

The Church has always held a far more compassionate, scientific and logical position on the value of human life than does today's secularized, pro-abortion, medical-legal fraternity. The Church has taught that we never cease to grow into our full humanity from conception onward. Indeed, since at *every age* we *all* depend on being part of the human community for physical as well as spiritual sustenance, we learn from the Church that none of us are ever individually "viable." We are never "independent" of other human beings or of God, any more than a newborn baby is less dependent on her mother two minutes or two years after her birth than two minutes before. It is only in the realm of politicized and schizophrenic old wives' tales that this truth is not self-evident.

To treat the unborn child as a patient is very much in the best moral, humanitarian, compassionate tradition of the historical Church. To treat the unborn child as a worthless "tumor" and pregnancy as if it were a "disability" is a contradiction of everything Christ and the Church, let alone legitimate science and medicine, have stood for until the very recent past.

To condemn the unborn child to death because she is dependent on her mother ("part of a woman's body") is to condemn the whole human race to death. We are *all* dependent on one another all of our lives. And the fact that a person is in the wrong womb at the wrong time or is the wrong sex or age or the wrong color or the wrong size, or has the wrong disability, is not reason enough to kill her.

[42]Richard John Neuhaus, "Butchered Logic," *First Things,* May, 1993.

THE BIG LIE

Author and humorist P. J. O'Rourke writes of the tortured absurdities of the political "theology" and lawlessness of the modern pro-abortion movement.

> The second item in the liberal creed, after self-righteousness, is unaccountability. Liberals have invented whole college majors—psychology, sociology, women's studies—to prove that nothing is anybody's fault. No one is fond of taking responsibility for his actions, but consider how much you'd have to hate free will to come up with a political platform that advocates killing unborn babies but not convicted murderers. A callous pragmatist might favor abortion and capital punishment. A devout Christian would sanction neither. But it takes years of therapy to arrive at the liberal point of view.[43]

In our age of lawlessness, and total disregard for logic, not to mention sanctity, many people who sin compound their sin by calling it "goodness." This is what "feminists" and "liberals" (a strange term to describe people who are reviving the Nazi eugenics program) have done in our day by extolling the "benefits" of abortion, conveniently re-labeling what is a self-evident horror as a "constitutional right" or a mere clinical "choice." It seems to me that in doing so they have disguised the ultimate degradation of women as "liberation."[44]

Since 1973, when abortion on demand in America—for any reason, by any person, of babies at any age of fetal gestation—was legalized, any fair observer of our society knows that the only people truly "liberated" by the abortion trade have been irresponsible males who refuse to be accountable for their sexual activity. It is no accident that among the first to support legalized abortion on demand in America, were the editors and owners of the largest pornography magazines.

---

[43]P. J. O'Rourke, "Liberals," *The American Spectator*, April, 1992.

[44]George Stephanopoulos, President Bill Clinton's first communications director and spokesman, spoke in glowing terms of abortion following Clinton's signing of the executive order providing government funding of medical experimentation on both living and dead aborted babies: "These executive orders made a tangible differences in persons' lives. . . . Women who go into abortion clinics Monday (the next day) are going to be treated differently. . . ." (*NY Times*, January 22, 1993).

In contrast to feminist political slogans, the aesthetic, spiritual and physical reality of having an abortion is degrading. It approximates a form of murderous medical rape. It is "liberating" to women and their babies in the same manner as Auschwitz was "liberating" to Jews. It does the same thing for women as hard-core pornography does—it exploits, denigrates and reduces women to the status of sexual serfs, on the one hand, and mere "productive citizens" with careers to protect on the other. It turns the life-giving womb into a death chamber in which a struggling, kicking, suffering child silently screams away her life as her brains are sucked out by a male abortionist.

The practice of abortion, "legal" or otherwise, reduces women to little more than the sexual chattel property of men and/or the property of businesses and corporations who regard the interruption of a career by a child as a "sin." In the sexually "liberated" climate of today, men have no reason to even *pretend* to view women as more than a means of selfish gratification. That the abortion mentality reduces women to sexual serfs—baby and sex machines—is well-illustrated by the growing use of aborted babies for medical experimentation and "therapeutic," even cosmetic, consumption. Women are now reduced by abortion to being glorified tissue banks, incubators for "fetal tissue," producers of "transplant material," organ and tissue factories, and "productive" careerists to whom children are a burden.

The results of the legalization of abortion, the acceptance of sexual "liberation," the degradation of women and the skyrocketing incidence of rape all converge in a twisted sort of symmetry.

As Leon Kass writes,

Regardless of their divergent motives, the deeds of rapist and harlot have a convergent inner meaning. Both are without modesty, shame, or sexual self-restraint. Both are indifferent to the generative meaning of (especially female) sexuality. Both regard sex purely as a matter of present and private (especially male) gratifications. Both are indifferent to the fact that sex points to future generations, those to whom we give life and nurture, paying back, in the only way we can, our debts to our own forebears. Both are especially indifferent to marriage and family, those conventional institutions whose main purpose is to provide a true home for fruitful and generous love and for the proper rearing of children.[45]

Sex has been reduced to the status of a casual contact sport in our society. This stripping away of meaning and love from sexuality has been deliberate. It has been the stated agenda of such "pioneers" in "sex education" as Dr. Sol Gordon who is famous for having said, "Sex is too important to glop up with sentiment." The acceptance of legal abortion and fetal experimentation as "normal" and "moral" has indeed reduced men and women to no more than "sexual partners"—tissue banks no longer "glopped up" with sentiment!

No one would accuse today's medical-industrial complex of sentimentality. As John Whitehead (attorney and founder of the Rutherford Institute) writes,

> The Roe redefinition was quickly and almost universally accepted by the medical profession. Only six months after the Supreme Court decision in Roe v. Wade (1973), Peter A. J. Adam, an associate professor of pediatrics at Case Western Reserve University in Ohio, reported to the American Pediatric Research Society on research he and his associates had conducted on twelve babies up to twenty weeks old who had survived hysterotomy abortions. These physicians cut the heads off of these tiny babies and placed tubes in the main arteries feeding their brains. The researchers kept the heads of these babies alive, much as the Russians kept the heads of the dogs alive in certain experiments in the 1950s. In response to questions raised about this "research," Dr. Adams said: "Once society declares a fetus dead, and abrogates its rights, I don't see any ethical problem. . . . Whose rights are we going to protect, once we've decided the fetus won't live?"[46]

In abortion, and in the kind of "fetal tissue" research described above, that in 1993 President Clinton began funding,

---

[45]Leon Kass, "Regarding Daughters and Sisters," *Commentary*, April 3, 1993.

[46]"Post-Abortion Fetal Study Stirs Storm," *Medical World News*, June 8, 1973, p. 21. As cited by John Whitehead, *Strategy on the Abortion Issue* (Charlottesville, VA, 1993). The federal funding of this type of "research" was outlawed by the Reagan Administration. In 1993, President Clinton began to provide federal funding for all "fetal tissue" research.

personhood is treated as if it were worthless. In the name of "women's rights" motherhood has now been reduced to just another cold, calculated medical-economic "option." Pregnancy has become an unfortunate medical "complication" of sex. Women have been stripped of the status of nurturing creatures and stripped of the extra protection that is due to them as the first, sacred, homes of all human beings. Science has become a fascist nightmare on the threshold of reviving the Nazi eugenics program. The "feminist" agenda has weirdly converged with that of the pornography industry. The sex educator's curriculum has converged with the career aims of the local pimp. The medical practitioner's career has become indistinguishable from the concentration camp guard.

The type of moral reversal that we see in the legalization of abortion (not to mention the search and destroy mission against "imperfect" babies, implicit in prenatal testing), in which ultimate evil is sold to the public as "good" and the word "choice" describes the robbery of a child's entire future of choices, is the type of supreme evil of which Saint Evagrios the Solitary spoke when he writes:

> Now what am I to say about the demon who makes the soul obtuse? . . . How at his approach, the soul departs from its own proper state and strips itself of reverence and the fear of God, no longer regarding sin as sin, or wickedness as wickedness; it looks on judgment and the eternal punishment . . . as mere words; it laughs at the fire which causes the earth to tremble; . . . You may beat your breast as such a soul draws near to sin but it takes no notice . . . it ignores you, like a pig that closes its eyes and charges through the fence.[47]

---

[47]Saint Evagrios the Solitary, *On Discrimination: The Philokalia*, vol. 1, translated by G. E. H. Palmer, Philip Sherrard, and Kallistos Ware, p. 44.

CHAPTER NINETEEN
THE JOURNEY

One of the root problems contributing to our present lawlessness is that in most Protestant theology conversion seems to have been confused with salvation. As a result Protestantism has implicity taught that people can do as they please since salvation and character formation— works —are unrelated. But, according to the historical Church, conversion and salvation are two very different things.[1] We are taught by the Church that the crown of salvation goes only to those who *finish the race*, not to the so-called Elect or to those who merely believe they are "born again," regardless of the content of their characters or actions.

In the parable of the sower we see that the majority of those converted failed to persist to salvation (Mt 13.3-9). On the other hand, we read of Jesus saying that the Roman Centurion had the greatest faith Jesus had found in Israel. Yet the Centurion, while on the road to salvation, had no conversion experience at all and was almost certainly not a Jew, let alone a Christian (Mt 8.5-13).

According to the teaching of the Church, conversion is that

---

[1] "St. Paul writes that we 'are children of God, and if children, also heirs, heirs on the one hand of God, co-heirs on the other hand, of Christ' (8.17). But all this has a condition, has a proviso, for there is the all important "if indeed." Our glorification, according to St. Paul, is contingent upon a mighty 'if' and that 'if' leads us to the spiritual reality, the spiritual reality of 'co-suffering.' The very use of the word 'co-suffer' presupposes the reality of the idea of 'co-suffering' and both presuppose an active, dynamic spiritual action or activity on the part of the one who co-suffers, else there is no meaning to the 'co.'

In the *Epistle to the Romans* (12.1) St. Paul uses language that would be meaningless if man were merely a passive object in the redemptive process, if justification by faith was an action that took place only on the Divine level. 'I appeal to you therefore, brethren, through the compassions of God, to present your bodies a living sacrifice, holy and well-pleasing to God, which is your reasonable service.' " Georges Florovsky, *The Byzantine Ascetic and Spiritual Fathers*, pp. 33-34.

process by which we start over — change our behavior — do an about-face. At its most dramatic, conversion may involve an inaugural and powerful encounter with Christ. Conversion consists of a sudden recognition of the fact that Christ is Lord, Savior and King, as in the story of the conversion of Zaccheus. (Lk 19.1-10)

The Church has always taught, however, that salvation is a journey, not a one-time experience.[2] Christ called it a difficult journey, one in which there are many pitfalls, as the parable of the sower, or the wise and foolish virgins illustrates so graphically. Christ told Zaccheus that he should do certain specific things in order to begin his journey; belief was not enough.[3]

Because Protestants, since the beginning of the Reformation, have tended to reduce the way of salvation to a sort of magical one time, "predestined" conversion experience, they have unwittingly reduced to near zero the importance of the sacraments.[4] After all, if one can be instantly "saved," what need does one have of the spiritual tools — crutches, if you will — provided by a sacramental form of worship? Indeed why even bother to do the hard work to become Christ-like at all if one is already saved? Why bother to read the Sermon on the Mount or the Beatitudes, let alone try to become like Christ? Why not simply read John 3.16 once, "believe," and forget the rest of Scripture?

If salvation is a one-time experience, then the teachings of

---

[2] ". . . Whoever wishes to travel the shortest road to Christ — the road to dispassion and spiritual knowledge — and joyfully to attain perfection, should not turn either to the right or the left, but in his whole way of life should journey diligently along the royal way." St. Peter of Damaskos, *The Seven Forms of Bodily Discipline: The Philokalia*, vol. 3, trans. G. E. H. Palmer, Philip Sherrard, and Kallistos Ware, p. 88.

[3] "Synergism does not mean that two energies are equal. Rather it means that there are two wills — one, the will of God which precedes, accompanies, and completes all that is good, positive, spiritual and redemptive, one that has willed that man have a spiritual will, a spiritual participation in the redemptive process; the other is the will of man which must respond, cooperate, 'co-suffer.' . . . St. Paul exhorts us to cleave to the good' . . . for there are always two wills in the process of redemption — the Divine, which initiates; and the human, which responds and is, in the very response active in that grace which it has received.' " Georges Florovsky, *The Byzantine Ascetic and Spiritual Fathers*, pp. 34-35.

[4] In the words of the Helvetic Confession of 1556, (the basic statement of the Calvinist creed, before the Council of Dort, 1618) the Eucharistic feast was nothing special: "This spiritual eating and drinking takes place even apart from the Lord's Supper, whenever and wherever someone believes in Christ." *Helvetic Confession* (post 21, Niesel 265) Once again Reformation theology internalized the Christian faith. Each Christian could partake in the "Eucharist" by merely feeling Christian!

Christ, the Beatitudes for instance, become absurdities. The Christian's attempt to hunger and thirst after righteousness, and to learn good habits of mind, body and spirit, are wasted if the outcome of the spiritual journey is already decided, if there is no need to run the race, fight the good fight, or finish the course.

By confusing conversion with the lifelong journey of salvation, Protestantism has also made nonsense of Christ's warnings about the dire consequences of failing to pursue holiness as an ongoing quest. Salvation as Christ reveals it means a search for the "pearl of great price" for which we are to be willing to sell all we have in the course of a lifetime struggle to become perfect even as God is perfect. Indeed if salvation could be easily or instantly achieved, then the majority of the Bible's teaching on how to live a moral, lawful, sacramental life makes no sense. In fact, Christ was wasting His time when he preached the Sermon on the Mount. And all the Saints, monks and ascetics who have struggled to live holy lives have been deluded.

A sad consequence of the modern Protestant confusion regarding the way of salvation is the disillusionment of so many would- be Christians who have been sold a false bill of goods: instant, easy "salvation" and the promise of instant, painless change in their characters. They have been given to understand that after being "born again," all will be well; God will bless; and their troubles will be behind them, if they only have sufficient "faith." They have been taught to "name and claim" the promises of God and that all they need will be granted to them instantly if they only "trust God." According to the Holy Tradition, this is a diabolically false teaching. It is an idea that actually leads people away from God. This is because the Church teaches that we can only imitate Christ and become like God through ascetic perseverance, that there are no short cuts to sanctity.

The thief on the cross found salvation because he was being crucified alongside of Jesus. Jesus did not magically help the suffering thief come down off his cross. The thief's conversion in no way altered his excruciating circumstances, nor was it possible without them. There was no easier way for him because he had a personal encounter with Christ.

The simplistic "born-again" formula for instant painless "salvation" is not only a misunderstanding; I believe it is a heresy. It contradicts the teaching of Christ in regard to the narrow, hard, ascetic, difficult way of salvation.[5] The thief on the cross — brief as his spiritual journey was — nevertheless had to complete his hard journey, his road of faith. He could have lost hope in his last hour. He could have let his pain lead to despair. He could have changed his mind and railed and jeered at Jesus, along with his fellow condemned companion, when he saw that he was not going to be saved from pain and physical death by Christ.

Even in the thief's case more was required than a mere "conversion experience." The thief, like the rest of us, needed to travel his own particular road of pain toward God through the imitation of Christ. To the extent that his knowledge of Christ permitted him to imitate Christ, the thief had to finish his course, just as we must.

As is well illustrated by the parable of the fig tree (Lk 13.6-9), the ultimate salvation of our souls — as distinct from conversion and repentance — is not found in simplistic formulas but in choosing to grow into the people God created us to be and by a life-long ascetic, sacramental struggle for holiness.

> Then he said to the keeper of his vineyard, "Look, for three years I have come seeking fruit on this fig tree and find none. Cut it down; why does it use up the ground?" But he answered . . . "Sir, let it alone this year also, until I dig around it and fertilize it. And if it bears fruit, well. But if not, you can cut it down."

Anthony M. Coniaris summarizes what the journey of salvation entails.

> What does it mean to be saved? What is salvation in Christ?
>
> Salvation is freedom — freedom from the tyranny of self-centeredness, freedom from the bondage of fear and death.
>
> Salvation in Christ is being freed from myself so that I can become the person God created me to be and intends me to become. . . .
>
> Salvation for the Orthodox Church has not meant only 'justification' or forgiveness of sins: it means the renewing and restoration of God's image in man, the lifting up of fallen humanity through Christ into the very life of God.[6]

---

[5] Mt 5.3-12, Mt 6.19-21, Mt 7.13-14, Mt 7.21-23, Mt 10.16-24, Mt 12.33-37, Mt 13.3-9 and 18-23, Mt 17.24-26, etc.

[6] Anthony M. Coniaris, *Introducing the Orthodox Church*, pp. 50-51.

If we are truly seeking God our question should not be: Am
I saved? Rather it must be: Am I becoming more like Christ?
"For if when we were enemies we were reconciled to God through
the death of His Son, much more, having been reconciled, we
shall be saved by His Life" (Rom 5.10).

Christ describes the journey of salvation as the quest to
become like God. "Therefore you shall be perfect, just as your
Father in heaven is perfect" (Mt 5.48). So humanly impossible
is this journey — this quest to be God-like — that "there are few
who find it" (Mt 7.14). For some salvation is as unattainable as
a camel passing through the eye of a needle. Nevertheless, the
Church teaches that Christ gives us all the opportunity and grace
to come to Him if we choose to do so. But, as the story of the
rich young ruler illustrates, saying we are coming to Him should
not to be confused with actually persevering to salvation.[7]
There is a narrow gate to pass. There is the necessity to sell all
we have, in order that we may purchase the one true thing. There
is the necessity to become monks, literally or in our hearts, and
to curb our passions in order that we might imitate our Lord.
We are told that many turn aside and refuse to enter. They want
a wider, easier, more inclusive, or perhaps more "ecumenical"
door. They want to "feel good about themselves" without having
to change their behavior. They want to perfect the art of self-
esteem without having to practice self-discipline. In fact, to many
misled people faith is just another form of self-centeredness. It
is focused on how to "feel good," not on how to imitate Christ's
own ascetic struggle.

According to Holy Tradition, Christ is the narrow gate, and
only by Him are we saved. There is no other gate. There is not
a wider, less exclusive or more democratic gate. Nor is there
any tradition of inter-faith dialogue with those outside of the narrow way of Christ to be found in the historic Church's teaching,
as if the means of salvation can be defined as a

---

[7] "Orthodox Spirituality is, essentially and basically, Christocentric and Christological.
The Christocentric emphasis is conspicuous in the whole structure of Orthodox devotional
life: sacramental, corporate, and private. The Christological pattern of Baptism, Eucharist,
Penance, and also Marriage, is obvious. All sacraments are, indeed, sacraments of the
believer's life *in Christ* . . . The utter reality of this encounter is vigorously stressed in the
office of preparation for Communion, as also in the prayers of thanksgiving after Communion. The preparation is precisely for one's meeting with Christ in the Sacrament, personal and intimate. Indeed, one meets Christ only in the fellowship of the Church . . ."
Georges Florovsky, *Aspects of Church History* (Vaduz, Flanders, 1987), p. 23.

consensus of points of view between men and women of good will. The Church teaches that we can only pass through the gate by imitating Christ. Thus the consistent prayer of the Saints has always been Christ's prayer: ". . . not as I will, but as You will." (Mt 26.39)[8]

According to Holy Tradition, Christ was exclusive in His statements because God's love is changeless, constant and non-negotiable. God's love is the final immovable reality.[9] Christ did not establish many ways to the Father. Nor did He establish many "churches" or "denominations," but only One Church, One Holy Tradition and One Truth that inexorably leads to God whose loving character is absolute.

> Whoever wishes to travel the shortest road to Christ — the road of dispassion and spiritual knowledge — and joyfully to attain perfection, should not turn either to the right or to the left, but in his whole way of life should journey diligently along the narrow way.[10]

The false "churches" of multi-denominationalism may, like amoebas, endlessly subdivide again and again but that does not mean that the one true historical Orthodox Church does not exist, any more than the fact that the divorce rate has been going up means that marriage is no longer a valid Christian sacrament. It only reveals that many people have gone sadly astray from God and refuse to obey His Church's sacramental and apostolic authority.

Christ's "narrow" teaching in today's pluralistic, pragmatic, democratic world of relativistic, academic fundamentalism, will appear very out of date and politically incorrect to many people. It is not fashionable to say that there is only one way to do anything. To have *no* fixed moral absolutes and beliefs is now understood to be a virtue. But for those who reject the myth of salvation through the theological sleight-of-hand of

---

[8]"According to Saint Maximus the Confessor: Salvation defined as deification (becoming like God) was the theme of Christian faith and the biblical message. The purpose of the Lord's Prayer was to point to the mystery of deification." Jaroslav Pelikan, *The Spirit of Eastern Christendom*, p. 10.

[9]"God became man, to set man free. . . God became human in order that man might become divine. . .'an image of the future deification by grace.' "(Maixus. Ambig. 64. PG 91.1389) Ibid. p. 11.

[10]St. Peter of Damaskos, *On the Seven Forms of Bodily Discipline: The Philokalia*, vol. 3, trans. G. E. H. Palmer, Philip Sherrard, and Kallistos Ware, p. 88.

"sensitivism" and good feeling, and who choose instead to pass through the narrow gate onto the royal way, there remains the real test: the difficult way on the hard road that leads to life and the journey of faith from death to life.

As Clement of Alexandria wrote in A.D. 202,

> When we hear, "your faith has saved you" (Mt 9.22), we do not understand (the Lord) to say simply that they will be saved who have believed in whatever manner, even if works have not followed.[11]

Christ promised that His way is difficult and He provided only one path toward God for us to tread: the lifelong ascetic-sacramental path of worship, sacrifice and obedience.

St. John Cassian wrote of meeting the famous African desert monk, Abba Moses. He asked him: "What is the purpose with which we are to pursue the Kingdom of heaven?" Abba Moses replied,

> The goal . . . as we have said is the Kingdom of God. Its immediate purpose, however, is purity of heart, . . . And, should it ever happen that for a short time our heart turns aside from the direct path, we must bring it back again at once, guiding our lives with reference to our purpose as if it were a carpenter's rule.[12]

Christ's own life was one of ascetic struggle. He often went into the desert to pray and fast. According to Holy Tradition, the false church has lied to people when it taught that following God would be easy or automatic. It lied when it taught that there is some spiritual formula through which Christians, like the unbelievers around them, can "have it all," including purity of heart and so-called spiritual gifts absent from struggle and a lifelong monastic hungering and thirsting for righteousness.

Contrary to the false "prosperity gospel" preached by many of the materialistic modern, so-called charismatic, Protestant denominations, Christ made no promise of material well-being or physical healing in this life as a "reward" for faith. Quite the contrary:

[11]Clement of Alexandria, *Stromateis*, A.D. 202, in *The Faith of the Early Fathers*, vol. 1, trans. W. A. Jurgens, p. 184.

[12]*The Philokalia*, vol. 1, trans. G. E. H. Palmer, Philip Sherrard, and Kallistos Ware, p. 95.

But woe to you who are rich, for you have received your consolation. Woe to you who are full, for you shall hunger. Woe to you who laugh now, for you shall mourn and weep. Woe to you when all men speak well of you, For so did their fathers the false prophets (Lk 6.24-26).

Christ promises woe to people who enjoy the very selfsame "blessings" that many Protestant denominations teach is the birthright of a Christian, as one of the "Elect" practitioners of the American Dream. Yet St. Mark the Ascetic writes, "(H)e who does something good and expects a reward is serving not God but his own will."[13]

Christ did not "have it all." He gave freely of Himself, receiving nothing in return. Christ's teaching, by example, is the opposite of the contemporary prosperity gospel which seeks to baptize the American Dream as if it were part and parcel of the ancient Christian faith. It is also the opposite of the secular "religion" of our day: belief in the "right" to be happy at all times. The psalmist, writing what might be a fitting epitaph to modern America, said, "The righteous also shall see and fear, and shall laugh at him, saying, 'Here is the man (nation) who did not make God his strength, but trusted in the abundance of his riches, and strengthened himself in his wickedness.'" (Ps 52.7). According to the Church, the struggle against sin, and its consequences, is the lot of true Christians.[14] Our dream is of righteousness, not wealth.[15] Our hope is in God, not politics or a new social order.

The Church teaches that there will be true peace for the followers of Jesus. But it is not the peace of this world. Nor is it the "inner peace" of modern psychological counseling and "therapeutic" religion, of the sort that deadens our consciences in the name of self-love. Nor, according to the Fathers, is it the financial prosperity promised to the duped audiences of

---

[13]St. Mark the Ascetic, *On Those Who Think that They Are Made Righteous by Works: The Philokalia*, vol. 1, trans. G. E. H. Palmer, Philip Sherrard, and Kallistos Ware, p. 130.

[14]"We have, 'put our hand to the plow'; yet we look back, forgetting and even strongly rejecting our duties, and so do not become 'fit for the kingdom of heaven' (of Luke 9.62)." St. Neilos the Ascetic, *Ascetic Discourse: The Philokalia*, vol. 1, trans. G. E. H. Palmer, Philip Sherrard, and Kallistos Ware, p. 203.

[15]"Let all involuntary suffering teach you to remember God, and you will not lack occasion for repentance." St. Mark the Ascetic, *On the Spiritual Law: The Philokalia*, vol. 1, trans. by G. E. H. Palmer, Philip Sherrard, and Kallistos Ware, p. 114.

"Christian" television who send in their money hoping for a material blessing in return.[16]

PERSECUTION

Far from making life easy, Christ predicted His followers would suffer. "Behold, I send you out as sheep in the midst of wolves. Therefore be wise as serpents and harmless as doves" (Mt 10.16). The promise of suffering is such an insistent theme in the Gospels that we might wonder if those who do not suffer for their faith are actually following Christ.

Christ told His disciples to have no illusions about the brotherhood of man. The picture He painted of the unbelieving world was one of ravaging wolves, a harsh world in which his followers needed the wariness, guile and canniness of serpents to survive the onslaught. At the same time, Jesus also told His disciples to be harmless, to be as clever as serpents in protecting themselves from temptation and demons, but without venom. "Beware of men, for they will deliver you up to councils and scourge you in their synagogues" (Mt 10.17). We are to pray for the best for all people; but, because we know all men are sinners and will sin against us, we must also expect persecution for our faith.

CONCLUSION

Think of the banal cheerful little ditties that children are routinely taught to sing in Protestant Sunday Schools. Think of the bouncy humanistic little tunes that the modern American Roman Catholic Church has introduced into its "liturgies." Now try and imagine how the words of Christ in Mt 10.21-33 would sound set to such mindless musical paeans to well-being, self-esteem, inclusiveness and good feeling.

---

[16]"The demon of avarice . . . after deceiving the soul, little by little he engulfs it in avaricious thoughts and then hands it over to the demon of self-esteem. . ." Evagrios the Solitary, *On Discrimination: The Philokalia*, vol. 1, trans. G. E. H. Palmer, Philip Sherrard, and Kallistos Ware, p. 51.

Now brother will deliver up brother to death, and a father his child; and children will rise up against parents and cause them to be put to death. And you will be hated by all for My name's sake. But he who endures to the end will be saved.

Holy Tradition teaches that those who follow Christ do not do so to feel good, or to improve their self-esteem, or because it will be "good for America," or even necessarily good for them in the present world. The Church teaches us that the one reason to follow Christ and to strive to be like Him — that is, to change the content of our characters through fasting, prayer, confession, sacrament and obedience — is so that "he who endures to the end will be saved." This is what it means to seek first the kingdom of God, that we struggle toward God by obeying Christ and practically imitating Him. This is what being saved from our sin requires. We are asked to join in the life of the historical Church and come to God in the only way His Son told us to.

Matta el Meskin (Matthew the Poor), the most famous of the twentieth-century Egyptian Coptic monks, articulates the historical Christian view of the true nature of the hungering to know God.

A sincere and humble acceptance of obedience to God that springs from a heart undefiled by falsehood, hypocrisy, love of display, or exhibitionism, and not looking for any particular (material benefits or) results, may be considered the beginning of the true way to the knowledge of God. . . . All this is to say that the spiritual understanding of the Gospel and of God is the result of the formation of a relationship with God through obedience to His commandments.[17]

[17]Matthew the Poor, *The Communion of Love* (Crestwood, NY, 1984), p. 21.

CHAPTER TWENTY

THE HEART OF CHRISTIANITY

According to Holy Tradition, Christian faith is a living sacrament. It has no human time frame. Christ has come and is coming again and the two events are happening simultaneously. The marriage supper of the lamb is now and yesterday and tomorrow; it is all now in the same sense as God is I AM. For this reason, the Church teaches, God cannot be fully described in human language. Rigid conceptions like predestination and election are inapplicable to God because He stands *outside of time*. His essence is indescribable.[1] When the Biblical authors and the Fathers speak about God they necessarily use words to do so, but with the understanding that human language is not up to the task. "For flesh and blood has not revealed this to you, but My Father who is in heaven" (Matthew 16.17).

St. Gregory the Theologian, in his Oration on Easter (A.D. 385), writes,

> God always was, and is, and will be; or better, He always
> *IS, Was* and *Will Be* . . . He is ever existing; and that is how
> He names Himself in treating with Moses on the mountain.
> He gathers in Himself the whole of being because He has
> neither a beginning nor will He have an end. He is like some

---

[1] "In the life and existence of the Church time is mysteriously overcome and mastered; time, so to speak *stands still* . . . it stands still, because of the power of grace, which gathers together in catholic unity of life that which had become separated by walls built in the course of time. Unity in the Spirit embraces in a mysterious, time-conquering fashion, the faithful of all generations. This time-conquering unity is manifested and revealed in the experience of the Church, especially in its Eucharistic experience." Georges Florovsky, *Bible, Church, Tradition: An Eastern Orthodox View*, p. 45.

great sea of being, limitless and unbounded, transcending every conception of time and nature.[2]

Augustine of Hippo writes: "Eternity itself is the substance of God, which has nothing that is changeable. There is nothing there that is past, as if it were no longer; nothing that is future, as if it not yet were. There is nothing there except IS."[3] John A. Hardon, S. J., in *The Catholic Catechism,* expresses the concept of the timelessness of God in this way: "There was no time before creation, since there were no changeable beings whose change could be measured (which is time) until the immutable God brought creatures into existence."[4]

According to the Church, Christian conversion in the true sense of the word is no more than the first realization of God's timeless presence. This new awareness is combined with a sincere desire to change the content of one's character so as to be able to joyfully enter into a relationship with God by becoming like Him. The Church teaches us that we may enter into God's presence by worshipping Him even *before* we are truly like Him.

We are not sentenced to worship God alone, arbitrarily, or capriciously, each pursuing an intuitive journey along a self-directed spiritual or psychological path. The Church teaches that when true worship takes place, it is in the presence of every Christian who has ever lived and every creature in heaven, whether Cherubim, Seraphim, Saints, Martyrs or the countless faithful who have gone before.[5]

Because all of life is sacramental, life, according to the Church, is much more than a guilt-ridden exercise in pietistic virtue on the one hand, or a political, materialistic quest for

---

[2] St. Gregory the Theologian, *Second Oration on Easter,* A.D. 383, in *The Faith of the Early Fathers,* vol. 2, trans. W. A. Jurgens, p. 38.

[3] Augustine of Hippo, *On the Psalms,* A.D. 392, in *The Faith of the Early Fathers,* vol. 3, trans. W. A. Jurgens, p. 21.

[4] John A. Hardon, *The Catholic Catechism* (New York, 1974), p. 72.

[5] "The fullness of the Church was then interpreted in a static manner, and the attitude to Antiquity has been accordingly distorted and misconstrued. After all, it does not make much difference, whether we restrict the normative authority of the Church to one century, or to five, or to eight. *There should be no restriction at all.* Consequently, there is no room for any 'theology of repetition.' The Church is still fully authoritative as she has been in the ages past, since the Spirit of Truth quickens her now no less effectively as in the ancient times." Georges Florovsky, *Bible, Church, Tradition: An Eastern Orthodox View,* pp. 111-12.

well being on the other.

As St. Clement wrote in A.D. 80,

> This is the way, beloved, in which we found our salvation,
> Jesus Christ, the high Priest of our offering, the Defender
> and Helper of our weakness. Through Him we fix our gaze
> on the heights of Heaven; through Him we see the reflec-
> tion of the faultless and lofty countenance of God; through
> Him the eyes of our heart were opened; through Him our
> foolish and darkened understanding shoots up to the light;
> through Him the Master willed that we should taste a
> deathless knowledge.[6]

Orthodox liturgical worship is the act of embracing the
"deathless knowledge" of which St. Clement writes. The Church
provides the means by which we come to the mystery of God,
and enter, through Christ, into His eternal presence.[7]

Jaroslav Pelikan writes concerning the attitude of the early Church to the passage of time and the theme of salvation,

> The coming of Christ was 'already' and 'not yet': He had
> come already in the incarnation, and on the basis of the
> incarnation would come in the Eucharist; He had come
> already in the Eucharist, and would come at the last in the
> new cup that He would drink with them in the Father's
> Kingdom.[8]

According to Holy Tradition, Christ's presence in the
Eucharist is seen as an eternal mystical reality. Christ was

---

[6] St. Clement of Rome, *Letter to the Corinthians*, A.D. 80, *The Faith of the Early Fathers*, vol. 1, trans. W. A. Jurgens, p. 9.

[7] "What is the basic character of Christian existence? The ultimate aim and purpose of human life was defined in the Patristic tradition as theosis, divinization. The term is rather offensive for the modern ear. It cannot be adequately rendered in any modern language, nor even in Latin. Even in Greek it is rather heavy and pretentious. Indeed, it is a daring word. The meaning of the word is, however, simple and lucid. It was one of the crucial terms in the Patristic vocabulary. It would suffice to quote at this point but St. Athanasius: 'He became man in order to divinize us in Himself. (De Incarnatione 54)' St. Athanasius actually resumes here the favourite idea of St. Irenaeus: 'Who, through his immense love became what we are, that He might bring us to be even what He is Himself (Adv. Haeres. V, Praefatio) . . . *Theosis meant a personal encounter*. It is that intimate intercourse of man with God, in which the whole of human existence is, as it were, permeated by the Divine Presence." Georges Florovsky, *Bible, Church, Tradition: An Eastern Orthodox View*, pp. 114-15.

[8] Jaroslav Pelikan, *The Christian Tradition*, vol. 1, *The Emergence of the Catholic Tradition*, p. 126.

manifest in the Incarnation, but is *actually present* in the Sacrament. As the beloved Orthodox scholar, the late Fr. Alexander Schmemann wrote,

> All that exists is God's gift to man, and it all exists to make God known to man, to make man's life communion with God. It is divine love made food, made life for man. God blesses everything He creates, and, in biblical language, this means He makes all creation the sign and means of His presence and wisdom, love and revelation.[9]

Kallistos Ware, Orthodox scholar and Bishop of Oxford, England, expresses the Orthodox view of the Christian life in these terms:

> Mysticism, spirituality, moral rules, worship, art: these things must not be kept in separate compartments. Doctrine cannot be understood unless it is prayed. A theologian, said Evagrios, is one who knows how to pray, and he who prays in spirit and in truth is by that very act a theologian. And doctrine, if it is to be prayed, must also be lived; theology without action, as Saint Maximus put it, is the theology of demons. The Creed belongs only to those who live it. Faith and love, theology and life, are inseparable.[10]

WORSHIPPERS

According to Holy Tradition, man is a being created to worship — be in communion with — God. We are still half-formed. We are spiritual "fetuses," still being made and re-created in Christ's Image. All people are born worshippers. Indeed before birth we worship by inhabiting that shrine Jesus Christ graced with His unborn infant body — the female life-giving womb. In that holy place, all men and women are worshippers. The very existence of life praises God. The person who does not know he or she is a worshipper — needs to be in communion with God — is lost, like a frightened puppy in a rain storm who has wandered foolishly from home, running in panic from one dark street to the next seeking shelter.

[9] Alexander Schmemann, *For the Life of the World* (Crestwood, NY, 1973), p. 14.
[10] Kallistos Ware, *The Orthodox Church* (London, 1963), p. 215.

St. Luke tells us that when Mary greeted Elizabeth, the babe who was St. John the Baptist leapt in her womb (Luke 1.41), and was able to praise God as he recognized Christ in some mysterious way. Mary provided of her own free will a home in her womb for the Christ, the Savior whom the unborn St. John mystically worshipped even before birth. We read in the Luke account that as the baby leapt, Elizabeth "was filled with the Holy Spirit" (Luke 1.41). Thus the circle of worship was made complete. The freely-made choice of Mary to bear the Son of God inspired worship and joy by the unborn baby John. John's worship — communion — in turn mystically filled Elizabeth with the Holy Spirit and the desire to praise God.

It is following our birth that we make the choice either to abide in God or to depart from Him. We may choose to continue as we began in *utero*, as innocents with the guileless attitude of a little child, or we may choose to depart from our fully human beginnings to become something empty of ultimate purpose. We may degenerate to become less than we were created to be, beings that, brick by selfish brick, construct our own intellectual and spiritual prisons, our own hells.

Georges Florovsky writes,

> In the fullness of the communion of the Church the *catholic transfiguration of personality is accomplished*. But the rejection and denial of our own self does not signify that personality must be extinguished, that it must be dissolved within the multitude. Catholicity is not corporality or collectivism. On the contrary, *self-denial widens the scope of our own personality; in self-denial we possess the multitude within our own self; we enclose the many within our own ego. Therein lies the similarity with the Divine Oneness of the Holy Trinity*. In its catholicity the Church becomes the created similitude of Divine perfection.[11]

True worship in the historical Church is guileless, unselfish and childlike. As the great Roman Catholic theologian Romano Guardini writes,

> It is in the highest sense the life of a child, in which everything is picture, melody and song. Such is the wonder-

---

[11]Georges Florovsky, *Bible, Church, Tradition: An Eastern Orthodox View*, p. 43 (Italics original).

ful fact which the liturgy demonstrates: it unites act and reality in a supernatural childhood before God.[12]

The Church teaches us that conversion, that leads to true salvation, is more than simply turning from the world to Jesus. It is the turning off of the futile human clock. It is the destruction of the tyranny of time and ambition, by choosing to enter into the eternal present in which God always IS. As St. Clement of Alexandria writes: "The first cause, (God), therefore, is not located in a place, (He) is above place and time, and name and conception."[13]

The Church teaches us that we can live eternally with God, starting now because death has trampled death through Jesus Christ. The resurrected Christ is *truly present* in the Eucharistic feast and is available to us now in a practical way. Bishop Kallistos Ware writes: "Just as the three persons of the Trinity 'dwell' in one another in an unceasing movement of love, so man, made in the image of the Trinity is called to 'dwell' in the Trinitarian God."[14] The Church teaches that to fulfill our true destiny we must worship God. For we do not dwell in Him as co-equals but as servants dwell in the house of their master.

REAL LIFE

If worship is not a utilitarian means to self-realization, but rather the means of becoming God-like, the point of life — and if all of life, including our suffering, is fundamentally sacramental — then the rationalist, utilitarian view of life is the *exact opposite* of what God intended for His creatures. If worship is not only the preparation for the life to come but also the beginning of that future life itself — communion and union with God — then it will positively effect all of our existence. If we are not predestined to be saved or lost, but if free will is real, and we *can* choose God, then worship, as a practical daily means of helping us to grow to be like Christ makes sense.

[12]Romano Guardini, *The Church and the Catholic, and the Spirit of the Liturgy* (New York, 1950), p. 181.

[13]St. Clement of Alexandria, *Miscellany*, Refs. 5,11; 71, 3, A.D. 202, in *The Faith of the Early Fathers*, vol. 1, trans. W. A. Jurgens, p. 183.

[14]Kallistos Ware, *The Orthodox Church*, p. 236.

Worshippers are sometimes martyred. This is because those people desiring communion with God have an entirely different view of reality than non-worshippers who believe in utilitarianism or fatalism as their guiding principle. "Thou shalt not get in my way" — the modern rationalist dogma — is on a collision course with the historical Church which teaches that life is sacred, that our meaning is found in worship, that communion with God requires sacrifice, and that our ultimate destiny can only be realized by imitating Christ. This ascetic belief is the opposite of today's selfish, inward-looking, romantic pietism.

Thus worshippers aggravate a society that is dedicated to ulitarianism, self-realization and consumerism like unwelcome sand in the gears of an engine. For example, if life itself is sacramental, then whether a newly conceived baby is "useful," "convenient," "good for society," "wanted," "perfect," "white" or will be "happy" is not the issue. Rather the newly created child must be allowed to fulfill his or her life as a child of God even if that life includes a measure of sorrow and imperfection or physical or mental handicap. That is why "Thou shalt not murder" was inscribed in stone, not as a "social policy" of convenience, but as a reflection of respect for the Divine order of reciprocal love which applies to each person.

If life is sacramental, and the purpose of life is communion with God, then we can have a very clear idea of what is and what is not of permanent importance. We can examine how each aspect of life and creation amplifies or diminishes our ability to worship God and forgive others as we would ourselves be forgiven. This attitude of forgiveness includes forgiving people who are inconvenient to us, and allowing them to live. There is a word for forgiving even those whom we find "inconvenient": it is *mercy*.

In the fourth century, St. Evagrios the Solitary wrote, "Do you have a longing for prayer? Then leave the things of this world and live your life in heaven, not just theoretically but in angelic action and godlike knowledge."[15] If the whole of life is sacramental, then sentimental pietism of the Lutheran-Quaker variety is exposed as the fraud it really is. There is no longer

---

[15]St. Evagrios the Solitary, *On Prayer: The Philokalia*, vol. 1, trans. G. E. H. Palmer, Philip Sherrard and Kallistos Ware, p. 70.

a need to attempt to be falsely and pietistically "spiritual." There is no longer a need to hide our heads in the sand and let evil triumph. We can, and must, involve ourselves in all of life, and make it part of the heavenly realm of which St. Evagrios speaks.

Worship in the historical Church is therefore not "religious" but is rather an integral part of life lived out in the ancient yet timeless Christian cycles of fasting, prayer and sacrament.[16]

WORSHIP IN CHURCH

In the Orthodox Church much of the structure of the liturgical services is derived from the common worship that belonged to the Jews who were the first Christians.[17] The worship services of the historical Orthodox Church are also patterned after heavenly praise and worship as it is described in the book of Revelation.

Jaroslav Pelikan writes,

> The earliest Christians were Jews, and in their new faith they found a continuity with the old. . . . From the early chapters of the Book of Acts we get a . . . picture of a Christian community that continued to follow the (Old Testament) Scriptures, the worship, and the observances of Jewish religious life. . . . The church, therefore, was the inheritor of the promises and prerogatives of the Jews.[18]

According to the Holy Tradition, Orthodox liturgy is not just another "optional" or "denominational" approach to church worship but the living unbroken continuity of practice and tradition instituted by the living God, His Son, the Apostles, the Church Fathers and every Christian down to our own time.[19]

---

[16]"All that exists is God's gift to man, and it all exists to make God known to man, to make man's life communion with God. It is divine love made food, made life for men. . . And in the Bible to bless God is not a 'religious' or a 'cultic' act, but the very *way of life*." Alexander Schmemann, *For the Life of the World*, pp. 14-15.

[17]See Chapter 1, "The True Israel," by Jaroslav Pelikan, *The Emergence of the Christian Tradition*, pp. 12-27.

[18]Jaroslav Pelikan, *The Christian Tradition*, vol. 1, *The Emergence of the Catholic Tradition*, pp. 13-26.

[19]"The Church always stresses the permanence of her faith through the ages, from

Moreover there *never* was a time when worship in the early Church was "primitive" in the sense of being un-liturgical or unsophisticated. Early Christian worship began in the context of the *highly sophisticated* Jewish liturgy.[20]

THE FALSE CHURCH

The absence of historical legitimacy (and thus of true communal worship) in the counterfeit "worship experiences" of the non-Orthodox "denominations" today is, I believe, one reason why so many sincere Christians have a sense of being cheated by their self-invented, commercialized and trendy "liturgies." Many Roman Catholics and Protestants seem to know they are participating in a sham. But they are not sure why this is so. Many bewildered Roman Catholics and Protestants long for a deeper, more eternal spirituality that is awe-inspiring, respectful of God, has majesty and a sense of changeless dignity about it.[21] Yet they are unable to find such depth in the irreverent entertainments or dry sermonizing that have come to constitute "church."

The words of the Protestant hymn are poignant:

. . . O worship the King, all glorious above!

O gratefully sing His power and His love!

Our shield and defender, the Ancient of Days!

Pavilioned in splendor and girded with praise.

---

the very beginning. This identity, since the Apostolic times, is the most conspicuous sign and token of right faith — always the same. . . .

'Tradition' in the Church is not a continuity of human memory, or a permanence of rites and habits. It is a living tradition — *depositum juvenescens*, in the phrase of St. Irenaeus. Accordingly, it cannot be counted among dead rules. Ultimately, tradition is a continuity of the abiding presence of the Holy Spirit in the Church, a continuity of Divine Guidance and illumination . . .

'*Following the Holy Fathers*' . . . This is not a reference to some abstract tradition, in formulas and propositions. It is primarily an appeal to holy witnesses. Indeed, we appeal to the Apostles, and not just to an abstract 'Apostolicity.' In the similar manner do we refer to the Fathers." Georges Florovsky, *Bible, Church, Tradition: An Eastern Orthodox View*, pp. 105-06.

[20]Ben Williams, *Orthodox Worship* (Minneapolis, 1990).

[21]See Thomas Howard, *Evangelical Is Not Enough* (Nashville, 1984), and Peter Gillquist, *Becoming Orthodox* (Ben Lomond, CA, 1992).

Yet how are sincere Christians to fulfill this call, if they only know a "Jesus" who is a concoction of revivalist, romantic, nineteenth century Protestantism on the one hand, or trendy post-Vatican II "liturgies" on the other? This is a "Jesus" who changes from local church to church and who is no longer witnessed to by the history of the whole Church, but only by the subjectively interpreted Bible and politically correct trends of the moment. This is a "Jesus" who has been re-invented as an icon of the comfortable American white middle class. This is a "Jesus" who only "lives" in clever lengthy sermons, or in one's "heart," or in self-induced "charismatic" hysteria and entertainments, but who has been banished from the ancient Christian altar! If, that is, you can even find an altar in today's trendy Roman churches or gymnasium-style Protestant "sanctuaries." The "Jesus" of such "worship" is not the Timeless One but rather a very time-bound human invention.

MARY'S CHOICE

Judging by their addiction to "politically correct" fashion, Protestant denominations and Protestantized American Roman Catholics abhor embarrassment. They want desperately to keep up with the latest trends, to be "relevant." Yet the desire to be respectable and "politically correct" denies the historic origins of the Christian faith. Mary, the blessed God-bearer, the Mother of Christ, was willing to be pregnant as a single unmarried woman in a day and age in which she risked becoming an outcast or worse for such socially condemned behavior. Mary risked more than embarrassment. Her humility and desire to do God's will — to be in communion with Him, to freely choose to bear an unwanted "crisis pregnancy," in spite of what people would think — set the precedent for her Son's selfless life. Christ, in imitation of His blessed mother, Mary, put truth ahead of respectability.

Mary responded to the angel of the Lord in a way that reflected her extraordinarily pure humility. Far from selfishly seeking respectability and personal fulfillment, or social conformity and pietistic non-involvement, she reacted to God's call by initiating an act of worship through prayer. She willingly involved herself in fighting evil, in vanquishing the Devil, in putting truth and love ahead of other more pragmatic considerations. She said in response to the news that she was to bear an unexpected pregnancy (Luke 1.47): "My soul magnifies the Lord . . ." No wonder Elizabeth said of Mary, "Blessed are you among women, and blessed is the fruit of your womb!" (Luke 1.42).

And it is no wonder the Orthodox Church gathers to honor Mary in the service of the Akathist Hymn and to lovingly sing of her,

> Hail, Treasure-house of purity, through which we rose up from our fall;
>
> Hail, Lady, sweet-scented Lily perfuming the faithful; fragrant Incense and most precious Myrrh. . .
>
> Hail, O radiant Dawn, who alone bore Christ
>
> the Sun, the Dwelling place of Light;
>
> Hail, for you dispel the darkness and reduce to nothing the demons of gloom.

Mary's voluntary sacrifice, her communion with God through worship, her unselfish desire to involve herself in the fate of all human beings, earned her the unique title of "The Undisputed Intercessor" and "Champion Leader." And she has been the hope of the millions who have asked her to intercede for them. For it is of Mary alone that we can ask, "O Mother of the Most High God, O Righteous One, defend all those who seek refuge."

CHAPTER TWENTY-ONE
TASTE AND SEE

Saint Ambrose writes,

Who, then, is the author of the Sacraments if not the Lord
Jesus? . . . You may say "My bread is ordinary". . . . where
the consecration has entered in, the bread becomes the
flesh of Christ. . . . How can what is bread be the Body of
Christ? By the consecration. The consecration takes place
by certain words; but whose words? Those of the Lord
Jesus. Like all the rest of the things said beforehand, they
are said by the priest.[1]

Anything and everything has been used to fill the aching
vacuum created by the abandonment of the ancient Christian
liturgical tradition centered on Eucharistic worship. Many
pseudo-sacraments are now being used to fill the void — sermons, the "Inner Light" of the Quakers, the "twice-born" mantra
of the Anabaptists, the schizophrenic, pseudo-liturgical pietism
of the Lutherans, the "politically correct," feminized "liturgies"
of the Episcopalians, the harsh perfectionism of modern fundamentalism, political activities, Bible study groups, today's
trendy Roman Catholic folk and pop "liturgies," singles groups,
"coming forward" at revival meetings, Sunday school, pot luck
suppers, counseling sessions, "praise and worship" gatherings,
the "charismatic" movement, religious radio and television programs, books and lectures, have all been used. What was once
the common inheritance of all Christians, the

[1] St. Ambrose of Milan, *The Sacraments*, Ref. 1338-39, A.D. 390, in *The Faith of
the Early Fathers*, vol. 1, trans. W. A. Jurgens, p. 176.

Eucharistic feast, the bloodless sacrifice, the glory of the Church, is but a little understood memory to even many sincere Christians. Nevertheless, the voice of the Church, as to the centrality of the Eucharist, and by extension the whole way of life that prepares one to receive it, is unequivocal. Saint Cyril wrote in A.D. 350,

> Let us, then, with full confidence, partake of the body and blood of Christ. For in the figure of bread His body is given to you, and in the figure of wine His blood is given to you, so that by partaking of the body and blood of Christ, you might become united in body and blood with Him. For thus we become Christ-bearers, His body and blood being distributed through our members. And thus it is that we become, according to the blessed Peter, sharers of the divine nature.[2]

Worship becomes a counterfeit of the authentic article when Christ is removed from the altar. The fraud is just as much perpetrated when the sacraments are devalued, replaced, "updated," or otherwise trivialized. This is because if it is to inspire awe, something that is claimed to be eternal cannot be treated as if it were changeable or open to human tinkering on the basis of its "popularity."[3] This is why Saint Cyril of Jerusalem speaks

[2] St. Cyril of Jerusalem, *Catechetical Lectures*, Ref. 845, A.D. 350, in *The Faith of the Early Fathers*, vol. 1, trans. W. A. Jurgens, pp. 360-61.

[3] In the words of Fr. Georges Florovsky, "The Church is the unity of charismatic life. The source of this unity is hidden in the sacrament of the Lord's Supper and in the mystery of Pentecost. And Pentecost is continued and made permanent in the Church by means of the Apostolic Succession. It is not merely, as it were, the canonic skeleton of the Church, Ministry (or 'hierarchy') itself is primarily a *charismatic* principle, a 'ministry of the sacraments,' or 'a divine oeconomia.' Ministry is not only a *canonical* commission, it belongs not only to the *institutional* fabric of the Church — it is rather an indispensable constitutional or *structural* feature, just in so far as the Church is a body, an organism. Ministers are not, as it were, 'commissioned officers' of the community, not only leaders or delegates of the 'multitudes,' of the 'people' or 'congregation' — they are acting not only *in persona ecclesiae*. They are acting primarily *in persona Christi*. They are 'representatives' of Christ Himself, not of believers, and in them and through them, the Head of the Body, the only High Priest of the New Covenant, is performing, continuing and accomplishing His eternal pastoral and priestly office. He is Himself the only true Minister of the Church. . . . The unity of every local congregation springs from the unity in the Eucharistic meal. And it is as the celebrant of the Eucharist that the priest is the minister and the builder of Church unity. But there is another and higher office: to secure the universal and catholic unity of the whole Church in space and time. This is the episcopal office and function. On the one hand, the Bishop has an authority to ordain, and again this is not only a jurisdictional privilege, but precisely a power of sacramental action beyond that possessed by the priest. Thus the Bishop as 'ordainer' is the builder of Church unity on a wider scale. The Last Supper and Pentecost are inseparably linked to one another. The Spirit Com-

for the Church regarding the keeping of the *traditional* liturgical Communion feast and the ascetic way of life that prepares one to partake of it: "Keep these traditions inviolate, and preserve yourselves from offenses. Do not cut yourselves off from Communion, do not deprive yourselves, through the pollution of sins, of these holy and spiritual mysteries."[4]

Tragically, it is these very spiritual mysteries — fasting, prayer, confession, communion — from which Protestantism and trivialized modern American Roman Catholicism, have departed. I believe many sincere Christians struggle to be believers both within the Protestant denominations and within the tragically modernized American Roman Church. Yet I also believe that when compared to the historical continuity of ascetic struggle and worship found in the historical Orthodox Church, the modern "churches" suffer by spiritual, historic and aesthetic comparison.

Protestants and modernized Roman Catholics have unwittingly denied the physical reality of the Incarnation. They seem to be embarrassed by the physicality of Christ's birth, life, death, resurrection and redemptive work. Modern Roman Catholic church buildings —bare rooms stripped of imagery— often look like some United Nations meditation center rather than a Christian church. They seem to be even more "Protestant" than the Protestant churches themselves. They seem to have been built by people who have turned their backs on the historic Christ who gives Himself to His people in the Eucharist. They represent a truncated faith akin to a Buddhist experience — subjective, de-personalized, bare of life. This contrasts sharply with the faith of the Fathers — robust

---

forter descends when the Son has been glorified in His death and resurrection. But still they are two sacraments (or mysteries) which cannot be merged into one another. In the same way the priesthood and the episcopate differ from one another. In the episcopacy Pentecost becomes universal and continuous, in the undivided episcopate of the Church, the unity in space is secured. On the other hand, through its bishop, or rather in its bishop, every particular or local Church is linked with the past and with all ages. In its bishop every single Church outgrows and transcends its own limits and is organically united with the others. The Apostolic Succession is not so much the canonical as the mystical foundation of Church unity. It is something other than a safeguard of historical continuity or of administrative cohesion. It is an ultimate means to keep the mystical identity of the Body through the ages. But, of course, Ministry is never detached from the Body. It is in the Body, belongs to its sturcture. And ministerial gifts are given inside the Church (cf. 1 Cor 12). Georges Florovsky, *Bible, Church, Tradition: An Eastern Orthodox View*, pp. 65-66.

[4] St. Cyril of Jerusalem, *Catechetical Lectures*, Ref. 853M, A.D. 350, in *The Faith of the Early Fathers*, vol. 1, trans. W. A. Jurgens, p. 366.

earthly, physical, present, external as well as internal, historical and actual. The faith of the ages can be touched, seen, smelt, held and felt. "That which was from the beginning, which we have heard, which we have seen with our eyes, which we have looked upon, and our hands have handled, concerning the Word of life . . ." (1 Jn 1.1).

Saint John of Damascus writes,

> Visible things are corporeal models which provide (an) understanding of intangible things. . . . In former times God, who is without form or body, could never be depicted. But now (following the Incarnation) when God is seen in the flesh conversing with men, I make an image (icon) of the God (Christ) whom I see. I do not worship matter; I worship the Creator of matter who became matter for my sake, who willed to take His abode in matter; who worked out my salvation through matter.[5]

The whole historical Church seems to rise up to condemn Protestant anti-sacramentality and the post-Vatican II, modernized reductionism of today's Roman Catholics. Saint Gregory of Nyssa writes,

> The bread again is first common bread; but when the mystery sanctifies it, it is called and actually becomes the body of Christ. So too the mystical oil, so too the wine; if they are things of little worth before the blessing, after their sanctification by the Spirit each of them had its own superior operation. This same power of the word also makes the priest venerable and honorable, separated from the generality of men by the new blessing bestowed upon him. Yesterday he was that one of the multitude, one of the people; suddenly he is made a teacher of piety, an instructor in hidden mysteries.[6]

By cutting themselves off from the centrality of the Sacraments, the Eucharist, the icons, fasting, the liturgical

---

[5] St. John of Damascus, *On the Divine Images*, trans. by David Anderson (Crestwood, NY, 1980).

[6] St. Gregory of Nyssa, *Sermon on the Day of Lights*, Ref. 1062, *The Faith of the Early Fathers*, vol. 1, trans. W. A. Jurgens, pp. 58–59.

calendar, confession to a priest and the physical side of spirituality, many Christians have also cut themselves off from all other believers in history. They may have "updated" their faith but they have also excommunicated themselves from the cloud of witnesses: "For you are not nourished by one body while someone else is nourished by another body; but rather, all are nourished by the same body."[7]

The abandonment of the ancient, awe-inspiring Eucharistic feast and the whole church calendar cannot be mitigated by tambourine-banging, speaking in "tongues," guitar-strumming, hymn-singing, long sermons, expository preaching, passing out balloons, Sunday School or mediocre popular "inspirational" music of the kind with which modern American Roman Catholics have polluted their sadly reduced "liturgies" in imitation of the worst of American pop culture.

And yet in spite of the desacralized culture in which we live, there is hope. The hope is where it has always been. It is in the historical Church, the unchanged, Orthodox Christ-bearing community that bears witness to the Lover of Mankind — the Christ who sat down with sinners like us in physical communion.

> And when Jesus was in Bethany at the house of Simon the leper, a woman came to Him having an alabaster flask of very costly fragrant oil, and she poured it on His head as He sat at the table. But when His disciples saw it, they were indignant, saying, "To what purpose is this waste? For this fragrant oil might have been sold for much and given to the poor." But when Jesus was aware of it, He said to them, "Why do you trouble the woman? For she has done a good work for Me. For you have the poor with you always, but me you do not have always. For in pouring this fragrant oil on My body, she did it for My burial. Assuredly, I say to you, whenever this gospel is preached in the whole world, what this woman has done well will also be told as a memorial to her" (Mt 26.6-13).

---

[7] St. John Chrysostom, *On First Corinthians*, Ref. 1194, A.D. 392, *The Faith of the Early Fathers*, vol. 1, trans. W. A. Jurgens, p. 117.

"USELESS" BEAUTY
AND ICONIC REALITY

In our desacralized Western world, we have often been confused as to the purpose of our physical existence. We have become utilitarian and one-dimensional in our understanding of reality. Yet the Orthodox Church does not view the purpose of the material world only in terms of its so-called "usefulness." Saint Maximus the Confessor speaks for the Holy Tradition concerning the meaning of life.

> All immortal things and immortality itself, all living things and Life itself, all holy things and holiness itself, all good things and goodness itself, all blessings and blessedness itself, all beings and being itself are manifestly works of God . . . For God is the Creator of all life, immortality, holiness and goodness; and He transcends the being of all intelligible and describable beings.[8]

The Church teaches us that through ascetic discipline, the Eucharist, liturgical worship, repentance and confession, we can come again into a vital physical and spiritual contact with God. We can discover that all of life is sacramental. The false distinctions between spirituality and secularity, between piety and worldliness, between the flesh and the spirit, are dissolved into one reality in which we again may come to God through worship into a right relationship with His creation.

Holy Tradition makes quite clear that far from being a mere empty religious rite, the Eucharist is the actual meeting point between God and man.[9] Christ's presence in the wine and bread is the most immediate thing we will encounter in this life. It rebuilds the broken bridge between the supernatural and what we call the natural world.

As Augustine writes

> Although the little one has not yet that faith which resides

---

[8] St. Maximus the Confessor, *The First Century on Theology: The Philokalia*, vol. 2, trans. G. E. H. Palmer, Philip Sherrard and Kallistos Ware, p. 124.

[9] John 6.51; 1 Corinthians 11.23-52; Luke 22.20; Matthew 26.27-28; Mark 14.23-24; 1 Corinthians 10.17; 1 John 1.7; 1 Corinthians 11.29; Matthew 26.28; John 6.56-58; etc.

in the will of believers, the sacrament of that same faith already makes him one of the faithful. For since response is made that they believe, they are called faithful, not by any ascent of the mind to the thing itself but by their receiving the sacrament of the thing itself.[10]

In the Orthodox Church, even babies receive the Eucharistic Feast since that sacrament makes them one of the faithful. Christ told each one of us to come to Him as a little child. The Orthodox Church extends this teaching literally to children. They too partake of Christ through baptism, Chrismation and the Eucharistic Feast. Nurtured on Christ's body and blood, even as they are nurtured by the blood of their mothers before birth, children too come to the Feast in the historic Church since they too are members of the human family.

The Fathers teach us that all of the world, all of existence, all matter, all spirit is mysteriously supernatural. All life is miraculous. All life is one spiritual-physical reality. In the Eucharist we are, for an instant, whole people — transported to the timeless heavenly realm while yet on earth. Jesus' Body and Blood mystically unite the physical and mundane together with the transcendent and eternal in a spiritual Mystery.

According to Holy Tradition, all physical existence has been redeemed by the Incarnation. God honored Mary's bold humility. God uses a placental sac, flesh, bone, blood, baptismal water, tears, amniotic fluid, bread and wine, mother's love, oil and breast milk, to bring us back to Himself. What we do in a monastery, a church, at breakfast or in our work is all done in the presence of the Lord when it is done in thanksgiving for the fact that Christ our Creator has once more allowed us into the garden.

The Church is not ashamed of our physical Lord. Saint John of Damascus writes,

The Body is truly united to Divinity, the Body which was from that of the Holy Virgin; not that the Body which was taken up comes back down from heaven, but that the bread itself and the wine are made over into the Body and Blood of God. If you inquire into the way in which this happens

---

[10]St. Augustine of Hippo, *Letter to Boniface*, A.D. 408, in *The Faith of the Early Fathers*, vol. 3, trans. W. A. Jurgens, p. 651.

let it suffice for you to hear that it is through the Holy Spirit, just as it was through the Holy Spirit that the Lord took on Himself from the Holy Mother of God, the flesh that subsisted in Himself. More than this we do not know, except that the word of God is true, effective, and all powerful . . . For those who partake worthily and with faith, it is for the remission of sins and everlasting life, and a safeguard to soul and body . . . the Bread and Wine are not a type of Body and Blood of Christ, − perish the thought! − but the deified Body Itself of the Lord, since the Lord Himself has said: "This is My Body."[11]

THE ETERNAL FEAST

Father Alexander Schmemann writes that at the end of the Eucharistic Feast "All is clear. All is simple and bright. Such fullness fills everything. Such joy permeates everything. Such love radiates through everything. We are again in the beginning, where our ascent to the table of Christ in his kingdom began."[12]

Individual Christians languishing in today's various sects may do many useful, even many spiritual, things that they naively label as "worship." But, according to the continuous witness of the historical Church, they have not joined that cloud of witnesses at the true, holy and eternal Eucharistic feast, administered by authentic priests, who have the legitimate authority of Jesus vested in them, through the unbroken actual physical historic apostolic succession. Therefore they have not worshipped − communed with − the Christ in the way He expressly told all Christians to do. Nor have they partaken of the brotherhood and sisterhood of all believers, for they are among the first Christians in history to ignore that which has been the central fact of life for all other Christians − the Eucharistic feast, and the sacramental ascetic life that prepares one to partake. We cannot expect to truly grow to be like Christ, however spiritual we say we feel, outside of His historical Church.[13]

---

[11]St. John of Damascus, *On the Source of Knowledge*, Ref. 2371, A.D. 733, in *The Faith of the Early Fathers*, vol. 3, trans W. A. Jurgens, p. 339.

[12]Alexander Schmemann, *The Eucharist* (Crestwood, 1988), p. 245.

[13]"Christianity is the Church, i.e., a Community, the New People of God, leading its

Nor will we ever understand why the whole historical Church has, for two thousand years, placed such a premium on sacramental worship, and a life lived in the context of a liturgical calendar, because we will have never participated in the real thing ourselves. There is no book, including this one, that will bring the Protestant skeptic or modernized, "post-Vatican II" Roman Catholic, closer to the authentic Eucharistic tradition of the ancient Church, if that person is waiting to be convinced by a rationalistic theological argument. In the end we must all humble ourselves and learn in the *doing* of authentic worship, not in the mere study of it. This is true faith in action. True theology is prayer, and true prayer is worship, and true worship is participation in the communion of all the saints in unbroken continuity back to the beginning. This is the message of the living Holy Tradition. And this is what Christ told Peter: "For flesh and blood has not revealed this to you . . ." (Mt 16.17).

---

corporate life according to its peculiar principles. And this life cannot be split into departments, some of which might have been ruled by an other and heterogeneous principles." Georges Florovsky, *Bible, Church, Tradition: An Eastern Orthodox View*, p. 70.

CHAPTER TWENTY-TWO
GOOD NEWS

The historical Orthodox Church teaches us that physical existence is good. The world of matter needs no utilitarian justification for its existence because Christ has redeemed the world and He continues to redeem it with His sacramental presence through His Church. This is why Orthodox churches are full of relics, icons, incense, oil, wine, candles, holy water, ornate vestments, chalices, mosaics, carvings, music, art of every kind, and are so exuberantly physical and esthetic. In the Orthodox Church, we understand God's love to be apparent in the physical manifestation of His beautiful creation, not just in some "spiritual" realm.

Lactantius writes that God's love is apparent to all in His good creation.

> There is no one so uncivilized nor of such barbarous manners that he does not, when he raises his eyes to heaven, even if he know not by what god's providence all this which he beholds is governed, understand something from the magnitude of things, the emotion, arrangement, constancy, usefulness, beauty and proportion, and that this could not possibly be if there were not established a wonderful order, having been fashioned on some greater design.[1]

The Orthodox Church celebrates the physical creation. It teaches us that nature, love, art, beauty, motherhood, fatherhood, worship, prayer, charity, enjoyment of beauty and the physical sacraments are *good*. They need no justification of any kind to legitimize them. They are there for all to see when

[1] Lactantius, *The Divine Institutions*, A.D. 304, in *The Faith of the Early Fathers*, vol. 1, trans. W. A. Jurgens, p. 266.

we raise "our eyes to heaven." St. Athanasius says,

> For creation, as if written in characters and by means of
> its order and harmony, declares in a loud voice its own
> Master and Creator. . . . For this reason, God, by his own
> word, gave creation such order as is found therein, so that
> while He is by nature invisible, men might yet be able to
> know Him through His works.[2]

Creation, Holy Tradition teaches us, is good in itself because
God is good in Himself and He is the Author of Life. Sin has
not changed this basic fact. Christ has come that we might imitate Him and grow to be like God in order that we may again
participate fully in God, and that participation includes the enjoyment of creation.

Pietists tell us we must make false choices. We must choose,
for instance, between helping the poor, witnessing for Jesus,
or enjoying and making art.[3] Narrow-minded secularists have
done the same by asking people to choose between career fulfillment or having a child. Or between career "success" and taking care of an aged parent. Or between loving and protecting
children and a "population explosion." Pietists ask, "How can
you have time for liturgical worship, or art, music and literature
when you could be feeding the hungry or preaching the gospel?"
Secularists ask, "How can you have a baby now? It will inter-
rupt your school or career. It will impede your process of self-
realization. You owe it to yourself (or to ecology, or to society)
to have an abortion." According to Holy Tradition, Jesus, by
contrast, was at one moment telling us to help the needy, and
in the next He was defending what our utilitarian world would
regard as a "useless" creative act of "wasteful" worship and love,
a pouring out of precious resources that could have been "better
spent."

> And when Jesus was in Bethany at the house of Simon the
> leper, a woman came to Him having an alabaster flask of

---

[2] St. Athanasius, *Treatise Against the Pagans*, Ref. 746-747, A.D. 318, in *The Faith
of the Early Fathers*, vol. 1, trans. W. A. Jurgens, pp. 320-21.

[3] Typical of this type of shriveled "Christianity" is Ron Sider's book *Rich Christians
in an Age of Hunger* (Downers Grove, 1977) and the type of guilt-mongering and carp-
ing that is the life work of such "evangelical leaders" as Tony Campolo.

very costly fragrant oil, and she poured it on His head as He sat at the table. But when His disciples saw it, they were indignant, saying, 'Why this waste? For this fragrant oil might have been sold for much and given to the poor.' But when Jesus was aware of it, He said to them, 'Why do you trouble the woman? For she has done a good work for Me. For you have the poor with you always, but Me you do not have always. For in pouring this fragrant oil on My body, she did it for My burial. Assuredly, I say to You, wherever this gospel is preached in the whole world, what this woman has done will also be told as a memorial to her (Matthew 26.6-13).

The Orthodox Church has recognized the importance of this story and reflects upon its meaning in its prayers and hymnography.

Evil-smelling and defiled, the woman approached you, O Savior. She washed Your feet with tears, and proclaimed Your passion. She cried, How can I look upon You, O Master? Yet You have come to save the harlot. I am dead, raise me from the depths, as You raised Lazarus on the fourth day from the tomb. Accept me in my wretchedness, O Lord, and save me.[4]

Christ, as the Orthodox Church powerfully teaches us in its Holy Week services, is not only Lord of the spirit but is also Lord of the sinful woman's tears, the myrrh she brought Him, and the body of Lazarus whom He raised back to life in the physical world of flesh and blood. Moreover the whole calendar of the Orthodox Church teaches us that *both* ascetic struggle and the celebration of feast days are part of the Christian life.

The Fathers speak with one voice on the importance of recognizing the goodness of the physical world and Christ's redemption of it.

All beauty, miracle, magnificence reflects what is supremely beautiful, miraculous and magnificent . . . the Source that is above beauty, miracle and magnificence. . . If we have to use the senses, we should use them in order to grasp the Creator through His creation, seeing Him reflected in

---

[4] *Aposticha*, 2nd Plagal Tone. Holy Tuesday Evening. Holy Week. Orthodox Church.

created things as the sun is reflected in water.[5]

The sheer exuberant physicality of Orthodox worship appears strange to many people today. With its reliance on physical relics, sacraments, ancient liturgies, fast days, feast days, candles, incense, icons, bread, wine, oil and water, Orthodox worship seems primitive or childlike, perhaps even naive to those who have rejected the Biblical view that the physical world is an integral expression of God's goodness. In rejecting the goodness of God's creation many Christians have in fact become spiritual Buddhists, worshipping as if only the spirit world were of importance. Thus, perhaps unwittingly, they deny the physical Incarnation by how they worship, if not by what they say.[6]

Orthodox worship is dismissed by some as simplistic and credulous, too "down to earth." It is criticized as at once too commonplace yet at the same time too mystical. Some Protestants, and modernized Roman Catholics, judge Orthodox worship as "needlessly ornate." They say that it is "extravagant," "uselessly symbolic" or even "pagan" in its joyful majesty and "old-fashioned" sensory extravagance. They have even accused the Orthodox of "idolatry" because of the Orthodox Church's use of icons in worship.[7] Yet the Orthodox Church teaches that before God's altar it is precisely the ceremonial, the symbolic, the joyful, the iconic, the physical, the colorful, the dignified, the beautiful and the "useless" that make up the true fullness of worship.

"Taste and See!" is the invitation of the Eucharistic feast. "Behold," says the Christ, "My hands and My feet, that it is I

---

[5]St. Theodoros the Great Ascetic, *Theoretikon: The Philokalia,* vol. 2, trans. G. E. H. Palmer, Philip Sherrard, and Kallistos Ware, pp. 41 and 45.

[6]"Christ's Mystery is the center of Orthodox faith, as it is also its starting point and its aim and climax. The mystery of God's Being, the Holy Trinity, has been revealed and disclosed by Him, who is 'One of the Holy Trinity.' This Mystery can be comprehended only through Christ, in meditation on His Person. Only those who 'know' Him can 'know' the Father, and the Holy Spirit, the 'Spirit of adoption' — to the Father, through the Incarnate Son. . . .

'The Body of Christ' is not an 'appendix.' Indeed, the final purpose of the Incarnation was that the Incarnate should have 'a body,' which is the Church, the New Humanity, redeemed and reborn in the Head." Georges Florovsky, *Aspects of Church History,* pp. 24-25.

[7]See the three treatises of St. John of Damascus. All three defend the use of icons as an extension of the central teaching of Christianity: God became matter in the Incarnation. *On the Divine Images: Three Apologies Against Those Who Attack the Divine Images,* trans. David Anderson (Crestwood, 1980).

Myself. Handle Me and see, for a spirit does not have flesh and bones as you see I have" (Luke 24.39). This is the message of every relic, icon, candle, vestment, fast and feast in every Orthodox Church, in every part of the world: *Handle Me and see! I have come to redeem the real world where you live!*

The Orthodox Church has always held that we must be unashamed of our physical nature. In fact the Church has taught that we can come to know God more fully through a proper appreciation of His creation. St. Maximus the Confessor writes,

> We do not know God from His essence. We know Him rather from the grandeur of His creation and from His providential care for all creatures. For through these things, as though they were mirrors, we may attain insight into His infinite goodness, wisdom and power.[8]

As anyone who has had the good fortune to visit an Orthodox monastic community, like Simonopetra on Mount Athos will know, Orthodox monasticism has, for centuries, practiced a life of balance and beauty in a non-exploitative relationship with nature. Long before "ecological concerns" became fashionable the Orthodox appreciation for God's creation has not only been talked about but *lived* by countless ascetic monks and nuns whose conservation of creation is part and parcel of an ascetic sacramental life.

GENEROUS REALITY

The Church has taught that God is generous and that all His creation teaches us about His infinite goodness. The ascetic St. Peter of Damascus wrote: "The man of spiritual knowledge finds that everything contributes to his soul's salvation and to God's glory; indeed, it was because of this glory that all things were brought into existence."[9]

---

[8] St. Maximus the Confessor, *First Century on Love: The Philokalia*, vol. 2, trans. G. E. H. Palmer, Philip Sherrard, and Kallistos Ware, p. 64.

[9] St. Peter of Damaskos, *On Holy Scripture: The Philokalia*, vol. 3, trans. G. E. H. Palmer, Philip Sherrard, and Kallistos Ware, p. 263.

Whether we look at God's creation, the ancient liturgical worship of the Orthodox Church or at descriptions of heaven, in the book of Revelation, we do not see a dreary sameness — four white walls and a sermon — limited only to "spiritual" reality let alone some dreadful bureaucratic program, for processing the "elect," but a riotous, joyful, mysterious pageantry!

Immediately I was in the Spirit; and behold, a throne set in heaven, and One sat on the throne. And He who sat there was like a jasper and a sardius stone in appearance; and there was a rainbow around the throne, in appearance like an emerald. Around the throne were twenty-four thrones, and on the thrones I saw twenty-four elders sitting, clothed in white robes; and they had crowns of gold on their heads. And from the throne proceeded lightnings, thunderings and voices. And there were seven lamps of fire burning before the throne, which are the seven Spirits of God. Before the throne there was a sea of glass, like crystal. And in the midst of the throne, and around the throne, were four living creatures full of eyes in front and in back. The first living creature was like a lion, the second living creature like a calf, the third living creature had a face like a man and the fourth living creature was like a flying eagle. And the four living creatures, each having six wings, were full of eyes around and within. And they do not rest day or night, saying:

'Holy, holy, holy

Lord God Almighty,

Who was and is and is to come!' (Revelation 4.1-11)

God, Holy Tradition teaches, is the good and generous Creator. He is the Lord of the physical world and the heavenly realm. He is the Lord of physical worship because He is the Creator and He has sent His physical flesh and blood Son to us. He will even raise our corrupt bodies incorruptible.

The woman poured precious myrrh upon Your kingly, divine and awesome Head, O Christ. She grasped Your most pure feet with her impure hands and cried; 'Praise the Lord, all works of the Lord! Sing and exalt Him forever!'[10]

[10]Troparia, Holy Tuesday Evening. Holy Week. Orthodox Church.

It was at the very time when we might expect Jesus to have been most preoccupied with His own approaching death, that He had time for the sinful woman's demonstration of physical worship as she "wasted" her gift on Him. Yet it was in the context of suffering that Jesus *allowed* the woman to pour expensive perfume on Him. It was in the context of sorrow that the beauty of precious oil had even greater meaning. And it is in the realization that while we are in life yet we are in death, that the importance of external expressions of beauty take on their full lifesaving sacramental meaning.

The Church teaches us that it is in the pit of our self-created hell that we most urgently need to love God's creative beauty. This has been the teaching of the Church as expressed by the Fathers. St. John Chrysostom answered the heretical Manachaeans, the anti-physical pietists of his own day, as follows.

> Creation is not evil. It is both good and a pattern of God's wisdom and power and love of mankind. . . . It leads us to the knowledge of God (and) makes us know the Master better.[11]

Our sacramental creation is a testament to the fact that God is love. Christ's coming proves His love for His physical creation and His creatures. As the Psalmist said, and the Church prays: "May the glory of the Lord endure forever. May the Lord rejoice in His works" (Psalm 104).

Holy Tradition tells us that Jesus taught that we do not live by bread alone. Nor do we live by "useful" things alone. Even the usefulness of good social programs has a limit when it comes to redemptive work. Narrowly defined evangelization and "witnessing for Jesus" is not all there is to the Christian life. Beyond the good deeds of charity — even the preaching of the gospel — is something much more important, the whole point of life in the first place, the restoration of our relationship to our Creator as worshippers, as those who complete the circle of creation by offering it back to the Creator in constant thanksgiving, thereby completing the journey of deification through direct communion with God.

---

[11]St. John Chrysostom, *Homilies on the Devil*, Ref. 1117, A.D. 386, in *The Faith of the Early Fathers*, vol. II, translated by W. A. Jurgens, p. 88.

Bless the Lord, O My soul!

O Lord my God, you are very great!

You are clothed with majesty and splendor;

You cover Yourself with light as with a garment.

You stretch out the heavens like a curtain;

You lay the beams of Your upper chambers in the waters.

You make the clouds Your chariot;

You ride on the wings of the wind.

You make the grass to grow for the cattle,

and vegetation for the service of man, That he may bring forth food from the earth,

and wine that gladdens the heart of man, Oil to make his face shine,

and bread to strengthen man's heart.

The trees of the Lord are full of sap;

the cedars of Lebanon which He planted.

There the birds build their nests;

the stork has her home in the fir trees.

The mountains are for the wild goats;

the rocks are a refuge for the badgers.

May the glory of the Lord endure forever!

May the Lord rejoice in His works!

(Psalm 104.1-3; 14-18; 31)

The Orthodox Church teaches us that our ultimate human meaning is not found in economic theories, flow charts, social programs or even "Biblical teaching" and rule-keeping. Our ultimate meaning is found in the worship of God who has given us the love we share with Him: a monk's love of God and God's creation, a mother's love for her baby, the love of the sinful woman for Jesus, the love of a grandparent for a grandchild, the love of art, the love of beauty and nature, the love of strange and wonderful heavenly creatures, the love of our fellow human beings and of our Savior, the love we express when entering a Church as we make the sign of the Cross and reverently, tenderly, kiss an icon, in an act that *affirms life* and declares reality *redeemed, meaningful,* full of wonder, glory and *significance.*

In giving us the physical bread and wine, His body and blood, to be the focal point of our spiritual lives in a real, physical, yet mysterious way, the Church teaches us that Jesus has redeemed the physical world forever. This is why the Orthodox Church has icons. This is why the whole liturgy leads up to the *physical* Eucharist. This is why the Orthodox Church's monks and nuns treat nature with love and reverence. This is why we fast and feast with our physical bodies. This is why art, music, beauty and joyful extravagance are the stuff of authentic worship.

The Orthodox Church is not ashamed of the physical world or the physical representations of Christ and the Saints because Christ was not ashamed of us. "Take, eat; this is My body which is broken for you" (1 Corinthians 11.24). This is why the sacrament of marriage is consummated by physical, joyful, fruitful sexual intercourse. This is why the Church has protected unborn babies for twenty centuries. This is why the monks of Mount Athos treat their natural environment with the respect we should accord to creation. This is why things matter!

St. Ambrose of Milan tells us that God's love can hardly be understood outside of the physical creative process.

> You are a portrait, O man, a portrait painted by your Lord God. Yours is a good artist and painter. Do not deface the good picture, which reflects not deceit, but truth, which expresses not guile but grace.[12]

Holy Tradition teaches us that God's love should be returned to Him practically by helping the poor, but that this is not all there is to carrying on Christ's work. The answer to the question, "Why live?" comes through understanding that it is the things in life that are above price and description that give life its true meaning: the "useless" love of God; the "useless" love of one another; the "useless" expression of creativity through art; the "useless" sacraments and the "useless" Eucharistic feast; the love of "useless" unwanted human beings; the "useless" and even troublesome gift of free will; the "useless,"

---

[12]St. Ambrose of Milan, *Hexameron,* Ref. 1318, A.D. 389, in *The Faith of the Early Fathers,* vol. 2, trans. by W. A. Jurgens, pp. 167-68.

awe-inspiring beautiful worship of the historical Orthodox Church, the "useless" keeping of fasts, feasts and vigils, the "useless" veneration of "useless" old bones—relics. It is these "useless" things that we make truly useful by offering them back to our loving, generous Creator.

It is through coming to the understanding that we must ourselves become icons — images — of Christ, that we may begin our true journey toward God. Life becomes worthwhile when we begin to understand that the Holy Mysteries are not the same thing as irrationality, but are of the stuff of that timeless realm, in which we humble ourselves before the infinite God.

St. John Cassian quotes the famous African desert monk Abba Moses as saying,

> God is not only to be known in His blessed and incomprehensible being, for this is something which is reserved for His saints in the age to come. He is also to be known from the grandeur and beauty of His creatures, from His providence which governs the world day by day, from His righteousness and from the wonders which He shows to His Saints in each generation. . . . When we consider that He numbers the raindrops, the sand of the sea and the stars of heaven, we are amazed at the grandeur of His nature and His wisdom.[13]

When we are in awe of the grandeur of God — His beauty, mystery, and creativity — there is a reason to share His love, to help the poor so they too can spend their lives doing more than being hungry. There is a reason to worship. There is a reason to fast and learn to escape the slavery of our passions. There is a reason to do good works, for instance to protect our earth's environment and unborn babies. Not only because it can be shown to be selfishly or economically advantageous to do so, but because God created beauty. If we love Him we will not squander or abuse His great gifts, but choose to use our free will to creatively be good stewards and to offer life back to Him as the monks of Mount Athos do.

---

[13]St. John Cassian, *On the Holy Fathers of Sketis: The Philokalia*, vol. 1, trans. G. E. H. Palmer, Philip Sherrard, and Kallistos Ware, p. 97.

Joy, the Church teaches, is the reason to protect our physical and spiritual environment. Joy is the reason to dedicate ourselves to God, to become monks in our hearts or in fact. Prayer, fasting, green grass and grazing antelope, whales, newts, lizards, loving marriages, unborn babies, children, reading a good book, going for a long, rambling, "pointless" walk, kissing the hand of a beloved priest or bishop, painting a painting or writing a novel or poem: all these things are part of the sacramental life.

GOODNESS FOR ITS OWN SAKE

The mighty preacher St. John Chrysostom delivered the Easter homily in the cathedral in Constantinople on a fifth century Pascha morning long ago. He addressed those who had come to break their Lenten fast — to rejoice in the joy of the risen Lord. St. John Chrysostom spoke to them words of timeless hope. They are as fresh today as they were on the day St. John of the golden tongue stood before thousands of the faithful and said,

Is there anyone who is devout and a lover of God?
Come, and receive this bright, this beautiful feast of feasts!
Is there anyone who is a wise servant?
Rejoice, as you enter into the joy of your Lord!
Is there anyone who is weary from fasting?
Come, and receive your reward!
Is there anyone who has labored from the first hour?
Accept today your fair wages!
Is there anyone who came after the third hour?
Be glad, as you celebrate the feast!
Is there anyone who came after the sixth hour?
Have no doubts, for nothing is being held back!
Is there anyone who delayed until the ninth hour?
Come forward, without any hesitation!
Is there anyone who came up only at the eleventh hour?

Do not be afraid because of your lateness — For the honor and generosity of the Master is unsurpassed.

He accepts the last as well as the first;

He gives rest to the eleventh-hour arrival as well as to the one who labored from the first;

He is as merciful to the former as He is gracious to the latter;

He shows his generosity to the one, and His kindness to the other;

He honors the deed and commends the purpose.

Therefore, enter all of you into the joy of your Lord!

Both first and last, receive the reward;

rich and poor, dance and sing together;

abstemious and careless, honor this day;

fasters and non-fasters, enjoy a feast today.

The table is filled, and everyone should share in the luxury;

the calf is fatted, and no one must go away hungry.

Come, one and all, and receive the banquet of faith!

Come, one and all, and receive the riches of lovingkindness!

No one must lament his poverty,

for a kingdom belonging to all has appeared; no one must despair over his failings,

for forgiveness has sprung up from the grave; no one must fear death,

for the death of the Savior has set us all free.

By being held in its power He extinguished it,

and by descending into Hades He made Hades a captive.

He embittered it when it tasted His flesh.

And in anticipation of this, Isaiah exclaimed:

"Hades was in an uproar, meeting you below."

It was in an uproar, for it was wiped out;

it was in an uproar, for it was mocked;

it was in an uproar, for it was vanquished;

it was in an uproar, for it was bound in chains.

It took a body, and met up with God;

it took earth, and came face to face with heaven;

it took what it saw, and was struck down by what it did not see.

O death, where is your sting?

O Hades, where is your victory?

Christ is risen, and you are laid low;

Christ is risen, and the demons are struck down;

Christ is risen, and the angels rejoice;

Christ is risen, and life is abundant and free;

Christ is risen, and there are no dead left in the tombs!

For Christ, when He was raised from the dead,

became the first fruits of those who have fallen asleep.

Glory to him! and power, for ever and ever. Amen.[14]

If God exists and has sent His Son to show us the sacramental way to commune with Him, if Christianity is true, then the answer to the moral decline of our culture is the same now as it was in the fifth century: "Wherefore, enter ye all into the joy of your Lord!" The answer to our personal spiritual agonies is the same now as it was then: "Christ is risen, and life is liberated." The answer to the tragic consequences suffered by those who have lost their sense of sacramentality is the same now as it was then: "If any man be a wise servant, let him rejoicing enter into the joy of his Lord." This joy is found where it has always been, in the risen Christ and in His one true Holy Catholic and Apostolic Church, the living, Orthodox, Christ-bearing community, the living dwelling place of the One to Whom we sing: "To Him be glory and dominion unto ages of ages. Amen." We each have hope, not because we are "good," or "elect," but because, ". . . the Lord, who is jealous of His honor, will accept the last even as the first."

---

[14]St. John Chrysostom, Easter Homily, trans. Fr. David Anderson.

CHAPTER TWENTY-THREE
A FINAL WORD

Since becoming Orthodox I have not discovered "perfection" in the Church. In fact the Orthodox Church is as full of problems as it is of people. This is because each one of us is a sinner. The remarkable thing is that *inspite* of the problems that beset the Church, its altars are clean of theological corruption and its chalices are undefiled. In fact the Church transcends the sum of its parts in a wonderful and observable way.

Nevertheless for me to end this book with less than a fair and truthful account of the state of the Church, as I see it, would be disingenuous. Converts need to come to the Church with their eyes open and those already Orthodox need to wake up.

Therefore, let me speak frankly to my friends who may be seriously considering the historical claims of the Orthodox Church, or who are already Orthodox, but are perplexed by the state of the Church today.

The Orthodox Church in the United States is, at present, in a state of some considerable disarray. This, in a way, is a "normal" situation. The Orthodox Church claims to be the *true Church* but not the *perfect Church*. Yet a number of particular situations deserve some attention. Our problems seem to me to be due to two facts: In the first place, the Orthodox Church is under constant attack by the secular, pagan Western culture that surrounds her; secondly, unlike the ancient Orthodox Churches in various lands — Palestine, Africa, Greece, the Ukraine and Russia — the Orthodox Church in North America (with the exception of Alaska) is a wholly immigrant Church. Its founders were not monks and missionaries, but people wanting a better material life.

We Orthodox are newcomers to America. In most places we have been here less that one hundred years. The fact that the Orthodox Church in the United States is composed of recent immigrants from various national backgrounds, who (with the exception of St. Herman of Alaska) did not come to America as missionaries but rather seeking "the good life," means that a peculiar historical situation has arisen: the Orthodox Church in our country is under the jurisdictional guidance of various national, "ethnic" Orthodox Churches which were transplanted to our shores. This situation is atypical of the rest of Orthodox Church history. For instance, in Greece or in Russia, believers do not think of themselves as being "Greek" or "Russian" Orthodox, but simply as members of *The Church* in the same way as residents of Italy do not describe themselves as "Italian Roman Catholics" but simply as "Catholics."

THE IMMIGRANT CHURCH

In the United States, because of the Church's immigrant non-missionary and non-evangelistic origin, various jurisdictions, languages and ethnic backgrounds unintentionally separate Orthodox Christians from one another. This is so even though the various Orthodox communities are in communion with one another and share the same liturgies and doctrine. At least in theory, they recognize each other as co-equal partners in the historic Orthodox mission.

While measures are being taken by the Orthodox bishops of the diverse national jurisdictions to bring unity, and hopefully eventually to create *one* American Orthodox body, nevertheless there remain at the present time real and regrettable ethnic divisions between the various American Orthodox. These ethnic divisions tend to make us virtual competitors and such competition has contributed to what might be called the "Protestantizing" of Orthodoxy in America. As a result, one hears various Orthodox people refer to themselves as being part of the "Greek" or "Russian" Church rather than as "Orthodox."

The Protestantizing of Orthodoxy, while not as advanced as the near-total Protestantizing of the American Roman Catholic Church, nevertheless has resulted in various un-Orthodox forms of thought and behavior. For instance, many parish councils, which are constituted of those lay people charged with the practical, day-to-day running of the local Orthodox parishes, seem to operate almost autonomously — as if they were Protestant Congregationalists rather than true Orthodox. Such congregational-style "Orthodoxy" has led to a *de facto* situation in some local churches in which the Orthodox faithful are hardly responsible to, or effectively part of, the ancient Orthodox Church. For instance, there is squabbling between a number of local parish councils and their various Orthodox dioceses about the financial obligations that local churches have to support their diocese in order that the Orthodox mission of the Church in North America might be maintained. Sometimes there are disputes within local congregations, especially those arising between parish councils and priests, which are unwholesome and disrespectful of the priest's role as standing in the place of the bishop, and ultimately of Christ — as Holy Tradition teaches that bishops and priests do. Many an underpaid, overworked priest in many an Orthodox parish is treated more like a slave than with the respect that a priest, even an imperfect one, should be accorded. This is evidence of the Protestant disease of individualism and democracy run amok, wherein the priest must come, hat in hand, to the all powerful parish council for every last thing he wishes to do as if the parish council "owned" the church.

ETHNIC CLUBS

Another problem that has arisen, which is peculiar to our American situation, is that some Orthodox Churches seem to be more like ethnic social clubs than missionary-minded, evangelical representatives of the universal, ancient Church. The historical Orthodox Church became known for *reaching out*, not for looking inward. It evangelized huge portions of the globe: all of the Slavic nations, the whole Middle East, Alaska, huge tracts of Africa, Europe and Asia, including the world's greatest land mass, Russia. Yet in some American congregations today the petty maintenance of native languages, customs and national festivals, often seems to take precedence over welcoming outsiders, seeking new converts and, *most important of all,*

*teaching the faithful the basic doctrines of Orthodox theology,
worship, confession and ascetic moral living.*

It is not too far fetched to say that there are some "Orthodox" in America that even regard converts with hostility. In August of 1992, I received a letter from a fairly recent convert to Orthodoxy. It speaks eloquently. I have, of course, chosen to keep his name confidential.

Dear Mr. Schaeffer,

As I indicated in an earlier letter, I have struggled greatly since becoming an Orthodox Christian a year ago. On the one side, the Orthodox Church, while offering true worship, historic continuity, the sacraments, Apostolic order, also presented coldness, aloofness, nominalism, lack of evangelism and a missionary spirit and ethnicity. Although my priest has been an enormous support to me, only one couple has really welcomed me into the church (out of an average of 350 per Sunday!) For the most part I worship alone from week to week. I am not really a part of this corporate worship. It's such a contrast to my former evangelical denomination where you could hardly enter or exit the church without a swarm of people pumping your arm, thrusting a visitor's packet in newcomer's hands and begging you to stay for coffee in a fellowship time afterwards. In addition, there appears to be very little effort made to reach out to the community (really — no evangelism period!) . . .

Do you know, in a way I'm frustrated that I have come to Orthodoxy and in spite of all its warts and blemishes have experienced true worship. Now that I have seen, tasted and heard the truth, how can I return to Protestantism, even though being Orthodox is hard for me? . . .

While it is understandable that, for historical reasons, the original languages — modern Greek, Arabic, Church Slavonic, etc. — are still employed, to one degree or another, in various local Orthodox Churches in America, nevertheless it seems as if language is often used as a barrier with which to keep out "outsiders." This may be unintentional, but is nevertheless highly unfortunate and *un-Orthodox*. After all, consider the fact that Saints Cyril and Methodios invented a whole new alphabet (the Cyrillic alphabet) in order to evangelize the Slavs. Had they insisted that the illiterate Slavs had to learn Greek, Orthodoxy would have never spread beyond Byzantium and the false Roman Catholic claim that the Orthodox Church is the "withered branch" of the historical Church, would have proved to be true.

Because of clinging to the languages of the country of origin, many Orthodox Churches are even losing contact with their own children, or second and third generations effectively lost to the Church. They grow up knowing more about ethnic holidays and nationalist folklore than about the basics of Christian living.

DEAD WOOD

A far more serious problem in the contemporary American Orthodox Church than the petty squabbles over jurisdiction and language, is the fact that the Church seems to contain many lay people, and even some priests, who are far from fervent. It seems to me that the Orthodox Church in America is rather full of what appears to be dead wood of the hardest and driest kind. Nevertheless, in the midst of this forest of dead wood, otherwise known as "nominal Christianity," there are many tender green shoots, people who *are* following and imitating Christ. The good news is that, through faithfully living sacramental lives, there are *many* ethnic Orthodox and converts who are *truly fervent*. Nevertheless, to the new or prospective convert, perhaps used to the enthusiasms, false or misdirected as they may be, of some of the Protestant sects, some Orthodox congregations will seem to be places in which Greeks, Ukrainians, Palestinians, Russians or others gather to eat national food, speak in their native language, encourage their children to socialize (and marry within the ethnic clan), and where the fervent Christian sacramental life in Christ has been *all but forgotten*. To put it another way, the naive convert looking for Mount Athos may well be more likely to find a local "Orthodox" church that is nothing more than an ethnic version of the local Elks Club.

Evidence of this tragic deadness can be seen in how few of the American Orthodox faithful truly avail themselves of the life-giving sacraments in our Church. For instance, many "Orthodox" do not confess regularly to their priest or to another spiritual father. Thus, they see little spiritual growth in their lives and are not in good standing sacramentally in the Church. This dramatic break with the Holy Tradition is sad and foolish. Our secular culture spends millions of dollars a year counterfeiting authentic confession. Millions of dollars are paid for psychiatric and psychological care alone. Yet we who have access to *authentic confession* that leads to salvation often take no advantage of this divine gift!

In some Orthodox Churches the sacrament of communion is rarely taken by the majority of the people. Some "Orthodox" are so nominal that they have fallen into the habit of taking communion only once or twice a year. In addition to this, some priests seem to have accepted the status quo of an Americanized, Protestantized, nominal "Orthodox Church." Because of this, they appear to be failing to teach confession, Christian morality and the sacramental ascetic life lest they offend their secularized parishioners. Given the power of some local parish councils to twist the priests' arms financially — to stop paychecks and otherwise intimidate them — perhaps it is understandable that many priests lack the moral courage to do more than preside over Greek, Russian or Arab social clubs in which their "priesthood" has degenerated into simply being the local ethnarch. It seems that some bishops have been similarly reduced to becoming ecclesiastical bureaucrats, hungry for inclusion in "respectable" American secularized society, instead of spiritual fathers. This is a tragic loss to the Church.

TWO CHURCHES

Because of the nominalism in much of the American Orthodox Church, one can say there are in fact *two* Orthodox Churches in America. The one is the historical Orthodox Church, the other a sort of social-ethnic club.

Like the wheat and the tares, these two churches exist side by side, within the walls of each local congregation. No one has the right to judge the faith of another individual. Nevertheless, there are some practical realities about our contemporary Orthodox communities that new-comers to Orthodoxy will find shocking, even appalling.

One such reality is the pervasive lack of financial commitment by many Orthodox to their parishes. There are isolated acts of generosity — especially if the donor's name can adorn an icon, building or some other object — but most parishes are strapped for cash. This is not because their members are poor, but because too many "Orthodox" have become nominal in their faith and/or have developed terrible habits with respect to giving to the Church.

For instance, many Greek Orthodox who came to America had become accustomed to a "state Church." (In Greece, the Orthodox Church is financed by the government.) They seem to be waiting for someone *else* to pay the parish bills. This bad habit results in the fact that many parishes always are trying to sell something to the non-Orthodox rather than pay their own way. Rather than just donate regularly to the Church, some parishioners seem to think that food festivals, bingo and the like are the "Orthodox" way to raise money. Typically, this is because of a level of stinginess that Evangelical Protestants would find incredible. If most Orthodox simply gave two to three percent of their income, let alone tithed, all the bills of most parishes would be paid.

With the chronic shortage of funds come other problems: a lack of money to educate children, have a Church library and pay for evangelistic outreach. So a double price is paid. First, the witness of the Church is non-existent because the only time people, in the non-Orthodox community, ever hear of the Church is when the Church is having a fund-raising event. Second, the energy of the parish is spent on secular fund-raising rather than spiritual outreach and internal spiritual growth. Young people growing up in such an environment get the idea that their father's new car, or mom's new job, is a good deal more important than his or her Church. After all, he or she makes much larger car payments than donations and seems to think his or her duty is done when he or she gets up early one morning a year to help roast a lamb at the "food fest."

The irony is that the same parents who "can't afford" their church will then lament their children's departure from the faith and probably blame their priest! To illustrate the magnitude of this problem, consider the fact that a priest at a Greek Orthodox parish I visited confided in me that over a third of the annual budget was being provided by the donations of six families, out of one hundred and twenty families. All six *were*

converts who were tithing their income and they were not, by
any stretch, the weathiest people in the Church. In fact, the
reverse was the case.

THE QUEST FOR TRUTH

However to the seeker of truth none of the very *real imperfections* in the present American Orthodox Church should
dissuade his or her search. Unlike the modern person, who feels
like the world owes them niceness, fulfillment and sensitivity
at every turn, the seeker of truth will pursue that pearl of great
price *even when it hurts to do so.* In fact, according to the
Fathers, mistreatment − even at the hands of our fellow
believers − is a good source for learning humility.

The seeker of truth will hopefully find an Orthodox congregation that *will* open their arms and receive him or her. But if
the convert is not as well-received as they should be, the
authentic seeker will pursue Christ, *even if the door keepers are
less than helpful.* He or she should be grateful to have a place
in which to partake of the authentic sacraments, pray, participate in the liturgy, go to confession and follow Christ,
regardless of the imperfections in any given local Orthodox
community.

I was most fortunate in finding a local Orthodox Church in
which the strength of Greek ethnic tradition manifested itself
in welcoming outsiders and providing a nurturing environment
for families. I was welcomed and adopted as if I were a long
lost cousin. I was welcomed long before anyone in that church
knew I had once been "somebody" in Protestant circles. Thank-
fully, such places exist and in great numbers.

The hard-working immigrant founders of many Orthodox
Churches provided them with a rich tradition of warmth, community and family that is a rare treasure indeed in modern individualistic America. The convert must always express his or
her gratitude for having been taken in from out of the storm
and for the inspiring perseverance of the hardworking people
who, by the sacrificial sweat of their brows, built the hundreds
of Orthodox Churches that are here in America. It has been
a remarkable feat that outweighs all the very real deficiencies
in contemporary Orthodoxy.

Moreover, the ethnicity of many local congregations has been a sort of protection, even if unintended as such, from some of the worst ravages of secularism that have infected so much of the world today. Given the aggressively Protestant and secular climate that confronted the Greek, Palestinian and Slavic Orthodox Christians who emigrated to America, the fact that many Orthodox communities have tried to isolate themselves is understandable. In this sense, the language barrier has been a blessing in disguise.

But the tragedy is that by isolating themselves, some Orthodox, have taken a head-in-the-sand attitude in regard to the effects of secularism on their children and on them. Rather than confronting the secularizing and pagan realities of American culture they have tended to accommodate them. This has resulted in second-and third-generation Orthodox being insufficiently trained (or forewarned) regarding the anti-Christian onslaught they face in the larger world. The sad truth is that a whole generation of Orthodox have been and are being lost because their parents, and perhaps their priests, have put a greater priority on "success" and being "good Americans" than they have on being good Orthodox Christians. Perhaps in this regard, it is therefore not entirely coincidental that a number of highly secularized, even pro-abortion, politicians have come forward who have "Orthodox" ethnic backgrounds. Nor is it surprising, given the premium put on "success" in the American culture, by many Orthodox immigrants, that some bishops and priests have been eager to cozy up to secular, even anti-Christian, politicians.

SEDUCTION

We Orthodox Christians in America have not often been overtly persecuted as have the Orthodox in what was the Soviet Union or Turkey. Rather, we have been *seduced* by a combination of secular materialism, Protestant pluralism and the desire to "make it" in America. We have unthinkingly adopted a materialistic secular world view while keeping an outward show of "Orthodoxy." We Orthodox have come to see ourselves, far too often, as just one more "denomination," another "special interest" group, rather than the inheritors of the *one, true, Holy, Catholic, and Apostolic Church* who are dutybound to evangelize the surrounding non-Christian Protestant culture.

We Orthodox have been seduced by the materialism, consumerism and secularism of the age. We have failed to meet
the Protestant-secular juggernaut head on. Our Orthodox
young people have been battered by many challenges. For instance, by the sort of fundamentalist Protestants who tell them
they are not "real Christians" because they are not "born again"
or "saved." Orthodox young people have also been assaulted
by aggressive secularists, for instance, in the schools and
universities, who have taught Orthodox young people to question, mock, or, at least, to minimize not only their faith but
all religious ideas and ideals. Moreover, Orthodox young people
have not been trained to resist the moral decay of the age. They
too have abortions, become sexually active before they are
married and divorce.

Between Protestants, who tell Orthodox young people they
are "not real Christians" because they cannot articulate a trite
confession of a so-called born-again experience, and secularists,
who have attacked all traditional Christian sacramentality and
transcendent ideals, our ill-prepared Orthodox young people have
been sent out as cannon fodder into our secular Sodom. And
they are being seduced by the spirit of the age.

Many Orthodox young people are also understandably confused by the mixed signals that come from some individuals
in positions of Orthodox leadership. They are told to live holy,
sacramental lives on one day, then on the next, they see their
Orthodox leaders "schmoozing" with pro-abortion politicians.
They are told that the Orthodox Church is the authentic, unique
depository of Christian truth on one day, then on the next they
see some of their Orthodox leaders participating in an
ecumenism of unbelief with other "Christian theologians," some
of whom deny the Virgin birth, the divinity of Christ and the
moral teachings of Scripture. With such confusion muddying
the Orthodox witness in America, it is hardly surprising many
Orthodox have lost their faith or relegated it to the level of a
mere cultural experience. Many more have been reduced to
nominalism, their faith choked by the pursuit of materialistic
"happiness" and the cares of this world, their chief interest in
life reduced to a desire to "get ahead," to "share in the American
Dream," rather than to be steadfast Orthodox Christians seeking to imitate Christ.

Fortunately, in spite of our problems and unlike modernized Roman Catholicism or today's Protestant denominations, Orthodoxy does not stand or fall by any particular generation, "leader," bishop, priest, pope or ethnic group's dedication to the cause of Christ, or lack thereof. The worst it can be accused of, at present, is deadness and inward-looking ethnicity in some of its parts, and of wasting its time and squandering its reputation by seeking favor from secularized politicians and the so-called ecumenical movement.

THE ECUMENICAL DEBACLE

Not all Orthodox leaders have been duped by the ecumenical movement. Yet even some of the very best, like the late Fr. Georges Florovsky, had high hopes that "ecumenism" would produce results it has not. In hindsight, these hopes seem rather forlorn. In 1949, Florovsky wrote,

> I regard Orthodox participation in the Ecumenical Movement in the same way as missionary action. The Orthodox Church is specifically called to play a part in ecumenical exchanges of ideas, precisely because it is aware of its own role as guardian of apostolic faith and of Tradition in their full integral shape, and it is in this sense the only true Church; since it knows that it holds the treasure of divine grace through the continuity of the ministry and apostolic succession; and finally because in this way it can claim a special place among divided Christianity.[1]

How noble a sentiment the late Father Florovsky, of blessed memory, articulates. Yet how sad to think that such a great mind and spirit as Fr. Georges Florovsky could have been so blinded by his own innocent good will — as to the true nature of the Protestant debacle which has resulted in the disintegration of Western civilization, the acceptance of abortion on demand, the ordination of women, homosexuals and lesbians; the apostasy and heresy inherent in "liberal" Protestant

---

[1] Georges Florovsky, *The Collected Works*, vol. 13, *Ecumenism — A Doctrinal Approach* I (Vaduz, 1987), p. 160.

theology. How ironic that the very elements of Protestantism, the "Liberal" elements that have had the most to do with ecumenism, are the very elements that have become the most secularized and which represent less and less people as their numbers dwindle, plagued by the drumbeat of Protestant doubt. How strange that the only Protestants, Evangelicals and Fundamentalists, with whom Orthodox theologians, like the late Georges Florovsky, actually have much in common, at least theologically, are the very Protestants who *on principle* have had nothing to do with the failed "ecumenical movement."

It is clearly time for the Orthodox, even those with a considerable investment of time and prestige in ecumenism, to admit the truth: the ecumenical movement is a failure from the Orthodox point of view. It is a sordid fiasco on a par with the ill-fated League of Nations, another product of earthly twentieth-century utopianism run amok. Orthodoxy has *not* "leavened the whole lump." Rather, the reverse is true. The apostasy of liberal Protestantism and the Protestant denominations acceptance of immorality and perversity has grown exponentially during the "ecumenical era."

In hindsight, it seems to be clear that the innocent good will of the Orthodox in the ecumenical movement has been abused. The true result of Orthodox involvement has not been to bear witness to the truth, but to lend respectability to a scandal and to confuse the faithful as to the true character of apostate, relativistic Protestantism. It is ironic that the thousands of Protestants who have recently converted to Orthodoxy, including numerous ministers and priests from diverse denominational backgrounds, have *not* come into the Orthodox Church through the actions of the Orthodox "witness" in ecumenism, but *quite the contrary* is true. The wave of recent Protestant converts have come into the Church *not* because of its polite efforts at "dialogue," but because of its ageless, Patristic and Apostolic witness, including those portions of that witness that most forcefully claim the exclusive nature of the Orthodox Church to *be* the true Church.

Former Protestants such as myself, have not come into Orthodoxy, at great personal cost, because we had a "dialogue" or were told that "we are all one happy family of Christians," but in order that we might find the truth. Fr. Florovsky, whom I believe to have perhaps been misguided in regard to ecumenism but who, nevertheless, was one of the great Orthodox Christians of our age, makes this very point:

> In the early church the preaching was emphatically theological. It was not a vain speculation. The New Testament itself is a theological book. . . . What we need in Christendom 'in such a time as this' is precisely a sound and existential theology. In fact, both clergy and the laity are hungry for theology. And because no theology is usually preached, they adopt some 'strange ideologies' and combine them with the fragments of traditional beliefs. The whole appeal of the 'rival gospels' in our days is that they offer some sort of pseudo theology, a system of pseudo dogmas. They are gladly accepted by those who cannot find any theology in the reduced Christianity of 'modern' style.[2]

A CALL TO THE ORTHODOX

The call to those in the Orthodox Church, whether born into the Church, raised in the Church, or new converts, is, I believe, the same. It seems to me that it is *not*, to invent a "new and better" American Church, and therefore to simply become one more self-invented Protestant-style "denomination," madly trying to be "relevant." It is *not* to "update" the faith, or make it "easy," even "entertaining," in the way that the American Roman Catholics have unfortunately done by trivializing their liturgies, music and worship practices beyond all historic recognition, not to mention good taste. And it is *certainly* not to form committees of lay technocrats — so-called clergy/laity groups — to "reorganize" the Church, to make it more "efficient" or worst of all, to "democratize" or "feminize" the Orthodox Church and make its Apostolic leaders "accountable" to the whims of politicaly activist "theologians" or ignorant, nominally Orthodox, Americanized lay people who often know little of the Orthodox tradition.

It seems to me that the *last* thing the Orthodox Church needs is a dose of Protestantized "efficiency" or slick Wall Street-style managerial techniques which will further undermine its unique apostolic authority. The Orthodox Church is not, and

---

[2]Georges Florovsky, *Bible, Church Tradition: An Eastern Orthodox View*, p. 15.

must not become, "politically correct." Even less should it strive to be a "democracy." Its job is not to be "efficient," "sensitive to diversity" or "sensitive to feminist concerns," but to remain steadfast. It must please God, not desacralized American fashion. The Orthodox Church must resist those who have a lust for political power, like today's restless, rootless feminists and other special interest groups, as they try to seize control of one institution after another to remake in *their* image.

The Orthodox Church was, is and always will be governed by an apostolic hierarchy whose wheels grind exceedingly slowly and in which change is mercifully difficult to realize. The Church's time table is *not* a human timetable. There is no room in the Orthodox spiritual vocabulary for innovation: change for its own sake.

I believe that the true call of the Orthodox Christian, and by extension the Church, begins with the only change that counts eternally — the slow, difficult change of our hearts, minds, souls and habits of daily life. The true call of the Orthodox, who wish to see authentic spiritual life uplifted within our Church, is not a reorganization of the Church or updating of the Church, but rather *a return* to the *basic patristic teachings* found in our precious sacramental Holy Tradition and a rigorous defense of true, ascetic-monastic Orthodoxy against the pluralistic, political, materialistic and secularizing impulses of our age.

THE QUIET REVOLUTION

It seems to me that Orthodox Christians must work together to revitalize our spiritual life. As the late Fr. John Meyendorff of blessed memory said, we must work in pan-Orthodox projects *acting as if* Orthodox unity *has* been achieved in America, whether it has been officially realized or not. Most important of all, the dead wood in the Church must be given new life, not by political means, but by prayer and passionate spirituality within the Church as practiced by those who *do* care about their faith, their children, their Church and the defense of our unique sacramental tradition.

Those who love Orthodoxy, and treasure its inheritance, will take advantage of the great mercy the Church offers them by

going to regular confession, by weekly partaking of the
Eucharist, by honoring their priest, by supporting and participating in Orthodox monastic life, by keeping the Church's
calendar of prayer and fasting as best they can, by donating
generously to their local parish and to their local monastery,
and by finding a spiritual father (who may not necessarily be
the same priest as one's local parish priest), and being accountable to him. Above all, those who love Orthodoxy will refuse
to be seduced by the materialistic evil engulfing us, on the one
hand, or demand a "perfect" Church on the other.

We who love Orthodoxy will learn from and obey our imperfect, sinful priests. We will gird ourselves against the in-
sidiousness of the secular culture around us, against its Protestantizing schismatic effects and the secularistic scourge which
comes to us packaged as "choice," "pluralism," and
"democratization." We will reject the destruction of moral absolutes which we are constantly urged to adopt in the name
of "pragmatism," "political correctness," "tolerance of diversity," "sensitivity" and "inclusiveness."

The true call to the Orthodox faithful today is, I believe, that
of a quiet revolution. This is a revolution of the spirit against
the horror of today's relativism which renders all things
unstable, inhuman and unworkable. It is a revolution in which,
step by step, convert by convert, the failures of the corrupted
Roman Catholic Church and the reactionary "Reformation" it
inevitably spawned are *lovingly but firmly* corrected.

Individual Protestants and Roman Catholics must be invited
to come home to the true, ancient Church: the Orthodox Church.
Our altars are clean, our liturgies are pure, the Spirit dwells within
our sanctuaries. We have not changed. We must share this living water with a thirsty world. We Orthodox Christians should have
the courage to stand on our feet and no longer be those who make
the Orthodox Church invisible, "the best kept secret in America."

THE MONASTIC IMPERATIVE

It seems to me that one of the things that Orthodoxy in
America needs most desperately is a legitimate and indigenous
monastic movement. We need examples to live by and we need

prayer! If Orthodoxy is to bear witness to the truth it needs centers of Christian life, witness, teaching and inspiration available to it. Monasticism has always been the hidden inner strength of the Church and our desacralized age is crying out for the very things that only monasticism offers — prayer, asceticism, discipline, liturgy, worship, godliness — hospitals for our sick souls. As the Abbot of the monastery of Osiou Gregoriou on Mount Athos writes,

> The priority which monasticism gives to the worship of God is a reminder, both in the Church and in the world, that if the Divine Liturgy and worship do not once again become the centre of our life, our world will be unable to be united and transfigured. It will be incapable of surpassing its divisions, its imbalance, its emptiness and death . . . in spite of all the prideful, humanistic systems and plans intended to improve it.
>
> Again, monasticism reminds us that the Divine Liturgy and worship are not simply one thing in our life; they are its centre, the source of its renewal and its entire satisfaction.[3]

Today, in America, the Orthodox Church faces its sternest challenge. We need true spiritual guidance that only life-long monks and nuns can give us. We need the best the Church has to offer and the best is monasticism. The only real answer to the secular challenge is not words but deeds. Monastic life is the unique gift Orthodoxy has to offer the world because it teaches by *doing* not by saying.

CONCLUSION

The Communists showed the Orthodox Church the respect of putting some of its faithful adherents against a wall and shooting them. However backhanded that "compliment," at least it implied that religious faith mattered enough to kill, or imprison, people for. In America, in our pluralistic culture through which all religion has been diminished to mere interdenominational squabbling or "personalized" religiosity, there is a more deadly and insidious form of execution being performed daily against the Orthodox faithful; religion has been relegated to a nether world of irrelevance! The message of the American Knowledge

---

[3]Archimandrite George Capsanis, *The Eros of Repentance*, (Newbury, 1993), p. 52.

Glass is not, "we will shoot you for your faith," but rather "your faith does not matter. There is not such thing as truth. It's all just a matter of personal opinion. You may worship Christ, or Buddha, or nothing at all, so long as you also worship Caesar!" I believe that pluralistic secularism, in the long run, is a more deadly poison than straightforward persecution. In our country the Orthodox Church is not so much being persecuted as seduced by the selfish, grasping "American Dream." Orthodox Christians must stand with courage on religious, sacramental, moral and ethical issues. We, like the Church's martyrs, must be willing to be true to our rich inheritance. We, of all people, must defend the sense of the sacred. This does not mean that there is an "Orthodox political platform," or that the Orthodox Church must launch innovative social "political" programs to repair the ravages of sin in society. *Far from it!* It seems to me that the quest of the Orthodox Church, in our culture, must be that the Church be *true to itself,* true to the love its martyrs died for, true to Christ, as were our forefathers and foremothers as they stood up to Turkish persecution and Communist martyrdom.

While everything else in our culture changes, the Orthodox Church must have the courage to be timeless. Far from "updating," and making itself more "relevant," the Church must have the courage to stand uncompromisingly for goodness and, in the eyes of the world, to be "irrelevant." If need be, I believe that the Church should even be, like St. John the Baptist, obnoxious in Her defense of the timeless, as She reminds the world of the difference between good and evil. This may result in the active persecution of the Orthodox faithful by our ever-expanding, aggressively secularized state. America's state-endorsed godlessness — for instance, in the form of the feminist and homosexual movements' challenge to Church hiring practices — is on a collision course with the Church. From education to social policy on abortion, prenatal testing for "imperfect" babies, sex education, "gay" and "feminist" rights, we find the Church being challenged.

Just as the collapse of the Soviet Union proved that the Communist style of secularism could not triumph forever, so in our own country, American godlessness will, I believe, finally be self consuming. This is because secularism must always fail; its world view does not describe reality as it is. It strips people

of spiritual meaning. And so it may even be that many Protestants, modernized Roman Catholics, and even some
secularists, will soon be challenged to look anew at the spiritual
truths their forefathers squandered: truths that are non-
negotiable, above debate, vote or "democratic" or general
discussion. If that time comes, the Orthodox Church must be
ready to rise from the secularist ashes, as it has done so
remarkably in what was once the Soviet Union, and as it did
when the Turkish bondage in Greece was overthrown.

As the collapsing secular world looks for hope the Orthodox
Church must be distinguished, not by its "modernism,"
"ecumenism" or "political correctness," but by its *steadfastness,
purity* and *spiritual light*. The Orthodox Church must be seen
to have stood firm when all else was shaken, changed and swept
away. The Orthodox Church must be the one true thing, the
pearl above price, untarnished. It must hold faithful to its
original sacramental and evangelistic call. To achieve this we
must be willing to pay the price, even to be ridiculed,
persecuted and rejected, because we stand for love, beauty
and mercy in a loveless, ugly age.

We Orthodox Christians must defend our children against
the secularizing influences of our age by striving to become *living examples* of Orthodox piety and observance. We Orthodox
would do well to treasure the unique inheritance we have, *by
going to regular confession*, and realizing that while the con-
gregationalist attitude, of arrogant, politicized, secularized
"parish councils" may be a way to operate a Protestant
"church," it is *not* the *Orthodox* way! Orthodox Christians must
work hard at being faithful to what we believe, we must put
our money and time "where our mouth is" by supporting, in
every way we can, the expansion of monasticism in America.
We desperately need beacons of light in this darkening world.
We must train our children, largely by our own faithful, loving, sacramental example, to resist the secular — Protestant
onslaught and the new Dark Age which I believe has now over-
taken us.

Those lost and confused secularists, Protestants, Roman
Catholics and others who are looking for something *transcendent, sacred and steadfast* in a confused, desacralized world,
must be invited into the Church — the One, Holy, Catholic,
Apostolic Orthodox Church of the ages. *True*, lasting,

"ecumenical unity" will occur when all Christians come home.

I believe that the "program" of the Orthodox Church is therefore to *be Orthodox*! If this is done then the rest will take care of itself. I believe that the *true unity* of the American Orthodox Church can only be found in the unity of a common evangelistic purpose, not in grand schemes or signed documents. True oneness will come from the common bond people have when they share an important task: the task of turning our immigrant church into *a missionary church*, the task of evangelizing America with *authentic Orthodox Christianity* for the first time in history.

SELECT BIBLIOGRAPHY

What follows is a selection of reading, alphabetical by author, that I found helpful in analyzing the history and trends that shape our world and in my own spiritual journey to Orthodoxy.

This is by no means a comprehensive or scholarly reading list on the subject of Orthodoxy, secularism and Protestantism. Rather, this list is compiled on the basis of the books I read and re-read (between the years of 1980 and 1994) that had the greatest impact on my own spiritual and intellectual journey as regarding my conversion to the Orthodox Church and my life within it.

Archbishop Iakovos, *Faith for a Lifetime*. New York: Doubleday, 1988.

Archbishop Paul of Finland, *The Faith We Hold*. Crestwood, NY: St. Vladimir's Seminary Press, 1980.

Ashanin, Charles, *Essays on Orthodox Christianity and Church History*, available from Broad Ripple, 6302 N. Park Ave., Indianapolis, Indiana 46220 (1990).

Athanasius, *The Incarnation*, translated by a religious of CSMV, Crestwood, NY: St. Vladimir's Orthodox Theological Seminary, 1944.

Baltzell, E. Digby, *Puritan Boston and Quaker Philadelphia*. New York, Beacon Press, 1982.

Bauer, Lord P. T., *Equality, the Third World, and Economic Delusion*. Cambridge, MA: Harvard University Press, 1981.

Bishop Alexander, *The Life of Fr. John of Kronstadt*. Crestwood, NY: St. Vladimir's Seminary Press, 1979.

Bloom, Alan, *The Closing of the American Mind.* New York, NY: Simon and Schuster, 1987.

Bork, Robert H., *The Tempting of America.* London and New York: The Free Press, McMillan Publishers, 1990.

Braudel, Fernand, *The Mediterranean and the Mediterranean World in the Age of Philip II,* 2nd revised edition. New York, San Francisco, and London: Harper and Row Publishers, 1966.

Bruce, Steve, *A House Divided: Protestantism, Schism, and Secularization.* London and New York: Rutledge, 1990.

Callinikos, Rev. Constantine, *The History of the Orthodox Church.* Brookline, MA: Holy Cross Seminary Press, 1954.

Chamberlin, E. R., *The Bad Popes.* New York: Dorsett Press, 1969.

Chesterton, G. K., *Thomas Aquinas.* New York, NY: Doubleday Image Books, 1956.

Cramer, Rita, *In Defense of the Family: Raising Children in America Today,* New York, NY, 1983.

Christensen, Monk Damascene, *Not of This World: The Life and Teaching of Fr. Seraphim Rose, Pathfinder to the Heart of Ancient Christianity.* Seraphim Rose Foundation, P.O. Box 1656, Forestville, CA 95436, 1993.

Dawney, Glenville, *Constantine in the Age of Justinian.* University of Oklahoma Press, 1960.

Diehl, Charles, *Byzantium: Greatness and Decline.* New Brunswick, NJ: Rutgers University Press, 1957.

Eugeria, *Diary of a Pilgrimage.* New York, NY: Newman Press. Trans. George Gringas, 1970.

Eusebius, *The History of the Church.* Translated with an introduction by G. A. Williams. New York: Dorsett Press, 1965.

Evdokimov, Paul, *The Sacrament of Love.* Crestwood, NY: St. Vladimir's Seminary Press. 1985.

Florovsky, Fr. Georges, *The Collected Works of Georges Florovsky.* Vaduz, Flanders: Buchervertriebsanstalt, 1987.

Vol. 1 — Bible, Church, Tradition: An Eastern Orthodox View.
Vol. 2 — Christianity and Culture.
Vol. 3 — Creation and Redemption.
Vol. 4 — Aspects of Church History.
Vol. 5 — Ways of Russian Theology: Part One.
Vol. 6 — Ways of Russian Theology: Part Two.
Vol. 7 — The Eastern Fathers of the Fourth Century.
Vol. 8 — The Byzantine Fathers of the Fifth Century.
Vol. 9 — The Byzantine Fathers of the Sixth to Eighth Century.
Vol. 10 — The Byzantine Ascetic and Spiritual Fathers.
Vol. 11 — Theology and Literature.
Vol. 12 — The Ecumenical Movement and the Orthodox Church.
Vol. 13— Philosophy: Philosophical Problems and Movements.
Vol. 14 — Sermons and Writings on Spirituality.

Gavin, Frank, *Some Aspects of Contemporary Greek Orthodox Thought*. American Review of Eastern Orthodoxy. New York, 1962.

Gillquist, Peter, *Becoming Orthodox*. Ben Lomand, CA: Conciliar Press, 1992.

Griffin, Brian F., *Panic Among the Philistines*. Chicago: Regnery Gateway Publishers, 1983.

Hall, James, *Dictionary of Subjects and Symbols in Art*. Icon Editions. New York, San Francisco, London: Harper and Row Publishers, 1974.

Harakas, Stanley, *The Orthodox Church: 455 Questions and Answers*. Minneapolis, MN: Light and Life Publishing Company, 1987.

Hardon, John A., S. J., *The Catholic Catechism*. New York: Doubleday, 1974.

Hopko, Fr. Thomas, *The Orthodox Faith*, vols. 1-4, published by the Department of Religious Education in the Orthodox Church in America, New York, 1979.

Howard, Thomas, *Evangelical Is Not Enough*. Nashville, TN: Thomas Nelson Publishers, 1984.

Isaac, Rael Jean and Isaac, Erich, *The Coercive Utopians: Social*

Deception by America's Power Players. Chicago: Regnery Gateway Publishers, 1983.

Johnson, Paul, *Modern Times*. New York: Harper and Row Publishers, 1983.

Jurgens, W. A. (ed. and trans.), *The Faith of the Early Fathers*, vols. 1-3. Collegeville, MN: Liturgical Press, 1979.

Kilpatrick, William K., *Why Johnny Can't Tell Right from Wrong*. New York: Simon and Schuster, 1992.

Kilpatrick, William, *Psychological Seduction: The Failure of Modern Psychology*. Nashville, TN: Thomas Nelson Publishers, 1983.

Litsas, Fotios K. (ed.), *A Companion to the Greek Orthodox Church*, Department of Communication, Greek Orthodox Archdiocese of North and South America, New York, 1984.

Letters of Marsilio Ficino, vols. 1-2, translated from Latin by members of the Language Department of the School of Economic Science, London, Shepherd Walyn, 1975.

Magoulis, Harry, *Byzantine Christianity*, Detroit: Wayne State University Press, 1982.

Matthew the Poor, *The Communion of Love*. Crestwood, NY: St. Vladimir's Seminary Press, 1984.

Meyendorff, Fr. John, *Imperial Unity and Christian Divisions*. Crestwood, NY: St. Vladimir's Seminary Press, 1989.

Meyendorff, Fr. John (ed.), *Catholicity and the Church*. Crestwood, NY: St. Vladimir's Seminary Press, 1983.

Meyendorff, Fr. John (ed.), *The Primacy of Peter*. Crestwood, NY: St. Vladimir's Seminary Press, 1992.

Neuhaus, Richard John, *The Naked Public Square*. Grand Rapids, MI: Eerdman's, 1984.

Nisbett, Robert, *The History of the Idea of Progress*. New York: Basic Books, 1980.

Noll, Mark A.; Hatch, Nathan O.; Marsden, George, *The Search for Christian America*. Westchester, IL: Crossway Books, 1983.

Novak, Michael, *The Spirit of Democratic Capitalism*, American Enterprise Institute and Simon and Schuster Publications, New York, 1982.

Obolensky, Dimitri, *The Byzantine Commonwealth, Eastern Europe 500-1453*. Crestwood, NY: St. Vladimir Seminary Press, 1971.

Ostrogorsky, George, *History of the Byzantine State*. New Jersey: Rutgers University, 1969.

Palmer, G. E. H.; Sherrard, Philip; and Ware, Kallistos (eds. and trans.), *The Philokalia*, vols. 1-3. London and Boston: Faber and Faber vols. 1-3, 1979.

Pelikan, Jaroslav (ed.), *The Preaching of St. John Chrysostom, Philadelphia: Fortress Press, 1967.*

Pelikan, Jaroslav, The Emergence of the Christian Tradition. Chicago: The University of Chicago Press, 1971-1991.

Vol. 1 — *The Emergence of the Catholic Tradition* (AD 100-600).
Vol. 2 — *The Spirit of Eastern Christendom* (AD 600-1700).
Vol. 3 — *The Growth of Medieval Theology* (AD 1300-1700).
Vol. 4 — *Reformation Church and Dogma* (AD 1300-1700).
Vol. 5 — *Christian Doctrine and Modern Culture* (Since 1700).

Postman, Neil, *Amusing Ourselves to Death*. New York: Penguin Books, 1986.

Poulos, George, *Orthodox Saints*, vols. 1-3. Brookline, MA: Holy Cross Seminary Press, 1991.

Quasten, Johannes, *Patrology*, vols. 1-3. Westminster, MD: Christian Classic, 1984.

Revell, Jean-François, *How Democracies Perish*. Garden City, NY: Doubleday, 1984.

Rose, Fr. Seraphim, *Orthodoxy and the Religion of the Future*. Platina, CA: St. Herman of Alaska Brotherhood, 1990.

Rose, Fr. Seraphim, *The Place of Blessed Augustine in the Orthodox Church*. Platina, CA: The St. Herman of Alaska Brotherhood, 1983.

Runciman, Steven, *The Great Church in Captivity*. New York:

Cambridge University Press, 1968.

Scammell, Michael, *Solzhenitsyn: A Biography*. New York and London: W. H. Norton and Company, 1984.

Schaeffer, Francis A., *The Great Evangelical Disaster*. Westchester, IL: Crossway Books, 1984.

Schlossberg, Herbert, *Idols for Destruction*. Nashville, TN: Thomas Nelson Publishers, 1983.

Schmemann, Alexander, *For the Life of the World*. Crestwood, NY: St. Vladimir's Seminary Press, 1973.

Scupoli, Lorenzo, *Unseen Warfare*, edited by Nicodemus of the Holy Mountain and revised by Theophan the Recluse. Trans. E. Kadloubovsky and G. E. H. Palmer. Crestwood, NY: St. Vladimir's Seminary Press, 1987.

Shaw, Peter, *The War Against the Intellect*. Iowa City: University of Iowa Press, 1989.

Simon, Julian L., *The Ultimate Resource*. Princeton: Princeton University Press, 1981.

Smith, Page, *A People's History of America*, vols. 1-5. New York: Penguin Books, 1976.

Smith, Page, *Killing the Spirit*. New York: Viking Press, a Division of Penguin Books, 1990.

Sobran, Joseph, *Single Issues*. New York: The Human Life Press, 1983.

Solzhenitsyn, Alexander, *From Under the Rubble*. Chicago: Regnery Gateway, 1974.

Sowell, Thomas, *The Economics of Politics and Race*. New York: William Morrow and Company, 1983.

Tyrrell, Jr., R. Emmett, *The Liberal Crackup*. New York: Simon and Schuster, 1984.

Vaporis, Nomikos M., *Father Kosmas: the Apostle of the Poor*. Brookline, MA: Holy Cross Orthodox Press, 1977.

Varghese, Abraham (ed.), *The Intellectuals Speak Out About God*. Chicago: Regnery Gateway Publishers, 1984.

Vasari, Giorgio, *The Artists of the Renaissance*, trans. George

Bull, New York: Viking Press, 1965.

Vasiliev, A. A., *The History of the Byzantine Empire*. Madison, WI: University of Wisconsin Press, 1952.

Vlachos, Archimandrite Hierotheos, *Orthodox Spirituality-A Brief Introduction*. Athens, Birth of the Theotokos Monastery, 1992. Available in the United States from: St. Nikodemos Publications, 2101 Ritchie St., Aliquippapa 15001.

Ware, Timothy Kallistos, *The Orthodox Church*. London and New York: Penguin Books, 1963.

Whitehead, John W., *The Second American Revolution*. Westchester, IL: Crossway Books, 1982.

Young, C. F., *The Medici*. London and New York: The Modern Library, 1921.

Periodicals

The Christian Activist
(a journal of Orthodox opinion) is available, free of charge from: P.O. Box 740
M.T. Hermon, CA 95041
Frank Schaeffer editor.

AGAIN Magazine
Conciliar Press
P.O. Box 76
Ben Lomond, CA 95005

First Things
156 5th Avenue
New York, NY 10010

Commentary
165 East 56th Street
New York, NY 10022

The Human Life Review
150 East 35th Street
New York, NY 10016

The Life Advocate
P.O. Box 13656
Portland, OR 97213

St. Vladimir's Theological Quarterly
575 Scarsdale Road
Crestwood, NY 10707

The American Spectator
2020 North 14th Street
Arlington, VA 22216

The Orthodox Word
St. Herman of Alaska Press
P.O. Box 70
Platina, CA 96076

INDEX

Printed in the United States
42918LVS00007B/35

9 780917 651366